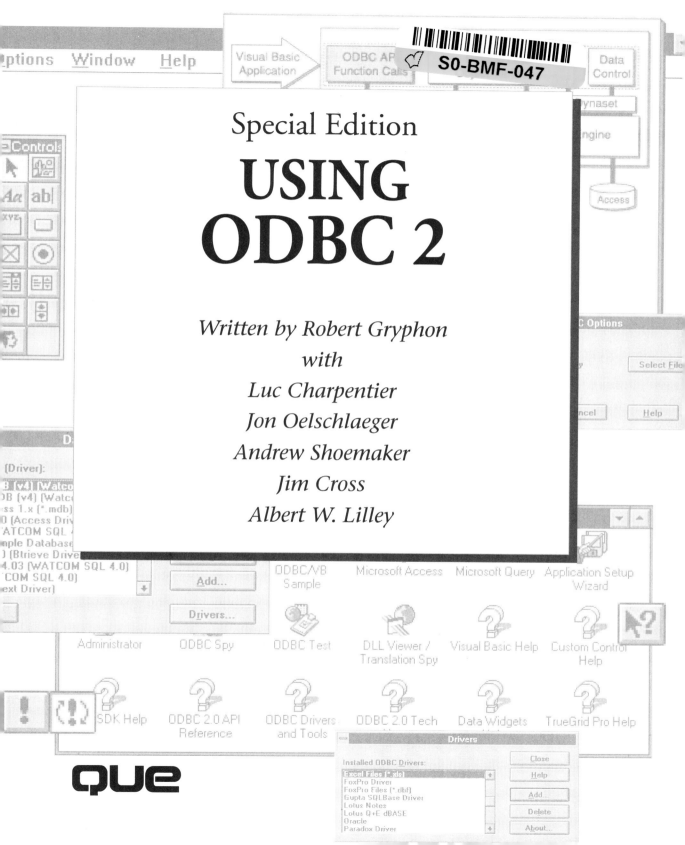

Special Edition

USING
ODBC 2

Written by Robert Gryphon

with

Luc Charpentier

Jon Oelschlaeger

Andrew Shoemaker

Jim Cross

Albert W. Lilley

que

Special Edition, Using ODBC 2

Copyright© 1995 by Que® Corporation.

Library of Congress Catalog No.: 95-67122

ISBN: 0-7897-0015-8

97 96 95   6 5 4 3 2 1

Interpretation of the printing code: the rightmost double-digit number is the year of the book's printing; the rightmost single-digit number, the number of the book's printing. For example, a printing code of 95-1 shows that the first printing of the book occurred in 1995.

Screen reproductions in this book were created with Collage Plus from Inner Media, Inc., Hollis, NH.

Publisher: David P. Ewing

Associate Publisher: Joseph P. Wikert

Associate Publisher-Operations: Corinne Walls

Managing Editor: Kelli Widdifield

Dedication

For Lou Abraham, Jim McCaffrey, and the McDowells.

Credits

Publishing Manager
Steven M. Schafer

Acquisitions Editor
Fred Slone

Product Director
Bryan Gambrel

Production Editor
Susan Ross Moore

Copy Editors
Patrick Kanouse
Julie A. McNamee

Technical Editor
Richard J. Simon

Acquisitions Coordinator
Angela C. Kowlowski

Operations Coordinator
Patricia J. Brooks

Editorial Assistant
Michelle R. Williams

Book Designer
Sandra Schroeder

Cover Designer
Dan Armstrong

Production Team
Claudia Bell
Don Brown
Kim Cofer
Amy Cornwell
Anne Dickerson
Michael Dietsch
Chad Dressler
Rich Evers
Lorell Fleming
John Hulse
Daryl Kessler
Bob LaRoche
Beth Lewis
Erika Millen
Victor Peterson
Kaylene Riemen
Kris Simmons
Michael Thomas
Scott Tullis
Jody York

Indexer
Michael Hughes

Composed in *Stone Serif* and *MCPdigital* by Que Corporation

About the Authors

Robert Gryphon is a consultant and computer author in Redmond, Washington. During his nine-year career in the computing industry, he has worked for law firms, major retailers, systems integrators, and as a contractor at Microsoft. He regularly writes for *Data Based Advisor* and *Infoworld*, among other publications. Robert holds a Master of Science in Information Systems and an MBA, as well as a variety of professional certifications.

Luc Charpentier is a consultant with over fourteen years of international experience. He specializes in database object-oriented programming with Smalltalk, and communications. As president and founder of LPC Consulting Services, he developed Smalltalk class libraries for interfacing to ODBC and Windows Sockets libraries. He has worked with major relational database management systems including Teradata, Sybase, and Oracle. He teaches logical and physical relational database design and SQL courses. He is a member of the Association for Computing Machinery and the IEEE Computer Society. Luc is a graduate of the University of Ottawa and holds an M.S. in Applied Mathematics from the University of Western Ontario.

Jon Oelschlaeger is founder and president of Ensemble Systems Corporation, a San Francisco area-based consulting firm specializing in business applications, training, and courseware development using Microsoft products. He is a Microsoft Certified engineer and instructor in Visual Basic, VBA Programming, and Windows—both Windows 3.x and Windows NT. He has thirty years of experience in the computer industry and has worked for Hughes Aircraft Company, General Electric, and numerous consulting clients in the design and development of application-specific computer systems and programs. Mr. Oelschlaeger holds a B.S.E.E. in Electrical Engineering from Valparaiso University, and has completed extensive post-graduate work in Computer Science at both U.S.C. and U.C.L.A.

Andrew Shoemaker has been programming since the seventh grade, when his father gave Andrew his first computer. While completing a masters degree in electrical engineering, Andrew helped a small company finish a document imaging application; he has been with that company ever since. He recently co-founded his own company. You can contact Andrew as Andrew.Shoemaker@bev.net on the Internet.

Jim Cross has more than thirteen years experience working with mainframe and personal computers in Atlanta, Georgia. Currently he is employed by Antinori Software and specializes in designing C++ applications for the banking and insurance industries.

Albert W. "Tripp" Lilley was diagnosed in the March 15, 1993, issue of *Forbes* magazine as suffering from "an incipient case of Geek Syndrome." Lilley has expanded his household network from two PCs to a "heterogenous, object-oriented, client-server, multimedia" network of eight fully buzzword-enabled machines. The experience Lilley brings to this book comes from his work in Windows and ODBC development while founding Perspex Imageworks, Inc., with Andrew Shoemaker. You can contact Lilley as Tripp.Lilley@bev.net on the very marketable Internet.

Trademark Acknowledgments

We'd Like to Hear from You!

As part of our continuing effort to produce books of the highest possible quality, Que would like to hear your comments. To stay competitive, we *really* want you, as a computer book reader and user, to let us know what you like or dislike most about this book or other Que products.

You can mail comments, ideas, or suggestions for improving future editions to the address below, or send us a fax at (317) 581-4663. For the on-line inclined, Macmillan Computer Publishing has a forum on CompuServe (type **GO QUEBOOKS** at any prompt) through which our staff and authors are available for questions and comments. The address of our Internet site is **http://www.mcp.com** (World Wide Web).

In addition to exploring our forum, please feel free to contact me personally to discuss your opinions of this book: on CompuServe, I'm at 75230,1556, and on the Internet, I'm **bgambrel@que.mcp.com**.

Thanks in advance—your comments will help us to continue publishing the best books available on computer topics in today's market.

Bryan Gambrel
Product Development Specialist
Que Corporation
201 W. 103rd Street
Indianapolis, Indiana 46290
USA

Contents at a Glance

Introduction   1

The ODBC API   **7**

1 What Is ODBC?   9

2 The Relational Database Model   19

3 The Client/Server Language: SQL   53

4 The Structure of ODBC: An Overview   93

5 Data Sources and Drivers   109

6 Creating the ODBC Environment and Connection   121

7 Catalog and Statistics Functions   137

8 The ODBC Statement: An Introduction   153

9 Creating Tables with the DDL   169

10 Inserting, Updating, and Deleting Rows   181

11 Queries and Result Sets   199

12 Setting Parameters with Prepared Statements   217

13 The Cursor Library and Positioned Operations   233

Visual C++   **263**

14 Using the Wizards   265

15 Using the Transfer Mechanism   287

16 Multi-Table Forms   315

Visual Basic   **331**

17 Using the Visual Basic Data Control with ODBC 2.0   333

18 Using Visual Basic Data Access Objects with ODBC 2.0   373

19 Using the ODBC API from within Visual Basic   407

Advanced Topics   **445**

20 Optimizing ODBC   447

21 Referential Integrity   459

22 Successful Downsizing   469

Appendixes   **491**

A Resources in the SDK   493

B ODBC Function Reference   507

C Contents of the Special Edition, *Using ODBC 2* CD-ROM   517

Glossary   523

Index   529

The ODBC API

Visual C++

Visual Basic

Advanced Topics

Appendixes

Contents

Introduction   **1**

Who Should Read This Book? 2
How the Book Is Structured 2

I The ODBC API   **7**

1 What Is ODBC?   **9**

What Is ODBC, Anyway? 9
How Does ODBC Work? 12
Where Did ODBC Come From? 12
Why You Should Use ODBC 13
What Do You Need to Use ODBC? 14
   Visual C++ 2.0 14
   Visual Basic Professional Edition 14
   The MSDN-II CD-ROM: The ODBC 2.0 SDK 15
   The Desktop Database Driver Set 15
What You Need to Learn to Use ODBC 17
   The Relational Model 17
   Structured Query Language Grammar 17
Where Is All This Going? 18
From Here… 18

2 The Relational Database Model   **19**

History of the Relational Model 19
Structure of the Relational Model 20
   Constructs of the Model 20
   Integrity Rules of the Model 21
   Operators of the Model 24
      Selection 24
      Projection 24
      Join 26
      Union 27
Relational Database Design 28
   Defining the Entities 29
   Defining the Relationships 35
      One-to-One Relationships 36
      One-to-Many Relationships 37
      Many-to-Many Relationships 38
   Defining Attributes 39
   Recursive Relationships 44
   History Tables 46

A Complete Example 48
From Here… 51

3 The Client/Server Language: SQL 53

SQL History 54
ODBC Data Types 54
Name of Objects 56
Data Definition Language 57
Tables 57
Indexes 60
Views 61
Data Control Language 66
Granting Privileges 66
Revoking Privileges 68
Data Manipulation Language 69
DELETE 69
INSERT 70
Simple *SELECT* 71
The *LIKE* Predicate 72
The *DISTINCT* Keyword 74
The *ORDER BY* Clause 74
The *IN* Predicate 75
The BETWEEN Predicate 76
Expressions 77
Functions 77
Date, *Time*, and *Timestamp* Literals 79
Simple Joins 79
Complex Joins 83
Aggregation 86
Subqueries 88
Union Queries 90
FOR UPDATE Clause 90
UPDATE 90
Call Procedure 91
From Here… 92

4 The Structure of ODBC: An Overview 93

Database-Specific Interfaces 93
Local Database Interfaces 94
Client/Server Database Interfaces 96
Halfway to ODBC: Intermediate Drivers 99
The ODBC Alternative 100
Single-Tier Drivers 100
Multiple-Tier Drivers 102
16-Bit and 32-Bit ODBC Drivers 104
A Typical ODBC Session 105
From Here… 107

5 Data Sources and Drivers   109

How To Install and Use the ODBC Administrator 109
How To Configure Logging 111
What Is an ODBC Driver? 112
The Different Types of ODBC Drivers 113
    API Conformance 113
    SQL Grammar Conformance 114
    Driver Type 116
How To Create Data Sources with the ODBC Administrator .. 117
Choosing Drivers and Approaches 118
    Multiple Targets 118
    Single Targets 119
From Here… 119

6 Creating the ODBC Environment and Connection 121

The Elements Needed to Enable a Project for ODBC 121
The ODBC Environment 122
Error Trapping 124
    Calling the *SQLError( )* Function 125
    Using Error Codes 127
How to Initialize and Free a Connection 128
How to Connect to a Data Source 129
    Connecting to a Specific Data Source 129
    Enabling Users to Choose a Data Source 131
        Choosing a Data Source with *SQLDriverConnect( )* .. 131
        Choosing a Data Source with
        SQLBrowseConnect( ) 132
How to Set and Get Connection Options 134
    Using *SQLSetConnectOption( )* 134
    Using *SQLGetConnectOption( )* 134
    Some Common Connection Options 135
How to Disconnect from a Data Source 135
From Here… 136

7 Catalog and Statistics Functions   137

Getting the Names of Tables in a Database 139
The Columns in a Table 140
    The *SQLTables( )* Result Set 140
    The *SQLColumns( ) Function* 140
    The *SQLColumns( )* Result Set 141
    The *SQLSpecialColumns( )* Function 141
    The *SQLSpecialColumns( )* Result Set 142
The Indexes Associated with a Table 143
    The *SQLPrimaryKeys( )* Function 143
    The *SQLForeignKeys( )* Function 144
    The *SQLForeignKeys( )* Result Sets 144
Learning What Stored Procedures Are Available 145
    The *SQLProcedures( )* Function 145

The *SQLProcedures( )* Result Set 145
The *SQLProcedureColumns( )* Function 146
The *SQLProcedureColumns( )* Result Set 146
The User Privileges in Force 148
The *SQLTablePrivileges( )* Function 148
The *SQLTablePrivileges( )* Result Set 148
The *SQLColumnPrivileges( )* Function 149
The *SQLTablePrivileges( )* Result Set 149
Where Do We Go from Here? 150
From Here… 152

8 The ODBC Statement: An Introduction   153

How to Create and Free a Statement 154
Creating a Statement Handle 155
Freeing a Statement Handle 155
How to Execute a Statement 156
Direct Execution 156
Prepared Execution 157
Configuring Statement Options 158
Getting Statement Options 158
Setting Statement Options 159
Synchronous and Asynchronous Execution 159
Synchronous Execution 159
Asynchronous Execution 159
Setting the Execution Mode 160
Query Result Sets 161
How to Reuse a Statement Handle 163
Performing Transactions 164
Grouping Statements into Transactions 166
Transaction Modes 166
ROLLBACK 168
From Here… 168

9 Creating Tables with the DDL   169

Creating Tables 171
How to Create Tables 171
When to Create Tables 172
Dropping Tables 172
How to Drop a Table 172
When It's Appropriate to Drop a Table 172
Creating Indexes on Tables 173
How to Create an Index 174
When to Create an Index 174
Dropping Indexes 175
How to Drop an Index 175
When It's Appropriate to Drop an Index 175
Altering Tables 176
How to Alter a Table 176

When to Alter a Table 177
Creating Views 178
    How to Create a View 178
    When to Create a View 179
Dropping Views 179
    How to Drop a View 179
    When It's Appropriate to Drop a View 179
From Here… 180

10 Inserting, Updating, and Deleting Rows   181

Inserting Rows into the Database 181
Updating Rows in the Database 184
Deleting Rows from the Database 186
Finding Out How Many Rows Were Affected 187
Maintaining Referential Integrity 188
    Watching for Inappropriate Relationships 188
    Organizing Operations into Transactions 190
    Returning Meaningful Data from a Trigger 196
Read-Only Mode 197
From Here… 197

11 Queries and Result Sets   199

The SQL *SELECT* Statement 200
The Order of Operations 201
Setting Up for a Query 202
Determining the Number of Result Columns 203
Getting Information about a Result Column 204
    SQLDescribeCol( ) 204
    SQLColAttributes( ) 205
Counting the Number of Rows Returned 207
Binding Columns 208
    Column-Wise Binding 209
    Row-Wise Binding 210
Working with the Data 212
    SQLGetData( ) 212
    SQLFetch( ) 213
    SQLExtendedFetch( ) 214
Cleaning Up after Queries 214
From Here… 215

12 Setting Parameters with Prepared Statements   217

Establishing Parameter Basics 218
Specifying Parameter Values 218
    Binding Parameter Values 219
    Passing Data at Execution Time 222
    Multiple Parameter Values 224
Getting Parameter Information 225
    Getting Detailed Parameter Information 226

Getting the Number of Parameters 226
Getting a List of Parameters and Related Columns 227
Passing and Accepting Procedure Parameters 229
Clearing Parameters 230
From Here… 231

13 The Cursor Library and Positioned Operations   233

The Cursor Library and Cursor Basics 234
Handling Result Sets with Cursors 236
Assigning a Cursor Name 236
The Result Set Cache 239
Setting the Cursor Position 239
Fetching Multiple Rows 242
Positioned Updates and Deletes 246
SELECT FOR UPDATE 246
WHERE CURRENT OF 246
Positioned Operations with *SQLSetPos()* 248
Checking Your Driver's Support for Cursors 249
SQL_CURSOR_COMMIT_BEHAVIOR 250
SQL_CURSOR_ROLLBACK_BEHAVIOR 251
SQL_BOOKMARK_PERSISTENCE 251
SQL_FETCH_DIRECTION 252
SQL_LOCK_TYPES 252
SQL_MAX_CURSOR_NAME_LEN 253
SQL_POS_OPERATIONS 253
SQL_POSITIONED_STATEMENTS 253
SQL_ROW_UPDATES 254
SQL_SCROLL_CONCURRENCY 254
SQL_SCROLL_OPTIONS 254
SQL_STATIC_SENSITIVITY 255
Connection and Statement Options 255
Setting Cursor Connection Options 255
SQL_ODBC_CURSORS 256
SQL_AUTOCOMMIT 256
Getting Cursor Connection Options 257
Setting Cursor Statement Options 257
SQL_CONCURRENCY 258
SQL_CURSOR_TYPE 258
SQL_KEYSET_SIZE 259
SQL_RETRIEVE_DATA 259
SQL_ROWSET_SIZE 259
SQL_SIMULATE_CURSOR 260
SQL_USE_BOOKMARKS 260
Getting Cursor Statement Options 261
Releasing a Cursor 261
From Here… 262

II Visual C++   263

14 Using the Wizards   265

The Application 266
Getting Connected 269
Using AppWizard 270
   Start AppWizard 271
   Complete Step 1 271
   Complete Step 2 271
   Select Data Source and Table 273
   Complete Step 3 273
   Complete Step 4 273
   Complete Step 5 274
   Complete Step 6 274
   Approve Project Information 274
   Build and Run the Application 274
Setting Up a View 275
   Open *IDD_RAIL_FORM* 276
   Lay Out the New Dialog 276
   Open ClassWizard 277
   Link Controls to Fields 277
   Build and Run the Application 278
How the Application Works 279
Creating Recordsets with ClassWizard 282
From Here… 286

15 Using the Transfer Mechanism   287

Navigating Through a Table 287
   Set Up the Pennsylvania Railroad Data Source 290
   Create a *CTrainSet* Class 290
   Add New Menu Items 291
   Create a Train List Dialog 291
   Create a *CTrainListDialog* Class 291
   Add a List Variable 292
   Add Member Variables 292
   Add Code to Load the List 292
   Add Message Handlers 293
   Add a Command Handler 294
   Build and Run the Program 294
Filtering and Sorting the Records 295
   Add a Member Variable 296
   Create a Hint 297
   Modify *OnTrainsSelect* 297
   Add an *OnUpdate* Function 297
   Add a Filter to the Record Set 298
   Build and Run the Program 298

Catching Errors with Exceptions 298
Adding and Updating Records 301
    Create an Add Record Menu Item 303
    Create Member Variable *m_InAddMode* 303
    Create a Handler for *ID_RECORD_ADDRECORD* 303
    Create an *OnMove* Function for *CRailView* 304
    Build and Run the Program 305
Deleting 305
    Create a Delete Record Menu Item 306
    Create a Handler for *ID_RECORD_DELETERECORD* 306
    Build and Run the Program 306
Aggregate Values 307
    Create a Compute Weight Menu Item 307
    Create a New *CRecordset* 308
    Remove Unnecessary Variables 308
    Change the Field Exchange 308
    Create a Handler for *ID_TRAINS_EMPTYWEIGHT* 308
    Build and Run the Program 309
Dynamic Binding to Columns 310
    Create the Browser Dialog 310
    Create a New Record Set Class 311
    Build a Dialog Class for the Dialog 312
    Create Maps and Variables 313
    Create a Browse Info Menu Item 314
    Create a Handler for *ID_TRAINS_BROWSEINFO* 314
    Build and Run the Program 314
From Here… 314

16 Multi-Table Forms   **315**

Performing Joins 315
    Update the *IDD_RAIL_FORM* 316
    Create a Member Variable 317
    Create a Message Handler 317
    Complete the List Box 317
    Create a Member Variable 317
    Modify the *GetDefaultSQL* Method 318
    Modify the *DoFieldExchange* Method 318
    Create a Function 319
    Build and Run the Program 320
Parameterizing a Record Set 321
    Add a New Member Variable to the *CRailSet* Class 321
    Add Initialization 322
    Add the New Member Variable 322
    Set Up the Filter 323
    Build the Parameterized Filter String 323
    Update the Parameterized Value 324
    Build and Run the Program 324
Working with Multiple Data Sources 324
    Add a Control 326

Create a Member Variable for the Control 327
Create a *CRecordSet* for the *RailroadDatabases* Table 327
Add an *OnInitDialog* Function 327
Complete the Control 327
Modify the *OnUpdate* Message 328
Build and Run the Program 329
Using SQL Statements 330
From Here... 330

III Visual Basic 331

17 Using the Visual Basic Data Control with ODBC 2.0 333

Choosing Possible Design Approaches 334
Defining Three Possible Design Strategies 334
Determining When to Use Each Approach 337
Typical Data Control Applications 337
Using Data Access Object Variables 337
Using ODBC 2.0 API Function Calls 338
Combining Several Different Techniques 339
Combining the Data Control and Data Access
Object Variables 339
Combining the Data Access Object with
ODBC 2.0 Function Calls 339
Combining All Three Approaches in
One Application 339
Building a Suitable Development Environment 340
Constructing an ODBC 2.0 Visual Basic Workbench 340
Adopting a Design Methodology—Some Suggestions 343
Beginning Your Visual Basic ODBC 2.0 Application 345
Packaging and Distributing Your Application 346
Visual Basic ODBC 2.0 Setup Wizard
Dialog Box Choices 347
Making Modifications to the SETUPWIZ.INI File ... 348
Making Modifications to the
SETUP1.MAK Project 348
Summarizing Visual Basic's Database Architecture 348
Understanding Visual Basic's Database Engine 350
Interfacing to ODBC 2.0 Facilities and Databases 351
Using the Data Control's *Dynaset* 351
Dynaset Characteristics 352
Visual Basic Application Considerations 355
Using the ODBC Administrative Dialog Boxes 355
Selecting an ODBC 2.0 Data Source 357
Configuring an ODBC 2.0 Data Source 357
Using Multiple Data Sources 357
Executing an SQL Query 357
Preparing the SQL Query 358

Using Microsoft Query for Ad Hoc Queries 359
Submitting the SQL Query 360
Evaluating the Success or Failure of Your SQL Query 360
Using the Data Control's Result Set 361
Using Visual Basic's Bound Controls 361
Programming Techniques to Use the Result Set 363
Incorporating Custom Controls.. 364
Browsing the Query Result Set 365
Preparing the Query Result Set for Printing.................... 366
Evaluating Data-Aware Custom Controls 368
Using Microsoft OCX Controls 368
Capitalizing on OLE 2.x Automation 369
Anticipating Future Visual Basic Directions 370
Trapping and Processing Errors.. 370
Dealing with ODBC 2.0 Errors 370
Interpreting ODBC Error Return Information 371
From Here… 372

18 Using Visual Basic Data Access Objects with ODBC 2.0   373

Understanding Data Access Object Variables 374
Programming with Database Object Variables 375
Using the Database Object 377
Using the *TableDefs* Object 377
Defining Objects 378
How to Create an Object from a Class.................... 378
Understanding Objects and Object Variables 378
Object Variables as C/C++ Pointers 380
Understanding Object Variable Arrays 380
Understanding the *TableDefs* Collection 382
Using Table Objects 384
Using the Table's Fields Collection 384
Using the Table's Indexes Collection 386
Using Snapshot Objects 387
Creating a *Snapshot* Object 388
Moving the Row Pointer within a
Snapshot Object 389
Using *Dynaset* Objects 391
Dynaset Object Methods 391
Dynaset Dynamic Behavior 392
Creating a *Dynaset* Object 394
Designing Database-Generating Applications 395
Creating a New Database 395
Creating the Database's Structure 396
Key Concepts in Using *NEW* 396
Cloning an Existing Database 397
Designing Query Result Applications 397
Preparing and Executing Your SQL Statements 397

Interacting with the Result Set 398
Obtaining the Values in the Result Set 399
Designing Transaction-Processing Applications 400
Using SQL Statements to Accomplish Your
Transactions 401
Using *Recordset* Methods for Transaction Processing 401
The *Dynaset*'s Refresh Method 402
Using the Dynaset's *EDIT* and *UPDATE* Methods .. 402
Deleting and Adding New Records 403
Managing Transaction Consistency 403
From Here… 405

19 Using the ODBC API from within Visual Basic   407

Deciding When to Use the ODBC 2.0 API Approach 407
Considering the Need for API-Level Control 408
Addressing Application Performance 410
Performance Effects of SQL Statement Processing .. 410
Performance Effects of Cursor Management 413
Types of Cursor Models 414
Forms of Cursor Behavior 414
Keyset-Driven Cursor Behavior 414
Mixed Cursors Behavior 415
Getting More Detailed Operations
and Error Information 416
Taking Direct Control with ODBC 2.0 API Calls 416
Understanding the Sequence of API Function Calls 417
Relating ODBC Function Calls to Your Application 418
Managing the Data Structures and Handles 421
Declaring ODBC 2.0 API Functions, Constants,
and Variables 421
Using the ODBC 2.0 SDK Visual Basic
Sample Program 421
Choosing the ODBC Conformance Level You Need 422
ODBC Core-Level Functionality 423
ODBC Extended Functionality—Levels 1 and 2 423
SQL Conformance Levels 424
Determining ODBC Conformance Level—API
and SQL 425
Structuring Your Visual Basic Code 427
Connecting to Data Sources 427
Initializing ODBC 427
Connecting to a Data Source 427
Other Connection Possibilities 429
Preparing Your SQL Statements 430
Direct Method SQL Statements 431
Prepared Method SQL Statements 431
Submitting Your SQL Statements 432
Retrieving the Result Set 433
SQLGetData Function Retrieval Operations 434

SQLBindCol Function Retrieval Operations 434
Using Status and Error Information 435
Terminating Statements, Connections,
    and the Environment 437
Programming the Result Set
    with the ODBC 2.0 API 438
    Working with Result Set Data Structures 439
    Manipulating the Result Set Cursor 440
Debugging and Testing with ODBC 2.0 Development Tools .. 440
    Using ODBC Trace to Log Data Source Operations 441
    Invoking ODBC Spy To Monitor ODBC Transactions 442
From Here… 443

IV Advanced Topics   445

20 Optimizing ODBC   447

Design Your Database Right in the First Place 448
Choose Optimized Drivers 449
Check Each Driver Capability Only Once 449
Avoid Disconnecting/Reconnecting 451
Make Judicious Use of Synchronous/Asynchronous Modes 452
Choose between *SQLExecute( )* and *SQLExecDirect( )* 453
    When to Use *SQLExecDirect( )* 453
    When to Use *SQLExecute( )* 453
Retrieve Results Judiciously 453
Always Bind the Primary Key Column 454
Turn Off Bookmarks If Not Needed 455
Select the Lowest Usable Transaction Isolation Level 455
Test Your Code with the Tracing Facility 456
    SQL_OPT_TRACEFILE 456
    SQL_OPT_TRACE 456
    Interpreting the Trace Results 457
From Here… 457

21 Referential Integrity   459

Integrity in the Relational Database Model 459
    Entity Integrity 460
        Enforcing Primary Key Validity 460
        Restricting Field Values 461
        Preventing Null Fields 461
        Preventing Duplicate Values 461
        Specifying Default Values 461
    Referential Integrity 462
Methods of Enforcing Integrity 462
    Enforcing Integrity through DBMS Services at
        Update Time 462

Enforcing Integrity through Application Code at
Entry Time 463
Enforcing Integrity through Post-Processing 463
A Look at SQL's Built-In Integrity Enforcement Keywords 465
Enforcing Primary Key Validity 466
Restricting Field Values 466
Preventing Null Fields 466
Enforcing Foreign Key Validity (Referential Integrity) 467
From Here… 467

22 Successful Downsizing 469

Picking a Downsizing Model 469
The Port 471
The Rewrite 473
The New Front End 473
Choosing the Hardware and Software Platform 475
Common Hardware Platforms 475
Personal Computer Databases 476
True Client/Server Databases 477
Using ODBC to Increase Your Options 478
Mix and Match for Cost and Performance 478
Integrate End-User Tools 479
Modeling the System 479
Identify the Critical Performance Elements 480
Make Sure All the Software Works Together 480
Simulate the System 481
Getting the Performance You Need 481
ODBC and Performance 482
Database Design 482
The Power of SQL 485
The Superstation 486
The Bottlenecks 486
Avoiding Common Pitfalls 487
Don't Mistake Small for Simple 488
Involve the Users 488
Understand the System 488
Develop System Deployment Techniques 489
From Here… 489

Appendixes 491

A Resources in the SDK 493

The ODBC Test Program 493
The ODBC Spy Program 495

The ODBC Help Files 496
    The API Reference 496
    The Release Notes 497
    The Tech Notes 497
    The ODBC Drivers and Tools 498
    The Sample ODBC Applications 498
The Sample ODBC Applications 498
    The Visual Basic Sample 498
    The C++ Sample 499
    The QueryDemo Sample 501
    The Cursors Sample 502
    The Admin Sample 503
    The DLL Viewer/Translation Spy Sample 504
    The Sample ODBC Driver 505
    The Quick Test 506
In Summation 506

B ODBC Function Reference   **507**

**C Contents of the Special Edition, *Using ODBC 2*
    CD-ROM**   **517**
Sample Code Used in the Book 517
A List of Databases 517
A List of Vendors 517
The Demos on This CD-ROM 518
    Paradox for Windows 518
    dBASE for Windows 5.0 518
    Jet Inspector v2.0 518
    ODBC Inspector v2.0 518
    SQL Inspector v2.0 519
    Help Files from South Wind Design 519
    Products 519
    Shareware 520
    White Papers 521
    Glossary of Terms 521

Glossary   **523**

Index   **529**

Introduction

Welcome to the ODBC revolution!

In the two years since its initial release, ODBC has taken over as the standard of choice for database communication. Its success has been the result of several elements, many of which could not have come together without a tremendous amount of effort by Microsoft. Perhaps the most important factor has been its timeliness: awareness of the lack of a standardized database communication method had been dawning throughout the industry since at least the late '80s. The second key success factor was its design: Microsoft took pains to co-develop and build off emerging standards such as the SQL Access Group's database call-level interface and the popular RDBMS language, SQL. The third pillar of ODBC's success is the support it has received throughout the industry, which has increased steadily over time and shows no signs of flagging. Finally, the fact that it *works* has been all the justification that most database-oriented software companies have needed to hop on the bandwagon.

One thing that has *not* worked in ODBC's favor is the scantiness of the available documentation. The ODBC 2.0 Software Development Kit itself comes with on-line help that's loaded with reference information, but without much of an introduction to the subject.

In this section, I'll talk about for whom this book is intended, give a brief overview of what you can expect from the rest of the book, and show how to get the most out of Special Edition, *Using ODBC 2*.

Who Should Read This Book?

This book is a cross between a tutorial guide and a reference manual. If you're a developer anxious to ramp up on ODBC as quickly as possible, this book lays the groundwork in the first few chapters, then dives into the details. Or, if you're just trying to understand the philosophy and theory behind ODBC, you can gloss over the program examples and read the text sections through Part I.

We'll start with the basics about ODBC (and database design in general), then look into specific techniques for performing standard ODBC maintenance and data processing tasks. Next, we'll go into detail about techniques for Visual C++ and Visual Basic programmers, and we'll wrap up with some discussions of topics beyond the scope of a simple tutorial/reference guide.

How the Book Is Structured

This book is not intended to provide complete information about every ODBC API call. Instead, in the programming technique chapters, we have chosen to focus on the most commonly used functions and explain those in some detail.

Throughout the programming chapters of this book, you'll notice the use of FAR * in the function prototypes and code listings. This syntax is used to retain compatibility with 16-bit compilers, such as Microsoft's Visual C++ 1.5. If you're writing 32-bit-only ODBC applications, the word FAR is extraneous and is not in keeping with the most graceful 32-bit programming standard. However, because it will be accepted (though ignored) by 32-bit compilers, we have left it in.

- In Chapter 1, "What Is ODBC?," we'll talk about the things that make ODBC unique and the real value that you can derive from using it in your applications.

- Chapter 2, "The Relational Database Model," introduces the relational model and describes a methodology for designing relational databases. You will learn about the structure, rules, and operators of the relational model. The methodology described will enable you to produce sound and stable database designs. You will learn how to define entities, attributes, and relationships. You also will learn how to handle dependent entities, subtypes, and recursive relationships. The chapter concludes with a complete design example.

■ Chapter 3, "The Client/Server Language: SQL," shows you the Structured Query Language (SQL). It describes the Data Definition Language (DDL), Data Control Language (DCL), and Data Manipulation Language (DML) statements. The ODBC minimum, core, and extended SQL levels are covered. It includes numerous examples illustrating the use of SQL to solve business problems.

■ In Chapter 4, "The Structure of ODBC: An Overview," you'll get a high-level look at the way ODBC is laid out. It's compared and contrasted with more conventional database communication methods, and you'll get a good idea of how ODBC fits into the overall database management picture.

■ Chapter 5, "Data Sources and Drivers," explains the different classifications and capabilities of ODBC drivers. This will help you decide what level of functionality your applications should expect from a driver.

■ Chapter 6, "Creating the ODBC Environment and Connection," begins the in-depth, how-to section of the book. It explains how and when to allocate and release the ODBC environment and connections in your programs.

■ Chapter 7, "Catalog and Statistics Functions," shows you how to get information about the databases and objects within a data source.

■ Chapter 8, "The ODBC Statement: An Introduction," discusses how ODBC statements are laid out and the methods used for running them.

■ Chapter 9, "Creating Tables with the DDL," explains how to use the ODBC API to create and drop tables, indexes, and views within your data source.

■ Chapter 10, "Inserting, Updating, and Deleting Rows," explains the proper method for modifying your data through ODBC.

■ In Chapter 11, "Queries and Result Sets," we introduce the art of querying your tables through the ODBC API—and dealing with the results that come back.

■ Chapter 12, "Setting Parameters with Prepared Statements," discusses the various methods of sending data to ODBC statements at run time.

■ In Chapter 13, "The Cursor Library and Positioned Operations," we present the more basic techniques for programmatically scrolling through result sets.

- Chapter 14, "Using the Wizards," begins the Visual C++ section of the book with an overview of the scenario that will be used for examples in these chapters. The rest of the chapter covers AppWizard and ClassWizard, two code generators included in Visual C++ that produce classes to interface to ODBC tables.

- Chapter 15, "Using the Transfer Mechanism," explains the classes of the Microsoft Foundation Class (MFC) library that encapsulate ODBC. Text and examples show how to use these classes to retrieve records and aggregate values and how to make updates and deletions to the table. The last part of the chapter shows how to use MFC classes to work with tables where the definition of the tables is not known when the code is written.

- Chapter 16, "Multi-Table Forms," concludes our VC++ section with using the MFC to perform joins to access multiple tables in a database and how one class can access tables in multiple databases. The remainder of the chapter discusses how to improve database performance by parameterized values and by directly executing SQL statements.

- Chapter 17, "Using the Visual Basic Data Control with ODBC 2.0," discusses the general design considerations and tradeoffs that a Visual Basic programmer needs to consider when developing an ODBC 2.0 Visual Basic application. Additional material is provided which describes what the relationship is between Visual Basic and ODBC 2.0, and the general characteristics of the Visual Basic Data Control's recordset.

- Chapter 18, "Using Visual Basic Data Access Objects with ODBC 2.0," treats another of the three possible ways to use Visual Basic to access ODBC 2.0 databases. The chapter delves into specific details about each of the Object Variables and the associated methods and properties of these variables.

- Chapter 19, "Using the ODBC API from within Visual Basic," addresses the techniques that would be used by Visual Basic programmers who want to make direct use of the ODBC 2.0 API function calls. The subject of ODBC conformance level is summarized so the programmer can determine what features his or her application might need.

- Chapter 20, "Optimizing ODBC," provides a variety of tips for improving the performance of your ODBC-enabled applications.

■ Chapter 21, "Referential Integrity," shows how ODBC can be used to enforce the validity of information in a database. The chapter explains entity integrity—defining rules for values in table columns, and referential integrity—enforcing references between different records. The chapter also provides an introduction to SQL's built-in integrity enforcement keywords.

■ Finally, in Chapter 22, "Successful Downsizing," we talk about the ultimate reason that many companies are interested in ODBC, and offer advice that can help you ride out that sometimes rocky road.

We've also included three appendixes and a glossary to move reference and general-interest material out of the main text:

■ Appendix A, "Resources in the SDK," describes the contents of the ODBC 2.0 Software Development Kit. You can use it as a brief guide to the sample applications and utilities included with the SDK.

■ Appendix B, "ODBC Function Reference," is a quick guide to all ODBC functions, organized by API conformance level.

■ Appendix C, "Contents of the Special Edition, *Using ODBC 2* CD-ROM," gives instructions for installing and using the programs and databases found on the accompanying CD-ROM.

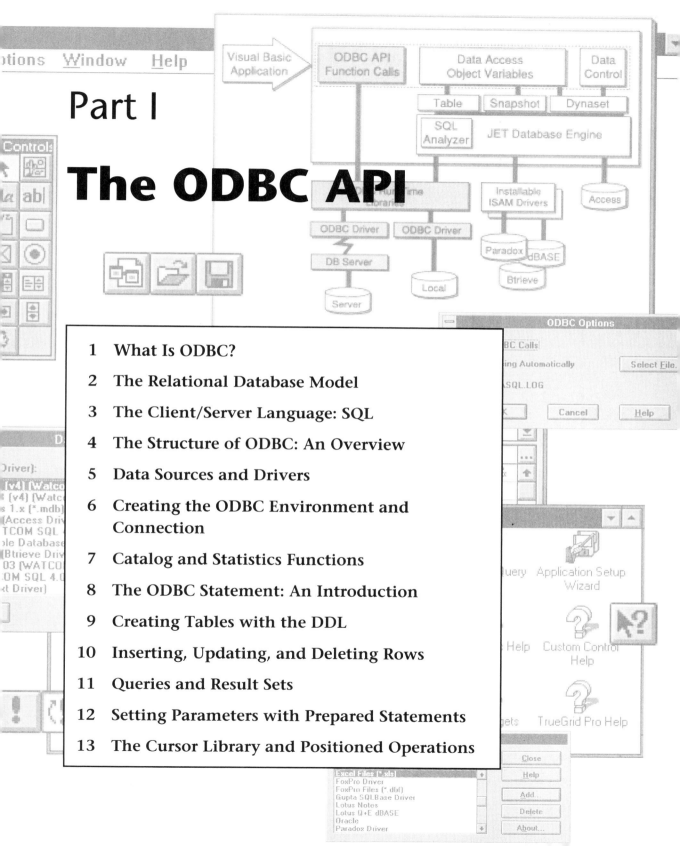

Part I

The ODBC API

1   What Is ODBC?

2   The Relational Database Model

3   The Client/Server Language: SQL

4   The Structure of ODBC: An Overview

5   Data Sources and Drivers

6   Creating the ODBC Environment and
    Connection

7   Catalog and Statistics Functions

8   The ODBC Statement: An Introduction

9   Creating Tables with the DDL

10 Inserting, Updating, and Deleting Rows

11 Queries and Result Sets

12 Setting Parameters with Prepared Statements

13 The Cursor Library and Positioned Operations

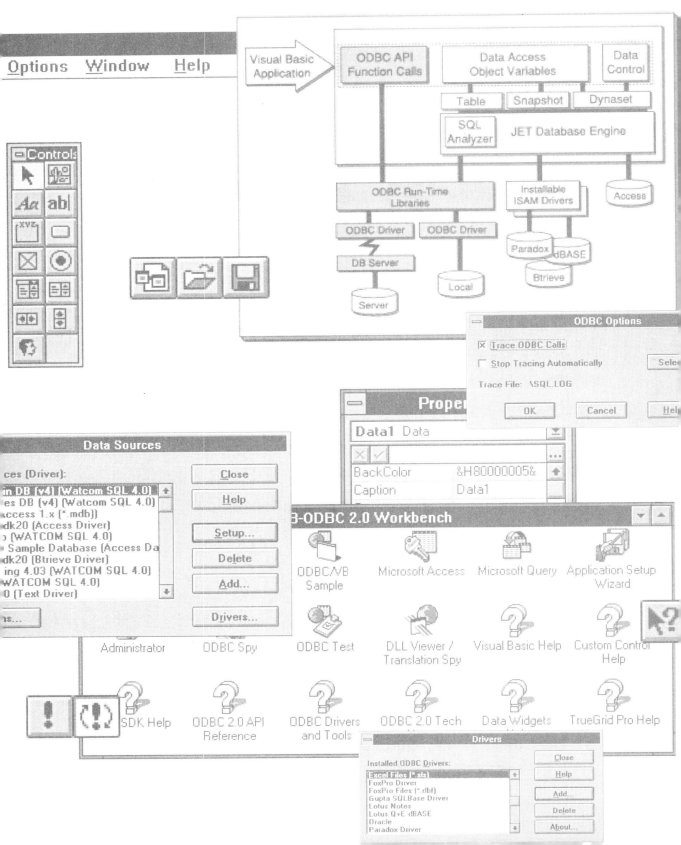

Chapter 1

What Is ODBC?

Open Database Connectivity (ODBC) is a uniform interface standard used to access databases. This chapter gives an introduction and overview of ODBC concepts. It also provides a road map to the rest of the book.

In this chapter, we discuss:

- What ODBC is
- How ODBC works
- Where ODBC came from
- Why you should use ODBC
- What you need to use ODBC
- What you need to learn to use ODBC
- Where ODBC is going

What Is ODBC, Anyway?

Open Database Connectivity is a database access library. It does just about the same thing as Sequiter's CodeBase, the Borland Paradox Engine, Informix ESQL, or dozens of other libraries. It allows your applications to manipulate data in a database.

What, then, is so different about ODBC? You probably have invested years of your life learning other database libraries. There is probably little appeal in learning another.

ODBC does have one major distinction. It can manipulate almost *any* database. It can access DB2 on an AS/400. It can manipulate bTrieve files on a laptop. It can access files that you might not even consider to be databases, like Excel spreadsheets or ASCII data.

Surely, there must be some shortcomings. The biggest limitation, at the time of this writing, is *where* ODBC operates. This book assumes that you're using one of Microsoft's Windows ODBC implementations, either the 16-bit Windows or the 32-bit Windows NT. Applications can use the ODBC Applications Programming Interface (API) on either platform with little or no change in the source code. A UNIX implementation is now available from Visigenic (see the following Note), and while this book does not specifically address any idiosyncrasies it may have, 90% of the material covered should apply equally to that platform.

> ### Note
>
> In Windows programming terminology, an API is a DLL or set of DLLs that gives the programmer access to a set of new functions. These functions can be incorporated into your applications wherever they are needed and can be mixed in with your own functions or those from other APIs.

> ### Note
>
> Microsoft has promised ODBC software for the Apple Macintosh and computers running under UNIX. There are also plans to make ODBC available from extended MS-DOS applications. In October of 1994, Microsoft exclusively licensed Visigenic Software, Inc. to provide ODBC APIs and drivers on non-Windows platforms. At this writing, Visigenic has thus far provided only a UNIX implementation.

You might be curious as to how ODBC can manipulate such diverse databases. That's the easy part. The vast majority of databases conform, in whole or in part, to the *relational* database concepts of E.F. Codd. Even products based on file management systems predating the relational model map well to it. ODBC looks at databases for what they have in common, not how they differ. For information about relational database concepts, see Chapter 2, "The Relational Database Model."

You won't have to make a radical change in how you think of your databases. The biggest change in dealing with relational databases is in *terminology*. You will still want to find the records that fit some criteria. The records are called *rows*, and the filter is a WHERE clause. The search itself is called a *query*.

Doesn't providing support for so many databases make ODBC complex? No; a typical application will use less than twenty different function calls. ODBC is based on the *Structured Query Language* (SQL). Using SQL greatly simplifies the API. It is the calculus of the relational database.

You might feel somewhat apprehensive about all this if most of your database programming experience is in an Xbase dialect or Parodox's application language (PAL). Isn't SQL supposed to be for client/server gurus or database czars in some corporate monolith? Nothing could be further from the truth. Most of the SQL grammar that you use in an ODBC application could be written to fit on the back of a postage stamp. To learn more about the Structured Query Language, see Chapter 3, "The Client/Server Language: SQL."

You also may have heard that ODBC itself is difficult to learn. This is not entirely true. The *documentation* for version 1.0 was poor, to be sure. Many prospective users gave up on ODBC because of it. To be fair, it was written to match ODBC in a pre-beta state, before many of the details of operation were settled. Just try to write documentation about nonexistent software some time.

This book specifically targets ODBC version 2.0. This release reflects the maturity that you would expect from a 2.x version. Most of the glaring omissions and errors have been corrected. Some new ideas have crept in, too. ODBC is no longer experimental.

Before proceeding, let me inform you of one thing that ODBC is not. *Using ODBC does not make your application instantly and completely database-independent.* That is not to say that it cannot or has not been done, however. The diversity of the underlying databases just makes absolute database independence an expensive and time-consuming prospect.

This revelation is often a shock to beginners. Unless you are writing a high-volume commercial application, you have little need for this capability. There is a certain level of functionality that you can *easily* support in your application that will work with the vast majority of databases.

This level of functionality and database support should suffice for all in-house development and most shrink-wrapped products. If you feel that your application *must* support all possible databases at a high level of functionality, you should make sure that:

■ The project is well-funded

■ Your organization is completely committed

■ You have developers with prior ODBC experience

If you go this route, prepare for a lengthy and expensive project.

The ODBC API

How Does ODBC Work?

ODBC provides a considerable amount of database independence through the use of *drivers*. Drivers are specific to a database. You use a Paradox ODBC driver to manipulate a Paradox database.

A driver is a module (usually a DLL) written to support ODBC function calls. Your application manipulates the database by calling these functions inside the driver. If you want to manipulate a different type of database, you dynamically link to a different driver.

The interface between ODBC and the driver varies little. Ideally, it would not vary at all. There is a certain set of functions, called the *core*, that all ODBC drivers support. The other functions that a driver supports are an important measure of ODBC support. Refer to Chapter 5, "Data Sources and Drivers," for a discussion of the different conformance levels that drivers can support.

Another component of ODBC is the *driver manager*. The driver manager is contained inside ODBC.DLL (or, in the 32-bit version of ODBC, in ODBC32.DLL), and is linked to all ODBC applications. It loads the desired drivers and manages the binding of ODBC function calls in your application to functions in the DLL.

ODBC drivers for large, client/server database management systems such as Oracle or Informix do not directly manipulate a database. These drivers are actually an interface to the network communication protocol that these databases use for remote operation. This could be NETBIOS (as with DB2/2), TCP/IP (as with Informix Online), or a proprietary protocol. In some cases, ODBC drivers for client/server DBMSs speak to the database engine *through* the proprietary interface provided by the DBMS' manufacturer. In other cases, the driver itself *is* the client side of the link, but this is less common.

Where Did ODBC Come From?

If you have used a client/server DBMS's native library, or embedded SQL, you will notice a strong resemblance to the equivalent components of the ODBC API. This is no accident. Two groups that often set standards in the UNIX world, the X/Open consortium and the SQL Access Group, came up with the basic design of what we now call ODBC.

Microsoft, the implementer of ODBC, has positioned it as a major part of WOSA, the Windows Open Systems Architecture. WOSA is Microsoft's vision of enterprise computing, along with the Telephony API (TAPI), the Messaging API (MAPI), and others.

Why You Should Use ODBC

There are many good reasons to use ODBC. Some are technical, while others are economic. Some are common sense. It's just hard to find a good reason *not* to use it.

Much of the motivation for using ODBC stems from its relative database independence. Changing databases is usually easy, and often trivial. It's often just a matter of changing drivers.

Let's say, for instance, that you are doing a downsizing. Your company is shopping for a client/server system to replace its aging mainframe. If you use ODBC, your development effort need not wait until a platform and database management system has been bid and delivered. You can develop on your PC with a database whose behavior is similar to a true client/server environment.

The ODBC API

Note

Many developers use PowerSoft's Watcom SQL system to simulate a typical client/server system. Its capabilities and behavior closely mimic a high-quality minicomputer-based database.

Database administration often proves to be more work than you might expect. If you have never handled these chores before, you need to learn how it is done before you have dozens of users and mission-critical data online. Watcom provides a safe but realistic environment for this.

Watcom SQL can be used in local, networked, or client/server mode. Its price (for local, single-user operation) is lower than some PC database libraries. If your volume is low, you may even want to consider using the Watcom product as your server.

Another good reason to use ODBC is to avoid using a different database API for each type of database that you use with an application. These database libraries usually take from a few weeks to several months to learn, even though they all operate in a similar manner.

A month's worth of salary, benefits, and administrative costs for a productive programmer can be quite expensive, approaching five figures. If five programmers must "retool" by learning a new API once a year, you may have wasted $50,000. Only in large companies would such an expense not be felt on the bottom line.

The only compelling reason to use a native API and avoid ODBC is if the slightly decreased performance of a well-written ODBC application is critical.

More often than not, insistence on using the fastest available API at any cost is more of an affectation than any real design consideration. We all like to be able to say that we did the best we could do. You must consider cost-effectiveness in the design of any system, however. To learn how to maximize ODBC performance, see Chapter 20, "Optimizing ODBC."

One non-technical reason to use ODBC is the fact that Microsoft implemented it and supports it. Microsoft can, by sheer mass, unilaterally impose standards and practices throughout the PC world, and for that matter, the entire computer world. Betting against Microsoft has been a very foolish bet, up to this point.

What Do You Need to Use ODBC?

There are several ways to use ODBC. The most convenient ways are to purchase one of the following:

- Microsoft Visual C++ 2.0

- Microsoft Visual Basic 3.0 for Windows Professional edition

- Level II of the Microsoft Developer's Network: the Development Platform CD-ROM

Any of these will provide you with the basic tools to use ODBC.

Visual C++ 2.0

To follow along with most of this book, everything you need is included with Microsoft's Visual C++ 2.0. It should include the libraries and headers for ODBC 2.0. It also includes the ODBC online help reference and various other items, many of which are discussed in Appendix A, "Resources in the SDK."

Visual C++ also includes the Microsoft Foundation Classes, or MFC. The MFC is a Windows application framework that includes extensive database classes based on ODBC. If you use these classes, you can distribute drivers from the Desktop Driver Set without royalty (see the documentation for details). To learn how to use the MFC database classes, see Chapters 16-18 in Part II, *Visual C++*.

Visual Basic Professional Edition

Visual Basic can access ODBC data sources through the JET Database Engine, a common interface used to access ISAM files and ODBC data sources. This interface provided the model that the MFC class designers used to implement the MFC database classes. This provides a simple, high-level interface to ODBC functionality. To learn how to use the Visual Basic Professional database functions, see Chapters 17-19 in Part III, *Visual Basic*.

The MSDN-II CD-ROM: The ODBC 2.0 SDK

The complete ODBC 2.0 SDK contains 16- and 32-bit versions of:

- The ODBC libraries and headers

- Several example programs

- Several utility programs

- ODBC application setup tools and examples

- Extensive online help

- The Desktop Driver Set (discussed in the next section)

- All the redistributable components of ODBC

If you are serious about ODBC, you really should get the SDK. In particular, the utility program called ODBCTest can be of great help when exploring the API or testing queries during development.

Having the SDK makes it easier to use ODBC with other vendors' compilers. There is nothing Microsoft-specific about ODBC.

The Desktop Database Driver Set

The Desktop Database Driver Set is a suite of ODBC drivers for the most common PC databases. The databases supported are:

- Microsoft Access

- FoxPro

- dBASE

- Paradox

- Excel spreadsheets

- ASCII delimited and fixed length files

Note that the Desktop Driver Set is included with all of the products mentioned in this list.

I

The ODBC API

> **Note**
>
> The Desktop Database Driver Set was previously available only in a 16-bit version. 32-bit drivers are now available, both from Microsoft and third-party vendors.

A partial listing of 32-bit drivers currently available is found in the following table.

File Format	Microsoft	Intersolv
Access	Available	
Clipper		Available
dBASE II, III, IV	Available	Available
Excel .XLS	Available	Available
FoxBase		Available
FoxPro 1, 2.5	Available	Available
Microsoft SQL Server	Available	Available
Oracle 7		Available
Paradox	Available	
Sybase SQL Server		Available
Text Files		Available

The vendors listed in the preceding table can be reached at the following locations:

Microsoft Developer Network
One Microsoft Way
Redmond, WA 98052-6339
Internet: msdn@microsoft.com
CompuServe: GO MSDN
(206) 936-7329 (fax) Attn: Developer Network

Intersolv (Q+E recently has been merged into Intersolv)
5540 Centerview Drive, Suite 324
Raleigh, NC 27606
(800) 876-3101
(919) 859-2220
(919) 859-9334 (fax)

What You Need to Learn to Use ODBC

To learn ODBC, you need a plan. Just poking about with the examples will make for rough going. This is because using ODBC requires a working knowledge of:

- Relational operations and terminology

- SQL grammar

- ODBC architecture

- How to use the API

If you make an honest effort to learn (or review) the first three items, learning the API will pose little problem. This book contains almost all the information that you need. You also will find the ODBC online help useful.

The Relational Model

If you know how to use any PC database, you already know something about relational databases. It's not necessary to memorize all the requirements and rules. What you need, at first, are the *terms*.

After you have read enough about the relational model to understand the terms and the basic operations, you might be interested in learning about database design. One standard way to model relational databases is to use entity-relationship (or E/R) diagrams.

Structured Query Language Grammar

SQL grammar defines the operations that may be performed on databases and tables. There are only a few of these, so you should be able to make your own SQL quick reference on a single sheet of paper. Some SQL statements you will often use are:

- CREATE: permits the creation of tables and indexes

- DROP: allows the destruction of tables and indexes

- INSERT: adds new rows to a table

- UPDATE: changes values in one or more rows in a table

- DELETE: removes rows from a table

There is one statement that bears more study than the above. It is the SELECT statement, used to query a table. You will likely use it most often. You may also find its grammar more complex than any other statement.

The ODBC API

You can use the SELECT statement to perform a *join*, or multi-table query. This operation enables you to show the relationships in tables directly. This is a very powerful concept.

Where Is All This Going?

Just as C++ enables the implementation of object-oriented concepts, SQL enables the implementation of relational concepts. SQL differs from C++ in that it has no real competitors within its domain.

SQL is also backed up by much more rigorous methods of validation than C++. It is derived directly from *set theory*, a well-established branch of mathematics. What all this means to developers is that a knowledge of SQL should be relative to transfer between different DBMS platforms. There have already been several major efforts to standardize SQL across the industry.

Database function call-level interfaces are much more arbitrary in nature. We are fortunate that the X/Open and SAG groups have together suggested a standard that was both well-designed and had a resemblance to several existing systems.

We will all benefit if the call-level interfaces continue to converge as much as SQL itself has done. In just a few years, all DBMSs could be manipulated with a single set of source code. The database world would find itself in a position of greater uniformity than computer languages may ever find themselves.

ODBC will be obsolete when this happens, but you will not be adversely affected. Your source code will require few changes to move from one DBMS to another. Best of all, it will all look like ODBC.

From Here...

- To learn about relational databases, refer to Chapter 2, "The Relational Database Model."

- If you're already completely familiar with relational databases, you can skip to Chapter 3, "The Client/Server Language: SQL" and learn about SQL.

- To dive right into programming topics, skip ahead to Chapter 5, "Data Sources and Drivers."

- To read about some of the more interesting items packed into the ODBC SDK, look at Appendix A, "Resources in the SDK."

Chapter 2

The Relational Database Model

The majority of ODBC-compliant data sources are Relational Database Management Systems (RDBMS). ODBC not only specifies an application programming interface to DBMSs but also Structured Query Language (SQL) as a database language. SQL is the standard database language for RDBMS. If you use ODBC, your data is most likely stored in an RDBMS.

In this chapter, you look at:

- The constructs, rules, and operators of the relational model

- The process of designing relational databases

- A complete database design example

History of the Relational Model

The relational model was developed in the 1970s; Dr. E.F. Codd is credited with its creation. The first commercial RDBMS implementations appeared in the early 1980s with products such as Ingres and Oracle.

Although today commercial database management systems based on newer models (such as the Object Data model) have appeared on the market, RDBMSs dominate the commercial database market and are likely to do so for a number of years.

The relational model introduced many improvements over its predecessors (Hierarchical and Network models). These improvements include:

- *Set processing*—the ability to manipulate sets of rows at a time versus a record at a time

- *Logical data independence*—the relational model provides better facilities to isolate applications from database changes (such as views)

- *Database navigation performed by the database management system*—in the previous models, the application was responsible for choosing the access path and decided how to navigate through the data (by using pointers). In RDBMSs this is performed by the database optimizer.

Structure of the Relational Model

The *relational model* is the foundation on which RDBMSs are implemented. It consists of the following:

- *Constructs*—the objects on which the model operate

- *Integrity rules*—must be satisfied for a database to be valid

- *Operators*—specify how we manipulate the objects of the model

Constructs of the Model

The relational model uses only one construct: two-dimensional tables consisting of rows and columns. All the rows of a table must be distinct. The column values must be *atomic* (cannot be decomposed). Repeating groups or arrays are not allowed in relational tables. Figure 2.1 shows a table of employees.

Fig. 2.1
An example of a relational table.

Employee Number	First Name	Last Name	Date Of Birth	Date Of Hire
1001	John	Doe	Oct 19, 1946	Jan 01, 1975
1005	Bill	Smith	Jan 10, 1970	Mar 23, 1994
2009	Mary	Doe	Sep 07, 1945	Jan 17, 1986
1004	Tom	Martin	Mar 08, 1942	July 6, 1956
0998	Robert	Carpenter	Oct 19, 1946	June 27, 1987

Note

The order of rows and columns in a relational table is irrelevant.

There may be missing values in some columns. These missing values are referred to as *null*s. Figure 2.2 shows the employee table with an additional column: Date_Of_Termination. The rows of the active employees have a missing value or null in the Date_Of_ Termination column.

> **Note**
>
> Most databases do not allow embedded spaces or blanks in identifiers (for example, table and column names). For readability in all the figures, you use blanks to separate words in column names. In the text, you use an underscore as the word separator (as in, Date Of Termination in a figure becomes Date_of_Termination) in the body of the text.

Employee Number	First Name	Last Name	Date Of Birth	Date Of Hire	Date Of Termination
1001	John	Doe	Oct 19, 1946	Jan 01, 1975	Jun 01, 1994
1005	Bill	Smith	Jan 10, 1970	Mar 23, 1994	
2009	Mary	Doe	Sep 07, 1945	Jan 17, 1986	
1004	Tom	Martin	Mar 08, 1942	July 6, 1956	May 01, 1994
0998	Robert	Carpenter	Oct 19, 1946	June 27, 1987	

Fig. 2.2
A relational table with missing column values.

> **Note**
>
> Although in the figures, null values appear like blanks, a missing value or null is differ-ent from a blank or zero. When comparing entries in columns, entries containing blanks or zeroes will be equal to each other. However, two entries containing nulls will not be equal to each other.
>
> In the database literature, tables are sometimes called *relations*—hence the name Relational. The terms *tuple* and *attributes* are also used to refer to rows and columns respectively.

Integrity Rules of the Model

A table's rows must be distinct. There is always a column or group of columns that is unique for every row. You will choose one column or group of col-umns to uniquely identify each row. This is called the *primary key* of the table. In your Employee table (refer to fig. 2.2), you could choose Employee Number or First Name and Last Name as the primary key.

Therefore, the primary key is a column or group of columns that uniquely identifies the rows of the table.

Note

There may be more than one column or group that can uniquely identify the rows of a table. One is chosen as the primary key. The other columns or groups are sometimes called *candidate keys* or *alternate keys*.

Figure 2.3 shows the Employee table with a primary key of Employee_Number.

Fig. 2.3
The primary key is Employee_Number.

Employee Number	First Name	Last Name	Date Of Birth	Date Of Hire
1001	John	Doe	Oct 19, 1946	Jan 01, 1975
1005	Bill	Smith	Jan 10, 1970	Mar 23, 1994
2009	Mary	Doe	Sep 07, 1945	Jan 17, 1986
1004	Tom	Martin	Mar 08, 1942	July 6, 1956
0998	Robert	Carpenter	Oct 19, 1946	June 27, 1987

Figure 2.4 shows the Employee table with a primary key consisting of the columns First_Name and Last_Name.

Fig. 2.4
The primary key is First_Name and Last_Name.

Employee Number	First Name	Last Name	Date Of Birth	Date Of Hire
1001	John	Doe	Oct 19, 1946	Jan 01, 1975
1005	Bill	Smith	Jan 10, 1970	Mar 23, 1994
2009	Mary	Doe	Sep 07, 1945	Jan 17, 1986
1004	Tom	Martin	Mar 08, 1942	July 6, 1956
0998	Robert	Carpenter	Oct 19, 1946	June 27, 1987

Note

In this example, the column Last_Name (by itself) could not be chosen as a primary key as there are two entries with a Last_Name of Doe. The Last_Name does not uniquely identify the rows of the Employee table. Therefore, it cannot be the primary key.

In RDBMs that enforce primary key constraints, any attempt to insert rows with duplicate primary key values is rejected with an error.

If your DBMS does not enforce the uniqueness of the primary key, use a unique index on the primary key columns to prevent the insertion of rows with duplicate primary key values.

This is not allowed by the Relational Model. Primary keys *must* be unique. If the DBMS allows the definition of primary keys, it will enforce it. Otherwise, a unique index is used to enforce uniqueness. When you think about relationships and foreign keys, if you used LAST_NAME as the primary key, and another table referred to the employee table and contained only LAST_NAME, to which Smith would it refer?

The relational model imposes the following rule on primary keys: A column that is part of a primary key cannot be null. This is the *entity integrity* rule. The primary key is used to identify the rows of a table. It wouldn't make sense to use a column that has a missing value to identify rows.

When you implement relational databases, you must be able to represent the relationship between tables. To do this, a table may contain columns that are the primary key of another table. This is called a *foreign key*. In figure 2.5, some employees have company cars. In figure 2.5b, Car_Number is the primary key of the Company_Car table. In figure 2.5a Car_Number is a foreign key in the Employee table (it refers to the primary key of the Company_Car table).

(a)

Employee Number	First Name	Last Name	Date Of Birth	Date Of Hire	Car Number
1001	John	Doe	Oct 19, 1946	Jan 01, 1975	10005
1005	Bill	Smith	Jan 10, 1970	Mar 23, 1994	
2009	Mary	Doe	Sep 07, 1945	Jan 17, 1986	81002
1004	Tom	Martin	Mar 08, 1942	July 6, 1956	
0998	Robert	Carpenter	Oct 19, 1946	June 27, 1987	

Fig. 2.5
An example of a foreign key.

(b)

Car Number	Make	Model	Year
10005	Ford	Tempo	1992
20003	Chrysler	LeBaron	1990
81002	Saturn	SL1	1993
09876	Ford	Escort	1992

The ODBC API

Foreign key columns must either be null or equal to an existing primary key value of the table to which they refer. This is the second integrity rule of the relational model and is called *referential integrity*.

In your example, the only valid values that could appear in the Car_Number column of the Employee table are 1005, 2003, 81002, and 09876. Therefore, you cannot insert a row in the Employee table with a Car_Number that is not in the Company_Car table. If your RDBMS enforces referential integrity, it would reject such an attempt with an error. Likewise, if you try to delete a row from the Company_Car table, you either can delete all the employees using this company car, replace the Car_Number column value for the employees by another one or null, or prevent the deletion.

Operators of the Model

The relational model is simple but powerful. Its strength comes from the expressive power of its operators. The relational model defines many operators. In this section, you examine the most important ones: selection, projection, join, and union.

Selection

The `selection` operator returns a subset of the rows of a table. It enables you to pick a horizontal slice from a table. In figure 2.6 you apply the selection operator against the Employee table of figure 2.6a. You select only the rows where the Last Name is equal to Doe. The results of the select are shown in figure 2.6b.

> **Note**
>
> The `Select` statement in SQL is not the same as the relational operator selection. Select in SQL is used to apply most of the relational operators including selection, projection, join and union.

Projection

The `projection` operator returns a subset of the columns of a table. It enables you to pick a vertical slice from a table. In figure 2.7, you pick only the First Name and Last Name columns from the Employee table (see fig. 2.7a). The results of the projection are shown in 2.7b.

(a)

Employee Number	First Name	Last Name	Date Of Birth	Date Of Hire
1001	John	Doe	Oct 19, 1946	Jan 01, 1975
1005	Bill	Smith	Jan 10, 1970	Mar 23, 1994
2009	Mary	Doe	Sep 07, 1945	Jan 17, 1986
1004	Tom	Martin	Mar 08, 1942	July 6, 1956
0998	Robert	Carpenter	Oct 19, 1946	June 27, 1987

(b)

Employee Number	First Name	Last Name	Date Of Birth	Date Of Hire
1001	John	Doe	Oct 19, 1946	Jan 01, 1975
2009	Mary	Doe	Sep 07, 1945	Jan 17, 1986

Fig. 2.6
The selection operator.

(a)

Employee Number	First Name	Last Name	Date Of Birth	Date Of Hire
1001	John	Doe	Oct 19, 1946	Jan 01, 1975
1005	Bill	Smith	Jan 10, 1970	Mar 23, 1994
2009	Mary	Doe	Sep 07, 1945	Jan 17, 1986
1004	Tom	Martin	Mar 08, 1942	July 6, 1956
0998	Robert	Carpenter	Oct 19, 1946	June 27, 1987

(b)

First Name	Last Name
John	Doe
Bill	Smith
Mary	Doe
Tom	Martin
Robert	Carpenter

Fig. 2.7
The projection operator.

Join

The join operator combines tables. Although there are many variations of the join, you will look at the most common one: the *natural join*. This operator joins tables based on one or more columns whose values in one table match the one in the other table. Both tables usually will contain a column with the same name. The natural join will eliminate one of them from the result. Figure 2.8 illustrates a natural join between the Employee and Company_Car tables (see figs. 2.8a and 2.8b). The join is performed on the Car_Number column. Since only two rows in the Employee table have non-null values in the Car_Number column, only two rows are included in the result (see fig. 2.8c).

Fig. 2.8
The natural join operator.

(a)

First Name	Last Name	Car Number
John	Doe	10005
Bill	Smith	
Mary	Doe	81002
Tom	Martin	
Robert	Carpenter	

(b)

Car Number	Make	Model	Year
10005	Ford	Tempo	1992
20003	Chrysler	LeBaron	1990
81002	Saturn	SL1	1993
09876	Ford	Escort	1992

(c)

First Name	Last Name	Car Number	Make	Model	Year
John	Doe	10005	Ford	Tempo	1992
Mary	Doe	81002	Saturn	SL1	1993

If you wanted all the rows from the Employee table (including the non-matching one), you can use the *outer join* operator. Figure 2.9 illustrates the result (see fig. 2.9c) of an outer join between the Employee (see fig. 2.9a) and the Company_Car tables (see fig. 2.9b). Note how nulls are put in the columns of the rows for which there was no match.

Note

To reiterate, although null values appear blank in the figures, they are different from blanks or zeroes.

(a)

First Name	Last Name	Car Number
John	Doe	10005
Bill	Smith	
Mary	Doe	81002
Tom	Martin	
Robert	Carpenter	

(b)

Car Number	Make	Model	Year
10005	Ford	Tempo	1992
20003	Chrysler	LeBaron	1990
81002	Saturn	SL1	1993
09876	Ford	Escort	1992

Fig. 2.9
The outer join operator.

(c)

First Name	Last Name	Car Number	Make	Model	Year
John	Doe	10005	Ford	Tempo	1992
Bill	Smith				
Mary	Doe	81002	Saturn	SL1	1993
Tom	Martin				
Robert	Carpenter				

Union

With the join operator you were able to combine tables vertically (concatenating columns from different tables). Union enables you to concatenate rows from different tables. The union of two tables can only be performed when the tables have union-compatible columns. That is, the columns must have the same or similar types. It would not make sense to perform a union in which one column of the result would contain both numeric and alphabetic entries.

In the example in figure 2.10, you perform a union between a Part-Time Employee (see fig. 2.10a) and Full-Time Employee (see fig. 2.10b) table to obtain a list of all the employees working for a company. The result of the union is shown in 2.10c.

> **Note**
>
> Each table in the example contains a row for Bill Smith (Employee_Number 1005). Since relational table rows must be unique, the duplicate rows are eliminated. The UNION ALL clause in SQL enables you to retain duplicate rows in an answer set.

The union is one of the set operators. The other set operators are *intersection*, *difference*, and *Cartesian product*. The intersection returns the rows which are in both tables. The difference returns the rows which are in the first but not in the second table. The Cartesian product is not used in practice and has mostly academic interest.

(a)

Fig. 2.10
The Union
operator.

Employee Number	First Name	Last Name
1001	John	Doe
1005	Bill	Smith
2009	Mary	Doe

(b)

Employee Number	First Name	Last Name
2001	Susan	Smith
1005	Bill	Smith
1004	Tom	Martin
0998	Robert	Carpenter

(c)

Employee Number	First Name	Last Name
1001	John	Doe
1005	Bill	Smith
2009	Mary	Doe
2001	Susan	Smith
1004	Tom	Martin
0998	Robert	Carpenter

Tip
In database design, it is common practice to always use the singular when naming tables or entities.

Tip
Primary key columns should be static and never change. Primary key updates are expensive since all foreign key references also must be updated.

Relational Database Design

One of the objectives of the relational model is to make the database understandable by both end users and programmers. To achieve this and to produce stable systems, you must pay special attention to the design of your databases. This section describes a process that leads to simple and stable databases. The process consists of three steps:

1. Defining the entities

2. Defining the relationships

3. Defining the attributes

It is important to perform the steps in the given order. If you proceed to a step before completing the preceding one, you most likely will miss some entities or relationships. Following a process will enable you to deal with large databases with confidence.

> **Note**
>
> When designing databases for large and complex systems, you may want to organize the database design around the major subjects of the systems. In business application some subjects are: customers, products, transactions, and so on.
>
> If you organize your database around these subjects, you will be able to share the data across many applications.

Defining the Entities

The first step in developing a database is to define the entities. These entities will be implemented as tables in your database.

An *entity* is a person, thing, or concept that the database must store. Entities in commercial applications may include employee, product, transaction, invoice, and line item. To qualify an item as an entity you must be able to distinguish between different occurrences of an entity (otherwise you could not define a primary key). If you cannot distinguish the different occurrences, you are most likely not dealing with an entity.

Once you have identified an entity, you choose its primary key. The primary key must be unique and cannot allow nulls.

If an entity has many occurrences, it is better to choose a primary key that is automatically generated by the system. Sequences in Oracle, Identity in Sybase, or any auto incrementing column feature implemented by the DBMS can be used. If the DBMS does not support such features, procedures in the database or the application can be used to generate the primary keys.

Figure 2.11 illustrates two entities: Invoice (see fig. 2.11a) and Invoice_Status (see fig. 2.11b).

Tip
In RDBMSs that do not enforce the entity integrity rule, use a unique index over the primary key columns to enforce uniqueness.

Tip
Use a NOT NULL constraint when defining the primary key columns.

Tip
Use the SQLPrimaryKeys ODBC function to retrieve primary key information on existing tables.

(a)

(b)

Invoice Number
1
3
2

Status Code
P
I

Fig. 2.11
Modeling two entities.

Some entities depend on other entities for their existence. For example, an invoice line cannot exist without an invoice. These entities are called *dependent entities*. The entity on which their existence depends is called the *parent entity*. Dependent entities always have a primary key that consists of multiple columns. One of these is the primary key of the parent entity.

In figure 2.12, the Invoice_Line is a dependent entity.

(a)

(b)

Fig. 2.12
A dependent entity.

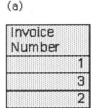

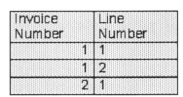

Caution

Before modeling an entity as a dependent you should ensure the following applies to the dependent entity:

- It must always have a parent (its existence depends on the parent)

- It must have at most one parent (otherwise, it is a relationship)

- It must always have the same parent (no update to primary keys)

You now have come to your last topic on entities. Consider the following situation: a company employs full-time and part-time employees. Both types of employees have employee number, first, and last names. However, only full-time employees have salaries. Part-time employees have hourly wages. The entities Part-Time Employee and Full-Time Employee are *subtypes* of Employee. Employee is called the *supertype*. In this example, an employee must be either a part-time or a full-time employee but not both. Therefore, these subtypes are mutually exclusive. In this example, the set of employees is equal to the union of Part-Time and Full-Time employees (since an employee *must* be Part-Time or Full-Time).

Therefore, a supertype is an entity that generalizes a concept. It contains attributes that are common to its subtypes. The subtypes represent the specialization of a concept. They have attributes that are unique to them.

You can implement these subtypes in three different ways:

- Only one table (which would contain all the attributes). Figure 2.13 illustrates this implementation. In this implementation you must be careful to ensure an employee cannot have both a salary and an hourly wage. You also should check that the Salary_Amount is specified when the Employee_Type is F (Full-Time), and the Hourly_Wage_Amount is specified when the Employee_Type is P (Part-Time).

Employee Number	First Name	Last Name	Employee Type	Salary Amount	Hourly Wage Amount
1001	John	Doe	F	50,000	
1005	Bill	Smith	P		23.00
2009	Mary	Doe	F	65,000	

Fig. 2.13
Using one table to implement mutually exclusive subtypes.

- Tables that only represent the subtypes (the attributes of the supertype are placed in the subtype tables). Figure 2.14 shows this implementation. When inserting into one of the subtype tables, you should check that the employee does not exist in the other table. The Full-Time and Part-Time employees are shown in figures 2.14a and 2.14b respectively.

- Separate tables for the supertype and its subtypes. This is illustrated in figure 2.15. When you insert rows in the subtype table, you should ensure that the insert is consistent with the employee type. The Employee table in 2.15a implements the supertype. The Full-Time and Part-Time subtypes are shown in 2.15b and 2.15c respectively.

Note

You use an Employee Type in the Employee table to differentiate between part-time and full-time employees. Although this is not strictly required, it helps maintain integrity and will provide better performance. Without this column, in the third alternative you would have to check the subtype tables to determine whether an employee is a part-time or full-time employee. If there were a large number of subtypes, this would degrade performance.

Fig. 2.14
Using subtypes
table only.

(a)

Employee Number	First Name	Last Name	Salary Amount
1001	John	Doe	50,000
1005	Bill	Smith	
2009	Mary	Doe	65,000

(b)

Employee Number	First Name	Last Name	Hourly Wage Amount
1001	John	Doe	
1005	Bill	Smith	23.00
2009	Mary	Doe	

There are two other variations of subtypes. Consider the previous example, and let's change the definition so that you allow employees that are neither full-time nor part-time (such as retired employees). In this case, the subtypes are not complete, since they do not cover all the employees. For this case you only can use the first or third alternative. These tables are shown in figures 2.16 and 2.17. Note that Robert Martin (Employee_Number 1002) is neither a full-time nor a part-time employee.

The last case is when the subtypes are not mutually exclusive. Consider a business that has customers and employees. For your example, customers and employees are subtypes of persons (with attributes Last_Name and First_Name). Employee has attribute Salary amount and Customer has attribute Credit_Limit. A person can be both a customer and an employee. This case is similar to incomplete subtypes: you can use either the first or third alternative. These are illustrated in figures 2.18 and 2.19.

(a)

Employee Number	First Name	Last Name	Employee Type
1001	John	Doe	F
1005	Bill	Smith	P
2009	Mary	Doe	F

Fig. 2.15
Using separate tables for the supertype and its subtypes.

(b)

Employee Number	Salary Amount
1001	50,000
2009	65,000

(c)

Employee Number	Hourly Wage Amount
1005	23.00

Employee Number	First Name	Last Name	Employee Type	Salary Amount	Hourly Wage Amount
1001	John	Doe	F	50,000	
1005	Bill	Smith	P		23.00
2009	Mary	Doe	F	65,000	
1002	Robert	Martin			

Fig. 2.16
Incomplete subtypes using one table.

Note

When you use only one table to model subtypes, you will have many rows with null values. This is typical of this implementation. Also, the validation rules to ensure the required values are input for the appropriate type are usually complex. For these reasons, I recommend always using separate tables for the supertype and its subtypes.

(a)

Fig. 2.17
Incomplete
subtypes using
tables for the
supertype and
its subtypes.

Employee Number	First Name	Last Name	Employee Type
1001	John	Doe	F
1005	Bill	Smith	P
2009	Mary	Doe	F
1002	Robert	Martin	

(b)

Employee Number	Salary Amount
1001	50,000
2009	65,000

(c)

Employee Number	Hourly Wage Amount
1005	23.00

Fig. 2.18
Non-exclusive
subtypes using
one table.

Person Number	First Name	Last Name	Salary Amount	Credit Limit Amount
1001	John	Doe	50,000	10,000
1005	Bill	Smith		2,300
2009	Mary	Doe	65,000	
1002	Robert	Martin	30,000	5,000

(a)

Employee Number	First Name	Last Name
1001	John	Doe
1005	Bill	Smith
2009	Mary	Doe
1002	Robert	Martin

Fig. 2.19
Non-exclusive
subtypes using
tables for the
supertype and
its subtypes.

The ODBC API

(b)

Person Number	Salary Amount
1001	50,000
2009	65,000
1002	30,000

(c)

Person Number	Credit Limit Amount
1001	10,000
1005	2,300
1002	5,000

Defining the Relationships

Now that you have defined your entities, you are ready to move on to relationships. You can proceed in a fairly mechanical fashion and check whether every pair of entities in your database is related.

Relationships come in three varieties:

- One-to-one

- One-to-many

- Many-to-many

You implement the first two by placing the primary key of one of the entities in the related entity. Many-to-many relationships always require a separate table.

One-to-One Relationships

A relationship is one-to-one when an entity relates to at most one other entity. For example, in a company some employees are assigned, at the most, one company car. There is a one-to-one relationship between the entities Employee and Company_Car.

> **Note**
>
> To implement a one-to-one relationship, a unique index must be defined over the foreign key column. The only difference between a one-to-one and a one-to-many relationship is the uniqueness of the foreign key column(s).

Tip

Don't combine entities with one-to-one relationships into a single table. You should model distinct entities as distinct tables.

To model the one-to-one relationship, the primary key of one of the entities is placed in the other entity. You could place the primary key of the Employee table in the Company_Car table as shown in figure 2.20. The other option is to place the primary key of the Company_Car table in the Employee table as illustrated in figure 2.21.

(a)

(b)

Fig. 2.20
Employee_Number is a foreign key in the Company_Car table.

Employee Number
1001
1005
1004
1003
1009

Car Number	Employee Number
01	1004
07	
03	1003
06	1005

(a)

(b)

Fig. 2.21
Car_Number is a foreign key in the Employee table.

Employee Number	Company Car
1001	
1005	06
1004	01
1003	03
1009	

Car Number
01
07
03
06

Where should you put the foreign key? The rule is to place the foreign key in the table that has the fewest rows. In your example, the Company Car table has four rows and the Employee table has five. Therefore, you choose the solution illustrated in figure 2.20, where the Employee Number (the primary key of the Employee table) appears as a foreign key in the Company Car table. If you look at the Company Car table in figure 2.20, there is one null value in the Employee Number column. In figure 2.21 there are 2 null values in the Car Number column of the Employee table. You put the primary key in the table with the fewest rows to minimize the number of null values in the foreign key column.

Note that you cannot allow duplicate values in the foreign key column(s). The Car_Number and the Employee_Number values must be unique in both the Employee and Company_Car tables. Otherwise, the relationship would not be one-to-one since you would allow many cars per employee or a car to be shared by many employees.

> **Caution**
>
> One-to-one relationships are rare. I have never come across a data model that had more than one one-to-one relationship. If you have a data model with many one-to-one relationships, check that you have not used one-to-one relationships instead of subtypes.

One-to-Many Relationships

One-to-many relationships are the most common type of relationships. These occur when one entity—let's call it "A"—is related to at most one other entity—let's call it "B"—and entity B can be related to more than one instance of entity A.

Consider the following example: Employees can work in at most one department, and a department has many employees. There is a one-to-many relationship between employees and departments. This relationship is implemented by placing the foreign key in the "many" side of the relationship. In your example, since a department can have many employees, you will place the foreign key in the Employee table. This is illustrated in figure 2.22.

Note how the Department code SALES occurs twice in the Employee table. This is legitimate since a department can have many employees. In your example, employees 1001 and 1004 both work in the Sales department. The non-uniqueness of the foreign key column(s) is the only difference between one-to-one and one-to-many relationships.

Tip

If the relationship is mandatory—the entity must always be related to the other entity—place a NOT NULL constraint over the foreign key column.

I

The ODBC API

(a)   (b)

Fig. 2.22
One-to-many
relationship:
foreign key placed
on the "many"
side.

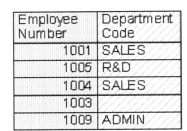

Let's see what happens if you put the foreign key in the wrong table (in your example, the Department table). Figure 2.23 shows this situation.

When you place the foreign key in the wrong table, you are unable to model the situation correctly. In figure 2.23, an employee can work in at most one department. When you use sample data in your models, it is easy to catch errors before you implement.

(a)   (b)

Fig. 2.23
One-to-many
relationship:
putting the
foreign key on
the wrong side.

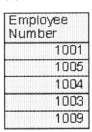 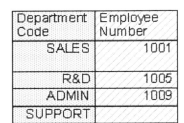

Many-to-Many Relationships

You handle many-to-many relationships differently from the other two types of relationships. You always have to add a new table.

A many-to-many relationship occurs when an entity can relate to more than one instance of another entity and vice versa. A student can take many courses and a course may be taken by more than one student. There is a many-to-many relationship between courses and students. To implement the relationship you will define a new table whose primary key will consist of the primary keys of the related entities. Figure 2.24c shows the new table, called Enrollment, that is created. The Student and Course entities are shown in figures 2.24a and 2.24b.

(a)

Student Number
1001
1005
1004
1003
1009

(b)

Course Code
MAT101
ENG107
PHL203
SOC406

Fig. 2.24
Many-to-many relationship: the Enrollment table implements the relationship.

(c)

Student Number	Course Code
1001	MAT101
1001	ENG107
1004	MAT101
1003	SOC406
1009	MAT101

For one-to-one and one-to-many relationships, a null value in the foreign key column told you that there were no relationships. For many-to-many relationships, the absence of rows in the relationship table tells you that there are no relationships. In your example, no students are taking course PHL203 and student 1005 is taking it easy this year: he/she is taking no courses. You know this because there are no rows in the enrollment table with Course Code PHL203 and Student Number 1005.

Defining Attributes

After you have completed the previous two steps, the definition of attributes is a straightforward process. Your objective in database design is to produce databases that are easy to maintain and where data redundancy is minimized.

Normalization is a process based on mathematical theory that leads to databases that exhibit desirable properties. The rules of normalization help you decide where you should put your attributes.

Normalization is based on the concept of *normal forms*. A table is in a normal form if it satisfies certain properties or constraints. In this section you examine informally the first three normal forms.

A table is in *first normal form* (*1NF*) if every column contains atomic data values. This is the reason why RDBMSs do not support repeating groups, arrays, lists, and nested relations. Figure 2.25 shows a table that is not in 1NF. This table violates 1NF because each cell in the Courses column contains more than one course.

Fig. 2.25
Table violating
1NF: repeating
group in the
Courses column.

Student Number	Courses
1001	MAT101 ENG107 SOC203
1005	MAT203 PHY105
1004	
1003	PHL432
1009	

To make the table conform to 1NF, you just need to eliminate the repeating course entries. The 1NF equivalent tables (Course and Enrollment) are shown in figure 2.26.

Fig. 2.26
Changing a table
to 1NF: eliminat-
ing repeating
groups.

(a)

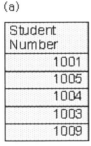

Student Number
1001
1005
1004
1003
1009

(b)

Student Number	Course Code
1001	MAT101
1001	ENG107
1001	SOC203
1005	MAT203
1005	PHY105
1003	PHL432

Note

You cannot create relations that are not in 1NF in a relational DBMS. However, if you frequently apply operations (such as substring) to decompose columns, the columns do not contain atomic data values. You should split the column into multiple columns.

Second normal form (*2NF*) applies only to tables having a primary key with multiple columns. A table is in 2NF if it is in 1NF and all the non-primary key column values depend on all the primary key columns. The table in figure 2.27 is not in 2NF. The values in the column Course_Description do not depend on Student_Number, which is part of the primary key.

Student Number	Course Code	Course Description
1001	MAT101	Calculus
1001	ENG107	Mechanical Engineering
1001	SOC203	Advanced Sociology
1005	MAT101	Calculus
1005	PHY105	Quantum Physics
1003	PHL432	The Body and Mind

Fig. 2.27
Table violating 2NF: Course_Description does not depend on Student_Number.

Tables that violate 2NF suffer from a number of problems. In your example, when you update a course description, you must update all the rows of the enrollment table. If you delete the last student enrolled in a course, you lose the description for the course (as well as the fact that the course existed in the first place). 2NF eliminates these anomalies.

To transform the table in 2NF, you remove the description column and place it in a course table. The 2NF tables are shown in figure 2.28.

A table is in *third normal form* (*3NF*) if it is in 2NF and all the columns depend only on the primary key or an alternate key.

Tables that are not in 3NF also exhibit anomalies. In figure 2.29 you have courses offered by departments. The Course table is not in 3NF since the Department_Description depends on the Department_Code. If you update a Department Description you must update all the appropriate rows in the Course table.

The equivalent 3NF tables are shown in figure 2.30.

When you design databases, your databases will be normalized if you follow common sense. Although normalization may seem complex, it is really about putting columns in the right tables. In your examples, it should be obvious that the course description belongs in the course table and not in the enrollment table. As well, why would you put the department name in the course table!

Tip
To remember normalization, remember this phrase: *The Key, The Whole Key, Nothing But The Key!*

(a)

Fig. 2.28
Tables in 2NF.

Student Number	Course Code
1001	MAT101
1001	ENG107
1001	SOC203
1005	MAT101
1005	PHY105
1003	PHL432

(b)

Course Code	Course Description
MAT101	Calculus
ENG107	Mechanical Engineering
SOC203	Advanced Sociology
MAT101	Calculus
PHY105	Quantum Physics
PHL432	The Body and Mind

(a)

Fig. 2.29
Table violating
3NF: Department
_Description
depends on the
Department_Code.

Course Code	Course Description	Department Code	Department Name
MAT101	Calculus	MATH	Mathematics and Statistics
ENG107	Mechanical Engineering	ENG	Engineering Sciences
SOC203	Advanced Sociology	SOC	Sociology and Anthropology
MAT101	Calculus	MATH	Mathematics and Statistics
PHY105	Quantum Physics	MATH	Mathematics and Statistics
PHL432	The Body and Mind	PHL	Philosophy

(b)

Department Code
MATH
ENG
SOC
PHL

(a)

Course Code	Course Description	Department Code
MAT101	Calculus	MATH
ENG107	Mechanical Engineering	ENG
SOC203	Advanced Sociology	SOC
MAT101	Calculus	MATH
PHY105	Quantum Physics	MATH
PHL432	The Body and Mind	PHL

(b)

Department Code	Department Name
MATH	Mathematics and Statistics
ENG	Engineering Sciences
SOC	Sociology and Anthropology
PHL	Philosophy

Fig. 2.30
Tables in 3NF: removing attributes not dependent on non-primary key columns.

Now that you know the rules to place attributes in tables, you need to do the following before you implement your design:

- Choose the data type of each column: integer, character, and so on

- Choose the length, precision, or scale of each column

- Decide whether null values should be allowed or not

- Decide whether default values should be supplied by the DBMS when the user does not supply a value

- Decide whether the values in the column must be unique

- Document any other constraints that the column values must satisfy (such as range constraints)

Very often the applications accessing the database will require values that must be computed on some rows of the database. For example, an application dealing with employees may require the average employee salary per department. Figure 2.31 shows a database with the Average_Salary_Amount column in the department table.

This is called a *derived attribute or column*. We can obtain the average salary per department with the following SQL statement:

```
Select Department_Code
      ,AVG(Salary_Amount)
   from Employee
   Group by Department_Code
```

(a)

Fig. 2.31
Department table
with derived
column:
`Average_Salary`
`_Amount.`

Employee Number	First Name	Last Name	Salary Amount	Department Code
1001	John	Doe	20,000	SALES
1005	Bill	Smith	30,000	SALES
2009	Mary	Doe	25,000	ENG
1004	Tom	Martin	20,000	ADMIN
0998	Robert	Carpenter		ENG

(b)

Department Code	Average Salary Amount
SALES	25,000
ENG	25,000
ADMIN	20,000

Do not introduce derived columns in your database unless you have performance problems. They make updates to the database more expensive and require procedures to keep them synchronized. In your example, any insert or delete against the Employee table would require an update of the Average_Salary_Amount column in the Department table. Updates to the Salary_Amount of any employee would also require an update to the Department table.

Recursive Relationships

You now have all the tools to go and design your databases. Before you look at a complete design example, let's look at two special cases of relationships.

A table has a *recursive relationship* when it is related to itself. Consider the following typical situation in a company: an employee reports to one employee (a manager) and another employee (the manager) can have many employees reporting to him or her. Unless you introduce role names (in your example, manager) talking about recursive relations can be pretty confusing. Like other relationships, they can be one-to-one, one-to-many, or many-to-many.

Recursive relationships are modeled exactly the same way as any other relationships. Since column names in a table must be unique, when you place the foreign key you will prefix it with the role name.

Figure 2.32 models the employees of your company.

Employee Number	First Name	Last Name	Manager Employee Number
1001	John	Doe	
1005	Bill	Smith	1001
2009	Mary	Doe	1005
1004	Tom	Martin	1005
0998	Robert	Carpenter	1005

Fig. 2.32
A one-to-many recursive relationship.

In this example Mary, Tom, and Robert report to Bill, who reports to John. This was handled like any other one-to-many relationship by placing a foreign key on the "many" side of the relationship.

You handle many-to-many recursive relationships like other many-to-many relationships. You create a new table. The classic example of a many-to-many recursive relationship is found in manufacturing. An assembly contains parts. These parts can themselves be assemblies. Therefore you have the following: a part (assembly) can contain many parts and a part can be used in many parts (assemblies). Figure 2.33 illustrates the situation.

(a)

Part Number	Part Description
001	Bicycle
002	Wheel
005	Hub
098	Spoke
104	Pedal
003	Handlebar

Fig. 2.33
A many-to-many recursive relationship.

(b)

Part Number	Component Part Number	Quantity
001	002	2
001	104	2
001	003	1
002	005	1
002	098	32

The ODBC API

The assembly table in figure 2.33b implements the many-to-many recursive relationship. You can see that a bicycle (Part Number 001) requires two wheels, two pedals, one frame, and one handlebar. A wheel (Part Number 002) requires a hub and 32 spokes. The primary key of the Assembly table consists of the primary keys of the Part table twice: the first one as a part, the other as a component. To find out if a part is used somewhere as a component, you just check if its Part_Number appears in the Component_Part_Number column.

History Tables

Often an application must maintain historical values of data. History tables are required to keep track of changing attributes or relationships.

A payroll application must maintain a history of employee salaries. To do this, you must implement a Salary_History table. The primary key consists of the Employee_Number and the effective date of the salary. Figure 2.34a shows the original table and figures 2.34b and 2.34c the equivalent history tables.

(a)

Fig. 2.34
Implementing a history table for an attribute.

Employee Number	First Name	Last Name	Salary Amount
1001	John	Doe	20,000
1005	Bill	Smith	30,000
2009	Mary	Doe	25,000
1004	Tom	Martin	20,000
0998	Robert	Carpenter	

(b)

Employee Number	First Name	Last Name
1001	John	Doe
1005	Bill	Smith
2009	Mary	Doe
1004	Tom	Martin
0998	Robert	Carpenter

(c)

Employee Number	Salary Effective Date	Salary Amount
1001	Jan 01, 1993	15,000
1001	Mar 01, 1994	20,000
1005	Jun 01, 1992	30,000
2009	Feb 10, 1987	22,500
2009	Jul 10, 1993	25,000
1004	Mar 01, 1994	20,000

Note that there are no rows in the Salary_History table for Robert Carpenter (Employee_Number 0998) since his salary was null in the original table. You must include the Effective_Salary_Date as part of the primary key in the

Salary_History table as there may be many rows for the same employee. To find an employee's current salary, you pick the row for the given employee with the most recent effective date from the Employee_Salary_History table.

You also may need to maintain a history for relationships. Consider a company where you need to keep track of the departments where an employee has worked. To create the history you remove the foreign key from the Employee table (see fig. 2.35a) and create an Employee_Department_History table (see fig. 2.35c). This is illustrated in figure 2.35.

(a)

Employee Number	Department Code
1001	SALES
1005	R&D
1004	SALES
1003	
1009	ADMIN

Fig. 2.35
Implementing a history table for a one-to-many relationship.

(b)

Employee Number
1001
1005
1004
1003
1009

(c)

Employee Number	Effective Date	Department Code
1001	Jan 01, 1982	SALES
1005	Feb 01, 1986	R&D
1004	Mar 01, 1982	SALES
1004	Jul 01, 1990	ADMIN
1009	Aug 10, 1994	ADMIN

Note that the primary key of the history table consists of the Employee_Number and the Effective_Date. You could not use only Employee_Number and Department_Code for the primary key since an employee could be transferred to a department and later come back. History for one-to-one and one-to-many relationships is handled in a similar way.

History for many-to-many relationships requires a modification to the existing relationship table. Let's look again at the many-to-many relationships for students enrolling in courses. Since students may drop, fail, or repeat courses, you should keep track of the student enrollment history. This is depicted in figure 2.36. Figure 2.36a shows the original table. Figure 2.36b shows the equivalent history table.

I

The ODBC API

Fig. 2.36
Implementing a
history table for a
many-to-many
relationship.

(a)

Student Number	Course Code
1001	MAT101
1001	ENG107
1001	SOC203
1005	MAT203
1005	PHY105
1003	PHL432

(b)

Student Number	Enrollment Date	Course Code
1001	Jan 01, 1992	MAT101
1001	Jul 05, 1993	ENG107
1001	Jan 01, 1992	SOC203
1005	Jul 05, 1993	MAT203
1005	Jul 05, 1993	PHY105
1003	Jan 01, 1992	PHL432

Note

You rarely allow deletions of rows from a history table. If, in your Employee and Department examples, it is possible for an employee not to be assigned to a department, you would need to add a Termination_Date column to the Employee_Department_History table. The rows that reflect the current assignments would have a null in this column. In figure 2.37b, from May 01, 1990 to Jul 01, 1990 Employee 1004 was not assigned to any department.

Fig. 2.37
Handling gaps in
history tables.

(a)

Employee Number
1001
1005
1004
1003
1009

(b)

Employee Number	Effective Date	Termination Date	Department Code
1001	Jan 01, 1982		SALES
1005	Feb 01, 1986		R&D
1004	Mar 01, 1982	May 01, 1990	SALES
1004	Jul 01, 1990		ADMIN
1009	Aug 10, 1994		ADMIN

A Complete Example

You now have a solid foundation to design databases. You have just been assigned the following project—to design a database for a publishing house.

At your first meeting with the user, she tells you: "Well, I have so many things to keep track of that I don't know where to begin. First, we have authors. We need their names. Then we have books, lots of them. We use an internal number to identify them. What did you say? ISBN number! Boy, you are sharp! In fact, our book number is derived from the last four digits of the ISBN number. We'd like to keep it that way. We keep track of the title, the number of pages, and the retail price. Some books are written by more than one author. Can an author write more than one book? Yes, of course! A book may have many printings. The good ones may have over a dozen printing runs. I need to know the printing dates and the number of copies printed. Also, I need to have monthly sales figures. Every month I have to know how many copies of each book we have sold. We classify books according to their topics. For example, we have RO for romance, MY for mysteries, WE for westerns, and so on. Books can only belong to one category. Oh, by the way, I forgot to tell you, some authors do not use their real names; they use 'pen names'. I need to know the author's real name. They hate it when we send them a check under their pen names. You see, they cannot cash the checks! Some authors use many pen names. Can you handle all this in your database?"

The first step is to define the entities and choose the primary keys. From the above description you have:

- Author

- Book

- Category

- Printing (an entity dependent on book)

- Book Sales History

The tables and their primary keys are shown in figure 2.38.

The next step is to identify the relationships. You have the following relationships:

- Many-to-many between Book and Author

- One-to-many between Category and Book

- One-to-many between Author (Real) and Author (Pen Name)

Figure 2.39 shows the tables with the foreign keys.

Now you are ready to place your attributes. Since you defined all your tables already, this is a simple task. Table 2.40 shows the completed data model.

Fig. 2.38
A design example:
defining the
entities.

(a)

Book Number
1
2
3

(b)

Author Number
1
2
3

(c)

Category Code
RO
MI
WE

(d)

Book Number	Printing Number
1	1
1	2
3	1

(e)

Book Number	Year Month
1	Jan 91
1	Feb 91
1	Mar 91

Fig. 2.39
A design example:
defining the
relationships.

(a)

Book Number	Category Code
1	RO
2	RO
3	WE

(b)

Author Number	Real Author Number
1	
2	1
3	1
4	

(c)

Category Code
RO
MI
WE

(d)

Book Number	Printing Number
1	1
1	2
3	1

(e)

Book Number	Year Month
1	Jan 91
1	Feb 91
1	Mar 91

(f)

Book Number	Author Number
1	2
1	4
2	3
3	4

(a)

Book Number	Category Code	Title	Number Of Pages	Retail Price Amount
1	RO	Tea for two	150	24.95
2	RO	Love at first sight	200	29.95
3	WE	Fight at the Coral	129	14.95

(b)

Category Code
RO
MI
WE

Fig. 2.40
A design example: placing the attributes.

(c)

Book Number	Printing Number	Printing Date	Copies Printed
1	1	Jan 1, 1994	10,000
1	2	May 5, 1994	25,000
3	1	Jul 17, 1993	5,000

(d)

Book Number	Year Month	Copies Sold
1	Jan 91	7,890
1	Feb 91	2,654
1	Mar 91	1,023

(e)

Book Number	Author Number
1	2
1	4
2	3
3	4

(f)

Author Number	Real Author Number	Author Name
1		Doe
2	1	Casanova
3	1	Don Juan
4		Smith

You examine the database language SQL in the next chapter, so after completing that chapter you will be able to implement your database design, query, and update your databases.

From Here...

- To learn how to define, query, and update your databases, consult Chapter 3, "The Client/Server Language: SQL," Chapter 9, "Creating Tables with the DDL," Chapter 10, "Inserting, Updating, and Deleting Rows," and Chapter 11, "Queries and Result Sets."

- To find out about your existing databases, look at Chapter 7, "Catalog and Statistics Functions." The ODBC catalog functions enable you to obtain information about the tables, columns, and keys in your databases.

- Details on how to enforce referential integrity can be found in Chapter 21, "Referential Integrity."

Chapter 3

The Client/Server Language: SQL

ODBC specifies Structured Query Language (SQL) as its database language. SQL is the *de jure* standard for relational database access. It has become so pervasive in the database industry that it is also used by databases supporting other models. It is now used for file, network, and object-oriented database access.

Database vendors have extended SQL far beyond a database language. Some dialects include logic flow constructs (such as IF-THEN-ELSE or DO-WHILE). Where SQL has been extended, it can be used as a full-fledged programming language. These SQL extensions offer opportunities to partition client/server applications in an optimal fashion.

In this chapter, you examine the dialect of SQL mandated by ODBC. You will learn:

- How to create relational database objects such as tables, views, and indexes

- How to control access to your data using the GRANT and REVOKE SQL statements

- How to update, delete, and insert rows in your tables

- How to use the full power of the SELECT statement to retrieve the data stored in your databases

SQL History

SQL was developed in the seventies by IBM as part of a relational database prototype called System R. It was adopted by the early implementation of RDBMSs such as SQL/DS and Oracle.

In the early eighties, the American National Standards Institute (ANSI) began work on a standard for SQL. The first ANSI standard was produced in 1986.

The current SQL standard was produced in 1992 and is the "International Standard ISO/IEC 9075:1992, Database Language SQL." This version is often called SQL2.

Work on the SQL language still continues. At this time, SQL3 is under development and includes extensions for Object Oriented Programming.

> **Note**
>
> The ODBC core SQL grammar is equivalent to the X/Open and SQL Access Group SQL CAE specification. The extended ODBC SQL grammar is very similar to the SQL2 standard.

ODBC Data Types

Each data source defines the SQL data types that it handles. The names used by each data source may vary. Use the function SQLGetTypeInfo to get the names of the data source types. In this section you will use the data type names used by Watcom SQL. Check your data source documentation or use SQLGetTypeInfo to find out the names used by your data source.

> **Note**
>
> To create or alter tables you must use the names returned in the TYPE_NAME column by the SQLGetTypeInfo call.

The ODBC SQL defines three levels of conformance: minimum, core, and extended. These levels of conformance also apply to the data types. A data source may not support all of the data types at a conformance level.

The minimum conformance level defines the character data types:

- CHAR(*n*)—a character string of fixed length *n*

- VARCHAR(*n*)—a varying length character string of maximum length *n*

- LONG VARCHAR—a varying length character string

> **Note**
>
> The maximum length of the character string that can be stored in the datatype is returned in the PRECISION column of SQLGetTypeInfo.

The core conformance level defines the numeric data types:

- DECIMAL(*p*,*s*) or NUMERIC(*p*,*s*)—an exact numeric of precision *p* and scale *s*

- SMALLINT—a 2 byte integer

- INTEGER—a 4 byte integer

- REAL—a 4 byte floating point

- FLOAT or DOUBLE PRECISION—an 8 byte floating point

> **Note**
>
> Use SQLGetTypeInfo to find out the precision, maximum, and minimum scales and whether the data type is signed or unsigned.

The extended conformance level defines the following additional data types:

- BIT—a single bit

- TINYINT—a one byte integer

- BIGINT—an 8 byte integer

- BINARY(*n*)—fixed length binary data of length (*n*)

- VARBINARY—varying length binary data with maximum length (*n*)

- LONG VARBINARY—varying length binary data

- DATE—date

The ODBC API

■ `TIME`—time

■ `TIMESTAMP`—date and time

The data source may also define other datatypes (such as money). As well if the data source allows the definition of user defined data types, you may use these in your data definition statements.

Note

`SQLGetTypeInfo` will not return any information about user defined data types. This information can be obtained from the appropriate catalog tables of your data source.

Note

Although your data source may support a given SQL conformance level, it may not support all the datatypes at that level. Choose your datatypes carefully if you want your applications to be portable.

Tip

Use `SQLGetInfo` with `fInfoType` of `SQL_ODBC_SQL_ CONFORMANCE` to check the data types supported by your datasource.

Tip

Use `SQLGetInfo` with `fInfoType` `SQL_ODBC_SQL_OPT _IEF` to find out if your data source supports the Integrity Enhancement Facility.

Name of Objects

In this section we use unqualified object names. This is the only requirement at the Minimum SQL Conformance level. The only restriction on unqualified object names is that they must start with a letter.

However, the ODBC SQL Grammar (and many data sources) supports qualified object names.

If the data source supports owners, then the following formats are supported:

■ *objectName*

■ *ownerName.objectName*

■ *qualifierName.ownerName.objectName*

If the data source does not support owners, then the following is also supported:

```
qualifierName.objectName
```

> **Note**
>
> I have used a period (.) as the separator between *qualifierName* and *ownerName*. It is data source dependent and you should use a separator for your data source as returned by SQLGetInfo with an fInfoType of SQL_QUALIFIER_NAME_SEPARATOR.

> **Note**
>
> Use SQLGetInfo with the following fInfoType to obtain information on the name of objects, use qualifiers and owners for your data source: SQL_MAX_OWNER_NAME_LEN, SQL_MAX_QUALIFIER_NAME_LEN, SQL_OWNER_USAGE, SQL_QUALIFIER_LOCATION, and SQL_SPECIAL_CHARACTERS.

Data Definition Language

A data definition language (DDL) is a language or a subset of a language that enables you to define objects. SQL uses three verbs for the definition of SQL objects:

```
CREATE

ALTER

DROP
```

In this section you will see how to use these verbs to define, modify, and remove tables, indexes, and views.

Tables

Tables are defined using the CREATE TABLE statement. To define the Book table from Chapter 2, "The Relational Database Model," you could use:

```
CREATE TABLE Book
      ( BookNumber          INTEGER
      , CategoryCode        CHAR(2)
      , Title               VARCHAR(100)
      , NumberOfPages       SMALLINT
      , RetailPriceAmount   NUMERIC(5,2)
      )
```

Tip
Use SQLGetInfo with an fInfoType of SQL_IDENTIFIER_CASE to check your data source's case sensitivity for identifiers.

Using the preceding statement is the simplest way to create a table. However, you should specify whether columns allow null values and, if your datasource allows it, specify a default.

Note that it is a trade-off between portability and database integrity. If the application is responsible, then *all* applications which may insert rows in the table may have to supply defaults. In shared database environments, it is too difficult to ensure that all applications provide suitable defaults. Coming from a database administration background in these trade-offs, I always favor database integrity.

In your Book table, it does not make sense to have a null value in BookNumber, CategoryCode, and Title. As most of your books are romance novels (CategoryCode = 'RO'), you will specify this value as your default. Because you may not know the number of pages or the retail price until the book is completely written, you will allow nulls in these columns.

Your create table now looks like this:

```
CREATE TABLE Book
     ( BookNumber        INTEGER                        NOT NULL
     , CategoryCode      CHAR(2)        DEFAULT 'RO'     NOT NULL
     , Title             VARCHAR(100)                   NOT NULL
     , NumberOfPages     SMALLINT
     , RetailPriceAmount NUMERIC(5,2)
     )
```

If you try to insert rows in the table without specifying a BookNumber or Title, you will get an error. If the CategoryCode is not specified, the book will have a CategoryCode of 'RO' (the default value).

If the data source supports it, you can specify the primary keys, uniqueness constraints, and referential integrity constraints when you create your table. The Book table create statement would be:

```
CREATE TABLE Book
     ( BookNumber        INTEGER              PRIMARY KEY
     , CategoryCode      CHAR(2)              DEFAULT 'RO'    NOT NULL
                                              REFERENCES Category CategoryCode
     , Title             VARCHAR(100)                         NOT NULL
                                              UNIQUE
     , NumberOfPages     SMALLINT
     , RetailPriceAmount NUMERIC(5,2)
     )
```

Note

The REFERENCES clause specifies referential integrity constraints. You have defined the title as unique because you don't want to have two different books with the same title.

> **Note**
>
> Use `SQLGetInfo` with `fInfoType` of: `SQL_MAX_COLUMN_NAME_LEN`,
> `SQL_MAX_COLUMNS_IN_TABLE`, `SQL_MAX_ROW_SIZE`,
> `SQL_MAX_ROW_SIZE_INCLUDES_LONG`, `SQL_MAX_TABLE_NAME_LEN`,
> `SQL_NEED_LONG_DATA_LEN`, and `SQL_NON_NULLABLE_COLUMNS` to obtain limits and
> restrictions on table and column names, size, names, and so forth.

To drop a table (for example, delete all the rows and remove the table definition), use the `DROP TABLE` statement. To drop our Book table, you would use

```
DROP TABLE Book
```

If your data source supports it, you could use:

```
DROP TABLE Book CASCADE
```

With the `CASCADE` keyword, if views or integrity constraints reference the table, they are also dropped.

If you do not want to drop the table if views or constraints reference the table, use the `RESTRICT` clause as in the following:

```
DROP TABLE Book RESTRICT
```

ODBC SQL allows columns to be added (core conformance) or dropped (extended conformance) to or from an existing table. The `ALTER TABLE` statement is used to modify a table. If you want to add the `PrintingCostAmount` column to our Book table, you would use:

```
ALTER TABLE Book ADD COLUMN PrintingCostAmount NUMERIC(5,2)
```

> **Note**
>
> The ODBC grammar does not allow default values or constraints to be specified
> when adding a column. Note that existing rows will contain a null value in the newly
> added column.

To remove a column from a table you also use the `ALTER` statement. This is an extended conformance level statement. The following removes the column you just added to the Book table:

```
ALTER TABLE Book DROP COLUMN PrintingCostAmount
```

If your data sources support it, you could use:

```
ALTER TABLE Book DROP COLUMN PrintingCostAmount RESTRICT
```

or

```
ALTER TABLE Book DROP COLUMN PrintingCostAmount CASCADE
```

The CASCADE option will drop views and integrity constraints (in other tables) referencing the dropped column. If RESTRICT is specified and views or integrity constraints in other tables reference the column, the column will not be dropped and an error will ensue.

Indexes

Indexes are usually btree or btree+ structures used to provide quick retrieval under some conditions. However, they slow updates, deletes, and inserts against tables. They also can be used to enforce uniqueness on columns.

An index may speed joins, and *clustered indexes* also may eliminate sorting. A clustered index is an index where the rows of the table are maintained in the same sequence as the index values.

On selection, an index is only useful if the selectivity is high, such as where the number of rows retrieved is much less than the number of I/Os required to read all the rows of a table.

Let's look at the following example:

- A table has 200,000 rows

- There are 50 rows per block

- The query retrieves more than 4,000 rows

Using an index in this case will be more costly than performing a table scan (such as reading all the rows in the table). Reading all the rows would require 4,000 I/Os (200,000 / 50). Using the index would require every block in the table to be read, because you retrieve at least one out of every 50 rows (200,000/4,000). An index in this case would only help if the query consistently retrieved less than 4,000 rows or if the index was clustered and the selection was based on a GREATER THAN or BETWEEN operator.

Most RDBMSs have a facility to examine the plan generated by the optimizer. This facility is usually called Explain or Show Plan. You should check whether the indexes you define are used effectively in your queries.

A cost-based optimizer is an optimizer that evaluates the cost (usually in terms of CPU and I/Os) of different plans, and chooses the cheapest plan to execute a query. The other type of optimizer (syntax-based) will only look at your SQL statement and generate a plan regardless of the data contained in the tables. Cost-based optimizers rely on up-to-date statistics about the amount and the distribution of data in your tables to do their job properly. You should ensure the statistics are updated frequently on volatile tables. Among other things, the job of a cost-based optimizer is to decide when to or not to use an index in a query.

The CREATE INDEX command defines an index. To create an index on the BookNumber of your book table, you would use:

```
CREATE UNIQUE INDEX BookNumberIndex ON Book (BookNumber)
```

If you want an index on CategoryCode and BookTitle, you would use:

```
CREATE INDEX CategoryTitleIndex ON Book (CategoryCode,Title)
```

Normally, the index is created in ascending key order. You can explicitly specify ascending or descending sequences by using the ASC or DESC clause. This will work only if your data source supports it.

Therefore, for an index in ascending key order, you could use:

```
CREATE INDEX CategoryTitleIndex ON Book (CategoryCode,Title) ASC
```

or, for an index in descending order, you could use:

```
CREATE INDEX CategoryTitleIndex ON Book (CategoryCode,Title) DESC
```

There are no statements to modify indexes. It would not make sense to alter an index. Instead, you just drop it and re-create a different one. To drop an index, you use the DROP INDEX statement.

The following statement would drop the index you just created in the previous example:

```
DROP INDEX CategoryTitleIndex
```

Views

Views are one of the most important concepts in RDBMSs. Views are virtual tables. They behave almost like tables, but they do not really exist. When a query against a view is submitted, the DBMS will resolve the view; in other words, it rewords the query so that it is evaluated against the tables in the database. To a user, there is no difference between views and tables. The only difference is that updates on views are limited by most DBMSs.

You can use them for a number of purposes. One of these is *logical data independence*, which enables you to make changes to the database without impacting application code.

Tip

SQLGetInfo with fInfoType of SQL_MAX_COLUMNS_IN _INDEX and SQL_MAX_INDEX_SIZE returns the limits on the maximun number and combined length of the columns of an index.

Consider the following. An application needs to retrieve the title and the total number of copies sold of our books. Given the tables you described in Chapter 2, "The Relational Database Model," you could use the following SQL statement to perform the query:

```
SELECT  BookTitle
      , SUM (CopiesSold)
   FROM  Book
      , BookSaleHistory
   WHERE Book.BookNumber = BookSaleHistory.BookNumber
   GROUP BY BookTitle
```

There is nothing wrong with the query. A few months later, you realize the query is run every minute by an over-anxious executive. You then decide to carry the derived column TotalSales in the Book table. Now you have to go back and change all the applications that contain the above query.

If you had used a view, there would have been no changes to the application.

Let's say you had created the view TotalBookSales as follows:

```
CREATE VIEW TotalBookSales
      ( BookTitle
      , TotalSales
      )
AS
SELECT  BookTitle
      , SUM (CopiesSold)
   FROM  Book
      , BookSaleHistory
   WHERE Book.BookNumber = BookSaleHistory.BookNumber
   GROUP BY BookTitle
```

Now all the applications would use the following query:

```
SELECT  BookTitle
      , TotalSales
   FROM  TotalBookSale
```

When you change your Book table to include the derived column TotalSales, no changes are required to the application. You just change your view to pick up the new column as follows:

```
CREATE VIEW TotalBookSales
      ( BookTitle
      , TotalSales
      )
AS
SELECT  BookTitle
      , TotalSales
   FROM  Book
```

You can see that views are a powerful tool to isolate applications from database changes.

You can also use views to enforce security. In your publishing application, you want to let authors see the number of copies sold for the books they have authored or co-authored. However, you do not want them to see this information for all books.

For the example, you will assume that the AuthorName in the Author table is the same as the user's authorization name (as returned by the USER() function).

If you only grant access to the authors on the following view:

```
CREATE VIEW MyBookCopiesSold
    ( BookTitle
    , TotalCopiesSold
    )
AS
SELECT  BookTitle
     , SUM(CopiesSold)
   FROM  Book
     , BookSaleHistory
   WHERE Book.BookNumber = BookSaleHistory.BookNumber
     AND Book.BookNumber in (
              SELECT BookNumber
              FROM  BookAuthor
              , Author
              WHERE BookAuthor.AuthorNumber = Author.AuthorNumber
                     AND AuthorName = USER()
```

the authors now can only see the number of copies sold for the books that they have authored.

You may have noticed that you do not handle the books written by authors using a pen name. The following view handles these correctly:

```
CREATE VIEW MyBookCopiesSold
    ( BookTitle
    , TotalCopiesSold
    )
AS
SELECT  BookTitle
     , SUM(CopiesSold)
   FROM  Book
     , BookSaleHistory
   WHERE Book.BookNumber = BookSaleHistory.BookNumber
     AND Book.BookNumber IN (
           SELECT BookNumber
             FROM  BookAuthor
                , Author
```

```
WHERE BookAuthor.AuthorNumber = Author.AuthorNumber
    AND AuthorName = USER()
OR ( BookAuthor.AuthorNumber = Author.RealAuthorNumber
    AND RealAuthorNumber IN (
        SELECT AuthorNumber
        FROM Author
        WHERE AuthorName = USER()))
```

You also can use views to present a simplified and customized view of your database to your users.

The model in the last figure of Chapter 2, "The Relational Database Model," has six tables (refer to fig. 2.40). If a user wants to see only books with sales and number of copies printed and only the real names of authors, with views you could only make him aware of the views shown in figure 3.1.

Fig. 3.1

A different logical model of the example database.

(a)

Book Number	Title	Copies Sold	Copies Printed
1	Tea for two	11,567	35,000
2	Love at first sight	354	1,000
3	Fight at the Coral	765	5,000

(b)

Book Number	Author Real Name
1	Doe
1	Smith
2	Doe
3	Smith

Therefore, each group of users can deal with its own representation of the database (a logical model) based on a common set of underlying tables (the conceptual model).

Most databases place restrictions on views. Update, delete, and insert are usually restricted to views meeting certain criteria (such as single table views, no aggregation, and so forth). You should consult the data source documentation to find out the limits imposed on views.

As you may have guessed from the preceding examples, you use the CREATE VIEW statement to define views.

The simplest way to define a view is shown in the following example:

```
CREATE VIEW MyAuthor
AS
  SELECT * from Author
```

The MyAuthor view will inherit the column names from the underlying table. Therefore, the view would have the columns Author Number, Real Author Number, and Author Name.

A view definition also can contain references to other views (as well as tables). It is perfectly acceptable to define the following:

```
CREATE VIEW UselessViewOnMyAuthor
AS
  SELECT * from MyAuthor
```

In the previous statement, the view UselessViewOnMyAuthor is defined on top of the view MyAuthor.

The ODBC SQL grammar does not allow the UNION operator in views. Also, an ORDER BY clause is not allowed.

When you define a view, you also can explicitly name the columns of the view. You must do so when, for example, retrieving two columns with identical names (but from different tables).

The following statement explicitly names the columns:

```
CREATE VIEW ShortenedAuthor
      ( AuthNo
      , RealAuthNo
      , AuthName
      )
AS
  SELECT * from Author
```

There is no ALTER view statement. One must drop the view and re-create it. A view is deleted by using the DROP VIEW statement. The following statement removes the view MyAuthor:

```
DROP VIEW MyAuthor
```

As in the case for tables, if your data source supports it, you could use

```
DROP VIEW MyAuthor CASCADE
```

In this case, if views or integrity constraints reference the view, they are also dropped.

The ODBC API

If you do not want to drop the view if other views or integrity constraints reference it, use the RESTRICT clause as in the following:

```
DROP VIEW MyAuthor RESTRICT
```

Note

Do not use SELECT * statements in your view definitions. The changes may not be reflected in the view until the view is dropped and re-created. You also lose the benefits of logical data independence.

Data Control Language

A Data Control Language (DCL) is the subset of a database language that enables you to define the privileges or restrictions placed on the users of the database.

Note

Data control statements are part of the core SQL grammar and therefore may not be supported by your data source.

Granting Privileges

Use the GRANT statement to grant privileges to users.

The reserved keyword PUBLIC refers to all currently defined users in a database.

The following statement allows all current users to perform selects against the Author table:

```
GRANT SELECT ON Author To PUBLIC
```

The following statement allows the user named Joe to perform inserts, updates, and deletes against the Book table:

```
GRANT DELETE, INSERT, UPDATE ON Book TO Joe
```

With a single statement you can grant privileges to more than one user, as in the following:

```
GRANT SELECT,UPDATE ON Book TO Joe, Bill, Mary
```

It is not possible to grant privileges on more than one object in one statement.

The privileges that may be granted are:

> DELETE
>
> INSERT
>
> SELECT
>
> UPDATE
>
> REFERENCES

The UPDATE and REFERENCES privileges can apply to tables or selected columns from a table.

The following statement:

```
GRANT UPDATE ON Book to PUBLIC
```

allows all current users to update any columns in the Book table.

If you want to allow updates on the Title column, you would use:

```
GRANT UPDATE(Title) ON Book to PUBLIC
```

You can specify multiple columns, as in

```
GRANT UPDATE(Title, NumberOfPages) ON Book to PUBLIC
```

The REFERENCES privilege allows a user to reference the columns of a table specified in an integrity constraint. If a user is granted access to a table whose referential integrity constraints refer to the column(s) of another table, then the user must be granted access to the referenced table or its columns referred to by the constraint.

The REFERENCE privilege is handled like the UPDATE privilege. To allow a user to reference the CategoryCode in the Category table (required when inserting rows in the Book table), you would execute:

```
GRANT REFERENCES ON Category TO Joe
```

or

```
GRANT REFERENCES ON Category(CategoryCode) TO Joe
```

Revoking Privileges

The REVOKE statement is used to revoke privileges from a user. Its syntax is identical to the GRANT statement.

The following statements revoke the privileges that were granted in the previous section:

```
REVOKE SELECT ON Author FROM PUBLIC

REVOKE DELETE, INSERT, UPDATE ON Book FROM Joe

REVOKE SELECT, UPDATE ON Book FROM Joe, Bill, Mary

REVOKE UPDATE ON Book FROM PUBLIC

REVOKE UPDATE(Title) ON Book FROM PUBLIC

REVOKE REFERENCES ON Category FROM Joe

REVOKE REFERENCES ON Category(CategoryCode) FROM Joe
```

Note

The ODBC SQL grammar does not state that UPDATE and REFERENCES can specify columns in a REVOKE statement. However, the SQL2 (SQL92) standard allows it.

The REVOKE statement has an optional CASCADE or RESTRICT clause.

Let's say you have granted SELECT privileges to user Joe on the view JoeAuthor where the view JoeAuthor is defined as:

```
CREATE VIEW JoeAuthor as SELECT * FROM Author
```

Bill, who is the owner of the table Author, has his SELECT privilege on Author revoked. Joe's privilege on JoeAuthor is useless because he will not be able to access the table Author.

If you use the following to revoke the privilege from Bill,

```
REVOKE SELECT ON Author FROM Bill CASCADE
```

then Joe's SELECT privilege on JoeAuthor would also be revoked.

On the other hand:

```
REVOKE SELECT ON Author FROM Bill RESTRICT
```

would generate an error, and the privilege would not be revoked.

Data Manipulation Language

The Data Manipulation Language (DML) portion of SQL is the set of statements that enables you to manipulate the data in your tables. All the statements you have looked at so far were concerned with the administration of your database.

SQL's DML contains only four verbs:

- DELETE
- INSERT
- SELECT
- UPDATE

Tip

Use the functions SQLColumnPrivileges and SQLTablePrivileges to display the privileges granted on existing objects in the database.

The ODBC API

In addition, some data sources support procedures and use the verb EXECUTE.

DELETE

The DELETE statement removes rows from a table.

To delete all the rows from the Author table, you would use:

```
DELETE FROM Author
```

To delete only the rows for AuthorNumber 1, you use:

```
DELETE FROM Author WHERE AuthorNumber = 1
```

The WHERE clause in the DELETE statement can include any clause that is allowed in a SELECT statement. Although some data sources may allow joins to appear in a DELETE statement (for example, Sybase), the ODBC SQL grammar does not allow them in a DELETE statement.

When processing answer sets with cursors, if your data source supports it you may use positioned delete statements. Positioned deletes are a Core Conformance Level feature in ODBC 1.0 but are an Extended Conformance Level in ODBC 2.0. To delete the current row (where the cursor is positioned) you would use:

```
DELETE FROM Author WHERE CURRENT OF MyCursor
```

> **Note**
>
> In the preceding statement, you have assumed that a SELECT statement was being processed against the Author table and the name of the cursor was MyCursor (the cursor name was set with the SQLSetCursorName function). The SELECT statement must include a FOR UPDATE clause.

INSERT

Tip
Use `SQLGetInfo`
with `fInfoType`
`SQL_POSITIONED`
`_STATEMENTS` to
check if positioned
deletes are sup-
ported.

The INSERT statement enables you to add rows to your tables.

To add a row to the Book table, you could use:

```
INSERT INTO Book
       VALUES(5,'WE', 'High Noon',120,17.50)
```

In the preceding statement, you did not specify the column names. Therefore, values for all columns must be supplied.

Another way to insert the same row in the table is to explicitly specify the
column names, as in:

```
INSERT INTO Book
      (BookNumber, CategoryCode, Title, NumberOfPages, RetailPriceAmount)
      VALUES(5,'WE', 'High Noon',120,17.50)
```

To specify a null value, use NULL instead of a literal. The following statement
puts NULL in the NumberOfPages and RetailPriceAmount columns:

```
INSERT INTO Book
      (BookNumber, CategoryCode, Title, NumberOfPages, RetailPriceAmount)
      VALUES(5,'WE', 'High Noon',NULL.NULL)
```

Parameters also can be used instead of literals. With the following statement,
the application would have to supply the parameters:

```
INSERT INTO Book
      (BookNumber, CategoryCode, Title, NumberOfPages, RetailPriceAmount)
      VALUES(5,'WE', 'High Noon',?,?)
```

> **Note**
>
> Chapter 13, "The Cursor Library and Positioned Operations," will teach you how to
> prepare, set parameter values, and execute statements with parameters.

When you do not specify column names explicitly, values for all columns
must be supplied.

When naming the columns explicitly, columns that have been defined with a
DEFAULT clause may be omitted. The following statement:

```
INSERT INTO Book
       (BookNumber, Title, NumberOfPages, RetailPriceAmount)
       VALUES(6, 'Romance for two',198,5.95)
```

inserts a row with a CategoryCode of 'RO' (the default for the column) in the Book table.

All the preceding statements have supplied values for the insert. You can insert in a table the rows returned by a query. This is supported at the SQL Core Conformance level. To populate the Book Sale History table for the month of January 91, you could use:

```
INSERT INTO BookSaleHistory
      SELECT  BookNumber
            , 'Jan 91'
            , 0
         FROM Book
```

This statement will insert a row for every Book in book table, setting the Month Year to "Jan 91" and the Number Of Copies Sold to "0".

Just as the INSERT statement uses the VALUES clause, you also can explicitly specify the column names. In fact, you must do this if you do not supply values for all the columns through the SELECT statement.

Simple *SELECT*

The SELECT statement is used to execute queries against ODBC data sources. It is a powerful statement with many features. With it you can perform all the relational operations described in Chapter 2, "The Relational Database Model."

The following statement retrieves all the rows and columns from the Book tables:

```
SELECT * FROM Book
```

If you only want to select some columns, you use:

```
SELECT  Title
      , RetailPriceAmount
   FROM Book
```

The two previous statements retrieved all the rows. To filter the rows returned, you use the WHERE clause.

To retrieve only the Title of books that sell for more than twenty dollars, you would use:

```
SELECT  Title
   FROM Book
   WHERE RetailPriceAmount > 20.00
```

You have used the > comparison in the preceding example. ODBC SQL supports the following operators: <, >, <=, >=, =, and <>.

You can place more than one condition in a WHERE clause. In the next statement, you use AND to retrieve all the books costing more than $20.00 and having fewer than 100 pages.

```
SELECT *
  FROM Book
  WHERE RetailPriceAmount > 20.00
    AND NumberOfPages < 100
```

You can also connect the conditions of a WHERE clause with OR. The following query returns all the romance or western books (CategoryCode of 'RO' or 'WE'):

```
SELECT *
  FROM Book
  WHERE CategoryCode = 'RO'
    OR  CategoryCode = 'WE'
```

You can use negation in the condition as well.

```
SELECT *
  FROM Book
  WHERE NOT CategoryCode = 'RO'
```

The above query returns all the non-Romance books. This is equivalent to:

```
SELECT *
  FROM Book
  WHERE CategoryCode <> 'RO'
```

You use a null predicate to filter columns containing NULLs. The following statement returns all the real names of authors (all the authors who have a null value in the RealAuthorNumber column):

```
SELECT AuthorName
  FROM Author
  WHERE RealAuthorNumber IS NULL
```

The next one does the reverse. It returns the pen names used by authors.

```
SELECT AuthorName
  FROM Author
  WHERE RealAuthorNumber IS NOT NULL
```

The *LIKE* Predicate

You use the LIKE predicate to perform pattern matching on strings. In the matching pattern the character '%' matches 0 or more of any character and '_' matches exactly one of any character.

The following query returns the rows for any book whose title contains `'ght'` in any position. The result of the query is shown in figure 3.2b. The original table is shown in figure 3.2a.

```
SELECT *
  FROM Book
  WHERE Title LIKE '%ght%'
```

The next query returns the rows for any book whose title contains `'e'` in the second character position. The results are displayed in figure 3.2c.

```
SELECT *
  FROM Book
  WHERE Title LIKE '_e%'
```

(a)

Book Number	Category Code	Title	Number Of Pages	Retail Price Amount
1	RO	Tea for two	150	24.95
2	RO	Love at first sight	200	29.95
3	WE	Fight at the Coral	129	14.95

(b)

Book Number	Category Code	Title	Number Of Pages	Retail Price Amount
2	RO	Love at first sight	200	29.95
3	WE	Fight at the Coral	129	14.95

(c)

Book Number	Category Code	Title	Number Of Pages	Retail Price Amount
1	RO	Tea for two	150	24.95

Fig. 3.2
Using the LIKE predicate for pattern matching.

Note

How can your search for the `'%'` or `'_'` characters in a string? They will be interpreted as zero, one, or more of any characters. An escape clause enables you to do this. Use SQLGetInfo with an fInfoType of SQL_LIKE_ESCAPE_CLAUSE to find out if escape clauses are allowed by your driver.

The ODBC API

The *DISTINCT* Keyword

Let's say you want to find all the Category Codes that are present in the Book table. If you use the following statement:

```
SELECT CategoryCode from Book
```

you will get many duplicate rows. If your book table contained 1,000 romance books, the answer set would contain 1000 'RO' rows.

You use the DISTINCT reserved word to eliminate duplicate rows from an answer set. The next query returns only as many rows are they are distinct Category Codes in the Book table. This is illustrated in figure 3.3. Figure 3.3a shows your Book table, 3.3b the result of the select without the DISTINCT, and 3.3c the results of the SELECT DISTINCT.

```
SELECT DISTINCT CategoryCode from Book
```

Fig. 3.3

Using DISTINCT to eliminate duplicate rows.

(a)

Book Number	Category Code	Title	Number Of Pages	Retail Price Amount
1	RO	Tea for two	150	24.95
2	RO	Love at first sight	200	29.95
3	WE	Fight at the Coral	129	14.95

(b)

Category Code
RO
RO
WE

(c)

Category Code
RO
WE

The *ORDER BY* Clause

The rows returned by a query are in an arbitrary order. That is, the order in which rows are returned is determined by the RDBMS unless you defined the order explicitly. To order the rows of an answer set, use the ORDER BY clause.

The following queries show how to use the ORDER BY clause. For each column that appears in the order, you may specify whether it is in ascending or descending order. If unspecified, the column is sorted in ascending order.

```
SELECT CategoryCode
      ,Title
  FROM Book
  ORDER BY Title


SELECT CategoryCode
      ,Title
      ,RetailPriceAmount
      ,NumberOfPages
  FROM Book
  ORDER BY RetailPriceAmount DESC, NumberOfPages ASC
```

You may use ordinal numbers instead of column names in an order by expression. The following statement is equivalent to the previous one:

```
SELECT CategoryCode
      ,Title
      ,RetailPriceAmount
      ,NumberOfPages
  FROM Book
  ORDER BY 3 DESC, 4 ASC
```

> **Note**
>
> Some data sources allow results to be sorted by columns that do not appear in the select list (as in the columns are not returned in the answer set). Use SQLGetInfo with fInfoType of SQL_ORDER_BY_COLUMNS_IN_SELECT to find out if your data source supports this.

All the previous features of the SELECT statement are at the Minimum Conformance level of the SQL grammar.

The next two predicates are supported at the Core Conformance level.

The *IN* Predicate

Sometimes you need to select rows of a table based on the values of columns belonging to a set of values. You could always use OR to do this but it is much simpler to use the IN predicate.

The following two queries are equivalent:

```
SELECT *
  FROM Book
  WHERE CategoryCode = 'RO'
     OR  CategoryCode = 'WE'
```

Tip

The maximum number of columns that may appear in an ORDER BY clause are returned by SQLGetInfo with fInfoType of SQL_MAX_COLUMNS_IN_ORDER_BY.

Tip

To find out how null values will be sorted, check the value returned by SQLGetInfo with fInfoType of SQL_NULL_COLLATION.

```
SELECT *
  FROM Book
  WHERE CategoryCode IN ('RO', 'WE')
```

You also can use the negated form of the IN predicate. The following queries are equivalent and return all books that are neither romance nor westerns.

```
SELECT *
  FROM Book
  WHERE CategoryCode NOT IN ('RO', 'WE')
```

```
SELECT *
  FROM Book
  WHERE CategoryCode <> 'RO'
    AND CategoryCode <> 'WE'
```

The *BETWEEN* Predicate

Sometimes, you may need to select all the rows where the value of a column is between two values (a range query). You use the BETWEEN predicate to perform such a query.

```
SELECT  Title
  FROM Book
  WHERE RetailPriceAmount BETWEEN 20.00 AND 35.00
```

All the books whose price is $20.00 or more and less than and including $35.00 will be returned. Therefore the above query is equivalent to:

```
SELECT  Title
  FROM Book
  WHERE RetailPriceAmount >= 20.00
    AND RetailPriceAmount <= 35.00
```

Just like the comparison operators, the BETWEEN predicate may be applied to non-numeric columns.

You also can use its negated form. The following two queries are equivalent:

```
SELECT  Title
  FROM Book
  WHERE RetailPriceAmount NOT BETWEEN 20.00 AND 35.00
```

```
SELECT  Title
  FROM Book
  WHERE RetailPriceAmount < 20.00
    OR RetailPriceAmount > 35.00
```

Expressions

So far you always have used columns in your select statements without performing any transformations on them. In place of numeric columns you often can use numerical expressions.

For example, to find out the number of copies unsold from the view shown in figure 3.1a, you would use:

```
SELECT  Title
      , CopiesPrinted - CopiesSold
    FROM BookCopiesView
```

You also can use expressions in the WHERE clause. The following statement only returns the books whose number of unsold copies is two times greater that the number of sold copies.

```
SELECT  Title
      , CopiesPrinted - CopiesSold
      , CopiesSold
    FROM Book
    WHERE ((CopiesPrinted - CopiesSold) / CopiesSold)> 2.0
```

The valid operators in expressions are +, -, /, and *. The + and - operators also can be used as *unary operators*. Unary operators only require one argument. They are used to sign numbers as in +5 or -12.0.

Functions

A data source may support a number of functions in SQL. The functions are broken down in the following categories:

- String functions

- Numeric functions

- Time and date functions

- System functions

- Data type conversion functions

SQLGetInfo with the following fInfoType will return information on the supported functions:

Tip

Not all data sources support expressions in an ORDER BY clause. SQLGetInfo with fInfoType of SQL_EXPRESSIONS_IN _ORDER_BY tells you if this is supported by your data source.

The ODBC API

fInfoType	**Information Returned**
SQL_CONVERT_FUNCTIONS	Supported conversions by the CONVERT function
SQL_NUMERIC_FUNCTIONS	Supported numeric functions
SQL_STRING_FUNCTIONS	Supported string functions
SQL_SYSTEM_FUNCTIONS	Supported system functions
SQL_TIMEDATE_ADD_INTERVALS	Supported timestamp intervals by the TIMESTAMPADD function
SQL_TIMEDATE_DIFF_INTERVALS	Supported timestamp intervals by the TIMESTAMPDIFF function
SQL_TIME_DATE_FUNCTIONS	Supported date and time functions

The ODBC SQL grammar specifies either of the following forms to invoke functions:

```
{ fn funtionName }

--(* VENDOR(Microsoft),PRODUCT(ODBC) fn functionName *)--
```

where *functionName* is the name of the function you want to invoke. Because most drivers will support the native SQL format as well, you could try one of the following formats to get the book's title and length of title:

```
SELECT Title
     ,LENGTH(Title)
  FROM Book


SELECT Title
     ,{ fn LENGTH(Title) }
  FROM Book


SELECT Title
     ,--(* VENDOR(Microsoft),PRODUCT(ODBC) fn LENGTH(Title) *)--
  FROM Book
```

The syntax for other functions is similar to the previous statements. Functions can be used anywhere a column name is used (except for ORDER BY—see the "Expressions" section of this chapter).

Date, *Time*, **and** *Timestamp* **Literals**

You already have looked informally at numeric and string literals. Data sources may support different formats for Date, Time, and Timestamp literals. If you use the format specified by the ODBC SQL grammar, you will ensure portability between data sources.

The ODBC formats for a date literal are:

```
{ d 'yyyy-mm-dd'}

--(* VENDOR(MICROSOFT),PRODUCT(ODBC) d 'yyyy-mm-dd' *)--
```

The ODBC formats for a time literal are:

```
{ t 'hh:mm:ss'}

--(* VENDOR(MICROSOFT),PRODUCT(ODBC) t 'hh:mm:ss' *)--
```

The ODBC formats for a timestamp literal are:

```
{ ts 'yyyy-mm-dd hh:mm:ss'}

--(* VENDOR(MICROSOFT),PRODUCT(ODBC) ts 'yyyy-mm-dd hh:mm:ss' *)--
```

You also can use the native format supported by your data source. However, your code will not be portable.

Simple Joins

So far you have looked at SQL statements involving only one table. You will now learn how to work with multiple tables in SQL.

The following statement performs a join between two tables. It is actually a *Cartesian product* between the Printing and the Book Sale History tables. The Cartesian product takes each row from the first table and creates (for each row of the first table) a new row for every row of the second table. The columns of the result consists of the columns of the first table followed by the columns of the second table. Every row of the Printing table is joined to each row of the Book Sale History table. The results are shown in figure 3.4c.

```
SELECT *
  FROM  Printing
     , BookSaleHistory
```

Fig. 3.4
A Cartesian product.

(a)

Book Number	Printing Number	Printing Date	Copies Printed
1	1	Jan 1, 1994	10,000
1	2	May 5, 1994	25,000
3	1	Jul 17, 1993	5,000

(b)

Book Number	Year Month	Copies Sold
1	Jan 91	7,890
1	Feb 91	2,654
1	Mar 91	1,023

(c)

Book Number	Printing Number	Printing Date	Copies Printed	Book Number	Year Month	Copies Sold
1	1	Jan 1, 1994	10,000	1	Jan 91	7,890
1	1	Jan 1, 1994	10,000	1	Feb 91	2,654
1	1	Jan 1, 1994	10,000	1	Mar 91	1,023
1	2	May 5, 1994	25,000	1	Jan 91	7,890
1	2	May 5, 1994	25,000	1	Feb 91	2,654
1	2	May 5, 1994	25,000	1	Mar 91	1,023
3	1	Jul 17, 1993	5,000	1	Jan 91	7,890
3	1	Jul 17, 1993	5,000	1	Feb 91	2,654
3	1	Jul 17, 1993	5,000	1	Mar 91	1,023

The previous statement is quite useless. What you really want to do is join the `Printing` and `BookSaleHistory` tables on the Book number column.

The following statement does an *equijoin* between the two tables. An equijoin is a join of two tables using the equality operator (=) to match the column(s). The results are shown in figure 3.5c.

```
SELECT *
  FROM  Printing
      , BookSaleHistory
  WHERE Printing.BookNumber = BookSaleHistory.BookNumber
```

Fig. 3.5
Equijoin: joining tables based on equality of column values.

(a)

Book Number	Printing Number	Printing Date	Copies Printed
1	1	Jan 1, 1994	10,000
1	2	May 5, 1994	25,000
3	1	Jul 17, 1993	5,000

(b)

Book Number	Year Month	Copies Sold
1	Jan 91	7,890
1	Feb 91	2,654
1	Mar 91	1,023

(c)

Book Number	Printing Number	Printing Date	Copies Printed	Book Number	Year Month	Copies Sold
1	1	Jan 1, 1994	10,000	1	Jan 91	7,890
1	1	Jan 1, 1994	10,000	1	Feb 91	2,654
1	1	Jan 1, 1994	10,000	1	Mar 91	1,023
1	2	May 5, 1994	25,000	1	Jan 91	7,890
1	2	May 5, 1994	25,000	1	Feb 91	2,654
1	2	May 5, 1994	25,000	1	Mar 91	1,023

You can specify individual columns, or all the columns of a table in the SELECT statement. The following statements are all equivalent to the preceding one:

```
SELECT  Printing.*
      , BookSaleHistory.*
   FROM  Printing
      , BookSaleHistory
   WHERE Printing.BookNumber = BookSaleHistory.BookNumber


SELECT  Printing.*
      , BookSaleHistory.BookNumber
      , YearMonth
      , CopiesSold
   FROM  Printing
      , BookSaleHistory
   WHERE Printing.BookNumber = BookSaleHistory.BookNumber
```

Note that you must use BookSaleHistory.BookNumber in the above statements, as using the unqualified column BookNumber would result in an error (ambiguous because both tables contain the column BookNumber).

> **Note**
>
> One of the most frequent sources of errors in an SQL statement is forgetting to specify a condition to join the tables in a WHERE clause, resulting in a Cartesian product between two tables.

Assume you want to get a list of books with their sales for the month of January, 1991. If you just use the following statement, then some books will not appear in the answer because there are no Book Sale History rows in the answer set. The tables are displayed in figure 3.6a and 3.6b. The result of the following query is shown in 3.6c.

```
SELECT  Title
      , CopiesSold
   FROM Book
      , BookSaleHistory
   WHERE Book.BookNumber = BookSaleHistory.BookNumber
     AND MonthYear = 'Jan 91'
```

Fig. 3.6

A join: picking up matching rows.

(a)

Book Number	Category Code	Title	Number Of Pages	Retail Price Amount
1	RO	Tea for two	150	24.95
2	RO	Love at first sight	200	29.95
3	WE	Fight at the Coral	129	14.95

(b)

Book Number	Year Month	Copies Sold
1	Jan 91	7,890
1	Feb 91	2,654
1	Mar 91	1,023

(c)

Title	Copies Sold
Tea for two	7,890

What we really want is to see all the books, and if there are no Book Sale History rows for January 91, put 0 in the Copies Sold column. The outer join will just do that. To do this, now write your query like this:

```
SELECT  Title
      , { fn IFNULL(CopiesSold,0) }
   FROM { oj Book LEFT OUTER JOIN BookSaleHistory ON
                Book.BookNumber = BookSaleHistory }
   WHERE MonthYear = 'Jan 91'
```

or

```
SELECT  Title
      , { fn IFNULL(CopiesSold,0) }
   FROM --(* VENDOR(Microsoft),PRODUCT(ODBC)
           oj Book LEFT OUTER JOIN BookSaleHistory ON
                Book.BookNumber = BookSaleHistory *)--
   WHERE MonthYear = 'Jan 91'
```

The result is shown in figure 3.7.

Fig. 3.7

A (LEFT) OUTER JOIN: joining non-matching rows.

Title	Copies Sold
Tea for two	7,890
Love at first sight	0
Fight at the Coral	0

> **Note**
>
> You have used the system function IFNULL to substitute the value zero if CopiesSold is null. You also could use the native SQL outer join from your data source, but your code would most likely be non-portable.

Tip
To check the level of OUTER JOIN support of your data source, use SQLGetInfo with an fInfoType of SQL_OUTER_JOINS.

The ODBC API

IF outer joins are not supported, but the UNION operator is, you always can use UNION. The following query is equivalent to the outer join one.

```
SELECT  Title
     , CopiesSold
  FROM Book
     , BookSaleHistory
  WHERE Book.BookNumber = BookSaleHistory
    AND MonthYear = 'Jan 91'
UNION
SELECT  Title
     , 0
  FROM Book
  WHERE BookNumber NOT IN (SELECT BookNumber FROM BookSaleHistory)
                       WHERE MonthYear = 'Jan 91' )
```

Complex Joins

In the previous section, all the joins you have looked at were between two tables. In this section, you will look at multi-way joins and recursive joins.

When a column appears in more than one table, you must qualify the column name. Actually, it is a good practice to always qualify your table names. When using descriptive names for columns, it is tedious to type the names in full. As well for recursive joins and some types of subqueries, you need to be able to refer to a table by an alternate name. Correlation names are used for this purpose.

For example, in the following query, the correlation names for the Book and Book Sale History tables are b and s. Any column qualified by b or s refers to the Book or Book Sale History tables.

```
SELECT  b.Title
     , s.CopiesSold
  FROM Book b
     , BookSaleHistory s
  WHERE b.BookNumber = s.BookNumber
    AND s.MonthYear = 'Jan 91'
```

To use a correlation name for a table, place it after the table name in the FROM clause.

Tip
SLGetInfo with
an fInfoType of
SQL_CORRELATION
_NAME will tell you
if your data source
supports correla-
tion names.

Let's see an example of a three-way join. You want to display the title, the name of the authors, and the monthly sales for your books.

```
SELECT  b.Title
      , a.AuthorName
      , s.YearMonth
      , s,CopiesSold
   FROM  Book b
      , Author a
      , BookSaleHistory s
   WHERE b.BookNumber = s.BookNumber
AND a.AuthorNumberNumber = b.AuthorNumber
```

Tip
When joining
tables, you should
ensure a join
condition is speci-
fied for every table
that appears in the
FROM clause. Oth-
erwise, you will
get a Cartesian
product.

When you join a table to itself, you are executing a recursive join. In order to express such queries, your data source must support correlation names.

If you want to display all the authors and their real names, you would use the following query:

```
SELECT  a.AuthorNumber
      , a.AuthorName
      , b.AuthorName
   FROM  Author a
      , Author b
   WHERE a.RealAuthorNumber = b.AuthorNumber
```

The results of the query are displayed in figure 3.8b.

Fig. 3.8
A Recursive Join:
joining a table to
itself.

(a)

Author Number	Real Author Number	Author Name
1		Doe
2	1	Casanova
3	1	Don Juan
4		Smith

(b)

Author Number	a.Author Name	b.Author Name
2	Casanova	Doe
3	Don Juan	Doe

Can you find out what's wrong with the query? Authors who do not use a pen name are not included in the result! To correct this, you need to use an outer join. The following statement corrects the above query. The results are shown in figure 3.9b.

```
SELECT  a.AuthorNumber
      , a.AuthorName
      , b.AuthorName
   FROM  { oj Author a LEFT OUTER JOIN Author b
         ON a.RealAuthorNumber = b,AuthorNumber }
```

(a)

Author Number	Real Author Number	Author Name
1		Doe
2	1	Casanova
3	1	Don Juan
4		Smith

(b)

Author Number	a.Author Name	b.Author Name
1	Doe	
2	Casanova	Doe
3	Don Juan	Doe
4	Smith	

Fig. 3.9
A recursive outer join.

Some data sources permit column aliases; that is, you can assign a different name to columns or expressions that appear after the SELECT keyword. This is useful in reports to substitute meaningful names for expressions or for recursive joins. The alias column name is placed after the column name. You could rewrite the previous statement as:

```
SELECT  a.AuthorNumber
      , a.AuthorName
      , b.AuthorName AS RealAuthorName
   FROM  { oj Author a LEFT OUTER JOIN Author b
         ON a.RealAuthoruNumber = b,AuthorNumber }
```

Tip
The AS alias key-
word is optional.
Use `SLQGetInfo`
with an
`fInfoType` of
`SQL_COLUMN`
`_ALIAS` to see if
the data source
supports column
aliasing.

Aggregation

SQL supports the following aggregate functions:

AVG

COUNT

MAX

MIN

SUM

To count all the rows in the Book table, you would use:

```
SELECT COUNT(*) FROM BOOK
```

If you use a WHERE clause, then COUNT(*) returns the number of rows that sat-isfy the selection criteria. If you wanted to know the number of books written by a given author (Author Number 1), you could use:

```
SELECT COUNT(*)
  FROM  BOOK
       , BookAuthor
  WHERE Book.BookNumber = BookAuthor.BookNumber
    AND AuthorNumber = 1
```

The COUNT function also can be applied to a specific column. Except for COUNT(*), nulls are always eliminated. Therefore, given the Author table in figure 3.8a, the next two queries return the same answer: 4.

```
SELECT COUNT(*) FROM Author
```

```
SELECT COUNT(AuthorNumber) FROM Author
```

However, the following query:

```
SELECT COUNT(RealAuthorNumber) FROM Author
```

would return 2. The two rows with null values are not included in the row count.

You can use the DISTINCT keyword within an aggregate to count only distinct values.

```
SELECT COUNT( DISTINCT RealAuthorNumber) from Author
```

would return the answer 1, as there is only one RealAuthorNumber in your table.

The following statement returns the average, maximum, and minimum price from your book table and the sum of the number of pages.

Aggregate function columns can be mixed with non-aggregate columns in a query. The non-aggregate columns must be specified in the GROUP BY clause.

```
SELECT AVG(RetailPriceAmount)
     , MAX(RetailPriceAmount)
     , MIN(RetailPriceAmount)
     , SUM(NumberOfPages)
   FROM Book
```

The following query computes the average, maximum, and minimum price per Category Code:

```
SELECT CategoryCode
     , AVG(RetailPriceAmount)
     , MAX(RetailPriceAmount)
     , MIN(RetailPriceAmount)
     , SUM(NumberOfPages)
   FROM Book
   GROUP BY CategoryCode
```

The result of the query is displayed in figure 3.10.

Category Code	AVG(Retail Price Amount)	MAX(Retail Price Amount)	MIN(Retail Price Amount)	SUM(Number Of Pages)
RO	27.45	29.95	24.95	350
WE	14.95	14.95	14.95	129

Fig. 3.10
Using GROUP BY with aggregate functions.

The WHERE clause restricts the rows returned by a query. The HAVING clause performs the equivalent function for aggregates. If you wanted to see only the CategoryCodes that have an average (RetailPriceAmount) greater than $25.00, you would use:

```
SELECT CategoryCode
     , AVG(RetailPriceAmount)
     , MAX(RetailPriceAmount)
     , MIN(RetailPriceAmount)
     , SUM(NumberOfPages)
   FROM Book
   GROUP BY CategoryCode
   HAVING AVG(RetailPriceAmount) > 25.00
```

The ODBC API

The conditions that may be specified in the HAVING clause are similar to the ones in a WHERE clause. These conditions may include comparisons, AND and OR clauses, negation, expressions, and so on. Of course, these conditions apply to aggregate functions.

In complex queries, the interactions between aggregation and the WHERE clause may seem confusing. You just need to remember the following order of processing:

1. The query is performed as if no aggregation takes place. The WHERE clause is applied and the queries return the rows, including the columns on which aggregation will be performed.

2. The aggregate functions are applied on the appropriate columns.

3. The HAVING clause is evaluated to filter the aggregated results.

> **Note**
>
> The key thing to remember is that aggregation is performed after the selection.

Tip
Use SQLGetInfo with fInfoType of SQL_GROUP_BY and SQL_MAX_COLUMNS_IN_GROUP_BY to check data source support and limits on aggregation.

Subqueries

So far all the conditions in a WHERE or HAVING clause you have looked at in-volved literals, sets of literals, or columns from other tables. In some cases, you need to compare to a value or values returned by evaluating another query. The query against which you evaluate our expression is called a subquery.

There are three kinds of subqueries:

- Subqueries introduced by an EXISTS predicate

- Subqueries introduced by an IN predicate

- Subqueries introduced by the quantified predicate ANY or ALL

Let's say you need to find all the CategoryCode in the Category table which are not used. That is, no books in these categories were ever published. You cannot use a join in this case. The next two statements would give you this list:

```
SELECT CategoryCode
  FROM Category
  WHERE CategoryCode NOT IN
```

```
            (SELECT CategoryCode
                FROM Book )


SELECT CategoryCode
  FROM Category
  WHERE CategoryCode NOT EXISTS
              (SELECT *
                  FROM Book )
```

When using the EXISTS (NOT EXISTS) predicate, it is customary to use SELECT* inside the subquery. The columns returned in this case do not matter as this is an existence check. The value true (or false) is returned if one or more (no) rows satisfy the subquery.

Consider the following request. You want a list of all the books whose price is greater than the price of the most expensive book in the romance category. The following statement accomplishes this:

```
SELECT b.Title
  FROM Book b
  WHERE b.Price >ALL ( SELECT b2.RetailPriceAmount
                          FROM RetailPriceAmount b2
                          WHERE b2.CategoryCode = 'RO' )
```

If you wanted the list of all the books whose price is greater than the price of any book in the romance category (in this case more expensive than the cheapest romance), you would use:

```
SELECT b.Title
  FROM Book b
  WHERE b.Price >ANY ( SELECT b2.RetailPriceAmount
                          FROM RetailPriceAmount b2
                          WHERE b2.CategoryCode = 'RO' )
```

Now you want a list of all the book titles that have been written by more than one author. You can use:

```
SELECT b.Title
  FROM Book b
  WHERE EXISTS (SELECT COUNT(ba.AuthorNumber)
                  FROM BookAuthor ba
                  WHERE ba.BookNumber = b.BookNumber
                  HAVING COUNT(ba.AuthorNumber) > 1 )
```

Notice that in the inner query the condition ba.BookNumber = b. BookNumber contains a reference to a column from the outer query. This is called a *correlated subquery*. This is a special class of subqueries as the data source cannot evaluate the inner or outer queries independently of each other.

Union Queries

Tip
Use SQLGetInfo
with an fInfoType
of
SQL_SUBQUERIES
to check the
subqueries support
that your data
source provides.

The relational operator union is implemented in SQL by the UNION keyword. The UNION operator eliminates duplicate rows from the answer set. The UNION ALL operator does not. The queries on which the union is performed must be union compatible (the data types of the columns must be similar).

If you want to sort the answer set, the only ORDER BY clause must be after the last query.

The following statement performs a union on the Book table and sorts the results on Title.

```
SELECT Title, RetailPriceAmount
  FROM Book
  Where CategoryCode = 'RO'
UNION
  SELECT Title, RetailPriceAmount
    FROM Book
    WHERE CategoryCode = 'WE'
ORDER BY Title
```

FOR UPDATE Clause

Tip
Use SQLGetInfo
with an fInfoType
of SQL_UNION to
check the level of
support of UNION
by your data
source.

To use positioned DELETE or UPDATE statements, the SELECT statement on which the cursor is defined must include a FOR UPDATE clause.

The following statement enables you to use positioned statements against the Book table:

```
SELECT * FROM Book FOR UPDATE OF
```

Tip
If you know that
the result will not
include duplicates,
use UNION ALL (if
supported) instead
of UNION. The
query will run
faster as the data
source will not
attempt to elimi-
nate duplicate
rows (this usually
requires an extra
sort).

A column list may be specified after the clause. If it is specified, only columns appearing in that list may be the target of an assignment in a subsequent positioned update.

```
SELECT * FROM Book FOR UPDATE OF RetailPriceAmount, NumberOfPages
```

After the above statement is executed, the only columns that may be updated in the SET clause of a positioned update statements are RetailPriceAmount and NumberOfPages.

UPDATE

The UPDATE statement updates rows of a table.

To increase the price by 10 percent of all the books, you would use the following code:

```
UPDATE Book
  SET RetailPriceAmount = RetailPriceAmount * 1.10
```

To increase the price of books that retail for more than $25.00, you use the following code:

```
UPDATE Book
    SET RetailPriceAmount = RetailPriceAmount * 1.10
    WHERE RetailPriceAmount > 25.00
```

The WHERE clause in the update statement can include any clause that is allowed in the WHERE clause of a select statement. Note that according to the ODBC SQL grammar, joins are not allowed in an update statement.

To set a column to a null value, you would use the following clause in your update statement:

```
SET columnName = NULL
```

You can update multiple columns in an update statement. The next statement increases the page count by 10 and the price by 20 percent for romance books.

```
UPDATE Book
    SET RetailPriceAmount = RetailPriceAmount * 1.20
        ,NumberOfPages = NumberOfPages + 10
    WHERE CategoryCode = 'RO'
```

When processing answer sets with cursors, if your data source supports it you may use positioned update statements. To update the current row (where the cursor is positioned), you would use:

```
UPDATE Book
    SET RetailPriceAmount = RetailPriceAmount * 1.10
    WHERE CURRENT OF MyCursor
```

Note

In the above statement, you have assumed that a select statement was being processed against the Book table and the name of the cursor was MyCursor (the cursor name was set with the SQLSetCursorName function). The Select statement must include a FOR UPDATE clause.

Call Procedure

Although the ODBC SQL grammar does not support the creation of procedures, it allows their invocation.

To invoke the procedure myProcedure, you would use either of the following statements:

```
{ call myProcedure }
```

Tip

Use SQLGetInfo with fInfoType SQL_POSITIONED _STATEMENTS to check whether positioned updates are supported.

```
--(* VENDOR(MICROSOFT),PRODUCT(ODBC) call myProcedure *)--
```

A procedure may have a return value and input or output parameters. The parameters to a procedure may either be literals or parameter markers. The following procedure returns a value and has an input string parameter and an output parameter:

```
{ call ?=myProcedure('abc',?) }
```

Now that you have the SQL knowledge to manipulate your databases, you are ready to learn the programming interface to ODBC. The rest of this book will teach you just that. This will enable you to submit your SQL statements to an ODBC data source and retrieve the results from these statements.

From Here...

- Chapter 9, "Creating Tables with the DDL," explains the creation of tables under ODBC.

- In Chapters 10, "Inserting, Updating, and Deleting Rows," and 11, "Queries and Result Sets," you will learn how to update and query your databases using the ODBC API.

- For details on parameterized statements, review Chapter 12, "Setting Parameters with Prepared Statements."

- The use of cursors and positioned statements is explained in Chapter 13, "The Cursor Library and Positioned Operations."

The complete ODBC SQL grammar can be found in:

- *ODBC 2.0 Programmer's Reference and SDK Guide*
  Microsoft Press
  ISBN: 1-55615-658-8

The following references contain details on the SQL/92 standard:

- *A Guide to THE SQL STANDARD*
  C.J. Date with Hugh Darwen
  Addison-Wesley Publishing Company
  ISBN: 0-201-55822-x

- American National Standards Institute Document
  ANSI X3.135-1992

Chapter 4

The Structure of ODBC: An Overview

The design of ODBC is innovative, but it is not difficult to understand. Having read the first few chapters, you are beginning to catch on to some of the design principles and capabilities of the ODBC API and its data source drivers. Now, a grasp of the big picture—a side view, if you will—will help you as you design your applications to take advantage of what ODBC has to offer.

In this chapter, we explore:

- Special interfaces that differ from DBMS to DBMS

- Intermediate drivers that incorporate some ODBC concepts

- The ODBC alternative

- Where 16-bit and 32-bit ODBC drivers can be used

- The steps involved in a typical ODBC session

Database-Specific Interfaces

Perhaps it is easiest to talk about what ODBC *is* by starting with describing what it *isn't*. Therefore, let's digress a little and talk about ordinary database-specific interfaces. Every database management system and vertical database application needs some way to talk to its native data format. The connection is known as the interface, and it can be as simple as direct file access or several layers removed.

To this day, modern user-oriented databases often work directly with their data. This is especially true of products that have been around for a long time, and are frequently considered by their manufacturers to be standard enough that they don't have to worry too much about accessing other formats. Also, a lot of vertical database applications written in lower-level languages (like C) often go directly to their data—it's easier for developers not to worry about the possibility that customers might want to choose a different back end than the one built into the product.

For better or for worse, the days of that type of thinking are numbered, at least in the world of Windows development. Even before ODBC's initial release a couple of years ago, the industry was beginning to turn from the notion that a DBMS need only read its native data format. When ODBC stepped in and provided a widespread basis for achieving this, it took its place as the *de facto* industry standard.

Speaking broadly, database interfaces fall into two categories:

- Local
- Client/server

Local Database Interfaces

Local DBMSs have been around since the early days of microcomputing. dBASE II, one of the earliest systems that's still around today in several modern incarnations, has always been based on this model of database access. Figure 4.1 illustrates the relationship between dBASE and its data.

Fig. 4.1
Local DBMSs access their data directly.

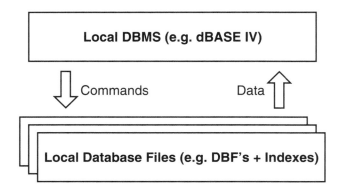

In figure 4.1, the local database management system is storing its data on a local hard drive. The DBMS (in this case, dBASE IV) accepts commands from the user or from a user-supplied program. These commands are usually in some proprietary database management language, in this case the Xbase language. The commands are translated into simple disk access commands, which are passed on to the file system. In return, the DBMS receives data from the disk, and then puts it to whatever use the user requested.

The database engine within a local DBMS application runs on the workstation. Although figure 4.1 implies that the data is on the workstation's local drive (through the absence of indications to the contrary), the data may also be stored on a file server elsewhere on the network. The database engine uses typical file I/O calls and record-locking techniques to read and write data directly.

In a network situation, there are a few more layers involved (see fig. 4.2), but it's really no different than opening word processor documents across the net.

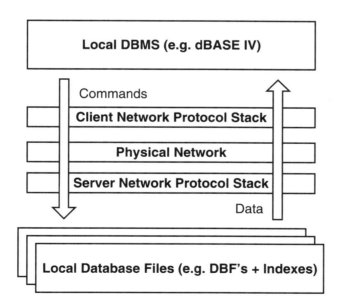

Fig. 4.2
Even across a network, local DBMSs work in the same way.

When the files in which data is stored are located on a server across the network, the DBMS behaves in exactly the same way as described earlier. It is up to the network operating system to make its server volumes emulate local drives, so that the DBMS will get the data it needs.

When the DBMS requests a block of data from the database per the user's commands, the request goes first to the workstation's (client's) network drivers, which direct it over the network to the appropriate server's network file system. The server operating system finds the data on the appropriate disk volume, and sends it back to the waiting workstation drivers. Finally, the data is passed to the DBMS, which uses it exactly as it would have used locally stored data. Unless the network is bogged down in a heavy-use period or the DBMS is requesting a large amount of data, the extra steps usually will not cause much of a delay as far as the user is concerned.

With a local DBMS, all significant work is done on the workstation side. Even if the data is stored on a file server and must be retrieved, it is still processed on the workstation. One major disadvantage to this model is that during any query in which a filtered subset of data is needed (such as all records where the last name is "Jones"), all of the data in the affected tables must still be sent over the network; the workstation needs to see all the data so it knows which to keep for the query and which to discard. It's easy to see how this can quickly clog up a network's bandwidth when several users are busily working with databases at the same time.

Under this model, the workstation must handle all data processing tasks as well as all user interface management. In modern database applications, especially those highly customized for ease of use, the user interface can be a complex affair. Graphical environments like Windows only make matters worse, in the sense that tremendous extra functionality (like fancy grid controls, pop-up help, and so on) is expected of the application. Upgrading your workstations to be able to handle all this responsibility can be an expensive business.

Client/Server Database Interfaces

Because server hardware technology has improved tremendously year after year, the database community has seen a paradigm shift over the course of the last five years or so. Local databases are giving way in large numbers to client/server systems, especially in medium-to-large companies.

As its name implies, a client/server database management system distributes the work load between the workstation and server machines. The server is used for more than just storing and retrieving database data to be passed across the net. It also is used to process the data before the workstation ever receives it. Because query result sets are narrowed down considerably before any data is sent, a lot less data is sent over the network, thus saving a great deal of network capacity. The workstation breathes easier too, because it doesn't have to do nearly as much thinking. Instead, it is left largely free to concentrate on user interface tasks.

An added benefit of processing data at the server is that multiple workstations profit from any caching mechanisms used by the server database engine. For example, imagine that one user requests a certain set of data, say, to populate a lookup table for the front-end (workstation-based) application. If another user comes along and asks for the same data, it can be retrieved almost instantly from a memory cache on the server.

The success of a client/server system depends heavily on the quality and capacity of the server hardware. The more users you have, the more processing the server will have to do, and an insufficient machine will soon be bogged down, resulting in even slower response times than characterize local databases. If you have the money, it often will pay to look into the "monster" PCs available from such companies as Compaq and Trident.

Figure 4.3 illustrates the basic client/server computing model. The front-end application sends commands to the server-based database engine, which takes over the task of reading data from the physical disk, processing it, and passing it to the front-end application.

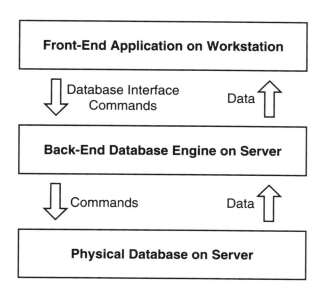

Fig. 4.3

In a client/server system, the server does the database work while the workstation manages the user interface.

The database interface between the client and server is necessarily more complex than in a local system. Several levels of translation are necessary to convey commands and result sets between the workstation and the server. Figure 4.4 shows a client/server database interface in more detail.

Fig. 4.4
In a client/server system, communication is the key.

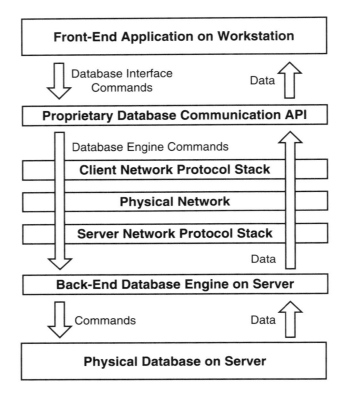

Client/server front-end applications virtually never talk directly to the database engine. Every client/server DBMS (such as Sybase or Oracle) comes with a database communication interface that runs on the front end. These interfaces use various names—database library, database communication API, and so on—but they all work in more or less the same way:

1. The front-end application sends commands to the database communication interface.

2. The interface passes the commands over the network to the database engine itself.

3. The database engine performs the work (such as a query or update operation) on the server side, working through the network file system to access the physical data.

4. The database engine passes any results back to the communication interface on the workstation.

5. The front end accepts the results from the interface and displays or otherwise makes use of them in a fashion the user can understand.

Client/server systems are actually closer to ODBC in principle than are local DBMSs. After all, they send commands from the front end to the database and receive results back without really knowing the details of how the orders were carried out. However, the important difference is that each client/server system manages the communication between its workstation and server portions in a proprietary fashion, incompatible with even other client/server systems. It's the same problem as with many local DBMSs: the lack of the ability to get data from different types of data sources.

Halfway to ODBC: Intermediate Drivers

Before ODBC was adopted as the most popular database interface standard, a number of other companies had thoughts along the same lines. They came up with tools for use in their own products that would provide some of the same benefits. A good example is the "PowerKeys" that work with the Approach end-user DBMS, now owned by Lotus.

Lotus' PowerKeys are drivers written for different data sources (such as dBASE, Paradox, and others). The main database application (Approach) talks to the drivers, and the drivers talk to the database. The benefit is that Approach only needs to know one way of communicating to data sources: the PowerKey way. The PowerKeys themselves know how to work with the different data sources in their own unique ways.

> **Note**
>
> Approach now supports ODBC as well as more direct PowerKey access to certain specific database formats.

This is the same principle on which ODBC is based—however, ODBC goes a couple of steps further. For one thing, ODBC is not a single-vendor solution: it is an open specification. This means that there are (at least theoretically) no secrets about ODBC between Microsoft and the general public; if you want to write an ODBC driver or an ODBC-enabled application, it is fairly easy to get your hands on the tools to do so. For another, ODBC is a standard based on other standards (see Chapter 1, "What Is ODBC?" for more information). This has resulted in less quibbling between companies about the details of the ODBC implementation—it's generally agreed that its design makes sense.

The ODBC Alternative

ODBC uses a layered approach to data management. At each layer in the database communication structure where there's a possibility of product-specific differences, ODBC gets in between the potentially incompatible components and provides a common interface.

From a structural point of view, there are two types of ODBC drivers:

- Single-tier

- Multiple-tier

Single-tier drivers do more work than multiple-tier drivers, but multiple-tier drivers are typically more complex because they normally must support higher levels of API and SQL grammar functionality.

Because the structure of ODBC looks different depending on which of these you're using, the next few sections take a look at the layout of each type in detail.

> **Note**
>
> For more information about single- and multiple-tier drivers, see Chapter 5, "Data Sources and Drivers."

Single-Tier Drivers

Single-tier drivers are, in ODBC terms, the approximate equivalent of the local DBMS. They sit between the application requesting the data and the database itself, providing a universal communication method benefit like "intermediate drivers" (discussed in an earlier section of this chapter) for non-client/server data. Figure 4.5 shows how a single-tier ODBC driver fits into the bigger picture.

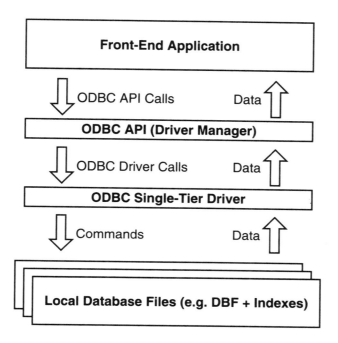

Fig. 4.5
A single-tier ODBC
driver acts as the
database engine.

When the user performs some action in the application that results in a need
for data or other database operations, the application passes an ODBC function call to the Driver Manager component of ODBC. The Driver Manager,
which is responsible for managing communications between the application
and the ODBC drivers it uses, determines what needs to be done. If it's something the Driver Manager can handle directly (such as certain types of cursor
operations), it will do so and pass any results (return codes, for example) back
to the application. If the Driver Manager needs to call a function in the driver
(such as an SQLExecute() call to obtain a result set), it will do that, and ferry
the results back to the application.

A single-tier driver *is* the database engine—it doesn't call anyone else for help;
it just does the job. It acts just like a local DBMS, completely self-contained but
also suffering from the same speed and network traffic disadvantages of any
local DBMS. Remember, the data itself may be stored on a file server elsewhere on the net, but single-tier drivers don't care; they just let the network
operating system go and get the pieces of the files they need.

Multiple-Tier Drivers

Multiple-tier drivers pass commands and data back and forth between the database engine and the client application. Rather than performing data processing functions themselves, they serve as relay stations. Figure 4.6 shows how a multiple-tier ODBC driver fits into the overall database communication structure.

Fig. 4.6
A multiple-tier ODBC driver sits between the client application and the database server.

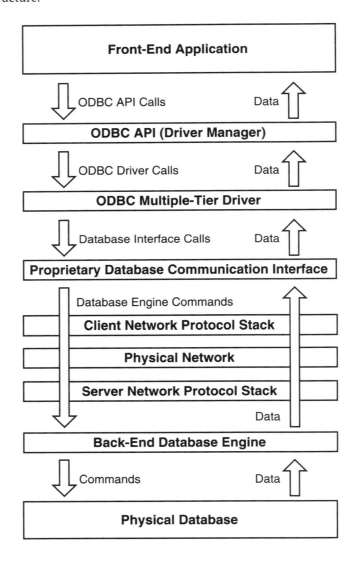

In a multiple-tier driver configuration, the flow of requests and results goes like this:

1. The front-end application issues a request for data or for some other type of database processing; this request goes to the ODBC driver manager.

2. The driver manager either fulfills the request or (usually) passes it on to the driver.

3. The multiple-tier driver translates the request into terms that the vendor-specific database communication interface (such as SQL Server's DB-Library) can understand, and passes it to the interface.

4. The interface sends the request over the network to the database engine on the server.

5. The server processes the request and sends the results, if any, back to the database communication interface.

6. The database interface forwards results to the multiple-tier ODBC driver.

7. The multiple-tier driver forwards the results to the application, usually directly into buffers where the data is expected.

8. The front-end application presents the data to the user in the appropriate fashion.

Theoretically, from an ODBC programmer's point of view, there is no more difference between a single-tier driver and a multiple-tier driver than there might be between two single-tier drivers. This means that as long as it's not too ambitious (as in requiring things that one of the drivers doesn't have) the same application could talk equally well to a dBASE data source and an Oracle data source. Unfortunately, in practice, single-tier drivers tend to have quite a bit less functionality than multiple-tier drivers. This is largely because the client/server systems supported by multiple-tier drivers perform most of the work, and usually provide a higher level of functionality (such as transaction processing) than the local DBMS systems that single-tier drivers strive to emulate.

In most cases, even in a client/server environment, there are no pieces of ODBC that reside and run on the server. The ODBC driver simply uses the native database client for communicating to the database. Some ODBC drivers require a program to reside on the server that handles the ODBC calls and translates them into native calls. This is the case with the Showcase AS/400 ODBC driver.

16-Bit and 32-Bit ODBC Drivers

The Developer's Network CD includes both 32-bit and 16-bit versions of the ODBC 2.0 SDK itself. ODBC 2.0 is capable of working with either 32-bit or 16-bit ODBC drivers.

It would be possible to have two different drivers that work with the same data source, one for a 32-bit operating system and another for a 16-bit OS. But this isn't normally necessary, due to some technical innovation by Microsoft.

Obviously, 32-bit drivers work under Windows NT and 16-bit drivers work under Windows. As you might expect, 16-bit drivers also will work under Windows NT. They run in the 16-bit subsystem, as do other 16-bit Windows applications, but they'll only work with 16-bit Windows programs. A native Windows NT application cannot use a 16-bit driver.

However, it's not so evident that 32-bit ODBC drivers will work under straight 16-bit Windows with Win32s installed. But they do! Based on demands from ODBC driver manufacturers, Microsoft used a technique called "thunking" to allow 16-bit applications to communicate with 32-bit drivers. This means that driver manufacturers with limited resources, but a strong desire to provide optimized support on 32-bit platforms, can get away with writing only a single driver, without leaving 16-bit users in the dust.

Some 32-bit drivers normally have the added ability to connect directly to a server database engine when the driver is running on the server as well, without worrying about all the across-the-net communication. For example, if you're running SQL Server under Windows NT and on the same machine you have a 32-bit app connecting to the DBMS with a 32-bit ODBC driver, the connection is optimized. By contrast, a 16-bit ODBC driver running on the server still acts as though it's connecting to the server across the network. Although this extra feature has limited application, it provides an additional level of optimization in a certain subset of installations.

As ODBC gains even more momentum, expect to see a mix of older 16-bit drivers and "futuristic" 32-bit drivers on most workstations with ODBC installed.

A Typical ODBC Session

In the following chapters, I'll go into detail about the things you need to do to make your application work with ODBC. Right now, let's take a look at the process from the top, to give you an idea of how applications in general communicate through ODBC. I'll talk about it in terms of the steps an ODBC-capable application takes during a typical running, and the things that ODBC has to do to fulfill each request.

1. The application starts up and creates an ODBC environment. This establishes a workspace for future ODBC function calls to utilize.

2. The application either creates an ODBC connection automatically, or first asks the user for a login, password, and possibly the name of the data source. The information provided by the application or by the user is passed to the ODBC API, which uses it in establishing a connection to the data source. In the case of a client/server DBMS that really pays attention to the login information, the info is translated into a form that its back-end engine can understand, and ODBC makes sure the connection was successful before proceeding—or returns an error to the application. For more information about creating your ODBC environment and connecting to data sources, see Chapter 6, "Creating the ODBC Environment and Connection."

> **Note**
>
> If the application needs to, it can connect to more than one data source. It doesn't need to do this all at once at the beginning of the program—it can do it at any appropriate time.

3. When the connection handle has been established, the application needs to create a statement handle through which it will execute ODBC commands. If your driver supports it, you may want to create more than one statement handle. For more information about statement handles, see Chapter 8, "The ODBC Statement: An Introduction."

4. Once the statement handle is available, the application will probably need to obtain information about the structure of the database with which it will be working. It may not need all the details at once, but it will probably need at least some of this information up front.

   The application can issue "catalog and statistics" function calls to inquire about table structures and other database-specific details. A single-tier ODBC driver will go out and grab this type of information directly; a multiple-tier driver will simply translate the request into the syntax expected by the database communication interface. Then ODBC returns the results to the application in a standard format, along with an error or success code and any auxiliary information. For more information about catalog and statistics functions, see Chapter 7, "Catalog and Statistics Functions."

5. Now you come to the central function of an ODBC application: queries and database updates. When the user activates a feature that requires information from the database, the application must formulate a query in proper ODBC SQL grammar. This looks a lot like a standard SQL statement, although special items such as functions and procedure calls can alter its appearance a little. The application sends the request to ODBC—then ODBC passes it to the data source driver. A single-tier driver must fulfill the request directly by plucking the information from the local database files. A multiple-tier driver will translate it into the exact syntax that the database engine is expecting, format and send the request, receive the results, and return them to the application in a standardized fashion. Of course, an error or success code and associated information are also returned.

   Database updates (insert, update, and delete statements, and the like) work in a similar fashion. The main difference is that instead of a result set, only error or success information is returned. For more information about queries and database manipulation, see Chapter 11, "Queries and Result Sets," and Chapter 10, "Inserting, Updating, and Deleting Rows," respectively.

6. When you close your application, it first needs to free the statement handle, then release any database connections you have made, and then release the ODBC environment itself. A single-tier driver will ensure that all local database files are closed correctly; a multiple-tier driver will close its sessions with the server database.

From Here...

- Refer to the next chapter for information about the categories and variations of data sources and ODBC drivers.

- Move on to Chapter 6, "Creating the ODBC Environment and Connection," to begin learning how to build ODBC functions into your applications.

Chapter 5

Data Sources and Drivers

ODBC applications obtain data by connecting to data sources. This chapter looks at ODBC database drivers and how data sources employ them to acquire data.

In this chapter, you learn:

- How to install and use the ODBC Administrator

- How to configure logging

- What ODBC drivers do for applications

- What the different types of drivers are

- How to create data sources with the Administrator

- What approaches to use for choosing drivers

How To Install and Use the ODBC Administrator

The ODBC Administrator is a Control Panel applet essential to the use of ODBC. The Administrator handles installed drivers and assists in managing data sources. It also provides access to call tracing of ODBC function calls. The Adminstrator (ODBCAD32.EXE or ODBCADM.EXE) also can be executed from the Program Manager.

If you do not see the ODBC icon on the Control Panel window (see fig. 5.1), you must install the Administrator. Installing the Administrator and its support files enables you to add sections of the registry needed for ODBC operation. This process also installs files such as ODBC32.DLL, called by ODBC applications.

Fig. 5.1
The ODBC Administrator appears in the Control Panel window as "ODBC."

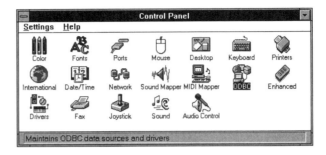

You can get the Administrator from several sources. One source is Microsoft Visual C++ 2.0. It also can be found in the ODBC 2.0 Software Development Kit distributed on the Microsoft Developer Network Development Platform, which is part of the Level II subscription. If you don't have access to any of these sources, and you don't need them for your intended use of ODBC, simply purchase or otherwise obtain an ODBC driver. For further information, consult the Vendor table in Chapter 1, "What Is ODBC?" All the components that you need for ODBC—including the Administrator—must be distributed with any driver.

Figure 5.2 shows the Administrator's main dialog box. It consists primarily of a list of data sources. Each item in the list has a user-defined name for the data source, followed by the name of the driver used by that source. This window is an interface to the ODBCINST.INI configuration file and the corresponding section of the Windows NT registry, where source configuration data is stored.

Fig. 5.2
The ODBC Administrator enables you to configure data sources.

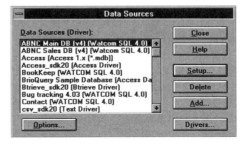

The Administrator's main dialog box has several functions available. Along with the usual **C**lose and **H**elp buttons, there are buttons to access other features. **A**dd, De**l**ete, and **S**etup manipulate the list of data sources. If you have the developer's version of the program, there is an **O**ptions button to enable the logging of function calls to a text file. The D**r**ivers button displays the Drivers dialog box. Figure 5.3 shows the Drivers dialog box. This dialog box is an interface to the ODBCINST.INI file under Windows, or the HKEY_LOCAL_MACHINE \SOFTWARE\ODBC\ODBCINST.INI section of registry, where driver information is kept. From here, you can add and delete drivers. To add a driver, browse for a copy of ODBC.INF on the disk containing the new drivers. This file contains information about the new drivers and any auxiliary files they may require. The drivers and related files are usually copied into the \WINDOWS\SYSTEM32 directory for 32-bit drivers and the \WINDOWS\SYSTEM directory for 16-bit drivers.

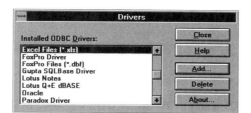

Fig. 5.3
The Drivers dialog box shows all available drivers.

How To Configure Logging

ODBC gives you a logging facility through the Administrator. This facility logs the ODBC function calls and the SQL statements passed to the driver. This is more accessible than using a full debugger. You can get an overview without becoming bogged down. Your users can even do the logging for you.

To configure logging, start the ODBC Administrator. Click the **O**ptions button to invoke the ODBC Options dialog box (see fig. 5.4).

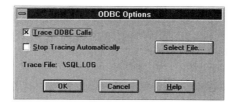

Fig. 5.4
The ODBC Options dialog box lets you configure the logging feature.

Listing 5.1 shows a log file that was generated during the execution of an ODBC application.

Listing 5.1   A Sample ODBC Log File

```
SQLFreeEnv(henv004A0F24);
SQLAllocEnv(phenv3B570000);
SQLAllocConnect(henv3B570000, phdbc42DF0000);
SQLDriverConnect(hdbc42DF0000, hwnd0B34, "DSN=NorthWind", 13,
➡ szConnStrOut, 256, pcbConnStrOut, 1);
SQLAllocStmt(hdbc42DF0000, phstmt42FF0000);
SQLExecDirect(hstmt0EC70000, "SELECT customer.CUSTMR_ID,
➡ customer.COMPANY, customer.CONTACT, customer.CON_TITLE,
➡ customer.ADDRESS, customer.CITY, customer.REGION,
➡ customer.ZIP_CODE, customer.COUNTRY, customer.PHONE,
➡ customer.FAX
FROM c:\windows\msapps\msquery\nwind\customer.dbf customer,
c:\windows\msapps\msquery\nwind\employee.dbf employee,
c:\windows\msapps\msquery\nwind\orders.dbf orders
WHERE orders.CUSTMR_ID = customer.CUSTMR_ID
AND orders.EMPLOY_ID = employee.EMPLOY_ID",  451);
SQLBindCol(hstmt0EC70000, 26, 1, rgbValue, 23, pcbValue);
SQLFetch(hstmt0EC70000);
```

What Is an ODBC Driver?

ODBC does not give applications direct access to a database. Instead, applications communicate with a driver through the ODBC driver manager. The driver manager passes SQL statements and other information from the application to a driver. The driver, in turn, passes the result sets from these statements back to the application.

ODBC Drivers are DLLs that provide an interface from your application to the data inside a specified database. This is not unlike the database library you may have used before. There is one major difference between ODBC and these libraries, however. ODBC provides a nearly uniform interface to all databases supported by a driver.

If a database management system (DBMS) you want to use is not supported by an ODBC driver, don't volunteer to write one without good cause! Writing drivers is a daunting task and is well beyond the scope of this book. If you must write a driver, be aware that most developers tackle this chore with the help of third-party tools. The Desktop Database Drivers (included with the MSDN Level II CD-ROM pack and with Visual C++) is a case in point. Microsoft used PageAhead's Simba library to simplify the development process.

The Different Types of ODBC Drivers

Drivers differ widely, both in capability and modes of operation. They are classified by the ODBC standard based on three criteria: API conformance levels, SQL grammar conformance, and driver type.

API Conformance

The API Conformance Level of a driver places limits on the functions that your application can call. Driver developers do not implement every ODBC function. They are encouraged to conform to one of three levels of functionality. These levels are:

- Core API conformance

- Extension Level 1 API conformance

- Extension Level 2 API conformance

These levels are general guidelines. Some drivers omit several functions from their claimed level of support. Almost all drivers implement functions belonging to a higher conformance level. Microsoft has announced no plans for a true certification program to enforce adherence to these levels. Until it does, the API conformance levels will continue to be viewed by driver developers as an informal guideline.

Core API conformance is a bare minimum of functionality. The 23 functions that make up the core involve allocating and freeing environments, database connections, and SQL statements. They provide basic support for passing parameters into statements, and accessing the results returned. Limited cataloging functions and error-message retrieval are available as well.

The Core API conformance level suffices for very basic applications. This level is adequate only if the schema for each table is known up front. If you must determine a table's schema at run time, hold out for a more capable driver. Fortunately, the number of strictly Core-level drivers is very small and decreasing.

> **Note**
>
> The best way to find the API conformance level of a function is to look at the ODBC API online help. Most versions of this file enable you to view functions by conformance level. This help file should be named ODBCAPI.HLP or ODBC20.HLP.

Extension Level 1 adds 19 more functions for your use in applications. Obtaining a table's schema is completely supported. You can learn what conceptual data types are available and what each is called. This ability is indispensable if your program is to work with several different drivers. You also can query the driver about support for different SQL conformance features (see the section "SQL Grammar Conformance" later in this chapter).

The majority of drivers conform to this level. If your application is to reach the widest possible audience, this is the target. You can write dynamic applications that know nothing about the tables they manipulate until run time.

Tip
Stored procedures are precompiled batches of SQL statements that run on the server side of certain client/server DBMSs, like Sybase. They're used for various types of processing that the client application doesn't need to be directly involved in.

Extension Level 2 extends Level 1 with 19 more functions. You now can get information about both primary and foreign keys. Among other additions, you can get information about table and column permissions, and stored procedures in the database. The most welcome features, however, might be enhancements to cursor control and concurrency control (see Chapter 13, "The Cursor Library and Positioned Operations").

Most of the Level 2 changes reflect support for advanced features found only in client/server databases. Consequently, you should not be disappointed if your PC database does not have a Level 2 driver available. Most don't have native support for the features needed for Level 2 compliance. Use this level only if you are writing applications intended for true client/server support. Make sure that Level 2 drivers are available for all platforms you plan to use.

SQL Grammar Conformance

The SQL conformance level of a driver determines what structured query language grammars may be used in ODBC statements. It also specifies what data types are available. The conformance levels defined for ODBC are:

- Minimum SQL grammars

- Core SQL grammars

- Extended SQL grammars

This measure of a driver is complicated by the nature of SQL. It seems that no two DBMS vendors use the same grammars. Two may use two different SQL grammars to implement the same feature. The term "Standard SQL" could mean ANSI 1989, ISO SQL-92, or just a particular vendor's interpretation.

> **Note**
>
> The data types named in this section are conceptual data types. The real names of data types are often unique to the database or driver. Use the `SQLGetTypeInfo()` function to get a result set containing the string to use in a table creation statement.

The minimum SQL grammar contains most of the features that you need. You can CREATE and DROP tables, and SELECT, INSERT, UPDATE, and DELETE records. There are some variations of the character field type. That type may correspond most closely with the standard types CHAR, VARCHAR, or LONG VARCHAR.

The minimum grammars might be enough for many developers. The character data type alone, however, is not sufficient for most situations. You won't find many drivers of this SQL conformance.

> **Note**
>
> A survey of drivers turned up zero drivers having only the character as a field type. Even the humble Text File Driver (from Microsoft's Desktop Database Drivers) supports character, date, float, short, and long integer types.

The core grammar adds a number of useful features. There are grammars to ALTER tables and CREATE and DROP indexes and views. It is possible to GRANT and REVOKE permission to create and read and write records to particular users. Subqueries add power to your SELECT statements here (see Chapter 3, "The Client/Server Language: SQL," and Chapter 11, "Queries and Result Sets," for information on queries and subqueries).

Several new data types are added. Integer types are introduced for both short and long integers. Floating point types of both single and double precision are added, as well.

If you have done much work with traditional PC databases, such as Paradox or Xbase, you would not think of creating a set of related tables without indexes. From the standard, it appears that you must have a driver of core conformance or better to create an index. Is this a possibility? What if the DBMS does not support granting and revoking permissions?

Many databases don't support the user permission concept. They still claim to have core conformance. You just have to look the other way. The grammar conformance levels were probably never intended to be applied to local databases on a PC.

> **Note**
>
> Most client/server DBMSs have a hierarchical security system in place with the database administrator (DBA) at the top. They can GRANT and REVOKE permission to perform various operations to users. The DBA can even give other users the right to GRANT and REVOKE. The SQL statement
>
>   GRANT SELECT ON INVOICES TO JKRANTZ
>
> enables the user JKRANTZ to search and read records from the INVOICES table.

The extended grammar introduces some very sophisticated new grammars. The concept of cursor control is added (see Chapter 13, "The Cursor Library and Positioned Operations"). The extended grammar also adds the date field type, in addition to several somewhat obscure field types.

Why is such a basic field type as the date deemed to be an extended feature? There seems to be no explanation worthy of repeating. Almost all drivers at the lower conformance levels include a date field type.

If you get the impression that grammar conformance levels are at odds with reality, you're not alone. The API conformance levels reveal much about a driver's usefulness. The SQL grammar conformance level, by itself, says a lot less. To be useful, a driver should support most of the core SQL conformance items.

Driver Type

Driver type is a characterization of the division of labor between the driver and the associated database management system. There are two basic types:

- Single-tier drivers
- Multiple-tier drivers

Single-tier drivers process both the ODBC function calls and the SQL statements. The driver is the DBMS. Take, for example, the dBASE driver from Microsoft's Desktop Drivers. The driver itself can manipulate dBASE tables and indexes like a stand-alone DBMS. It also contains an SQL parser to translate into function calls the strings passed to the driver. This is a common characteristic of single-machine systems. None of the traditional database products available on the PC started as SQL-based products.

Single-tier drivers are most often of Core or Extension Level 1 API compliance. This is because Level 2 compliance entails extending the DBMS to support features and concepts that were never present in the original product,
which is probably quite expensive. Also, some more advanced SQL concepts
at Level 2 might not be appropriate for simple file managers such as Btrieve.

Multiple-tier drivers have a separate DBMS. The driver must still process function calls from ODBC applications; however, it doesn't have to process the
SQL statements. That is a job for the DBMS.

A multiple-tier driver is often a communication manager for a true client/
server DBMS. The ODBC driver normally uses the native DBMS client to communicate to the server. The driver doesn't directly manipulate data files and
doesn't have to parse any SQL statements. It can just pass them directly to
the DBMS client. Because multiple-tier drivers are usually front ends for powerful client/server systems, they usually have support for most Level 1 and
Level 2 functions and data types. The amount of support is limited by the
abilities of the specific database.

How To Create Data Sources with the ODBC Administrator

Later you'll learn how to create data sources through the ODBC API. For now,
you set up a data source through the Administrator using the following steps.
Installed data sources are stored in the ODBC.INI file (Windows)
HKEY_CURRENT_USER\Software\ODBC\ODBC.INI section of the registry
(Windows NT).

1. Start by invoking the Administrator. Its icon should appear on the Control Panel's window.

2. Click the **A**dd button and choose a driver from the list.

3. After you choose a driver, a driver configuration dialog box appears.
   Figure 5.5 shows the ODBC Microsoft Access Setup dialog box. Other
   sources may look different.

4. Enter whatever information is needed to link your data source to the
   actual database. Read the driver documentation to find out what information is needed.

Fig. 5.5
The ODBC
Microsoft Access
Setup dialog box
enables you to
configure a data
source that uses
the Access ODBC
driver.

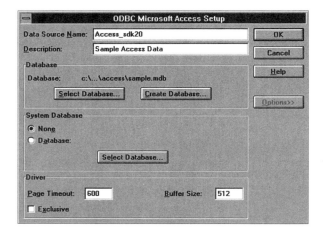

Choosing Drivers and Approaches

Developers cite several reasons for using ODBC. Before choosing the drivers
your applications support, you should examine your motivations. It might
save some missed deadlines and frayed nerves.

Multiple Targets

The most popular reason to use ODBC is that it enables you to support all
databases with one application. If your product is to be used with every type
of DBMS imaginable, ODBC is probably your best option. Perhaps this aspect
of ODBC has been oversold, however. It's not usually practical to support
every single driver, because you'll usually want to use functions or options
that aren't supported by the more basic drivers.

If you are going to support all drivers, there are two avenues that you might
follow. If you want to write a minimum amount of code, you have to use the
minimum set of features found in the most modest of drivers; however, your
application is slow and supports few data types.

If the performance penalty is unacceptable, you might try to use advanced
features in an effort to improve efficiency. If you want to use them, your
application has to query the driver about each advanced feature. If the feature
is not implemented by the driver, you have to find a way to perform the
operation without it.

This strategy can be quite expensive. The increase in size and complexity
might be enough to put your project in peril. Testing and support costs alone
could be prohibitive. Don't let it happen to you.

Do you really need to support all drivers? If you are using scalability as a selling point, maybe your application could support only a small number of DBMSs. Watcom SQL could serve as the platform for local and networked access. Informix Online could be the platform for client/server customers. Look for drivers with above-average compliance.

Because both the Watcom and Informix drivers support a similar level of ODBC functionality, there is no need to *special case* every database operation. You can use many of the advanced features, giving your application good performance. Even your testing and support costs are lower.

Single Targets

There is no reason to avoid using ODBC if you are targeting a single DBMS. There are several advantages in doing so. Unless someone in your organization is convinced that ODBC can't meet the requirements, look into using it.

ODBC developers can avoid wasting time learning yet another database API. Each learning curve costs your company a lot of money. If you never use that DBMS again, it is money wasted.

Client/server developers don't have constant access to the actual system they are targeting. You certainly do not want to bring your company's mission-critical computer system to its knees while developing an application. You should find a local DBMS with compliance characteristics similar to your target system. The worst that can happen is a reboot.

You can postpone the actual decision concerning which DBMS to use until later in the development cycle. You may find your first choice impractical for various reasons. Development need not wait until all benchmarking is complete.

If you are beginning to believe that there is much database development that should be done through ODBC, the point is made. As databases become more standardized, reasons to use native APIs become fewer. A programmer's time is a very expensive commodity. Don't waste it in learning a new API every time you start working with a new DBMS.

From Here...

- To begin learning how to program in ODBC, continue on to the next chapter, "Creating the ODBC Environment and Connection."

- To take a closer look at some of the contents of the ODBC SDK, turn to Appendix A, "Resources in the SDK."

Chapter 6

Creating the ODBC Environment and Connection

ODBC applications are written to issue SQL statements and perform queries. Before this can happen, you must set up the ODBC environment and connection.

In this chapter, you learn:

- What elements are needed to enable a project for ODBC
- How to initialize and free the ODBC environment
- How to trap and use ODBC error messages
- How to initialize and free a connection
- How to connect to an ODBC data source
- How to enable your users to choose a data source
- How to configure options for a data source
- How to disconnect from a data source

The Elements Needed to Enable a Project for ODBC

Before your application can make ODBC function calls, you must add the correct header files and libraries. If you are using another vendor's compiler or another class library, add these elements manually. If you're using Visual C++ and the MFC ODBC classes, see the three chapters in Part II, "Visual C++," for instructions.

The basic function prototypes and structure definitions for ODBC appear in SQL.H. SQLEXT.H adds elements needed to use advanced features and itself includes SQL.H. Both files are dependent on WINDOWS.H for data types. ODBCINST.H includes functions for installing and managing ODBC drivers and data sources.

When using Microsoft's Foundation Classes or Borland's ObjectWindows Library, WINDOWS.H is already included. If you are not using a general Windows class library, you should include WINDOWS.H before SQLEXT.H.

You will need to link your application with ODBC32.LIB for 32-bit applications and ODBC.LIB for 16-bit applications. These are import libraries for ODBC32.DLL and ODBC.DLL, respectively. If you use functions from ODBCINST.H, also link to ODBCCP32.LIB or ODBCINST.LIB.

The ODBC Environment

The ODBC environment is created by calling `SQLAllocEnv()`. The `Environment::Environment()` constructor calls `SQLAllocEnv()`, as shown in the following code listing:

```
class Environment
{
private:
    RETCODE retcode;
    HENV    henv;

public:
    Environment();
    ~Environment();
};

Environment::Environment()
{
    retcode = SQLAllocEnv( &henv );
}
```

The possible return values for `SQLAllocEnv()` are `SQL_SUCCESS` and `SQL_ERROR`. If the return value is `SQL_SUCCESS`, a valid ODBC environment has been created and `henv` is a handle to that environment. If `SQL_ERROR` is returned, environment creation has failed and henv has been assigned the value `SQL_NULL_HENV`. This is likely to happen only in very low memory situations where your application is probably doomed anyway. It's important to advise your users of (and keep in mind yourself) the minimum RAM requirements for your application, which usually will be at least 4 MB of RAM, or more depending on the size of your application.

> **Note**
>
> You should, with very few exceptions, check the return value of *each* ODBC function call. If you do not, your application will likely halt the first time an unexpected error occurs. This is just good advice in general. It is a cardinal rule for ODBC programming. See the next section for details.

The ODBC environment can have the same lifetime as your application. Keeping the environment open involves few resources. The ODBC32.DLL is already in memory, in any case.

Before your application terminates, you should free the environment. You can do this by calling SQLFreeEnv() as shown in the following listing. This frees all memory associated with the environment.

SQLFreeEnv() returns a RETCODE. The return value is not checked in the following listing because it is in a destructor that cannot return a value.

> **Note**
>
> All ODBC API functions have the same return type, the RETCODE. There is a simple, uniform set of values RETCODE can assume:
>
> - SQL_SUCCESS: The function was successful.
>
> - SQL_ERROR: The function failed due to an error.
>
> - SQL_INVALID_HANDLE: The function failed due to an invalid handle (HENV, HDBC, or HSTMT).
>
> - SQL_NEED_DATA: The function was successful. Some functions return this value to request the calling of other functions to supply more data.
>
> - SQL_NO_DATA_FOUND: The function was successful. The query involved did not return any data, however.
>
> - SQL_SUCCESS_WITH_INFO: The function was successful, but an abnormal condition occurred. The SQLSTATE contains more information (see the SQLError() section "Calling the SQLError() Function," later in this chapter).

A return of `SQL_ERROR` indicates that the environment was not freed. You might have passed it an invalid handle, or one that has already been freed.

It is very important to avoid calling `SQLFreeEnv()` with an invalid handle. If your call to `SQLAllocEnv()` fails, calling `SQLFreeEnv()` with the same `HENV` may cause a general protection fault. This next listing shows how *not* to structure your code:

```
HENV henv;
RETCODE retcode;

retcode = SQLAllocEnv( &henv );    // Try to allocate henv

if( retcode==SQL_SUCCESS )         // How did it go?
{
                                   // Do some ODBC
}

SQLFreeEnv( henv );                // The henv may be invalid =>
GPF!!!
```

Never free any kind of ODBC handle unconditionally. If the handle was invalid, your program may crash. You and your users will have no idea why.

The return code of an `SQLAllocEnv()` call is not the only indication of a failed environment allocation. After an `SQLAllocEnv()` failure, the `HENV` will have a value of `SQL_NULL_HENV`. The following listing shows how you might make use of this:

```
HENV henv;
RETCODE retcode;

retcode = SQLAllocEnv( &henv );    // Try to allocate henv

if( retcode==SQL_SUCCESS )         // How did it go?
{
                                   // Do some ODBC...
}
                                   // Do some other clean up...
if( henv!= SQL_NULL_HENV )         // Was the handle valid?
{
    SQLFreeEnv( henv );            // Free the handle.
}
```

You can learn the exact cause of the error from the SQL State (see "Calling the `SQLError()` Function," later in this chapter).

Error Trapping

We, as C and C++ programmers, often ignore function return codes. Take, for instance, the lowly `print()` function. It returns the number of characters written or a negative number on failure. Few of us ever check the return value from `printf()`, or suffer as a result. This is a dangerous practice for ODBC programming. You should check the return value of all ODBC function calls.

There are several reasons the ODBC API requires more error checking than most other APIs, because there are many opportunities for disaster. An SQL statement might be invalid or refer to a table that no longer exists. A function may have been called out of order. ODBC will not function if the data source task ceases to run.

The largest source of ODBC errors during development is invalid SQL statements. Several major functions pass an SQL statement as a string. Of course, the compiler will never help you discover syntax errors in these statements. You are on your own for that.

> **Note**
>
> SQL grammar is not always simple. We don't have an SQL compiler to flag problems. Finding syntax errors has traditionally been a matter of trial and error. Fortunately, inexpensive and simple-to-use tools are now available.
>
> One such tool is Microsoft Query (see fig. 6.1). Query is an ODBC-based interactive query utility. It is part of the suite of applications that Microsoft includes with its flagship applications like Word and Excel. Query uses Wizards to lead you through the process of attaching to a data source and executing an SQL statement.
>
> If you don't have Query, Microsoft has provided you with an alternative. Visual Basic Professional includes a sample program called Vista. Vista is, for the most part, an equal to Microsoft Query. It is also an illustration of the power that Visual Basic wields from the addition of ODBC support. Not bad for a Visual Basic example program.

SQL Statements can fail if a table is empty or a field no longer exists—even if your syntax is pristine. This fact alone would justify very thorough error trapping. *Any* statement could fail. You are at the mercy of the elements.

Calling functions in the correct order is not as elementary as it sounds. ODBC is a moderately complex machine. You may call most functions only after meeting certain requirements. Wherever appropriate, the conditions required to use a function will be given.

Calling the *SQLError()* Function

It is not enough to know that an error has occurred. You should learn the exact cause of the error so your program can react appropriately. The `SQLError()` function can provide you with an abundance of information about an error. `SQLError()` is prototyped in SQL.H, as in the following listing:

```
RETCODE SQLError(
    HENV            henv,
    HDBC            hdbc,
    HSTMT           hstmt,
    UCHAR FAR *     szSqlState,
    SDWORD FAR *    pfNativeError,
    UCHAR FAR *     szErrorMsg,
    SWORD           cbErrorMsgMax,
    SWORD FAR *     pcbErrorMsg
);
```

Fig. 6.1

In Microsoft Query, you see graphical representations of the relationships between tables, and you can combine data from those tables simply by selecting fields from lists.

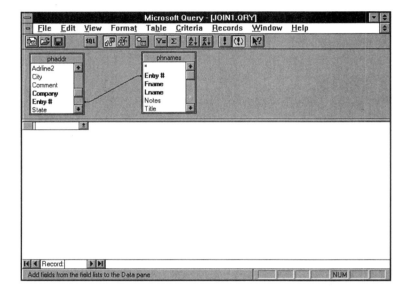

The first three parameters deal with the type of object used before the error: the environment, the connection, or the statement. For example, if the previous statement acted on the connection, pass the connection handle (HDBC) to SQLError(). The other handles should get the appropriate null handle: SQL_NULL_HENV, SQL_NULL_HDBC, or SQL_NULL_HSTMT.

> **Note**
>
> The type of the first parameter shows the type of object upon which a function call acts.

The szSqlState parameter should point to a character buffer of at least six bytes in length. This buffer will contain the SQLSTATE after SQLError() returns. SQLSTATE is a null-terminated string of five characters that indicates a warning or error state. You can find their meanings in Appendix A of the ODBC Programmer's Reference.

`pfNativeError` is the native error code. If the data source returns an error code, it will appear here. Some drivers never use this code. You will need to find the error code in the driver's documentation. There is no standardization of error codes among vendors.

The address of a buffer to hold error messages is passed to `SQLError()` in `szErrorMsg`. You should allow for a length of at least `SQL_MAX_MESSAGE_LENGTH` bytes. The buffer will contain practical information about the nature of the error. This is where text suitable to display in a dialog box can be found.

> **Note**
>
> SQL_MAX_MESSAGE_LENGTH is 512 bytes. You probably should dynamically allocate this buffer from the heap to avoid stack problems.

The `pcbErrorMsg` parameter is a pointer to the actual length of the error string placed in `szErrorMsg`. If you are using a language that handles null-terminated strings, you will not need to look at the result. It can be quite important to BASIC users, who need to know the length of their strings.

Using Error Codes

The `SQLError()` function has several applications. Both the `szErrorMsg` buffer and the `SQLSTATE` can be helpful. The situation determines which one to which you should refer.

During development, the buffer to which `szErrorMsg` points is most instructive. It will alert you to what part of ODBC has detected an error, such as the driver manager or driver. It usually will give a detailed explanation of the error, as well. At run time, you can put this string in a message box to notify your users of the nature of the error.

The `SQLSTATE` has many values that remain consistent between drivers, making it more useful for branching at run time. The values follow several conventions, but learning them will not spare you from looking them up in the ODBC API Reference help file. These values are probably too cryptic to use as error messages by themselves.

The following listing illustrates the use of the SQLSTATE to determine the whole cause of an error:

```
if( SQLConnect( ....... ) == SQL_SUCCESS )
{
    // Connection was successful
}
```

The ODBC API

```
else
{
    UCHAR  szSqlState[6];
    UCHAR  szErrorMsg[SQL_MAX_MESSAGE_LENGTH];
        // Could also be allocated on the heap.
    SDWORD dwNativeError;
    SWORD  wErrorMsg;

    SQLError(
                SQL_NULL_HENV, hdbc, SQL_NULL_HSTMT, szSqlState,
                &dwNativeError,             szErrorMsg,
SQL_MAX_MESSAGE_LENGTH-1,&wErrorMsg
            );
    // Connection failed, but why?
    if( !strcmp( szSqlState, "28000" )
        // 28000 is "invalid authorization specification"
    {
        MessageBox( hwnd, "INVALID PASSWORD OR USERID!",
                    "Logon Failure", MB_ICONHAND );
        // Log unauthorized attempt to logon...
    }
    else
    {
        MessageBox( hwnd, szErrorMsg, "Logon Failure",
        MB_ICONHAND );
    }
}
```

In the preceding listing, a user attempts to connect to a data source. On line 12, SQLError() fills in the szSqlState if he fails. We want to trap the particular case where failure is due to an unauthorized password. On line 19, szSqlState is compared to "28000" to determine if this has occurred.

A message box displays the szErrorMsg buffer on line 22. It is a common practice to notify the user of an ODBC error. In this case, the program takes no special action. The user is notified, in detail, about his error.

How to Initialize and Free a Connection

A *connection* gives an ODBC access to a data source. The SQLAllocConnect() function allocates connections before use. Before calling SQLAllocConnect(), you need to have a valid environment (HENV). You then can establish a connection with a data source (see the next section).

> **Caution**
>
> Before freeing the environment when the program is exited, you should free any connections you have established. The order in which you free the objects is significant. Resources will be lost if you fail to observe this order. More important, other ODBC applications may not be able to function. The following listing shows the correct order of events.

```
HENV henv;
HDBC hdbc;
RETCODE retcode;

retcode = SQLAllocEnv( &henv );                 // Allocate the
                                                // environment

if( retcode==SQL_SUCCESS )
{
    retcode = SQLAllocConnect( henv, &hdbc );   // Allocate the
                                                // connection

// More ODBC...

    if( hdbc != SQL_NULL_HDBC )
    {
        SQLFreeConnect( hdbc );                 // Free the
                                                // connection
    }
}

if( henv!= SQL_NULL_HENV )
{
    SQLFreeEnv( henv );                         // Free the
                                                // environment
}
```

How to Connect to a Data Source

Your application has laid a foundation for ODBC by allocating an environment and a connection. The next step is connecting to a data source. Now, you must make some decisions.

Connecting to a Specific Data Source

Are you going to determine, before run time, which data source your application will use? Custom or in-house applications usually do not. You probably have set up a data source specifically to hold your application's data. Your users may have no need or desire to choose their own data sources.

The ODBC API

If you are supporting a single driver or a small set of drivers, you should guide your users to them. Ideally, they should not even be aware that there is a choice of drivers available.

If you decide to guide your users to a particular data source, you use the `SQLConnect()` function (see the following listing). `SQLConnect()` connects your application to a particular data source and links the connection handle (`HDBC`) with that connection.

```
RETCODE SQLConnect(
    HDBC              hdbc,
    UCHAR FAR *       szDSN,
    SWORD             cbDSN,
    UCHAR FAR *       szUID,
    SWORD             cbUID,
    UCHAR FAR *       szAuthStr,
    SWORD             cbAuthStr);
```

The preconditions for using `SQLConnect()` are simple. You must have a valid connection handle. That connection handle must have been allocated with a valid environment handle (`HENV`). The connection handle passed as the first parameter must not currently be connected to another data source.

Three of the last six parameters are pointers to strings needed to perform a connection. The `szDSN` parameter is the name of the data source. The `cbUID` is the user id, while the `szAuthStr` is his or her password.

The `SWORD` parameters, `cbDSN`, `cbUID`, and `cbAuthStr` are the lengths of the string parameters that precede them. If you are using null-terminated strings, such as are available in C and C++, you don't actually need to determine these lengths. You can simply pass the constant `SQL_NTS`.

> **Note**
>
> The NTS in the constant SQL_NTS is for "Null-Terminated String."

The data source parameter should never be left blank. This would indicate that you want to connect to the default data source. A default data source may have been set in the registration database. If it is not set up, or another application has changed it, you will connect to the data. It should be clear that relying on the default is a gamble.

Most traditional PC databases have no security and do not require logging in. ODBC includes the user id and password strings primarily to support client/ server products. Using `SQLConnect()` directly removes even the appearance of security.

The parameters for SQLConnect() supply the information needed to connect to a data source. Some drivers do not even require all the parameters. You could even put up your own dialog box to fill its parameters. There is an easier way to do this, however. It is shown in the next section.

Enabling Users to Choose a Data Source

Are you going to let your end user choose a data source? Applications that emphasize connectivity certainly should. Most shrink-wrapped applications that advertise ODBC tout this feature. Choose carefully. The decision has serious implications.

If you choose this route, your application should support almost any driver. Enabling a user to connect to a data source that your application can't support is just poor public relations. Trying to support all drivers can hurt performance, break your budget, or both.

> **Note**
>
> You can find a discussion of "universal" driver support in Chapter 5, "Data Sources and Drivers."

Choosing a Data Source with *SQLDriverConnect()*

One way you can enable your users to choose a data source is to use the SQLDriverConnect() function (see the following listing). SQLDriverConnect() is quite versatile and can connect to any data source.

```
RETCODE SQLDriverConnect(
    HDBC    hdbc,                // Connection handle
    HWND    hwnd,                // Window to serve as parent to dialogs
    UCHAR FAR * szConnStrIn,     // Connection string
    SWORD   cbConnStrIn,         // Connection string length or SQL_NTS
    UCHAR FAR * szConnStrOut,    // Output string
    SWORD   cbConnStrOutMax,     // Length of buffer for output string
    SWORD FAR * pcbConnStrOut,   // Points to actual length of
                                 // output string
    UWORD   fDriverCompletion    // Flag indicating prompting for
                                 // information
);
```

The first four parameters are data you supply. The hdbc should be a valid connection not yet associated with a data source. The hwnd parameter provides a parent window for dialog boxes. The szConnStrIn is the connection string, while cbConnStrIn is the length of that string or SQL_NTS.

The connection string has its own special syntax. If you want your user to find a data source without any guidance, leave the buffer empty and pass the constant SQL_DRIVER_COMPLETE in the fDriverCompletion parameter. The driver manager will invoke a dialog listing all the available data sources.

If your user successfully selects a data source, SQLDriverConnect() returns SQL_SUCCESS. A connection is made to the selected data source with the defaults from the registry for 32-bit drivers or ODBC.INI file for 16-bit drivers. A return of SQL_ERROR means that a data source was selected, but an error prevented a connection. An SQL_NO_DATA_FOUND return will occur if the data source selection dialog was aborted.

One special side effect of a successful call to SQLDriverConnect() is left in the buffer to which the szConnStrOut parameter pointed. The buffer will contain the full connection string that was actually used to make the connection. This will include a data source name and perhaps a user id and password. It also may contain driver-specific tokens of no particular interest.

> **Note**
>
> The input and output connection strings usually contain several strings in the form:
>
>   KEYWORD=VALUE;
>
> The most common keywords are:
>
> - DRIVER: The name of the ODBC driver
> - DSN: The name of the data source
> - UID: The user id
> - PWD: The password

You may want to give the user a "hint" as to which data source to choose, but not actually limit the choices. To do this, call SQLDriverConnect() with a connection string containing DSN=SOURCENAME, where SOURCENAME is the name of the suggested data source. The fDriverCompletion parameter again should be SQL_DRIVER_COMPLETE.

Choosing a Data Source with *SQLBrowseConnect()*

Some client/server systems require more information than the user id and password to establish a connection. A host name may be required, for instance. Some RDBMSs, such as Informix, force a user to connect to a particular database (referring to the relational entity, not the RDBMS itself).

The `SQLBrowseConnect()` function (see the following listing) might be appropriate for such a situation. There are some special requirements, however. `SQLBrowseConnect()` is a Level 2 function, precluding its use with most single-tier drivers. You also must furnish the code necessary to parse the output buffer and handle user prompting and input.

```
RETCODE SQLBrowseConnect(
    HDBC         hdbc,            // Database connection handle
    UCHAR FAR *  szConnStrIn,     // Input connection string
    SWORD        cbConnStrIn,     // Length of input connection string
    UCHAR FAR *  szConnStrOut,    // Output connection string
    SWORD        cbConnStrOutMax, // Size of output buffer
    SWORD FAR *  pcbConnStrOut    // Length of output connection string
);
```

Using `SQLBrowseConnect()` is an iterative process. It will be called several times before an actual connection is established. The function is first called with `DSN=DATASOURCE` passed in the `szConnStrIn` parameter. For each succeeding iteration:

1. Parse the output buffer, `szConnStrOut`, to ascertain for what to prompt the user (see the following Note for the syntax).

2. Obtain user input using the appropriate prompts.

3. Form connection strings from the input and place them in the input buffer, `szConnStrIn`.

4. Call `SQLBrowseConnect()`. If the return value is `SQL_SUCCESS`, the connection has been established. If `SQL_NEED_DATA` is returned, repeat the process from step 1.

Note

The browse connection strings from the `SQLBrowseConnect()` function have the same general grammar as those used in `SQLDriverConnect()`. There are extensions to aid in prompting the user for more information.

A request to prompt for a particular item has the form:

    KEYWORD:PROMPT=?;

where PROMPT is the string with which the user should be prompted to acquire the associated data.

A request to present the user with a choice between several given items has the form:

(continues)

The ODBC API

(continued)

```
        KEYWORD:PROMPT={CHOICE1,CHOICE2,CHOICE3};
```

where CHOICE1, CHOICE2, and CHOICE3 are the choices to be presented.

Once the user has entered the information, it should be placed in the input buffer in the form:

```
        KEYWORD=USERINPUT;
```

where USERINPUT is the user's choice or input.

Using SQLBrowseConnect() is certainly the most difficult approach to establishing a connection. It should be used only when absolutely necessary.

How to Set and Get Connection Options

Extension Level 1 drivers enable you to control a connection's attributes. You can set these options before or after making a connection. These options will remain in effect while the connection handle exists. You do not have to reset them for whenever a connection is made.

Using *SQLSetConnectOption()*

The ability to control a connection's attributes is provided by the SQLSetConnectOption() function. The prototype is seen in the next listing. The first parameter, hdbc, associates it with a database connection. The fOption is a 16-bit value representing the option to be set. The vParam is a 32-bit value for that option. vParam can either be a 32-bit integer or a pointer to a null-terminated string:

```
RETCODE SQLSetConnectOption(
    HDBC        hdbc,
    UWORD       fOption,
    UDWORD      vParam
);
```

Using *SQLGetConnectOption()*

You may need to know the current value of a connection option. SQLGetConnectOption() determines the value of a connection option (see the following listing). Its operation is similiar to SQLSetConnectOption(). After calling the function, the pvParam parameter points to the value of the option referred to in the fOption parameter:

```
RETCODE SQLGetConnectOption(
    HDBC       hdbc,          // The database connection
    UWORD      fOption,       // The connection option
    PTR        pvParam        // The value of the connection option
);
```

Some Common Connection Options

ODBC defines several connection options. All options will not apply to all drivers. A particular driver may provide custom options as well. Drivers will disregard attempts to use invalid options or set invalid values to a valid option.

Here is a short list of connection option constants and their possible values:

- ■ SQL_ACCESS_MODE: The possible 32-bit values are SQL_MODE_READ_ONLY and SQL_MODE_READ_WRITE.

- ■ SQL_AUTOCOMMIT: The possible 32-bit values are SQL_AUTOCOMMIT_OFF and SQL_AUTOCOMMIT_ON. With AUTOCOMMIT set to on, the effects of each SQL statement are reflected immediately. Set to off, an explicit COMMIT is required before the statements affect the database.

- ■ SQL_LOGIN_TIMEOUT: The possible 32-bit values (in seconds) range from 1 to a driver-specific maximum. The value will be set at maximum if you attempt to set the value higher than it can accommodate.

How to Disconnect from a Data Source

After your application has completed its database operations, and before the database connection or ODBC environment is freed, you should disconnect from the database. This is done by calling the SQLDisconnect() function (see the following listing):

```
RETCODE SQLDisconnect(
    HDBC       hdbc
);
```

For the ODBC environment and connection, the order of events is important. In general, your application should follow these steps:

1. Start your application.

2. Allocate an environment handle.

3. Allocate a connection handle.

4. Connect to a data source.

5. Execute SQL statements and queries (see Chapter 7, "Catalog and Statistics Functions").

6. Disconnect from the data source.

7. Free the connection handle.

8. Free the environment handle.

9. Terminate your application.

From Here...

■ Continue on to Chapter 7, "Catalog and Statistics Functions," to learn how to get information about the data existing in a data source.

■ Chapter 8, "The ODBC Statement: An Introduction," continues your ODBC education, explaining how to formulate and issue statements to your ODBC data sources.

Chapter 7

Catalog and Statistics Functions

In writing ODBC applications, you do not always know the schema of each table and index in a database. You certainly will not always recognize each user and know what tables he has the right to access. You need a method of extracting such information about a database at run time. This requirement is fulfilled by the ODBC catalog functions.

In this chapter, you explore how to extract information about:

- The tables in a database

- The columns in a table

- The indexes associated with a table

- The stored procedures available

- The user privileges in force

- Where to go from here

All the catalog functions operate in the same manner. You first call the function with a parameter indicating the information you need. The requested information is returned in a result set and read the same way as you would any other query.

Before learning about the catalog functions, let's look at what they have in common. First of all, you need to learn about search patterns. Search patterns are used extensively in the parameters of the catalog functions. They require you to fetch rows of a result set.

Search patterns are probably not an alien subject to you. MS-DOS employs search patterns using special characters called *wildcards* for many commands. The command

```
DELETE *.bak
```

contains the search pattern *.bak.

Here, the asterisk is a wildcard meaning any combination of characters up to the period delimiter. ODBC uses the SQL standard wildcards:

- ___(the underscore): any single character

- % (the percent sign): any combination of zero or more characters.

You combine these special symbols with literal characters to form search expressions. For example, a search on the expression %ing% would find *ing* in any position in a field.

Several catalog functions use conventions for identifying tables, rows, and indexes; these conventions might be new to you. They reflect common, but not universal, practices in larger client/server DBMSs. They may not apply to others.

In traditional PC databases, a table name might consist of an MS-DOS file name and an extension. A client/server DBMS may take more items to describe its tables. A table might have:

- A qualifier, such as a database or server name

- An owner, usually the person who created the table

- The table name itself

While it may seem like overkill, such a scheme is needed where an RDBMS could consist of several names and serve many independent users. An example of such a table name is:

```
finance:"auditman".overruns
```

where the overruns table belongs to user auditman inside the finance database or server. Note that the delimiter combination used here is not necessarily what your DBMS will use. You will also need to know how to handle a result set, which is covered in Chapter 11, "Queries and Result Sets."

All the functions listed here may not be supported by your data source. In particular, a Level 1 driver will not support the functions about keys, procedures, or user privileges. If the DBMS has no security features, even a Level 2 driver will not support the user privilege functions.

Getting the Names of Tables in a Database

In an interactive system, the first description you might give a user about a database is a list of tables. If you want to limit the information to a particular set of tables, the SQLTables() function enables you to choose by several criteria.

A list of tables matching several search patterns is given by the SQLTables() function. The prototype of the SQLTables() function is:

```
RETCODE SQLTables(
HSTMT        hstmt,
UCHAR*       pQualifier,
SWORD        nQualifier,
UCHAR*       pOwner,
SWORD        nOwner,
UCHAR*       pName,
SWORD        nName,
UCHAR*       pType,
SWORD        nType
);
```

where the hstmt parameter is a valid statement handle. The pQualifier, pOwner, and pName are pointers to strings containing literals or search patterns for the qualifier name, the table owner, and the table name, respectively. The length parameters nQualifier, nOwner, nName, and nType should all be set to SQL_NTS.

The pType parameter is highly specialized. It specifies the types of tables and similar objects that will be returned in the result set. Although there are others, the most important of these are tables and views. When calling the function, you pass the string TABLES to return only tables, VIEWS to return only views, and TABLES,VIEWS to return both types. Be aware that not all DBMSs support views.

> **Note**
>
> A *view* is an object that is named like and can be queried as a table, but is actually the result set of another query. The result set is defined *at the time the view is queried*. Standard SQL syntax for view creation is:
>
> ```
> CREATE VIEW AS shortcut (SELECT LNAME, FNAME FROM custlist)
> ```
>
> where shortcut is the name of the new view. The contents of the view consist of the result set from the SELECT statement found within the parentheses. Chapter 3, "The Client/Server Language: SQL," provides several examples of views.

The Columns in a Table

Your user has browsed all the available tables and selected one for perusal. Now, he would like to know the names of the table's columns. To do this, you will call the SQLColumns() function.

The *SQLTables()* Result Set

The columns of the SQLTables() result set list information about the tables specified in the function call. The following table lists the columns in the result set:

Number	Name	Type	Length	Comment
1	TABLE_QUALIFIER	VARCHAR	128	Not supported=NULL
2	TABLE_OWNER	VARCHAR	128	N/A=NULL
3	TABLE_NAME	VARCHAR	128	Not NULL
4	TABLE_TYPE	VARCHAR	128	Type of table (TABLE, VIEW, SYSTEM TABLE, GLOBAL TEMPORARY, LOCAL TEMPORARY, ALIAS, SYNONYM, or database-specific type)
5	REMARKS	VARCHAR	254	Table description

The *SQLColumns()* Function

A list of columns can be found in the result set of the SQLColumns() function. This result set matches the given search patterns for qualifier, owner, table name, and column name. The function prototype for SQLColumns() is:

```
RETCODE SQLColumns(
HSTMT       hstmt,
UCHAR*      pQualifier,
SWORD       nQualifierLen,
UCHAR*      pOwner,
SWORD       nOwnerLen,
UCHAR*      pTableName,
SWORD       nTableNameLen,
UCHAR*      pColumnName,
SWORD       nColumnNameLen
);
```

where hstmt is a valid statement handle. All the parameters are the same as those in `SQLTables()`, with the exception of the last two parameters. The `pColumnName` parameter is a pointer to a null-terminated string containing a search pattern specifying tables of interest. The `pColumnName` should always be `SQL_NTS`.

The *SQLColumns()* Result Set

The columns of the `SQLColumns()` result set list information about the columns specified in the function call. The following table lists the columns in the result set:

Number	Name	Type	Length	Comment
1	TABLE_QUALIFIER	VARCHAR	128	Not supported=NULL
2	TABLE_OWNER	VARCHAR	128	N/A=NULL
3	TABLE_NAME	VARCHAR	128	Not NULL
4	COLUMN_NAME	VARCHAR	128	Not NULL
5	DATA_TYPE	SMALLINT	N/A	SQL data type (SQL_XXXX)
6	TYPE_NAME	VARCHAR	128	DBMS name for previous data type
7	PRECISION	INTEGER	N/A	Precision of column
8	LENGTH	INTEGER	N/A	Length of column
9	SCALE	SMALLINT	N/A	Scale of column
10	RADIX	SMALLINT	N/A	For numeric columns. Either a 10 or 2.
11	NULLABLE	SMALLINT	N/A	Not NULL
12	REMARKS	VARCHAR	254	Column description

The *SQLSpecialColumns()* Function

Special columns deal with uniquely specifying rows in a table. This may simply be a unique primary index. A special column could also be a DBMS-specific row identifier (*rowid*), such as used by Informix. A timestamp, marked each time a row is updated, is also a special column. With the exception of the index, *these columns do not appear in the schema!*

You might ask why anyone would want this information. One likely answer is that you wanted to discover relationships between tables from clues about column uniqueness. You also may need to temporarily identify a particular row that may have changing values. Finally, you may want to know when rows were updated, or in what order. In any case, the prototype for the SQLSpecialColumns() function is:

```
RETCODE SQLSpecialColumns(
HSTMT      hstmt,
UWORD      nColType,
UCHAR*     pTableQualifier,
SWORD      nTableQualifierLen,
UCHAR*     pTableOwner,
SWORD      nTableOwnerLen,
UCHAR*     pTableName,
SWORD      nTableNameLen,
UWORD      fScope,
UWORD      fNullable
);
```

where hstmt is a valid statement handle. The table qualifier, owner, name, and their lengths are similiar to the previous functions. The fNullable parameter is a Boolean value indicating if the given column can have a value of NULL. The nColType parameter is one of two values:

■ SQL_BEST_ROWID: if it is a unique index or rowid

■ SQL_ROW_VER: if the column is a time or version stamp

The fScope parameter indicates the minimum length of time a column value must be valid. Once this time has passed, the value of the row is no longer meaningful. The possible scopes, from shortest to longest, are:

■ SQL_SCOPE_CURROW: the rowid will only remain valid as long as it is the current row of the cursor. It may be updated at any time after that.

■ SQL_SCOPE_TRANSACTION: the rowid will remain valid during the current transaction.

■ SQL_SCOPE_SESSION: the rowid will remain valid throughout the user's session.

The *SQLSpecialColumns()* Result Set

Some columns of interest from the result set returned by the SQLSpecialColumns() function are as follows:

Number	Name	Type	Length	Comment
1	SCOPE	SMALLINT	N/A	Values found previously
2	COLUMN_NAME	VARCHAR	128	Name of the column
3	DATA_TYPE	SMALLINT	N/A	SQL data type
4	TYPE_NAME	VARCHAR	128	Data sources type name
5	PRECISION	INTEGER	N/A	Precision
6	LENGTH	INTEGER	N/A	Length
7	SCALE	SMALLINT	N/A	Scale
8	PSEUDO_COLUMN	SMALLINT	N/A	Whether column is not a normal column, such as an Oracle rowid column

The Indexes Associated with a Table

Indexes reveal a lot about the associated table. You can determine what column values are unique. They also can help you make an educated guess as to the table's relationship to other tables.

Primary keys usually are unique. They are placed on the most uniquely identifying attribute of a table. A foreign key is a set of columns that refers to a primary key in another table. There is a well-defined relationship between these two tables.

The *SQLPrimaryKeys()* Function

The columns that make up the primary key on a table are given in the result set of the SQLPrimaryKeys() function. Its function prototype is as follows:

```
RETCODE SQLPrimaryKeys(
HSTMT       hstmt,
UCHAR*      szTableQualifier,
SWORD       cbTableQualifier,
UCHAR*      szTableOwner,
SWORD       cbTableOwner,
UCHAR*      szTableName,
SWORD       cbTableName
);
```

where `hstmt` is a valid statement handle. All the other parameters serve to uniquely identify a table, as with the functions previously shown.

The *SQLForeignKeys()* Function

The `SQLForeignKeys()` function is much more complex than `SQLPrimaryKeys()`. This is partly because the function can be called to get several different result sets, as discussed in the next section. `SQLForeignKeys()`' function prototype is as follows:

```
RETCODE SQLForeignKeys(
HSTMT       hstmt,
UCHAR*      pPkQualifier,
SWORD       nPkQualifierLen,
UCHAR*      pPkOwner,
SWORD       nPkOwnerLen,
UCHAR*      pPkName,
SWORD       nPkNameLen,
UCHAR*      pFkQualifier,
SWORD       nFkQualifierLen,
UCHAR*      pFkOwner,
SWORD       nFkOwnerLen,
UCHAR*      pFkName,
SWORD       nFkNameLen
);
```

where `hstmt` is a valid statement handle. All parameters with the `Pk` prefix refer to the table containing the primary key. All parameters with the `Fk` prefix refer to the table with the foreign key. The two sets of parameters completely specify the two tables to test for the primary/foreign key relationship.

The *SQLForeignKeys()* Result Sets

If a primary key table is specified, `SQLForeignKeys()` returns a result set containing the primary key of that table and the foreign keys that refer to it. If a foreign key table is given, `SQLForeignKeys()` returns a result set containing the foreign keys in that table and the primary keys to which they refer. If both tables are given, `SQLForeignKeys()` returns the foreign keys in the foreign key table that refer to the primary key of the primary key table.

> **Note**
>
> Because of the great volume and complexity of the `SQLForeignKeys()` result sets, it is recommended that you refer directly to the on-line help file or Microsoft's Programmer's Reference.

Learning What Stored Procedures Are Available

Stored procedures are executable code stored with a database. Some stored procedures are linked to a particular event, such as SQL statements you want to be executed each time INSERT is performed on a particular table. The type of procedure of most interest here is one that takes parameters, returns a result set, and is to be called by users.

The *SQLProcedures()* Function

The SQLProcedures() function returns a result set with information about the stored procedures available on a system. Its prototype is as follows:

```
RETCODE SQLProcedures(
HSTMT       hstmt,
UCHAR*      pProcQualifier,
SWORD       nProcQualifierLen,
UCHAR*      pProcOwner,
SWORD       nProcOwnerLen,
UCHAR*      pProcName,
SWORD       nProcNameLen
);
```

where hstmt is a valid statement handle. The pProcQualifier, pProcOwner, and pProcName parameters specify a search pattern quite similiar to the way a table is specified in the other catalog functions. The length parameters, nProcQualifierLen, nProcOwnerLen, and nProcNameLen should be set to SQL_NTS as usual.

The *SQLProcedures()* Result Set

The SQLProcedures() result set returns information to completely specify the procedure. The columns of the result set are listed in the following table:

Number	Name	Type	Length	Comment
1	PROCEDURE_QUALIFIER	VARCHAR	128	Qualifier
2	PROCEDURE_OWNER	VARCHAR	128	Owner
3	PROCEDURE_NAME	VARCHAR	128	Name
4	NUM_INPUT_PARAMS	N/A	N/A	Future use
5	NUM_OUTPUT_PARAMS	N/A	N/A	Future use
6	NUM_RESULT_SETS	N/A	N/A	Future use

(continues)

Number	Name	Type	Length	Comment
7	REMARKS	VARCHAR	254	Procedure description
8	PROCEDURE_TYPE	SMALLINT	N/A	Type of procedure

The possible values of the *procedure type* column are as follows:

- SQL_PT_PROCEDURE: The procedure has no return value

- SQL_PT_FUNCTION: The procedure has no return value

- SQL_PT_UNKNOWN: It cannot be determined if the procedure has a return value

The *SQLProcedureColumns()* Function

The SQLProcedureColumns() function returns information about the input parameters that a procedure requires. It also describes the result set that the procedure returns.

```
RETCODE SQLProcedureColumns(
HSTMT       hstmt,
UCHAR*      szProcQualifier,
SWORD       cbProcQualifier,
UCHAR*      szProcOwner,
SWORD       cbProcOwner,
UCHAR*      szProcName,
SWORD       cbProcName,
UCHAR*      szColumnName,
SWORD       cbColumnName
);
```

where hstmt is a valid statement handle. All the parameters for SQLProcedures() are represented, plus parameters for a column name search pattern and its length. This parameter should be set to NULL for most situations, indicating that information should be retrieved for all procedures.

The *SQLProcedureColumns()* Result Set

The result set also resembles that of the SQLProcedures() function. The major difference is the addition of the column name and column type columns.

The columns of the result set are listed in the following table:

Number	Name	Type	Length	Comment
1	PROCEDURE_QUALIFIER	VARCHAR	128	Qualifier
2	PROCEDURE_OWNER	VARCHAR	128	Owner
3	PROCEDURE_NAME	VARCHAR	128	Procedure name
4	COLUMN_NAME	VARCHAR	128	Name of column
5	COLUMN_TYPE	SMALLINT	N/A	Column type (see previous)
6	DATA_TYPE	SMALLINT	N/A	Column data type
7	TYPE_NAME	VARCHAR	128	DBMS name for previous data type
8	PRECISION	INTEGER	N/A	Precision of column
9	LENGTH	INTEGER	N/A	Length of column
10	SCALE	SMALLINT	N/A	Scale of column
11	RADIX	SMALLINT	N/A	For numeric columns. Either a 10 or 2
12	NULLABLE	SMALLINT	N/A	Not NULL
13	REMARKS	VARCHAR	254	Column description

The *column type* may be one of the following values:

- SQL_PARAM_INPUT: Specifies an input parameter

- SQL_PARAM_INPUT_OUTPUT: Specifies an input *and* output parameter

- SQL_PARAM_OUTPUT: Specifies an output parameter

- SQL_RETURN_VALUE: Specifies the procedure return value

- SQL_RESULT_COL: The column named is contained in the result set of the procedure

The User Privileges in Force

Most commercial client/server systems have a security system. It limits each user's access to particular objects in the database. This helps protect the database's integrity from unauthorized changes.

Privileges are those actions that a particular user may perform on a particular object such as INSERT, UPDATE, DELETE, or SELECT. A user may also be granted a REFERENCE privilege to refer to a table or column in a join, as long as it does not appear in the list of output columns. Privileges may be granted at the table level, the column level, or both.

The *SQLTablePrivileges()* Function

The SQLTablePrivileges() function enumerates the privileges granted to all users on a particular table or tables matching a search pattern. Its parameters match those of the SQLTables() function discussed earlier. Its prototype is as follows:

```
RETCODE SQLTablePrivileges(
HSTMT       hstmt,
UCHAR*      szTableQualifier,
SWORD       cbTableQualifier,
UCHAR*      szTableOwner,
SWORD       cbTableOwner,
UCHAR*      szTableName,
SWORD       cbTableName
);
```

where hstmt is a valid statement handle and the other parameters define a search pattern for a table or tables, as with SQLTables().

The *SQLTablePrivileges()* Result Set

The result set of interest from the SQLTablePrivileges() function is shown in the following table:

Number	Name	Type	Length	Comment
1	TABLE_QUALIFIER	VARCHAR	128	Not supported=NULL
2	TABLE_OWNER	VARCHAR	128	N/A=NULL
3	TABLE_NAME	VARCHAR	128	Not NULL
4	GRANTOR	VARCHAR	128	User granting privilege
5	GRANTEE	VARCHAR	128	Owner of privilege

Number	Name	Type	Length	Comment
6	PRIVILEGE	VARCHAR	128	See previous table
7	IS_GRANTABLE	VARCHAR	3	Can grantee grant to other users: "YES" or "NO"

The *SQLColumnPrivileges()* Function

Column-level privileges are described by the result set of the SQLColumnPrivileges() function. The prototype of the SQLColumnPrivileges() function is as follows:

```
RETCODE SQLColumnPrivileges(
HSTMT      hstmt,
UCHAR*     szTableQualifier,
SWORD      cbTableQualifier,
UCHAR*     szTableOwner,
SWORD      cbTableOwner,
UCHAR*     szTableName,
SWORD      cbTableName,
UCHAR*     szColumnName,
SWORD      cbColumnName
);
```

where hstmt is a valid statement handle and the other parameters define a search pattern for a table or tables, as with SQLTables(), and similarly, a search pattern for column names.

The *SQLTablePrivileges()* Result Set

The result set of interest from the SQLTablePrivileges() function is described in the following table:

Number	Name	Type	Length	Comment
1	TABLE_QUALIFIER	VARCHAR	128	Not supported=NULL
2	TABLE_OWNER	VARCHAR	128	N/A=NULL
3	TABLE_NAME	VARCHAR	128	Not NULL
4	COLUMN_NAME	VARCHAR	128	Not NULL
5	GRANTOR	VARCHAR	128	User granting privilege

(continues)

Number	Name	Type	Length	Comment
6	GRANTEE	VARCHAR	128	Owner of privilege
7	PRIVILEGE	VARCHAR	128	See previous table
8	IS_GRANTABLE	VARCHAR	3	Can grantee grant to other users: "YES" or "NO"

Where Do We Go from Here?

Here is a excellent opportunity for an enterprising programmer to encapsulate the catalog functions into a set of C++ classes. It would certainly make them easier to use. Since they all operate the same way, perhaps they might even share a common base class.

The data members would follow the result set columns for the function. If you are not opposed to public data members, just declare everything in a struct. This shares all the characteristics of a class, but makes all data public by default.

There would be but a few member functions. The constructor and destructor would create and destroy the statement handle to be used by the catalog function. Each class would require one function that has parameters similiar to the catalog function to pass the input data to the class. The final method would simply perform a fetch on the next row in the result set. Listing 7.1 contains all the code for a simplified version of such a class.

Listing 7.1 The *TableList* Class Header

```
// FILE: Tablist.h


#include <windows.h>
#include "sql.h"
#include "sqlext.h"


class TableList
{
    HSTMT hstmt;            // Statement handle to get and
                           // manipulate the result set
public:
```

```
                              // Data from result set
                              // (note extra byte for the null
                              // character)
        char QUALIFIER[129];
        char OWNER[129];
        char NAME[129];
        char TYPE[129];
        char REMARKS[255];


        TableList( HDBC hdbc )    // Constructor that allocates hstmt
            { SQLAllocStmt( hdbc, &hstmt ); }

        ~TableList()              // Destructor to free hstmt
            { SQLFreeStmt( hstmt ); }

         RETCODE GetResultSet(    // See SQLTables() function

            UCHAR*        pQualifier,

            UCHAR*        pOwner,

            UCHAR*        pName,

            UCHAR*        pType,

        ) { return SQLTables( hstmt, pQualifier, SQL_NTS, pOwner,
        ➥SQL_NTS,
                     pName, SQL_NTS, pType, SQL_NTS ); }

        RETCODE BindColumns(); // Binds result set to data members

        RETCODE Fetch() { return SQLFetch( hstmt ); }

    };
```

Using the class would be easy. All you need is a valid connection handle and the information you might need to pick which tables to examine. Listing 7.2 gives such an example.

Listing 7.2 A *TableList* Class Example

```
// FILE: MyApp.cpp


#include "tablist.h"
#include "myapp.h"


RETCODE ShowTables( HDBC hdbc )
{
```

(continues)

Listing 7.2 Continued

```
        RETCODE retcode

        TableList* pTableList = new TableList( hdbc );

//  Get the result set
        retcode = pTableList-> GetResultSet(
                                            "",        // No qualifier

                                            "%"        // Any owner

                                            "%",       // Any name

                                            "%",       // Any type

        )
if ( retcode == SQL_SUCCESS )
    pTableList-> BindColumns();

    while( retcode==SQL_SUCCESS )
    {
// DO OUTPUT HERE, perhaps to a listbox.
        retcode = pTableList->Fetch();

    }

    delete pTableList;
    return retcode;
}
```

Now that you have seen how easy it is to do, try designing your own class around a catalog function. This technique is not limited to the catalog function. Try it on your result set.

From Here...

We've covered a lot of ground in this chapter. Certain topics were introduced that are discussed in their own chapters; for more information, you can go directly to one of these chapters:

- Chapter 11, "Queries and Result Sets," goes into detail about result sets and how to retrieve information from them.

- Chapter 13, "The Cursor Library and Positioned Operations," talks about the use of cursors to control the current row in a result set.

Chapter 8

The ODBC Statement: An Introduction

The *statement* is the workhorse of the ODBC API. It enables you to execute SQL statements and perform queries. ODBC statements also perform most of the manipulation on databases.

In ODBC terminology a statement is more than just a command to be sent to the database engine. It is a construct that is allocated in memory and which has a number of other constructs connected to it. You can attach options and parameters to a statement, and many statements (usually SELECT statements) bring back result sets. All of these are fully discussed in other chapters.

You can access any capability of a database engine through a statement, even if the syntax used is not standard ODBC SQL. Most of the examples throughout this book deal with only straight ODBC SQL in order to make them work with the widest possible variety of database drivers.

In this chapter, you explore:

- Creating and freeing a statement

- Executing a statement

- Understanding synchronous and asynchronous execution

- Understanding query result sets

- Reusing a statement handle

- Configuring statement options

- Performing transactions

How to Create and Free a Statement

Before you can execute a statement, you must create a statement handle or HSTMT. The statement handle is one of the basic ODBC object types, such as the environment (HENV) and connection (HDBC) handles. The HSMT handle is created and destroyed in much the same manner as the HENV and HDBC handles.

The lifetime of a statement handle is limited to its parent database connection handle. A simplified order of events around the creation of the statement handle is as follows:

1. Start the application.

2. Create the environment handle (HENV).

3. Create the connection handle (HDBC).

4. Connect to a data source, using the connection handle.

5. Create a statement handle (HSTMT).

6. Use the statement handle to execute statements.

7. Free the statement handle.

8. Disconnect from the database.

9. Free the connection handle.

10. Free the environment handle.

11. Terminate the application.

You should not create more than one ODBC environment handle. The environment manages your connection to the ODBC DLLs, and your application can have only one copy of an application in memory. Allocating a second environment is pointless.

Allocating and using more than one connection handle is perfectly legal and sometimes very useful. You later can connect to two data sources, making it easy to transfer data from one source to another. Don't make needless connections, as there is some resource use involved.

Some drivers support only one connection. Others may support only one statement handle. Both of these limitations are infrequent, but they are quite annoying. If you are writing to a single target driver or small number of drivers, you should read the driver documentation to see if it is subject to either limitation.

You also can connect and disconnect to a data source as often as you desire, but there is a down side. Connections to local, single-tier data sources may only take a fraction of a second. True client/server sources that run in a separate task from the application may take several seconds, leaving your application dead in the water (at least in synchronous execution). Connect and disconnect to a data source only when necessary.

Using two or more statement handles can be very useful—when your driver permits it (some do not). You can do things like compare columns of one result set to another. There are several other applications for using multiple statement handles that are outlined throughout the rest of the book.

Creating a Statement Handle

Before you can create a statement, you must have a valid connection. In turn, your connection must be created following the creation of an ODBC environment to be valid. For an explanation of how this is done, see Chapter 6, "Creating the ODBC Environment and Connection."

A statement is initialized by calling the SQLAllocStmt() function. The prototype is

```
RETCODE SQLAllocStmt( HDBC hdbc, HSTMT* phstmt );
```

where hdbc is a handle to a valid connection and phstmt is a pointer to an unused statement handle (HSTMT).

If SQLAllocStmt() succeeds, it returns a value of SQL_SUCCESS. If it fails, the return value is SQL_ERROR. If you somehow passed an invalid connection value to the function, the return value is SQL_INVALID_HANDLE.

Once you have successfully called the SQLAllocStmt() function, the HSTMT pointed to by phstmt is valid. If the function failed, for whatever reason, the statement handle has a value of SQL_NULL_HSTMT.

Caution

Do not initialize the value of an HSTMT to SQL_NULL_HSTMT. Your program will crash when you call SQLAllocStmt().

Freeing a Statement Handle

After you finish with a statement handle, you should free it before freeing the connection associated with the statement. Failing to do so causes a memory leak in your program and error messages when you try to free your connection.

A statement handle is freed by passing it to the SQLFreeStmt() function. The prototype for SQLFreeStmt() is

```
RETCODE SQLFreeStmt( HSTMT hstmt, UWORD nOption );
```

where hsmt is a valid statement handle and nOption is an integer constant. The nOption specifies what items associated with hstmt to free. To release everything belonging to the statement, use the SQL_DROP for the nOption parameter.

How to Execute a Statement

The real substance of an ODBC statement is the text of an SQL statement. ODBC parses this text and translates the SQL grammar into actions. These actions can be performed immediately or stored for later execution.

If you want to perform an action once, you probably want to use *direct* execution. If the statement performs an action repeatedly, you want to use *prepared* execution.

Direct Execution

The most straightforward way to execute an SQL statement is to use SQLExecDirect(). It parses and executes the statement immediately. The function prototype for SQLExecDirect() is

```
RETCODE SQLExecDirect(
    HSTMT       hstmt,
    UCHAR*      pSQLString,
    SDWORD      lnLength
);
```

where hstmt is a valid statement, pSQLString is a pointer to a valid SQL statement, and lnLength is the 32-bit signed integer length of the SQL string.

> **Note**
>
> The lnLength parameter of SQLExecDirect(), like most ODBC string-length parameters, is primarily for BASIC programs. Languages that use null-terminated strings, like C/C++, should pass SQL_NTS (NULL-Terminated String) for this parameter.

The RETCODE return value should always be checked after calling SQLExecDirect(). If the return value is SQL_SUCCESS, the ODBC statement executed. You may safely assume that the SQL statement contained inside the function has been executed.

If the return value is any other value, such as SQL_ERROR or
SQL_SUCCESS_WITH_INFO, you need to investigate. You should call SQLError()
to get the error message and the SQLSTATE value. Then you can make a decision to display the error message to your users or handle the situation with
program logic from the SQLSTATE. A discussion of the SQLError() function
can be found in Chapter 6, "Creating the ODBC Environment and Connection."

Prepared Execution

There are several reasons why you may want to delay the execution of a statement until well after its preparation. They are:

- The statement is to be executed many times.

- The text of the query has been entered by a user and may contain SQL
  grammar errors.

- Your error-handling strategy requires knowing if an error stems from a
  parsing error in the SQL statement or from a missing database object.

- The values for clauses in an SQL statement are not known until run
  time.

To prepare your SQL statement for execution, pass it to the SQLPrepare()
function. Depending on the driver, this may cause the text of the statement
to be parsed and the grammar to be translated. Some drivers do not actually
do the parsing until another ODBC function call that requires it is called; in
these cases, it will always return SQL_SUCCESS, so you can't rely on
SQLPrepare() as a sure method of testing the validity of your statement. In
any case, the statement is not yet executed. This pre-processing is performed
by a SQLPrepare() function like the following:

```
RETCODE SQLPrepare(
    HSTMT       hstmt,
    UCHAR*      pStatement,
    UDWORD      lnLength
);
```

where hstmt is a valid statement handle and pStatement is a pointer to a
character string containing a valid SQL command. If pStatement is a NULL-
terminated string, then lnLength should be SQL_NTS; otherwise, it should be
the length of the buffer pointed to by pStatement.

The RETCODE return value should be checked after calling SQLPrepare(). If the
return value is SQL_SUCCESS, the SQL statement passed in the pStatement

parameter is grammatically correct and is ready to be executed—if your driver does the parsing at that time. Otherwise, SQL_SUCCESS is not meaningful in itself.

If the return value is SQL_ERROR or SQL_SUCCESS_WITH_INFO, you need to investigate. You should not attempt to execute the statement; it can't be executed. You can call SQLError() to get the error message.

Many other aspects of statement management are dealt with in different chapters in this book. For example, Chapter 12, "Setting Parameters with Prepared Statements," talks about methods of passing data to a statement at run time so that you can reuse a statement, but fill in different data each time.

Configuring Statement Options

The process of controlling statement options consists of three different operations:

- Querying the driver to see if the option is supported

- Getting the current value of the statement option

- Setting the value of the statement option

> **Note**
>
> Some driver options are always supported. You don't need to query the driver for support. The SQL_OPT_TRACEFILE is an example of a universally implemented option. It turns ODBC function tracing output on and off.

Getting Statement Options

You can obtain the current value of any statement option by calling the SQLGetStmtOption() function. Its function prototype is

```
RETCODE SQLGetStmtOption(
HSTMT hstmt,
UWORD nOption,
PTR ptrParam
);
```

where hstmt is a valid statement handle. The nOption parameter is one of several constants. The ptrParam parameter is a 32-bit pointer to a buffer that receives a null-terminated string.

Each option may have several possible values. You have to search your documentation for these, as there are too many to list here.

Setting Statement Options

You can set the value of any statement option by calling the SQLSetStmtOption() function. Its function prototype is

```
RETCODE SQLSetStmtOption(
HSTMT hstmt,
UWORD nOption,
PTR ptrParam
);
```

where hstmt is a valid statement handle. The nOption parameter is one of several constants. The ptrParam parameter can be either a 32-bit value or a 32-bit pointer to a null-terminated string. Each option may have several possible values. Again, you will have to search your documentation for these, as there are too many to list here.

Synchronous and Asynchronous Execution

When you execute a C/C++ function from/in the runtime library, processing is always complete once a return value has been received. When code is executing on a single machine and in a single task, this might be a valid assumption. This is not necessarily the case with an ODBC statement.

Synchronous Execution

The default mode of statement execution is *synchronous*. A statement executed synchronously does not relinquish control of program flow until all processing has been completed. The time required to execute some statements, such as the deletion of all records from a huge table, can be lengthy. If your application has a single thread of execution, it may be prevented from doing important processing.

If you are waiting for another task to finish processing and that task is on another machine, there are several possible disasters that can prevent you from ever receiving your results. For example, the server can go down, or the network cable can be broken. In such cases, your application appears to lock, through no fault of your own.

Asynchronous Execution

Some drivers support asynchronous execution. When first called, the SQLExecute() function returns a value of SQL_STILL_EXECUTING. At this point your application is free to do other processing.

Periodically, your application should call `SQLExecute()` with the same statement handle as the original call. The other parameters should be valid but are ignored. The return value is `SQL_SUCCESS` if the statement has finished processing. If statement processing is still in progress, the function return value is `SQL_STILL_EXECUTING`.

Asynchronous execution may free up your application to do other things, but it is not without problems. The complexity of your code certainly increases. This is especially true if you are writing an interoperable application that also must be prepared to operate synchronously. Performance will probably suffer as well.

Asynchronous execution is recommended for applications that connect to large, heavily loaded client/server systems. Here is where you are most likely to encounter significant time delays in processing. Elsewhere, asynchronous execution is probably not worth the overhead.

If you implement asynchronous execution in an application, be prepared to handle a rather complex state machine. You must set up some facility to periodically check the state of your in-progress functions, monitoring the result codes to determine what should happen next. There are several ways to accomplish this.

You can set up a timer and handle `WM_TIMER` messages. You do not have to set up a timer if you use the `WM_ENTERIDLE` message instead; if you do, however, you lose some control over the calling frequency. Be aware that they are both very low priority messages.

Setting the Execution Mode

Not all drivers support asynchronous execution. In particular, local, single-tier, or Level 1 drivers probably don't support it. You should read the driver's documentation to learn if it supports this feature. If you are writing an interoperable application, you must find out at run time. This is done by allocating a statement, attempting to set it to asynchronous operation, and testing for success.

Caution

You can't call any other functions that use the same statement handle as the synchronously executing function until it has returned a value of `SQL_SUCCESS`, `SQL_SUCCESS_WITH_INFO`, or `SQL_ERROR`.

The availability of asynchronous execution is best determined by calling the SQLSetStmtOption() function. This option must be set at the statement level and not the connection level. SQLSetStmtOption() should be called as

```
retcode = SQLSetStmtOption( hstmt, SQL_ASYNC_ENABLE, 1 );
```

where hstmt is a valid statement handle. The constant SQL_ASYNC_ENABLE is the option, and the value 1 attempts to turn the option on. A retcode of SQL_SUCCESS means your driver supports the option and hstmt will now operate in the asycronous mode. A value of SQL_ERROR means the driver does not support this mode of operation.

Note

While we are most concerned here with the SQLExecute() function, there are over 20 other functions that can operate asynchronously:

SQLColAttributes()	SQLNumParams()
SQLColumnPrivileges()	SQLNumResultCols()
SQLColumns()	SQLParamData()
SQLDescribeCol()	SQLPrepare()
SQLDescribeParam()	SQLPrimaryKeys()
SQLExecDirect()	SQLProcedureColumns()
SQLExecute()	SQLProcedures()
SQLExtendedFetch()	SQLPutData()
SQLFetch()	SQLSetPos()
SQLForeignKeys()	SQLSpecialColumns
SQLGetData()	SQLStatistics()
SQLGetTypeInfo()	SQLTablePrivileges()
SQLMoreResutls()	SQLTables()

Query Result Sets

Most ODBC statements, such as an INSERT, UPDATE, or DELETE, execute and return an "error" code. All processing is complete once the function has returned. However, queries are different. Executing a query does not immediately return the information you requested. It creates a *result set*.

A *result set* is a series of rows that satisfies the requirements set forth in your query. By default, you must access the result set row by row, from the first to the last. This is done by calling the SQLFetch() function.

After you have called SQLExecDirect() or SQLExecute(), you have created a result set and associated it with your statement handle. At this point, there is no *current* row. The first row becomes current only after the first call to SQLFetch().

Unless a driver has the slightly unique functionality of being able to use the SQLRowCount() function to count the rows (which some do, although this is really intended for INSERT/UPDATE/DELETE statements), there is no direct way to know how many rows are contained in the result set. You simply call SQLFetch() and check the return code. As long as the function returns SQL_SUCCESS, you have fetched another row and made it the current row. When you receive a return of SQL_NO_DATA_FOUND, there were no rows to read.

> ### Note
>
> If you must know the number of rows in a result set in advance, and your driver does not support SQLRowCount() in this way, you should frame a query that replaces the column list with the count() scalar function. You would replace
>
> ```
> SELECT * FROM cards
> ```
>
> with the query
>
> ```
> SELECT COUNT(*) FROM cards
> ```
>
> This returns a result set consisting of one column in one row containing the number of rows in the result set of the original query.

The significance of the current row is that you can access the values of its columns. There are several ways to accomplish this. Only the most elementary method is covered here. More ambitious ways to access the result set are outlined in Chapter 13, "The Cursor Library and Positioned Operations."

You can extract the value of a column of the current row by calling the SQLGetData() function. The prototype of SQLGetData() is

```
RETCODE SQLGetData(
HSTMT     hstmt,
UWORD     nColumn,
SWORD     nCDataType,
PTR       vpValue,
SDWORD    nMaxValueLen,
SDWORD*   pnActualValueLen
);
```

where `hstmt` is a valid statement handle. The `nColumn` parameter is found by counting where this column appears in the column list of your query. This number is 1-based. The `nCDataType` parameter is a constant representing the C language data type that you want the `vpValue` parameter to point to.

If `nCDataType` is a string type, `nMaxValueLen` is the length of the buffer you passed a pointer to in `vpValue`. `pnActualValueLen` is a pointer to the actual length of the object. If `nCDataType` is a numeric or date type, these parameters are not valid.

Refer to Chapter 11, "Queries and Result Sets," for more information about getting and using query data.

How to Reuse a Statement Handle

Every time you need to execute a statement, you could conceivably allocate a statement handle, execute the statement, and free the statement handle with the `SQLFreeStmt()` function. You would certainly slow performance down somewhat. Soon, you'll see that repeatedly allocating statement handles is not usually neccessary.

If the last statement executed on a statement handle does not return a result set, you may prepare another statement using the same handle and execute the new statement without freeing the statement handle first. This includes such commands as, `INSERT`, `DELETE`, `UPDATE`, `CREATE`, and `DROP` statements, among others. Keep one statement handle reserved for these operations.

If your last statement was a `SELECT`, you probably have a result set or cursor associated with your statement handle. (A *cursor* is the current position or row within a result set. Closing a cursor destroys the result set.) The situation is somewhat more complicated. The `SQLFreeStmt()` function has several options to handle these situations. Its function prototype is

```
RETCODE SQLFreeStmt( hstmt, nOption );
```

where `hstmt` is the handle to a valid statement. The `nOption` parameter is one of the following:

- ■ `SQL_CLOSE`: Closes the cursor but does not destroy the statement handle

- ■ `SQL_DROP`: Closes the cursor and destroys the statement handle

- ■ `SQL_UNBIND`: Frees any output buffers that you have allocated with `SQLBindCol()`

■ `SQL_RESET_PARAMS`: Releases any input parameters you have set by using the `SQLBindParameter()`

It is a good policy to call `SQLFreeStmt()` in such a way as to disturb the smallest number of resources associated with the statement handle as possible. When in doubt, however, use the `SQL_DROP` option and allocate another handle.

Performing Transactions

To this point, the execution of a statement has been referred to as a discrete, atomic event, which is how you interact with a traditional PC file manager, such as bTrieve. Each statement succeeds or fails on its own. Advanced client/ server DBMSs provide *transactions* to provide a way to group these statements. The entire `transaction` succeeds, or it fails.

What if you're executing a series of statements related to a single event and one of the statements fails? Take, for example, an inventory database. One table might contain data about product deliveries. Another table contains data about products in stock. A third table records the billing `transaction` to a particular customer. A delivery consists of:

■ An adjustment (in this case, a decrease) in the inventory level

■ A delivery record to schedule transportation to the customer

■ A cash transaction to bill the customer

To process the delivery of a product, you must add a new record to the delivery table. This schedules a truck on the appropriate route at the loading dock. You also must update the product table to reflect new inventory levels. This prompts warehouse personnel to move items from shelves to the loading dock. You must update the outstanding balance customer record, which provides information to the accounting department for later billing.

For the sake of discussion, say that you are planning to deliver to a customer that has been removed from your customer table because they haven't paid their bills. Your order entry program attempts to process the transaction. Here is what happens.

1. The `INSERT` into the deliver table succeeds.

2. The `UPDATE` of the product table succeeds.

3. The `UPDATE` of the customer table fails. The record in question does not even exist.

Your application displays a dialog box indicating that the transaction failed because the customer is not listed. Your data clerk doesn't know why the customer wasn't in the list, but he lets it go.

The product was moved to the loading dock and loaded on the truck. A truck made a delivery to the deadbeat customer. Everything worked as designed, except that your accounting department has no one to bill. Later, an audit discovers a delivery without billing information.

A visit from your boss impresses you with your company's disdain for shipping products out for free. You begin to search for methods to prevent this career-threatening chain of events from recurring. Surely, there is a way.

Normal IF...THEN logic structures don't help you because it is the last transaction that fails. You can rearrange the order of the statements, but this just introduces other nonsensical scenarios. Customers are billed for orders that never took place. Empty trucks are sent driving about the countryside. One of your junior colleagues is spotted trying out your chair for size. You need a general solution and soon.

What you need is a way to group these statements so that they occur in an all-or-nothing fashion. You find that your database has transaction support. transactions are the answer. You are saved! Your next act is to reassign your junior colleague to a permanent slot in the data entry corps.

> **Note**
>
> It is possible to solve this problem without recourse to transactions. However, other solutions require much more coding and provide much less opportunity for melodrama.

This is how transactions work:

- Start a transaction and execute each statement.
- If all the statements succeed, execute a COMMIT.
- If any of the statements fail, execute a ROLLBACK.

Executing a COMMIT actually causes the the statements to effect the statements as permanent changes to the database. This removes any changes the statements would make. If your application exits without doing either, an implied COMMIT takes place.

The start of a transaction is actually an *implicit* event. There is no special function to call. A transaction is said to have started as you execute a statement after a COMMIT or ROLLBACK. A transaction has also started when you execute the first statement after connecting to a database.

Grouping Statements into Transactions

The most important aspect of transaction support is how statements are grouped into transactions. You should group your statements into transactions that map to the financial, physical, or logical transactions that you are recording. This is possible to do fairly early in the design process.

Developers new to the transaction concept are often confused about how to handle a transaction consisting of a single statement. Do these need to be committed or rolled back? The answer is yes. You must do so to provide a starting point for the next transaction. Otherwise, this single statement is considered part of the next transaction. If the next transaction rolls back, the results of the successful single statement are obliterated.

Your application should simply test the results from each statement. If they all succeed, your application can safely perform a COMMIT. If any statement should fail, you should:

- Stop the execution of any further statements

- Perform a ROLLBACK

- Report an error to your user that specifically states which statement caused the failure

The error message that a user gets from the failed transaction is very important. The message should give some clue as to how to fix the problem. If a record required for the transaction is missing, instruct the user to add the appropriate record. If there is inconsistent data, provide enough information to find the record in error.

Transaction Modes

To query the current connection for the available transaction capabilities, your application should call the SQLGetInfo() function with the following parameters:

```
retcode = SQLGetInfo( hdbc, SQL_TXN_CAPABLE, &nShort,
  ↪sizeof(nShort), NULL );
```

where hdbc is a valid connection handle and nShort is an unsigned 16-bit integer. The sizeof(nShort) provides the size of the receiving buffer, nShort.

After SQLGetInfo() is called successfully with the previous parameters, nShort contains one of the following values:

- SQL_TC_NONE: There is no transaction support

- SQL_TC_DML: Transactions are supported for DELETE, INSERT, SELECT, and UPDATE statements. CREATE and DROP statements in a transaction cause an error

- SQL_TC_DDL_COMMIT: As SQL_TC_DML, except CREATE and DROP statements cause an immediate COMMIT

- SQL_TC_DDL_IGNORE: As SQL_TC_DML, except CREATE and DROP statements are ignored

- SQL_TC_ALL: Transactions are supported for all the above statement types

CREATE and DROP statements are rarely a part of normal transaction processing. It is probably best to assume that these statements are not supported. This allows you to trap only the SQL_TC_NONE case in your code. Your application can operate successfully with any other value if this limitation is assumed.

If you must use CREATE or DROP statements and SQLGetInfo() resulted in a value of SQL_TC_DML, you must disable transaction processing. After executing the statement, transaction processing should be turned back on.

To start transaction processing call SQLSetConnectOption() with the following parameters:

```
retcode = SQLSetConnectOption( hdbc, SQL_AUTOCOMMIT,
➥SQL_AUTOCOMMIT_OFF );
```

where hdbc is a valid connection handle. Note that turning transaction processing on is the same as turning the AUTOCOMMIT mode off.

To stop transaction processing call SQLSetConnectOption() with the following parameters:

```
retcode = SQLSetConnectOption( hdbc, SQL_AUTOCOMMIT,
➥SQL_AUTOCOMMIT_ON );
```

where hdbc is a valid connection handle. Note that turning transaction processing off is the same as turning the AUTOCOMMIT mode on.

AUTOCOMMIT mode is a mode of operation without transactions. This is usually the only mode of operation available for single-tier drivers. It is also the

The ODBC API

default mode in most drivers. The only way that an ODBC driver can add `transactions` to a data source that does not support them is to cache the actual SQL statements. You are unlikely to find such a caching feature in any driver.

If you're not using `AUTOCOMMIT` mode, you should perform a `COMMIT` after the last ODBC function call involved in a successful `transaction`. This is done by calling the `SQLTransact()` function with the following parameters:

```
retcode = SQLTransact( henv, hdbc, SQL_COMMIT );
```

where `henv` is the environment handle and `hdbc` is a valid connection handle. The `COMMIT` is global to all statements open on the connection associated with `hdbc`.

ROLLBACK

You should perform a `ROLLBACK` after any ODBC function call that fails during a successful `transaction`. This is done by calling the `SQLTransact()` function with the following parameters:

```
retcode = SQLTransact( henv, hdbc, SQL_ROLLBACK );
```

where `henv` is the environment handle and `hdbc` is a valid connection handle. The `ROLLBACK` is global to all statements open on the connection associated with `hdbc`.

From Here...

You now know the basics of ODBC statements, including statement configuration options and different means of executing statements. You also have learned how transactions work. To investigate the use of other types of statements for specific tasks, you can refer to the following chapters:

- Chapter 11, "Queries and Result Sets," to learn the statements necessary to construct sophisticated queries, retrieve and handle information as efficiently as possible, and clean up after queries are complete.

- Chapter 12, "Setting Parameters with Prepared Statements," to learn how to establish parameters for statements before their execution.

- Chapter 13, "The Cursor Library and Positioned Operations," to learn statements for handling block and scrollable cursors, and for working with Recordsets.

Chapter 9

Creating Tables with the DDL

An SQL, or Structured Query Language, is one part of a complete database management language. It lets you perform queries on your data and tables. But another necessary area of database syntax is the DDL, or Data Definition Language. This part of the language lets you define tables and other aspects of your database.

Although it's usually an administrative task performed during the initial establishment of a database, there are a few different situations in which an application might need to create a table during a session. Here are a few examples of when this might be appropriate:

- The application itself is designed to initialize or upgrade a database. Many database application companies just provide cumbersome SQL scripts to make the required database changes, and others want to send consultants out to manually make the changes. You may be able to distinguish your product from others by including an easy-to-run, intelligent, and friendly Windows application that handles the entire upgrade for them (preferably including a database backup at the very beginning).

- The application is a tool that gives users administrative access to the database—for example, a database customization utility. Such programs are often included with vertical database applications that are billed as "customizable." When writing a tool like this, your primary concern is to give the user as much power as he needs without making it too easy to use the tool to mess up the database terribly.

- The program needs to create temporary tables under circumstances where a view won't fit the bill. This is a common circumstance, and it is discussed in various places throughout this chapter.

In this chapter you learn to use ODBC to create and modify tables. Throughout this chapter, assume that the database itself has already been created. Some data sources actually do allow you to create a database from within an ODBC application, by issuing a statement containing the data-source-specific syntax that would create the database. For example, with Microsoft's SQL Server driver, the following command will create a 10-megabyte database:

```
retcode = SQLExecDirect (hstmt,
➥"CREATE DATABASE mydatabase ON mydevice = 10", SQL_NTS);
```

but don't count on that syntax working on another DBMS platform.

> **Note**
>
> For more information about ODBC statements, refer to Chapter 8, "The ODBC Statement: An Introduction."

With many data sources, you must use whatever system administration facilities are provided with your DBMS. If this is an important feature for you, you'll have to experiment with a given driver to find out if a database can be created from within an application. There is no ODBC "get information" call that can be used to discover whether a driver is capable of this.

> **Note**
>
> This is a non-issue when we're talking about a local database that stores its tables in separate datafiles—in that case, the *directory* in which the files are stored is, in effect, the database.

Because Chapter 3, "The Client/Server Language: SQL," goes into SQL command variations in some detail, I won't give as many examples of each command in this chapter. Instead, I'll concentrate on using representative examples to illustrate the process of performing each of the following operations:

- Creating, dropping, and altering tables

- Creating indexes on tables

- Dropping indexes

- Creating and dropping views

> **Note**
>
> Refer to Chapter 7, "Catalog and Statistics Functions," to find out the names of the tables and other database objects that already exist within your database.

Creating Tables

Creating a table is a simple operation. This section will take you through the steps necessary to create a table and discuss when it is necessary to create a table.

How to Create Tables

To create a table within the active database in an ODBC data source, use the CREATE TABLE command. The statement can be issued as follows:

```
retcode = SQLExecDirect(hstmt, "CREATE TABLE mytable (id INTEGER,
➥field2 CHAR(20); field3 VARCHAR(200))", SQL_NTS);
```

The key to making CREATE TABLE statements work correctly is getting the data types right for your data source. Support for data types, especially unique ones like unlimited binary fields, is totally driver-dependent. Support for certain data types is part of what makes a driver fit into a particular SQL conformance level. If your application is intended to be interoperable among the widest possible variety of drivers, it is best to assume no more than a core SQL conformance level, which includes most character and numeric data types.

This point needs to be emphasized because it goes right to the heart of one of the foundation decisions during your application design phase. You need to consider carefully the consequences of attempting to support drivers at the lower levels of API and SQL conformance. If you wish to support only core SQL conformance, you must restrict carefully your selection of data types, along with many other aspects of SQL syntax. For more information about SQL conformance levels, refer to Chapter 5, "Data Sources and Drivers."

Some sources of data, such as a local dBASE III driver, create tables (and indexes, for that matter) as separate files on the disk. However, virtually all client/server systems simply create them within a preallocated or otherwise self-contained database space.

> **Tip**
> Use the SQLGetTypeInfo() function to learn whether a data source supports a particular data type.

When to Create Tables

Creating a table is not a difficult or time-consuming operation. It also doesn't interfere with other users' work, unless something goes badly wrong (for example, the allocated database space suddenly gets filled up). Therefore, generally speaking, it's appropriate to create a table at any time during an application's execution. This is especially true of temporary tables, which are usually created, used by one user only, and then dropped before the application is closed.

If you're creating permanent tables in the database, you do need to put some thought into it before finalizing them. You can't just create any old table and expect it to work within a database's framework. It's important to follow naming conventions and proper normalization guidelines when creating tables, for your sake and the sake of any analyst who has to work with the database after you have moved on. Refer to Chapter 2, "The Relational Database Model," for detailed information on database design.

When creating temporary tables, your primary concern is to give them unique names. Many algorithms are available for this purpose, such as deriving a name from the data and time or maintaining an incrementing counter that stores the next usable numeric or alphanumeric suffix.

Dropping Tables

Dropping a table is also a simple operation. This section will show you how to drop a table and discuss when it is acceptable to drop a table.

How to Drop a Table

To drop a table, use the DROP TABLE syntax. In the context of an ODBC application, it looks like the following:

```
retcode = SQLExecDirect (hstmt, "DROP TABLE mytable", SQL_NTS);
```

It's as simple as that.

When It's Appropriate to Drop a Table

Knowing when it's safe to drop a table is a little less obvious. Keep in mind that there are several consequences to dropping a table.

For one thing, another user may be working in the table you're trying to drop. Depending on the nature of the data source, the table may be locked by the other user, or it may not, but the user's application may be relying on the continued presence of the table. In the former case, your attempt to drop the table will certainly fail, and you'll need to deal with the resulting error. In the latter case, you'll probably succeed in dropping the table, but the other user's application will most likely crash. In any event, you have to ask yourself what business you have dropping a table in a production database while other users are working in it. Even if maintenance is your goal, and you intend to restore the table presently, you still have to wait until after hours, or at least kick everyone off the system first.

Another possible consequence of dropping a table is the loss of referential integrity in the database. If other tables refer to the table you're dropping, you have a breach. Many data sources, especially client/server systems, simply will not allow this to happen if you've set up integrity constraints (such as triggers) properly beforehand. However, many others (such as an Xbase driver) have no control over such matters, and it's in your hands to be careful.

In most cases, dropping a table is not a time-consuming process, but dropping a large table on a bogged-down server may affect other users' performance for a while.

Temporary tables are, once again, in a category by themselves. Many applications need to create temporary tables for storage of derived information, such as the contents of a two-stage report. Such tables usually are not large and typically are used by only one user at a time. Under those circumstances, it should be fine to create and drop them at will.

There is one other consideration with respect to temporary tables: your data source may have a limitation on the number of tables you can create in a database. If you create a lot of temporary tables, you can surpass that limit. Therefore, it is vitally important to be certain to drop all temporary tables after their use. Problems can arise when a workstation crashes or is shut off without exiting your application: temporary tables can be left in the database. It's good to provide an after-hours utility that can rampage through a database, recognize temporary tables, and blow them away.

If you're really worried about exceeding a limit on the number of tables, you might consider creating a separate database for temporary tables, which even can be shared between applications.

Creating Indexes on Tables

Creating an index on a table is a little more complex. This section will show you how to create an index and discuss when you should use an index.

How to Create an Index

To create an index on a table, use the CREATE INDEX statement. In the context of an ODBC application, it looks like this:

```
retcode = SQLExecDirect (hstmt, "CREATE INDEX id ON mytable (id)",
➥SQL_NTS);
```

This will create an index called "id" on the "id" column.

Insert the keyword UNIQUE to prevent duplicate index key values:

```
retcode = SQLExecDirect (hstmt,
➥"CREATE UNIQUE INDEX id ON mytable (id)", SQL_NTS);
```

If id is mytable's primary key, this second example actually makes more sense, because indexes on primary key columns should virtually always be unique to preserve entity integrity.

Many data sources support clustered indexes. A *clustered index* is really a *physical* sort order for the rows in the table. This may conjure up an image of sorting data on the fly to keep it in exactly the right order on the disk, and some data sources may treat it that way. However, most don't exactly sort the data. It would be more accurate to say that when you issue a CREATE CLUSTERED INDEX command, the database engine knows to organize the table's data in whatever fashion that allows for optimum retrieval in that order. This is in contrast to a regular index, which is nothing more than a set of row pointers arranged in the specified order. A clustered index has no associated array of row pointers—it's physical as opposed to logical. As a result, you can only have a single clustered index "attached" to each table.

Clustered indexes usually are unique, and often are placed on the primary key column of the table. This is especially true if the primary key acts as a foreign key in other (child) tables in the database. Therefore, the following command makes perfect sense and is the most likely of the three examples in this section:

```
retcode = SQLExecDirect (hstmt,
➥"CREATE UNIQUE CLUSTERED INDEX id ON mytable (id)", SQL_NTS);
```

When to Create an Index

Creating an index is a simple operation to request, but it can be quite time-consuming to execute. Indexing a large table can take seemingly forever, bringing an average server to its knees, and with it, everyone on the system. Clustered indexes are the worst, because at least some physical rearrangement of the table in question needs to take place. Therefore, creation of indexes on larger tables should be considered an after-hours maintenance task.

On most data sources, indexes are not necessary on very small tables (of, say, one to five or ten rows). The time spent in maintaining the index and searching it to find the appropriate rows when queries are executed often overbalances the time saved in scanning the whole table at those levels.

Dropping Indexes

Now that you have learned to create an index, how can you drop it? This section will take you through the steps of dropping an index and discuss when you need to drop an index.

How to Drop an Index

To get rid of an index, use the DROP INDEX command. Within an ODBC application, it looks like this:

```
retcode = SQLExecDirect(hstmt, "DROP INDEX index1", SQL_NTS);
```

Even if the index has special attributes like UNIQUE or CLUSTERED, you don't need to specify them on the DROP INDEX line.

Dropping a *clustered index* simply releases the database engine from the requirement of optimizing a particular sort order. The DBMS will not go back and rearrange the already existing data in a mixed order, of course.

When It's Appropriate to Drop an Index

Dropping an index usually is not a time-consuming process in itself. As with most database objects, when dropped, an index is usually either deleted from the disk (a quick operation) or its space is simply considered free within whatever type of data space construct the data source uses to store databases.

However, it is possible to severely affect other users by dropping an index at a bad time. If a user is about to perform a complex search that would rely on that index, the search could end up taking hours instead of minutes. Also, be aware that if you try to drop an index while someone else's application is actually in the process of using it, your program will fail, and you'll need to plan for that. In either case, dropping indexes should usually be an after-hours maintenance task except when you're working with temporary tables.

Another thing to keep in mind is that some data sources (usually client/server, and in my opinion, the better ones) will not allow you to drop a table until you've dropped all other database objects (such as child tables and stored procedures) that mention it. Other data sources will offer the option to "cascade" the drop, dropping all the associated objects. Check your data source's documentation for more information, because the results are potentially annoying in the former case and potentially devastating in the latter.

Altering Tables

Now that you know how to create and delete tables, and add and delete indexes, you need to learn how to alter these tables. The next sections cover in detail when and how to alter tables.

How to Alter a Table

Although there are very few reasons for which an application might need to change the structure of a table on the fly, it is something that ODBC SQL is capable of, and this chapter is the most appropriate place for it. Therefore, let's look at a couple of forms of the ALTER TABLE command. The following syntax will add a column to a table:

```
retcode = SQLExecDirect (hstmt,
➥"ALTER TABLE mytable ADD COLUMN newcolumn CHAR(15)", SQL_NTS);
```

The command given previously will add a character-type column called newcolumn, with a length of 15, to table mytable. New columns are added to the end of the table; you can't specify the order of the columns once you've initially created the table.

The following syntax will remove a column:

```
retcode = SQLExecDirect (hstmt,
➥"ALTER TABLE mytable DROP COLUMN newcolumn", SQL_NTS);
```

This doesn't work in all cases, however. Many data sources only support the ADD COLUMN syntax. In such cases, the usual procedure for removing columns (assuming they're not required to maintain referential integrity), or for making any kind of major changes to a table's structure (such as renaming or resizing columns), is as follows:

1. Lock all users out of the database during this delicate operation, to prevent them from trying to add.

2. Use the CREATE TABLE syntax discussed earlier in this chapter to create a new table with the exact structure you're looking for. You can create the appropriate indexes at this point or later, but this is definitely the right time to create the CLUSTERED index if you want one.

3. Use a series of INSERT operations, a data-source-specific command, or some sort of bulk-copy operation to copy the data from the old table into the new table.

4. Turn off any referential integrity constraints on the old table. The constraints that exist, if any, and the method for doing this, if applicable, will depend totally on the nature of your data source.

5. Drop the old table, using the DROP TABLE syntax.

6. Rename the new table to the old name. This will sometimes be easy with a data source-specific command or even a DOS RENAME command, but sometimes will require some behind-the-scenes snooping and tweaking in the data source's system database.

7. Restore the referential integrity constraints, if any.

8. Test thoroughly before letting users back on.

To those of you who are familiar with some DBMS' easy tools for totally reconstructing a table (as in most Xbase variants), this might seem like a pretty limited capability. But those are the breaks: it would be quite tricky for a client/server database engine to make major changes to a table structure while other users are trying to work in the system.

> **Note**
>
> You can find out whether your data source can accept the ALTER TABLE command by calling SQLGetInfo() with SQL_ALTER_TABLE in the fInfoType parameter. This also will tell you whether the DROP COLUMN syntax is supported.

When to Alter a Table

The only time you ever should alter a table is during a scheduled maintenance period. It can take quite a while to arrange the data space for a new column; this will slow things down for other users even if they aren't trying to use the table in question. If they are trying to use the table, the obvious horrors will occur: they'll be locked out, their applications will almost certainly crash, and they'll hunt you down like a dog.

You need to be very sure in advance that your changes will not affect the operation of your system at any level. The ALTER TABLE command usually will not affect the front-end application except that, until you update the application, it won't see the new column(s). However, the procedure described for making major database changes often will result in some interesting problems, such as changed column names that need to be updated throughout the application, or length differences that need to be ironed out (the application may be expecting the old length and ignore any additional space that has been added on). Be very sure that it's worth the effort when considering those kinds of changes.

ALTER TABLE often will play havoc with views and stored procedures. If you have a view or procedure that issues a SELECT * FROM mytable command, you would expect any added columns to automatically appear in the result set. But this is not so of some DBMSs, such as Microsoft's SQL Server: only the previously existent columns will be selected, due to the way the view/procedure was compiled. As a rule, you should recompile all views and database procedures that make any use of a table that has been altered.

You usually don't need to worry about ALTER TABLE messing up your tables, but since it is a reconstructive operation and therefore one of the most complex procedures for a DBMS, there's always the possibility of a disaster. It makes sense to do a database backup before altering a large or important table.

Creating Views

The following sections discuss how and when to create views.

How to Create a View

As discussed in great detail in Chapter 3, "The Client/Server Language: SQL," *views* are imaginary tables based on a subset of the rows and columns from one or more actual tables. Views are very useful for populating multi-column list and grid controls in your front-end application, and just for general convenience during all types of queries and data manipulation.

The following syntax creates a simple view, in the context of an ODBC application:

```
retcode = SQLExecDirect (hstmt,
➡"CREATE VIEW myview (field2, field3) AS
➡(SELECT field2, field3 FROM mytable)", SQL_NTS);
```

The result: a view that contains only field2 and field3 from table mytable.

Once a view is established, you can use the SELECT statement to query it, just as though it were a table:

```
retcode = SQLExecDirect (hstmt, "SELECT * FROM myview", SQL_NTS);
```

which will, of course, retrieve field2 and field3.

Some data sources also will allow updates to tables through views under certain conditions. The updates will take place in the original tables.

> **Note**
>
> The ability to support views is a core SQL conformance level specification. You can find out your data source's level of SQL conformance by calling `SQLGetInfo()` with `SQL_ODBC_SQL_CONFORMANCE` in the `fInfoType` parameter. However, it is possible that a driver that calls itself a core-level driver will not support views.

When to Create a View

Creating a view is not in itself a big deal. When you create a view, the database engine usually does very little work: no more than if you created a tiny database procedure. It compiles it, checks it for correct syntax and the existence of the objects mentioned, and stores it.

However, running a view is in some cases a different story. Just like there are good times and bad times to run a massive SELECT statement, there are good and bad times to use a view that will result in a large search-and-retrieve operation. A view is nothing more than a convenience. It is no quicker and no slower than the SELECT statement it replaces, because as far as the DBMS is concerned, it *is* that SELECT statement. You should discourage heavy SELECTs on large tables during peak periods, whether view-related or not.

Dropping Views

Now that you know how to create a view, it's time to learn how to drop one. This section shows you how and when to drop a view.

How to Drop a View

To dispose of a view, simply drop it:

```
retcode = SQLExecDirect (hstmt, "DROP VIEW myview", SQL_NTS);
```

When It's Appropriate to Drop a View

Dropping a view is a quick operation, and if we're talking about a view that was created for administrative use only, you should be able to drop it any time. This is also true of views on a temporary table, as long as you're finished with the table. However, if the view is used by the main application, dropping it while users are working will cause their apps to crash if they happen to try to use it before you can re-create it. This may be hazardous to your health.

From Here...

- Proceed to Chapter 10, "Inserting, Updating, and Deleting Rows," to learn about data manipulation commands.

- Skip to Chapter 11, "Queries and Result Sets," to learn how to request data from a data source and process the results.

Chapter 10

Inserting, Updating, and Deleting Rows

Although querying is the operation that gets the most publicity (admittedly, in this book as well), it is really only half the picture. Chances are, your users will spend almost as much time changing the data in their databases as they will examining it. There are many places in an application in which data is changed, some in direct response to users' inputs and others performed behind the scenes by the application.

Unlike the complicated affair that is a query, operations that work with the database are relatively simple to use. The only thing to worry about is whether the operation and all related operations were successful. This issue is covered in detail in this chapter's final section.

This chapter discusses the following methods and aspects of data manipulation:

- Inserting, updating, and deleting rows in a database

- Finding out what sections of a database were affected by updating

- Maintaining referential integrity

- Returning meaningful data from a trigger, such as an error message

- The potentially misleading read-only mode

Inserting Rows into the Database

From the programmer's point of view, there are many different sets of circumstances under which users will have to add data to the tables in the database. Input screens usually involve one main insertion, plus potentially many auxiliary ones into little tables related to the main one—such as a customer record plus several alternate address records. Grid controls may be set up to enable the users to insert rows; these may actually insert each row as it's put in, or wait to send a whole batch of inserts to the database.

Inserting is a simpler operation than updating or deleting, in the sense that it is not really possible to insert more than one row at a time. Although it may be appropriate for your front-end application to pass a whole set of new rows through ODBC to the database, the DBMS will in reality only insert one at a time. This means that your app will have to send the INSERT instructions one by one as separate ODBC statements.

One of the worst situations a program can face is when there's a problem right in the middle of a multiple-part operation, like the customer/address example mentioned earlier. If some of the information is inserted (or updated, for that matter), but then some sort of error occurs that prevents the rest from happening, you have a situation that's difficult to recover from. In fact, you're fairly likely to have a referential integrity breach on your hands: the links may be lost between records that are supposed to be related in a particular way. To address this type of situation, the last section of this chapter talks about different ways to maintain referential integrity between tables when something goes wrong.

Just in general, you need to be careful to retain the links between tables when inserting rows into child tables. Some DBMSs will catch your errors and return failure messages, but many will not. Proofread your code for relational awareness, because ODBC can't cure the GIGO (garbage-in, garbage-out) disease. This subject is discussed in more detail in Chapter 21, "Referential Integrity."

> **Note**
>
> Most database management systems, and that includes single-tier ODBC drivers, do not usually *insert* rows into the tables—in fact, they are actually appended. There are some exceptions to this, for example, dBASE's INSERT command (as opposed to its APPEND command), or a SQL Server table with a clustered index defined. But by and large, "insert" is a misnomer. To a normal application, that should make no difference.

To add rows to your tables, use the SQL INSERT command in an ODBC statement. There are basically two forms of the INSERT statement: with and without column names provided. The following instruction will insert a new row into a table called mytable, filling in certain specific columns whose names have been provided:

```
retcode = SQLExecDirect (hstmt,
➡"INSERT INTO mytable (firstname, lastname, phone)
➡VALUES ('George', 'Fredrickson', '(510) 555-1234'),
➡SQL_NTS);
```

Three columns are specified, and three values of the appropriate data types are supplied.

> **Caution**
>
> It is critical that you supply values for all columns in which NULLs are not allowed; otherwise, your DBMS will return a failure status through ODBC.

The other form of the INSERT command is handy when you intend to supply a value for every column. In this case, you simply specify the values in the order that the column names appear in the table structure. Here's an example of an INSERT command in that format, assuming that table mytable has a total of exactly eight columns:

```
retcode = SQLExecDirect (hstmt, "INSERT INTO mytable
➡VALUES ('George', 'Fredrickson', '(510) 555-1234',
➡'1234 Any Place', NULL, "Beverly Hills", "CA", "90125", SQL_NTS);
```

Notice the NULL keyword after the first address line, which is located where a second address line would logically appear. This is the syntax that enables you to place literally *no* data in a column, unless that column does not accept null values. A second address line is a good candidate for a column that should allow nulls. The keyword NULL should not be surrounded by quotation marks in the INSERT statement.

> **Note**
>
> The INTO keyword is essentially meaningless, and is optional in many SQL dialects (such as SQL Server), but it is specified as part of the ODBC-standard syntax for the INSERT command, and your ODBC programs should use it all the time.

The ODBC API

Some database management systems provide various mechanisms for preventing the insertion of duplicate rows—that is, rows in which certain fields designated as "unique" have values that are already present in other rows. Using UNIQUE indexes is normally the method used to enforce this restriction. This is one of only a few reasons why an INSERT command would ever fail.

Updating Rows in the Database

There are several types of scenarios in which update operations are likely to appear in your programs. On modification screens, the user generally will make changes to one row at a time. The program itself may need to make occasional updates to internally maintained system tables, for example, when the user changes items in a Preferences dialog. Adding a dimension of complexity that is not present (or possible) with the insert command, a SQL UPDATE command can potentially affect many or all rows in a table.

> **Note**
>
> For many client/server database management systems, especially those that support transaction processing, there is really no such thing as an update. Although the UPDATE command is still used, in reality what occurs is a pair of operations: a deletion of the old row and an insertion of the new one. The reverse is generally the case with local DBMSs: changes are written directly over the data in the tables, and additional space is allocated (or freed) as appropriate for variable-length fields.

The same referential integrity issues pertain to database updates as apply to insertions. In particular, one type of potential problem is more of a concern for UPDATE commands than for INSERT statements: updates to primary key columns. Generally, it makes no sense to change primary key values, because when properly implemented they will be arbitrary and meaningless, used for nothing other than uniquely identifying records. However, if you do have to update a field that is part of the primary key, you must *cascade* that update to any child tables that may use this primary key value in their foreign keys. More on this later.

If you want to update a single row in a table, the best way to isolate it is to refer to it by its primary key. The following command illustrates this method:

```
retcode = SQLExecDirect (hstmt,
➥"UPDATE mytable SET firstname = 'Giorgio', zip = '90126'
➥WHERE id = 117", SQL_NTS);
```

The other kind of UPDATE command is designed to make the same type of changes to multiple rows, usually either every single row (which is rare) or every row that meets the criteria of a WHERE clause. The following syntax shows how to make a change to every row in the table mytable; it will null out every address2 value:

```
retcode = SQLExecDirect (hstmt, "UPDATE mytable SET address2 =
➥NULL",SQL_NTS);
```

This one is particularly tricky for Xbase aficionados—in that language, the similar command REPLACE address2 WITH "" would only affect the "current record," which is a concept that doesn't exist in SQL (except, to some extent, with cursors).

> **Note**
>
> Chapter 13, "The Cursor Library and Positioned Operations," explains what cursors are and how to use them.

The following syntax will change every occurrence of the last name Griffin to the Gryphon spelling, whether there is one row to change or a plethora of them:

```
retcode = SQLExecDirect (hstmt, "UPDATE mytable SET lastname =
➥'Gryphon' WHERE lastname = 'Griffin'", SQL_NTS);
```

Under certain circumstances, there is a dichotomy to mass updates: a trade-off between simplicity and robustness. Some database servers choke when you try to make too many changes in one shot, especially if your server hardware is weak. There are a variety of reasons for such problems. For example, in a transaction processing DBMS, the transaction log can be filled up and the entire command would then have to be rolled back. Or, the number of changes required can simply bring a database to its knees.

In cases like this, you may want to design your program to make only a single update at a time, or to do updates in sets of 100 or 1000 rows where possible. This will leave you with less to recover from if there is in fact a problem. This is just a heads-up; if you're seeing this type of thing happen, your program certainly might be at fault. This dilemma is rare where single-tier ODBC drivers are involved, and it is never as pronounced during DELETE operations because deletions are much simpler than updates.

I

The ODBC API

Deleting Rows from the Database

There's too much data in the world, and there's only one way to get rid of the surplus: by deleting it. Personally, I don't think there's enough deletion going on in the world; this of course is a major contributor to slow database search speeds.

In the contexts in which they're issued by applications, deletions are usually done one at a time, such as when the user picks a particular row to be deleted. Even if the user chooses several rows for deletion (say, by Ctrl+clicking in a multi-pick list box or grid), the application will virtually always have to perform the deletions one at a time anyway, referring to each row by its primary key.

However, it is possible to perform mass deletions, deleting all rows in a table or all rows that match a particular WHERE clause. This is a valuable capability in *cascading delete* situations. Whenever a row is deleted in a parent table that has associated rows in one or more child tables, the related rows in the child table also must be deleted. If a user deletes a record in a table called *customer*, he may think only one row is being deleted, whereas in reality any associated rows in, say, the *address* table, must also be deleted. The first half of this operation might look like the following, assuming the value of id for the record we want to delete happens to be 7:

```
retcode = SQLExecDirect (hstmt, "DELETE FROM customer WHERE id =
➡7", SQL_NTS);
```

This is an example of a DELETE command that singles out one individual row for deletion.

The rest of the operation involves deleting the address rows associated with the now defunct customer row:

```
retcode = SQLExecDirect (hstmt,
➡"DELETE FROM address WHERE customer_id = 7", SQL_NTS);
```

In reality, these two operations normally will have to be reversed to preserve referential integrity throughout the operation. That is, since address rows must at all times be associated with valid customer rows, they aren't allowed to exist at all if their customer row is gone, even if you're just about to delete them.

> **Note**
>
> Cascading deletes are often handled at the back end through the use of special procedures called triggers. Triggers are discussed in the following section.

In any case, it's important to avoid issuing the simplest form of the DELETE command unless you are really sure of what you're doing:

```
retcode = SQLExecDirect (hstmt, "DELETE FROM address", SQL_NTS);
```

This will delete an entire table in one shot. Xbase users should be especially careful, because in Xbase a similar command will delete only the "current" row in a table.

Things aren't always as they appear to be, and that is clearly true of delete operations in some DBMSs. When is a delete not a delete? Some database formats are designed so that when your application issues a DELETE command, the affected record(s) are only *marked* for deletion, rather than being killed dead on the spot. Xbase is a good example of this phenomenon. Microsoft's single-tier ODBC driver for the DBF file format preserves this behavior. Some drivers provide special, driver-specific commands for the purpose of actually purging out the flagged records. But in some cases, including the Microsoft ISAM drivers, a separate *utility* is even required.

Finding Out How Many Rows Were Affected

To find out how many rows were affected by an INSERT, UPDATE, or DELETE statement, issue the SQLRowCount() function. Its function prototype looks like this:

```
RETCODE SQLRowCount (HSTMT hstmt, SDWORD FAR * pcrow);
```

> **Note**
>
> SQLRowCount() also can be used, on some ODBC drivers, to find out how many rows were obtained with a SELECT statement. See Chapter 11, "Queries and Result Sets," for details.

The return code from SQLRowCount() is one of the following:

- **SQL_SUCCESS:** The row count was obtained correctly.

- **SQL_SUCCESS_WITH_INFO:** The row count was obtained, but the driver sends a warning message.

- **SQL_ERROR:** There's a problem; check your variables and syntax and try again.

- **SQL_INVALID_HANDLE:** The statement handle was unusable.

Maintaining Referential Integrity

Modifications to records in relational databases are not as simple as issuing a couple of commands and moving on. There are a lot of things that can go wrong, and you need to be on top of this situation. Most potential problems relate to breaches of referential integrity—in other words, making mincemeat of the links between tables. In a truly relational database, referential integrity must be maintained 100 percent of the time. There can never for a moment be a child record with no parent records, yet it is certainly possible to make illegal modification requests through ODBC. At some level in the system, this contingency must be managed.

There are two basic problems to be addressed when your aim is to protect the integrity of your relationships:

- Watching for inappropriate modifications

- Organizing operations into transactions

These problems will be addressed in the next two sections.

Watching for Inappropriate Relationships

With some relational database management systems, preserving referential integrity is not a particularly difficult task because the database engine keeps careful watch over the database. A great deal of this can be handled through triggers, specialized back-end SQL procedures that are supported by quite a few of the most popular database servers (such as SQL Server and Oracle). *Triggers* are procedures that are attached to particular tables and are executed when the insert, delete, or update commands are issued on that particular table. There can be up to three triggers on a given table: one for inserts, one for deletes, and one for updates; some DBMSs allow you to create combination triggers that handle more than one of these operations for a given table, such as insertions *and* deletions.

A typical insert trigger on a child table will check to make sure that all foreign keys do in fact map to valid primary key values in the respective parent tables. If the operation fails, the row will not be inserted, and a SQL_ERROR state will be returned to the app through ODBC.

Update and delete triggers are usually a little more complicated. You need to plan for the situations where an update or deletion would affect other tables. If you attempt an update or deletion, the trigger has to check all related tables to see if anything additional needs to be done. If a change in one table *will* affect rows in another table, there are two ways a trigger can handle the situation:

- Cascades

- Complete rejection

A *cascade* is the action of carrying an update or deletion on to all related tables. Expanding on an earlier example, if a customer row is deleted, the delete trigger on the customer table could first delete all dependent address table rows, and *then* permit the customer row deletion. The address table could in turn pass on the deletion to any tables that might be dependent on it. Cascades are more often used for deletions, though they can be applied to updates as well—a cascading update would generally only apply if the primary key in a table is being changed, and that, in theory, should never happen.

The alternative to a cascade is complete rejection of any questionable modification. For example, if an UPDATE statement were to attempt to change the primary key for a given row, and one or more rows in other tables referred to that key as a foreign key, you just might want to prevent the whole thing from happening. Your UPDATE trigger on the main table should check for this condition and return an error if it is detected.

One key point about triggers is that they exist totally independently of ODBC, and ODBC has no control over them—it's more like the other way around. If anything, this makes your job as an ODBC programmer more rather than less complicated, especially if you're trying to write an application that will work with a wide variety of data sources. Triggers may be the best possible way to preserve the links between tables, but many data sources don't support them (virtually *no* single-tier drivers do). This means that you have to make an interoperability decision: you can decide to support all or most data sources in general, or you can opt to only work with data sources that support back end integrity controls such as triggers.

If you choose the second approach, although your life will be a lot easier, you will have thrown away a lot of what ODBC is good for. If you go with the Cascading option, you are faced with the necessity of performing all integrity control manually, directed through the front-end application. This involves a lot more than just checking your ODBC SQL syntax carefully. To truly prevent foul-ups, you have to keep track of all relationships at the front end, and check that everything is in sync after every database change, no matter how minor.

Organizing Operations into Transactions

Realistically, you will take great pains during your development cycle to ensure that your application does everything in the right order, avoiding any possibility of a clumsy integrity problem. However, you can't control every factor—it's possible that one of the links in the communication chain will break and only half of what you said to do is actually done.

This isn't quite so bad if the first operation in a sequence fails, because of course your program will be watching the return codes and will backtrack if things aren't working out from the beginning. But what if something fails after some of the work has already been done? The answer is simple, but its implementation can be overwhelming: you have to be able to undo any successful changes that were made before the failure occurred.

Imagine what this type of backtracking can entail if you have to accomplish it all yourself. Your program needs to closely monitor the results of every operation that occurs, so that if a failure occurs it can act. You need to keep track of each individual update made to the database in case you need to backtrack. And worst of all, you need to temporarily store any data you've deleted or overwritten in order to be able to restore it if necessary. This is beyond the scope of what most programmers want to address.

Most true relational DBMSs provide a built-in solution to this common problem: some level of *transaction processing* capabilities. Transaction processing enables you to organize your operations into units, and the database engine will make sure that either all or none of a set of modifications are committed in the database.

For example, let's say you want to insert a new customer row plus two related *address* rows. The series of commands to accomplish this (excluding error checking) might be as follows:

```
retcode = SQLExecDirect (hstmt,
➡"INSERT INTO customer (id, firstname, lastname, company)
➡VALUES (11, 'George', 'Fredrickson', 'IBM')", SQL_NTS);
retcode = SQLExecDirect (hstmt,
➡"INSERT INTO address (id, cust_id, address_type, address1,
➡address2, city, state, zip)
➡VALUES (100, 11, 'Home', '1234 No Way', NULL, 'Tacoma', 'WA',
➡'98123')", SQL_NTS);
retcode = SQLExecDirect (hstmt,
➡"INSERT INTO address (id, cust_id, address_type, address1,
➡address2, city, state, zip)
➡VALUES (100, 11, 'Office', '4321 Any Place', 'Suite 567',
➡'Olympia', 'WA', '98321')", SQL_NTS);
```

Notice the order in which the operations are arranged: the customer row is inserted first because the address rows depend on it.

Now, these operations belong as a set, and the user would rather get a single failure message back than have part of the data inserted and part not. The only sure way to accomplish this is by resorting to the transaction processing (TP) capabilities of your data source. Assuming you are willing to limit the compatibility of your application to only those ODBC drivers that support TP, you can make use of the transaction processing capabilities of ODBC through the use of the various functions described later.

Checking for Transaction Processing Capabilities

To check whether your data source supports transaction processing, issue the SQLGetInfo() function with an fInfoType of SQL_TXN_CAPABLE. You'll receive one of the following return values:

- SQL_TC_NONE: This indicates that transactions are not supported.

- SQL_TC_DML: Indicates that transactions can contain only data manipulation language (DML) statements, such as INSERT, UPDATE, and DELETE, and also SELECT statements—which aren't technically part of the "data manipulation" portion of the SQL language. Data definition language (DDL) statements, such as CREATE TABLE, will cause errors.

- SQL_TC_DDL_COMMIT: Transactions are only allowed to contain DML statements, but DDL statements within a transaction will be executed after causing the transaction to be committed, rather than causing errors.

- SQL_TC_DDL_IGNORE: Transactions are only allowed to contain DML statements, and DDL statements within a transaction will be totally ignored.

- SQL_TC_ALL: Transactions are supported for all DDL *and* DML commands.

I

The ODBC API

The isolation levels of a transaction processing system indicate the level of care with which it manages potential conflicts between two transactions that the database engine is attempting to process at the same time.

For example, assume transaction A is in the process of executing a series of operations (updates, deletes, or whatever) but they have not yet been committed. Then, transaction B appears on the scene and either makes changes to the same data that transaction A is working on, or reads it as transaction A has left it, perhaps in an intermediate stage. Transaction B commits, but then transaction A rolls back its changes. What does the data look like at this point?

It depends on the RDBMS. There are basically three types of potential problems that can occur with concurrent transactions: dirty reads, nonrepeatable reads, and phantoms. Some DBMSs prevent all of these issues, but others prevent only some, or even none, of them. (See the "Checking Supported Transaction Isolation Levels" sidebar for an explanation of how to find out what your data source can do.)

If a transaction processing system permits *dirty reads*, this means that if one transaction makes a change but it hasn't yet been committed, and another transaction reads the changed row, but then the first transaction rolls back, the second transaction will have returned an invalid row.

A *nonrepeatable* read occurs in the circumstance that a transaction reads a row, then another transaction changes the same row, and then the first transaction tries to reread the row only to find out it has been changed. This is not as large a problem as a dirty read, but it can be a nuisance in grid control synchronization situations.

A *phantom* is a situation wherein one transaction reads all rows that satisfy a WHERE condition, then another transaction inserts a row that would have satisfied the condition if it had been in there just a moment before. If the transaction rereads for the same condition, the set of rows retrieved will be different.

Checking Supported Transaction Isolation Levels

To get even more information about the transaction processing capabilities of your database driver (assuming it supports transactions at all), call SQLGetInfo() with fInfoType of SQL_TXN_ISOLATION_OPTION. The value returned will explain the transaction isolation problems your data source can prevent:

- SQL_TXN_READ_UNCOMMITTED: Watch out—all three problems previously described are possible.

- SQL_TXN_READ_COMMITTED: Dirty reads are avoided, but the other problems are possible.

- SQL_TXN_REPEATABLE_READ: Dirty and nonrepeatable reads are avoided, but phantoms can still occur.

- SQL_TXN_SERIALIZABLE: None of the described problems can occur.

- SQL_TXN_VERSIONING: An improved version of SQL_TXN_SERIALIZABLE. Concurrent execution of transactions is better optimized.

- SQL_TXN_SERIALIZABLE uses a locking method that reduces concurrency and SQL_TXN_VERSIONING uses a non-locking method such as record versioning. Oracle's Read Consistency isolation level is an example of SQL_TXN_VERSIONING.

Calling SQLGetInfo with fInfoType of SQL_DEFAULT_TXN_ISOLATION also will return one of the above result codes. However, in this case, rather than describing the capabilities of the driver, the value returned describes the default isolation level settings.

You can configure the driver's transaction isolation level settings by calling the SQLSetConnectOption() function with SQL_TXN_ISOLATION as your fOption parameter. Specify one of the SQL_TXN values listed in the "Checking Supported Transaction Isolation Levels" sidebar.

Why would you want to change the isolation level? A data source may support a greater level of isolation than its driver calls for by default, and you may need the extra degree of robustness. Or, the opposite may apply: for performance reasons, you may wish to downgrade the isolation level.

Note

Take care not to specify an isolation option that's not supported by one of the data sources with which you want to work.

To really make use of your database engine's transaction processing features, you need to set up your connection in *manual commit* mode. By default, a connection is set up in auto-commit mode, which means that every statement is immediately committed after successful execution. To group several statements into a single transaction, you need to call `SQLSetConnectOption()` with an `fOption` of `SQL_AUTOCOMMIT` and `vParam` of `SQL_AUTOCOMMIT_OFF`. (This is necessary for the current example, to which you'll return in a moment.)

The result of this is that the application must explicitly commit or roll back each set of statements. The core-level `SQLTransact()` function is used for this purpose; its function prototype is as follows:

```
RETCODE SQLTransact (HENV henv, HDBC hdbc, UWORD fType);
```

The first two parameters are the environment handle and the connection handle, respectively. You should pass only one of these, with the other being passed as `SQL_NULL_HENV` or `SQL_NULL_HDBC`. If `henv` is a valid environment, the driver manager will attempt to commit/roll back all currently open transactions on all connected connections. If `hdbc` is a valid connection handle, the current transaction on only that connection will be affected.

The third parameter, `fType`, can be one of the following:

- `SQL_COMMIT`: Commit the transaction(s)

- `SQL_ROLLBACK`: Roll back the transaction(s)

`SQLTransact()` will return one of the following return codes:

- `SQL_SUCCESS`: The transaction(s) were committed/rolled back properly.

- `SQL_SUCCESS_WITH_INFO`: Everything seemed to work properly, but the driver has returned an informational or warning message.

- `SQL_ERROR`: One of various possible errors occurred. See the ODBC API Help file for details.

- `SQL_INVALID_HANDLE`: This occurs if both of the first two parameters are passed as null.

After `SQLTransact()` is successfully called, then as soon as a new statement is executed a new transaction will begin.

If you forget to issue a `SQLTransact()` call after a group of statements, the transaction will be left open and any additional statements called will continue to become part of the transaction until a `SQLTransact()` is finally issued. There are two very bad potential consequences of this. First, if a rollback command is issued with the intent to roll back the second batch of statements, the first batch will of course roll back as well. The other possible problem is that most database engines have some limit on the total size of

a transaction (usually in terms of affected data pages), and you can exceed
that limit fairly easily if you aren't paying attention.

Now, as promised, back to your example. The following code sequence takes
the SQL example given earlier and turns it into an ODBC-directed transaction:

```
HENV henv;

BOOL AddCustomer( HDBC hdbc )
{
    HSTMT    hstmt;

    if ( SQLSetConnectionOption( hdbc, SQL_AUTOCOMMIT,
        ➥SQL_AUTOCOMMIT_OFF ) != SQL_SUCCESS )
    {
        // Could not enter transaction mode, display error.
        return( FALSE );
    }

    if ( SQLAllocStmt( hdbc, &hstmt ) != SQL_SUCCESS )
    {
        // Could not allocate statement, display error.
        SQLSetConnectionOption( hdbc, SQL_AUTOCOMMIT,
        ➥SQL_AUTOCOMMIT_ON );
        return( FALSE );
    }

    if ( SQLExecDirect( hstmt, "INSERT INTO customer (id, firstname,
                        ➥lastname, company)"
                                " VALUES (11, 'George', 'Fredrickson',
                                ➥'IBM')", SQL_NTS ) == SQL_SUCCESS )
        {
            if ( SQLExecDirect( hstmt, "INSERT INTO address (id, cust_id,
            ➥address_type, address1,"
                                " address2, city, state, zip) VALUES
                                ➥(100, 11, 'Home',"
                                " '1234 No Way', NULL, 'Tacoma', 'WA',
                                ➥'98123')", SQL_NTS ) == SQL_SUCCESS )
            {
                if ( SQLExecDirect( hstmt, "INSERT INTO address (id,
                ➥cust_id, address_type,"
                                        " address1, address2, city, state,
                                        ➥zip) VALUES"
                                        " (100, 11, 'Office', '4321 Any
                                        ➥Place', 'Suite 567',"
                                        " 'Olympia', 'WA', '98321')",
                                        ➥SQL_NTS ) == SQL_SUCCESS )
                {
                    SQLTransact( henv, hdbc, SQL_COMMIT );
                    SQLFreeStmt( hstmt, SQL_DROP );
                    return( TRUE );
                }
            }
```

```
    }

    SQLTransact( henv, hdbc, SQL_ROLLBACK );

    // Display Error.

    SQLFreeStmt( hstmt, SQL_DROP );
    return( FALSE );
}
```

> **Note**
>
> Those RDBMSs that support triggers usually also support transaction processing. Triggers make use of the database server's built-in transaction processing capabilities to roll back illegal insertions, deletions, and updates attempted by the application.

Transaction processing capabilities and triggers virtually never apply to single-tier drivers because they would have to be built in as part of the driver itself. It's possible but highly unlikely that a single-tier driver would support these features (although they are extremely rare in local DBMSs themselves). This means that if you choose to make your applications work with single-tier drivers, you must be prepared either to manage referential integrity constraints internally, or ignore them.

Returning Meaningful Data from a Trigger

A detailed examination of trigger syntax is beyond the scope of this book, and besides, it is a little different for every RDBMS that supports triggers. However, one thing that merits a special mention is the ability of a trigger to return useful data to your application. This applies to all three types of triggers: INSERT, UPDATE, and DELETE.

There are several reasons why you would want to return more detailed information to the application than an error code normally supplies. For example, you might want to send back a message that explains the problem in more detail than the application would be able to figure out on its own. Or, you want to return a value that was automatically generated by the trigger for use as a key.

In any case, it's sometimes possible to obtain the text returned by a trigger from within your ODBC application. Whether and how this is supported is dependent on the driver, but it's most frequently accomplished in the following manner:

1. Execute your statement.

2. The `SQLExecute()` or `SQLExec()` function will return `SQL_SUCCESS_WITH_INFO`.

3. Call the `SQLError()` function to obtain the text. Examine the information pointed to by `szErrorMsg`—that's what you're looking for.

Once you have received the text, you can parse it however you wish.

Read-Only Mode

One of the options that can be set with the `SQLSetConnectOption()` function is `SQL_ACCESS_MODE`. This can be set to either `SQL_MODE_READ_WRITE` (which is the default) or `SQL_MODE_READ_ONLY`.

You might think that setting a driver into read-only mode would prevent database changes from occurring. Although it's conceivable that a driver would go so far as to build that in, it is not required by ODBC specifications. When a program issues this command, it is really only an indication to the driver that it can optimize its operation without worrying about write operations. Any other behavior on the driver's part is purely data source-dependent.

From Here...

- Continue to the next chapter for a discussion of the numerous steps involved in the querying process.

- In Chapter 12, "Setting Parameters with Prepared Statements," you'll learn about a special technique for passing data to INSERT, UPDATE, DELETE, SELECT, and other statements at execution time.

- Chapter 13, "The Cursor Library and Positioned Operations," shows you how to perform convenient updates on individual rows within result sets using cursor techniques.

Chapter 11

Queries and Result Sets

Querying is really the central topic of this book, because it is the core of an ODBC program. All of the initialization, statement preparation, and parameter and option setting leads up to the rather complicated task of querying, managing the retrieved results, and presenting them to the users. The real meat of a program is its querying capabilities. This is fortunate, because it's also the heart of ODBC.

Users will judge a program more on its query results than on any other single component, because queries are often performed at critical moments in business processes. The factors that will impress users the most are:

- Speed of retrieval
- Convenience of presentation

The speed of retrieval is largely dependent on uncontrollable factors, such as the network line speed, the server hardware (if dealing with a multiple-tier driver), the workstation hardware, and the quality of the ODBC drivers you're using. However, some steps can be taken to optimize the front-end side of data retrieval, and these are covered in Chapter 20, "Optimizing ODBC."

Among other things, Parts II and III of this book talk about managing result sets in Visual C++ and Visual Basic. A complete discussion of modern techniques for presenting read-only and read-write result sets is beyond the scope of this book. However, suggestions on the types of controls to be used in conjunction with particular functions are interspersed throughout the sections in this chapter and Chapter 13, "The Cursor Library and Positioned Operations."

In this chapter, you examine the workings of the following concepts and functions:

- How queries are done: The SQL SELECT statement

- The order of operations: The components of a query

- Setting up for a query

- Determining the number of result columns

- Getting information about a result column

- Counting the number of rows returned

- Binding columns to facilitate easy retrieval

- Working with the data

- Cleaning up after queries

The SQL *SELECT* Statement

SELECT is the SQL statement that's used to perform all types of queries.

Like the majority of important database operations, queries are sent to ODBC via the SQLExecute() and SQLExecDirect() statements. This means that before you can execute a query, you must define a statement handle with SQLAllocStmt(), as described in Chapter 8, "The ODBC Statement: An Introduction."

The basic SELECT statement retrieves a set of rows from a table or a view, which, as far as the front end is concerned, are the same thing. Here is an example of the simplest form of a SELECT statement, which retrieves all columns and all rows in the table called customer:

```
SELECT * FROM customer
```

The asterisk is a wildcard referring to all *columns*, not all rows. This query also retrieves all rows by virtue of the lack of any WHERE clause. For more detail about the different variations of the SELECT statement, including multi-table joins, see Chapter 3, "The Client/Server Language: SQL."

> **Note**
>
> The SELECT * syntax is used for simplicity in some of the examples in this chapter. However, when you're designing the queries that your own applications will make, you should SELECT only the columns you need at a given time. SELECTing columns you won't be using is one of the worst performance killers possible, because it ties up the database engine, the network, *and* the front-end application all at once.

The WHERE clause is used to specify selection criteria. For example, the following query selects all customer records with the last name "Fredrickson":

```
SELECT * FROM customer WHERE lastname = "Fredrickson"
```

The examples in this chapter will not get more complex than that, because the focus will be on ODBC syntax rather than SQL grammar. However, the SELECT statement is in reality a good deal more versatile. You can use an ORDER BY clause to determine the order that the results will arrive in, and a GROUP BY clause to break the results into sets of like records. These clauses and others are covered in Chapter 3, "The Client/Server Language: SQL."

The Order of Operations

Because the process of querying a database through ODBC is fairly complex, it's appropriate to devote a section for the purpose of describing the process as a whole. Assuming you already have allocated an ODBC environment, made your connections, and allocated an appropriate statement handle, the sequence goes like this:

1. First, you need to use SQLPrepare()/SQLExecute() or SQLExecDirect() to send a preformulated SQL statement to the database through ODBC. Various options can be set to direct the behavior of the statement.

2. When the statement is issued, the application does not actually receive the data. Instead, the command is simply presented to the database engine, which will formulate a plan for its execution. Multi-tiered databases normally will build a result set at this point in preparation to be "fetched" by the application.

3. To figure out how to deal with the results, you'll typically want to know how many columns are present in the result set. This is especially important if the SELECT statement includes an asterisk (*). If you don't know the answer in advance, the SQLNumResultCols() function will tell you.

4. If you're not sure about the attributes of the columns you've retrieved, you can find out more about them by calling the `SQLDescribeCol()` and `SQLColAttributes()` functions.

5. With some DBMSs, such as WATCOM SQL, `SQLRowCount()` will tell you the number of rows retrieved/affected by the statement. For SQL Servers and many other DBMSs, `SQLRowCount()` will return -1.

6. `SQLBindCol()` is called for each column, or for a structure describing the columns, to provide a place for ODBC to put the results where your program can get at them.

7. Now you can begin actually retrieving the data. If you wish to obtain only a single field value, `SQLGetData()` does that. `SQLFetch()` will pull one row at a time from the result set and place the data in the appropriate bound columns. `SQLExtendedFetch()` enables you to retrieve multiple rows at once and scroll through them with relative ease.

The subsequent sections assume that the following SQL statement is being or has been issued:

```
SELECT id, firstname, lastname FROM customer
```

Setting Up for a Query

If you intend to execute a statement more than once, it will be more efficient in the long run to "prepare" it in advance. The `SQLPrepare()` function performs this service. Assuming you've already used `SQLAllocStmt()` to allocate the statement, the following line will prepare the `SELECT` command given above for execution:

```
retcode = SQLPrepare (hstmt,
➥"SELECT id, firstname, lastname FROM customer", SQL_NTS)
```

Whether or not you choose to use `SQLPrepare()` to prepare your statement for execution, you can set options for the statement with the `SQLSetStmtOption()` function. For example, the following line will set 100 as the maximum number of rows that can be returned by the data source:

```
retcode = SQLSetStmtOption (hstmt, SQL_MAX_ROWS, 100)
```

This is good for preventing massive result sets from bringing a network to its knees.

> **Note**
>
> Chapters 8, "The ODBC Statement: An Introduction," 10, "Inserting, Updating, and Deleting Rows," and 13, "The Cursor Library and Positioned Operations," talk about statement options that pertain to the topics covered in those chapters. For a complete list of statement options, consult the ODBC API Help file.

Also, the `SQL_QUERY_TIMEOUT` option specifies how long the application should wait for a statement to finish and return. By default, there is no timeout, meaning that a serious hangup can conceivably lock up the application.

> **Note**
>
> Statement options are not the same thing as statement parameters. Parameters are variables that can be filled in to a statement at execution time. They're covered in Chapter 12, "Setting Parameters with Prepared Statements."

Determining the Number of Result Columns

The number of columns in a result set is obtainable through the `SQLNumResultCols()` function, which is available at the core API conformance level. Its function prototype is as follows:

```
RETCODE SQLNumResultsCols (HSTMT hstmt, SWORD FAR * pccol)
```

`pccol` will end up containing the number of columns in the result set.

The return code from this function is one of the following values:

retcode	Description
SQL_SUCCESS	No problem; you can rely on the value at `pccol`
SQL_SUCCESS_WITH_INFO	`pccol` is accurate, but the driver has sent more information which can be obtained through the `SQLError()` function
SQL_STILL_EXECUTING	You're running the statement in asynchronous mode. You'll need to check again in a moment

(continues)

retcode	Description
SQL_ERROR	There's a problem; check your variables and syntax and try again
SQL_INVALID_HANDLE	The statement handle was not usable. Check your syntax or allocate another one

Getting Information about a Result Column

Depending on the context within the application, you may or may not know what to expect in the result set. In case you don't, two investigative functions are available to give you more information:

- SQLDescribeCol()

- SQLColAttributes()

SQLDescribeCol()

SQLDescribeCol() provides overall information about a column in the result set or the anticipated result set. This is a core-level function. Its prototype is listed here:

```
RETCODE SQLDescribeCol (
      HSTMT        hstmt,
      UWORD        icol,
      UCHAR FAR *  szColName,
      SWORD        cbColNameMax,
      SWORD FAR *  pcbColName,
      SWORD FAR *  pfSqlType,
      UWORD FAR *  pcbColDef,
      SWORD FAR *  pibScale,
      SWORD FAR *  pfNullable
)
```

If you were to run this function with an icol value of 3, then based on the result set derived from your example SELECT statement, the following values would be brought over:

Variable	Value	Description
szColName	"LASTNAME"	The name of the column
pcbColName	8	The length of the column's name—*not* the length of the column data itself

Variable	Value	Description
pfSqlType	SQL_CHAR	The SQL *type* of the column. A list of all SQL column types is available in the ODBC API Help File under the entry for this function
pcbColDef	The *precision* of the column (the maximum number of bytes it uses)	In the case of character fields, this is simply the defined length (or maximum length, in the case of VARCHAR columns) of the column, which in this case happens to be 20
pibScale	The *scale* of the column (the maximum number of digits to the right of the decimal point)	Because this does not apply to character data, the value returned in your example is 0
pfNullable	SQL_NO_NULLS	Your *customer* table definition requires a value in the lastname field; nulls are not acceptable

The return code from this function is one of the following values:

retcode	Description
SQL_SUCCESS	All available information was obtained
SQL_SUCCESS_WITH_INFO	All expected information was obtained, but the driver sends a warning message
SQL_STILL_EXECUTING	Returned if running in asynchronous mode. Check again in a moment
SQL_ERROR	There's a problem; check variables and syntax and try again
SQL_INVALID_HANDLE	The statement handle was unusable. Check syntax or allocate another handle

SQLColAttributes()

SQLColAttributes() obtains information about a specified "descriptor type" for a particular column. A descriptor is an attribute of a column. The function prototype is:

```
RETCODE SQLColAttributes (
     HSTMT        hstmt,
     UWORD        icol,
     UWORD        fDescType,
```

```
                    PTR          rgbDesc,
                    SWORD        cbDescMax,
                    SWORD FAR *  pcbDesc,
                    SDWORD FAR * pfDesc
          )
```

There are too many different descriptors to list them all here, but one example is `SQL_COLUMN_TYPE`, which of course returns the SQL type of the column. Does this sound familiar? Perhaps because you already obtained this information from `SQLDescribeCol()` above?

There are two substantial differences between `SQLDescribeCol()` and `SQLColAttributes()`. First, `SQLDescribeCol()` obtains several specific values in one shot, whereas `SQLColAttributes()` retrieves only one value at a time. Second, `SQLColAttributes()` is extensible: future versions of ODBC can add new descriptors without upsetting the whole sequence.

Let's say you were to call `SQLColAttributes()` on the third column of your example `SELECT` statement for the purpose of obtaining the column type. You would pass the statement handle, 3 as the `icol` value, and `SQL_COLUMN_TYPE` as the `fDescType`. The output variables would come back as follows:

Variable	Value
rgbDesc	N/A
pcbDesc	N/A
pfDesc	SQL_CHAR, the value for the SQL type CHAR

`rgbDesc` is a buffer used if the descriptor is intended to supply a character value, and `pcbDesc` would contain the length of that character value. However, the `SQL_COLUMN_TYPE` descriptor returns a numeric value, so `pfDesc` is where the result is placed.

Let's look at another example, one which returns a character value. This time you'll still call `SQLColAttributes()` on the third column, but this time you'll ask for the column name. The appropriate `fDescType` value is `SQL_COLUMN_NAME`. Output variables, as shown in the following table:

Variable	Value
rgbDesc	"LASTNAME"
pcbDesc	8, the length of the string "LASTNAME"
pfDesc	N/A

The return code from this function is one of the following values:

retcode	Description
SQL_SUCCESS	Attribute information was obtained correctly
SQL_SUCCESS_WITH_INFO	Attribute information was obtained, but the driver sends a warning message
SQL_STILL_EXECUTING	Returned if running in asynchronous mode. Check again in a moment
SQL_ERROR	There's a problem; check your descriptor value, variables, and syntax and try again
SQL_INVALID_HANDLE	The statement handle was unusable. Check syntax or allocate another handle

Counting the Number of Rows Returned

Some databases, such as WATCOM SQL, support the use of the SQLRowCount() function for finding out how many rows will be returned. Its function prototype looks like this:

```
RETCODE SQLRowCount (HSTMT hstmt, SDWORD FAR * pcrow)
```

Note

SQLRowCount() also can be used to find out how many rows were affected by an INSERT, UPDATE, or DELETE statement. See Chapter 10, "Inserting, Updating, and Deleting Rows," for details.

Tip

For optimum driver compatibility, call this function only after the result set rows have been fetched.

The code returned by SQLRowCount() is one of the following:

retcode	Description
SQL_SUCCESS	The row count was obtained correctly
SQL_SUCCESS_WITH_INFO	The row count was obtained, but the driver sends a warning message
SQL_ERROR	There's a problem; check your variables and syntax and try again
SQL_INVALID_HANDLE	The statement handle was unusable

Binding Columns

For your program to work with the data in the most efficient way, you should bind all of the columns you're interested in to specially prepared buffers. `SQLBindCol()` is the function responsible for this. This is a core-level function. Here is its prototype:

```
RETCODE SQLBindCol (
    HSTMT          hstmt,
    UWORD          icol,
    SWORD          fCType,
    PTR            rgbValue,
    SDWORD         cbValueMax,
    SDWORD FAR *   pcbValue
    )
```

Your program must prepare in advance the data space to which pgbValue will point. This is as simple as defining variables to hold the information. For example, the following line will prepare a place to put a single 20-position character last name value (allowing for the additional null terminator byte):

```
UCHAR szLastName[21]
```

A single-value data storage location is fine if you're just going to use the `SQLFetch()` function to obtain data. This is because `SQLFetch()` can retrieve only one row at a time. However, `SQLExtendedFetch()` adds a dimension to the situation, allowing you to retrieve multiple rows with one call. An appropriate definition for a 100-row result set for 20-character last names is, of course:

```
UCHAR szLastName[100][21]
```

> **Note**
>
> You must prepare a separate location for each column you're going to bind, *unless* you're using row-wise binding (discussed in a moment).

`SQLBindCol()` is a more complex function than it looks, because there are actually several variations on its functionality. You can use `SQLBindCol()` in the following ways:

■ Column-wise

■ Row-wise

The next sections discuss these two approaches.

Column-Wise Binding

Column-wise binding is a little simpler to conceptualize, so let's begin there. If you choose to bind in this way, you're telling ODBC that you want each column to be loaded into a particular, separate location that will be referred to by a unique name. You're allocating each column completely separately from all other columns.

As an example, let's bind some of the columns resultant from your sample SELECT statement above. Let's say that you're not too interested in the id value for your immediate purposes, and you don't think you need to bind it. (You can still obtain the value through SQLGetData() if you need to.) However, you want to bind the other two columns for purposes of using the storage locations with SQLFetch(). The commands you would execute are the following:

```
UCHAR szFirstName[21];      // In reality, this will only allow
                            // space for 20 characters,
                            // because the NULL terminator is also
                            // included.
UCHAR szLastName[21];       // Ditto the above comment.
SDWORD cbFirstName;
SDWORD cbLastName;

retcode = SQLExecDirect( hstmt,
➥"SELECT id, firstname, lastname FROM customer", SQL_NTS );
if ( retcode == SQL_SUCCESS )
{
  SQLBindCol (hstmt,
  ➥2,SQL_C_DEFAULT, szFirstName, 21, &cbFirstName);
  SQLBindCol (hstmt,
  ➥3,SQL_C_DEFAULT, szLastName, 21, &cbLastName);

                            // Fetch records...
}
```

> **Note**
>
> Passing SQL_C_DEFAULT in the *fCType* variable lets ODBC decide which C datatype to assign the column value. For character information, unless you're deliberately intending to convert to another type, you might as well specify this *fCType*.

If you're planning to retrieve a *set* of rows for use with the SQLExtendedFetch() function, you'll need to allocate enough space in the location pointed to by rgbValue. For example, let's take the previous example and rewrite it for the purposes of retrieving not just one row, but 100 rows at a time. Again, you'll only bind the last two columns, first name and last name:

```
UCHAR szFirstName[100][21];    // In reality, this will only allow
                               // space for 20 characters,
                               // because the NULL terminator is
                               // also included.

UCHAR szLastName[100][21];     // Ditto the above comment.
SDWORD cbFirstName;
SDWORD cbLastName;

retcode = SQLExecDirect( hstmt,
➥"SELECT id, firstname, lastname FROM customer", SQL_NTS );
if ( retcode == SQL_SUCCESS )
{
    SQLBindCol (hstmt,
    ➥2, SQL_C_DEFAULT, szFirstName, 21, &cbFirstName);
    SQLBindCol (hstmt,
    ➥3, SQL_C_DEFAULT, szLastName, 21, &cbLastName);

                               // Fetch data...
}
```

Notice that the value of 21 passed as the *cbValueMax* variable does not change. This value indicates to ODBC the maximum size of a single element in the array of data storage locations, rather than the size of the whole thing. Again, this value must include consideration for a null termination byte in the case of character data.

Row-Wise Binding

Row-wise binding is often more efficient than column-wise binding if you're planning to use all columns in immediate sequence in your application. It also requires only a single call to bind all your columns. The difference is, rather than allocating a separate storage location for the data that comes back for each column, you instead allocate space for an array of *structures* that look like the data that will be returned for all the bound columns combined.

The *rgbValue* variable points to the beginning of the entire storage location. You must also issue the SQLSetStmtOption() function and set the SQL_BIND_TYPE option to the length of the entire structure (you should use sizeof() to obtain this value). Based on this information, SQLExtendedFetch() automatically calculates the offset for each row and column.

For example, let's create a workspace for 100 rows of first and last names, bound in a row-wise fashion:

```
typedef struct
{
    UCHAR  szFirstName[21];
    SDWORD cbFirstName;
    UCHAR  szLastName[21];
    SDWORD cbLastName;
} PERSON;

    .
    .
    .

    PERSON people[100];

    SQLSetStmtOption (hstmt, SQL_BIND_TYPE, sizeof(PERSON));
    SQLSetStmtOption (hstmt, SQL_ROWSET_SIZE, 100);

    retcode = SQLExecDirect( hstmt,
    ➡"SELECT id, firstname, lastname FROM customer", SQL_NTS );
    if ( retcode == SQL_SUCCESS )
    {
        SQLBindCol (hstmt, 2, SQL_C_CHAR,
        ➡people[0].szFirstName, 21, &people[0].cbFirstName);
        SQLBindCol (hstmt, 3, SQL_C_CHAR,
        ➡people[0].szLastName, 21, &people[0].cbLastName);

        // Fetch data...
    }
```

The main advantage to row-wise binding is that all your data is contiguous, and you can read a whole row in one piece if you want.

The return code from the SQLBindCol() function is one of the following values:

retcode	Description
SQL_SUCCESS	The column was bound correctly
SQL_SUCCESS_WITH_INFO	The column was bound, but the driver sends a warning message
SQL_ERROR	There's a problem; check your variables and syntax and try again
SQL_INVALID_HANDLE	The statement handle was unusable. Check syntax or allocate another handle

Working with the Data

Once you have issued your statement and bound your columns (in either order), you can bring rows of data into the prepared data storage locations. There are basically three approaches to obtaining and working with data. If you prefer not to go through the process of binding, you can choose to deal with data one field at a time. If you choose to make use of SQLBindCol(), you can choose to bring down one row of data at a time, or you can read many rows into a special two-dimensional buffer. The functions used to perform these operations are, respectively:

- SQLGetData()

- SQLFetch()

- SQLExtendedFetch()

The following sections are devoted to discussing these operators.

SQLGetData()

SQLGetData() is the simplest way to get a piece of data from a result set. Basically, it reads a single column value from the "current" row. This is a core-level API function. Its prototype is as follows:

```
RETCODE SQLGetData (
      HSTMT         hstmt,
      UWORD         icol,
      SWORD         fCType,
      PTR           rgbValue,
      SDWORD        cbValueMax,
      SDWORD FAR *  pcbValue
)
```

Before you can obtain data from an unbound column, you must use SQLFetch(), SQLExtendedFetch(), or SQLColPos() to position the row pointer on the correct row. SQLGetData does not move the row pointer itself, because otherwise it would be inconvenient to get more than one value per row.

> **Note**
>
> SQLSetPos() is a cursor-related operation. Chapter 13, "The Cursor Library and Positioned Operations," describes cursors in detail.

The following example shows SQLGetData() obtaining the id value from the current row in your *customer* result set. Remember, you never bothered to bind that column:

```
UWORD iid;
SDWORD cbid;
retcode = SQLGetData (hstmt, 1, SQL_C_ULONG, &iid, 0, &cbid)
```

The cbValueMax parameter's value is 0 because that value is ignored for numeric data types.

SQLGetData()'s return code is one of the following values:

retcode	**Description**
SQL_SUCCESS	The column data was obtained correctly
SQL_SUCCESS_WITH_INFO	The column data was obtained, but the driver sends a warning message. For example, this code is returned if data had to be truncated
SQL_NO_DATA_FOUND	For some reason, there was no data for the function to retrieve
SQL_STILL_EXECUTING	Returned if running in asynchronous mode. Check again in a moment
SQL_ERROR	There's a problem; check your variables and syntax and try again
SQL_INVALID_HANDLE	The statement handle was unusable. Check syntax or allocate another handle

SQLGetData() has its place, but calling it over and over can drive you crazy, and can become just plain inefficient. SQLFetch() and SQLExtendedFetch() do a lot more work with a lot less coding.

SQLFetch()

SQLFetch() brings the next row of data in the result set into locations prepared with SQLBindCol(). This is a core-level function, and its simple function prototype is as follows:

```
RETCODE SQLFetch (hstmt)
```

When SQLFetch() is called, the query that was previously submitted only to the database engine for examination is actually executed. As the data is retrieved, it is placed in the appropriate storage locations that SQLBindCol() prepared for the various columns. As the data is fetched, it is converted and even truncated if necessary.

If you have elected not to bind a given column, SQLFetch() will ignore it. You can still get at unbound column data through the SQLGetData() function.

Because it's so simple, it's tempting just to use SQLFetch() all the time. This is not a bad practice while you're concentrating on learning the other vagaries of ODBC programming. However, during the development of production applications, you'll want to pay close attention to determining which of the different methods is most appropriate for a given set of circumstances.

The return code from SQLFetch() is one of the following values:

retcode	Description
SQL_SUCCESS	All column data was obtained correctly
SQL_SUCCESS_WITH_INFO	All expected data was fetched, but the driver sends a warning message. For example, this code is returned if data had to be truncated due to a mismatch between the data received and the column binding
SQL_NO_DATA_FOUND	You have gone past the end of the result set
SQL_STILL_EXECUTING	Returned if running in asynchronous mode. Check again in a moment
SQL_ERROR	There's a problem; check your column bindings and syntax and try again
SQL_INVALID_HANDLE	The statement handle was unusable. Check syntax or allocate another handle

SQLExtendedFetch()

SQLExtendedFetch() can be used to obtain more than one row at a time from a result set, or to go directly to a specific row and retrieve its data. Because a discussion of SQLExtendedFetch() is tied is with the concept of cursors, it's been saved for Chapter 13, "The Cursor Library and Positioned Operations."

SQLGetData(), SQLFetch(), and SQLExtendedFetch() can be used in conjunction to make your program as efficient as possible about returning result sets. Chapter 20, "Optimizing ODBC," discusses this and other strategies for speeding up your ODBC code.

Cleaning Up after Queries

After your application has finished with a query and the results are no longer needed, you should free the statement for reuse. This is accomplished by issuing the SQLFreeStmt() function. This is a core-level function, and its prototype looks like this:

```
RETCODE = SQLFreeStmt (HSTMT hstmt; UWORD fOption)
```

There are four possible values for fOption:

retcode	Description
SQL_CLOSE	If a cursor is defined for the specified statement, it is closed. Discussed in detail in Chapter 13, "The Cursor Library and Positioned Operations"
SQL_DROP	This completely blows away the statement. You must allocate a new one if you need to do more SQL
SQL_UNBIND	This option unbinds all columns from the data storage locations set up with SQLBindCol()
SQL_RESET_PARAMS	Resets all parameters set up for the statement with SQLBindParameter(). Discussed in detail in the next chapter

The possible return values for SQLFreeStmt() are:

retcode	Description
SQL_SUCCESS	The operation was performed as expected, depending on fOption
SQL_SUCCESS_WITH_INFO	The operation was performed, but the driver sends a warning message
SQL_ERROR	There's a problem; check syntax and try again
SQL_INVALID_HANDLE	The statement handle was unusable. Check syntax

From Here...

■ Chapter 12, "Setting Parameters with Prepared Statements," backtracks a little, explaining how to fill in parameters for statements before their execution.

■ After that, you'll move on to the complex topic of cursors in Chapter 13, "The Cursor Library and Positioned Operations."

Chapter 12

Setting Parameters with Prepared Statements

One reason to bother preparing a statement with SQLPrepare() instead of just whipping it out with SQLExecDirect() is that you may need to execute the same statement more than once. Rather than having to set all the options up each time you want to run a statement, you can put it together once and run it over and over. In fact, you can set up several statements in memory at once and call the right one for a particular purpose each time a common task needs to be done. Sounds pretty good, right?

Think about the issue a little further, and you may realize there's a slight flaw in this concept. That is, how often do you execute the exact same command more than once? Maybe in the case of SELECT statements, which are used to fill grids or input screens, but what about in data modification statements? How often do you make exactly the same UPDATE to a row, or DELETE the same row, or INSERT the exact same data? Almost never—although you'll often execute very *similar* commands with slightly different data.

Fortunately, ODBC provides a reconciliation between the desire to save time preparing statements and the fact that some aspects of the statements are likely to be different every time. The solution lies in the concept of ODBC statement *parameters*.

In this chapter, you look over statement parameters from the following angles:

- Parameter basics
- Specifying parameter values to supply to your statements
- Getting information about parameters

- Passing and accepting procedure parameters

- Clearing parameters from their associated statements

Establishing Parameter Basics

Two steps to establishing parameters in a statement are leaving markers and attaching parameter definitions. You can do these in either order, but it seems a little more intuitive to leave the markers first.

To indicate where parameters belong in a statement, you must leave markers for them. These placeholders are simply question marks, inserted in the appropriate locations within the *szSqlStr* variable in a SQLPrepare() function call.

For example, the following statement has three parameters, corresponding to the three values that should be stored by the following INSERT command:

```
retcode = SQLPrepare (hstmt, "INSERT INTO mytable VALUES (?, ?, ?)", 36)
```

Parameters are intended to represent values only. You can't use a parameter to stand for a piece of syntax that might change within the statement—only for values that may change during subsequent executions of the statement.

> **Note**
>
> It's possible use parameters in SQLExecDirect() statements, too. There's nothing wrong with this approach if it makes sense in context, but it does sort of go against the concept of running a statement several times—after all, that's what SQLPrepare() is for.
>
> If you want to use SQLExecDirect() with parameters, you'll have to bind parameters first (as discussed later in the "Binding Parameters" section).

Specifying Parameter Values

To specify a parameter value (or set of values), you must first define a buffer for the value(s) and put the value(s) into it. A pointer to that buffer is passed to the SQLBindParameter() function.

Binding Parameter Values

The process of attaching parameters to a statement is referred to as *binding* parameters. This is accomplished through the SQLBindParameter() function, which is defined at the core API conformance level. Its prototype is:

```
RETCODE SQLBindParameter(
       HSTMT          hstmt,
       UWORD          ipar,
       SWORD          fParamType,
       SWORD          fCType,
       SWORD          fSqlType,
       UDWORD         cbColDef,
       SWORD          ibScale,
       PTR            rgbValue,
       SDWORD         cbValueMax,
       SDWORD FAR *   pcbValue
  )
```

As you can see, this is one of the more complex ODBC function prototypes you've encountered. This may be a little surprising for such an apparently straightforward feature. However, SQLBindParameter() can operate in a couple of different ways. You can use it to specify parameter data directly, or in such a way that the data is retrieved at execution time—and in the latter case, you can provide a single value per parameter or an entire array of values for each.

The various input and input/output variables are passed as shown in table 12.1.

Table 12.1 Input and Output Variables

Variable	Description
hstmt	Statement handle, as usual
ipar	This is the parameter index. To determine the number of a given parameter in a statement, simply count the question mark parameter markers from left to right, starting with 1
fParamType	The I/O type of the parameter. There are three possible values for this argument: SQL_PARAM_INPUT, SQL_PARAM_INPUT_OUTPUT, and SQL_PARAM_OUTPUT. SQL_PARAM_INPUT parameters simply pass variable data to a statement. SQL_PARAM_OUTPUT parameters can be assigned values by procedures that are called within a statement. SQL_PARAM_INPUT_OUTPUT parameters pass read/write arguments to procedures called within a statement. They pass a value, then accept a different value from the procedure. The different parameter types will be discussed in more detail in the sections to follow

(continues)

The ODBC API

Table 12.1 Continued	
Variable	**Description**
fCType	The C data type of the parameter. If you specify SQL_C_DEFAULT, the C data type will automatically be derived from the fSqlType argument (follows). For a complete list of C data types, consult the ODBC API Help file
fSqlType	The SQL data type of the parameter. Again, see the help file for a complete list of SQL data types
cbColDef	The *precision* of the column to which the parameter is tied. This is the maximum length or number of digits for the parameter, depending on the data type. A list of precision constants for the various SQL data types is available under the "Precision" entry in the Help file
ibScale	The *scale* of the column/parameter, such as the maximum number of digits right of the decimal point. This doesn't apply to non-numeric data types. A list of scale constants for the various SQL data types is given under "Scale" in the Help file
rgbValue	A pointer to the parameter's data storage. This is the location of the data item or items that will actually replace the parameter marker at execution time
cbValueMax	The maximum length of the parameter within its buffer. If data is being retrieved at execution time (as explained later), this value indicates the length of each instance of the parameter within the buffer. This value is ignored for all data types except character and binary
pcbValue	A pointer to another data buffer, this one receives a value that indicates the actual length of the parameter data in rgbValue (*if* the parameter data is of the character or binary types). There are also some special values that can be placed in the buffer to trigger unusual behavior during SQLExecute() or SQLExecDirect(). These are: SQL_NTS, SQL_NULL_DATA, SQL_DEFAULT_PARAM, and two even more unique values: SQL_NTS indicates a null-terminated string; the length will be determined automatically. SQL_NULL_DATA indicates that the parameter value should be passed as a null. SQL_DEFAULT_PARAM instructs the procedure to which this parameter is being passed to use its default value for this parameter instead of using the value at rgbValue. This assumes that a procedure is involved, and that the procedure is set up with the appropriate default. SQL_LEN_DATA_AT_EXEC(*length*) is a macro that lets SQLPutData() provide the length value at execution time. This is discussed in the next section. *Length* must be non-negative, but it's ignored unless the data type of the value is SQL_LONGVARCHAR, SQL_LONGVARBINARY, or a

Variable	Description
	similar long data type specific to the data source. In that case, *length* must contain the number of bytes in the parameter value. For example, to specify that 10,000 bytes of data will be sent with SQLPutData() for an SQL_LONGVARCHAR parameter, an application sets pcbValue to SQL_LEN_DATA_AT_EXEC(10000). SQL_DATA_AT_EXEC: Use this parameter if you're calling an ODBC 1.0 driver from your ODBC 2.0 application and you intend to supply parameter values with SQLPutData() (as discussed later in the "Passing Data at Execution Time" section.)

Note

SQLBindParameter() can be called before or after SQLPrepare(), but must be called before SQLExecute() if a statement contains parameter markers.

Let's look at a basic example that employs the SQLBindParameter() function. The following listing illustrates the proper binding of two parameters to a prepared statement, and the actual execution of the statement:

```
RETCODE InsertRecord( HSTMT hstmt, LPCSTR lpszText, USHORT nValue )
{
    RETCODE retcode;
    char   szText[21]; // Maximum length of string will be 20
                       // characters.

    lstrcpy( szText, lpszText );

    retcode = SQLPrepare (hstmt,
    ➥"INSERT INTO mytable VALUES (?, ?)", SQL_NTS );
    if ( retcode == SQL_SUCCESS )
    {
        retcode = SQLBindParameter (hstmt, 1, SQL_PARAM_INPUT,
                ➥ SQL_C_CHAR, SQL_CHAR, lstrlen(szText),
                          0, (PTR)&szText[0], sizeof(szText), NULL );
        if ( retcode == SQL_SUCCESS )
           retcode = SQLBindParameter (hstmt, 2, SQL_PARAM_INPUT,
           ➥ SQL_C_USHORT, SQL_SMALLINT, 10,
                          0, (PTR)&nValue, sizeof(nValue), NULL );

        if ( retcode == SQL_SUCCESS )
           retcode = SQLExecute (hstmt);

        SQLFreeStmt (hstmt, SQL_RESET_PARAMS);
    }
}
```

```
            return( retcode );
    }

    .
    .
    .

      retcode = InsertRecord( hstmt, "Text", 13 );
    .
    .
    .
```

The SQL command that was actually sent to the data source was:

```
    INSERT INTO mytable VALUES ('Text', 13)
```

Possible return codes from `SQLBindParameter()`are as follows:

retcode	Description
SQL_SUCCESS	The parameter was bound without event
SQL_SUCCESS_WITH_INFO	The parameter was bound but more information was returned by the driver
SQL_ERROR	The binding failed. Check your syntax and variables
SQL_INVALID_HANDLE	The statement handle was invalid. Check syntax or allocate a new handle

Note

The `SQLBindParameter()` function in ODBC 2.0 replaces the ODBC 1.0 function `SQLSetParam()`. If you have any old applications that still call `SQLSetParam()`, the calls will be mapped by ODBC 2.0 drivers to `SQLBindParameter()`. Also, if an ODBC 2.0 application calls `SQLBindParameter()` in an ODBC 1.0 driver, the call will be mapped back to `SQLSetParam()`.

If you're able to replace the ODBC 1.0 API and 1.0 drivers with 2.0 throughout your organization/customer base, you may wish to go back and migrate your 1.0 applications to the new ODBC. This will save the inefficiency involved in the translation.

Passing Data at Execution Time

If you call `SQLBindParameter()` and specify `SQL_LEN_DATA_AT_EXEC(length)` for the `pcbValue` argument, this lets ODBC know that you'll be providing the parameter data at execution time. If this is the case, when `SQLExecute()` or

SQLExecDirect() is called to run the statement, the return code will be
SQL_NEED_DATA. This is your cue that the process needs to be completed using
a pair of additional functions: SQLParamData() and SQLPutData(). If you have
more than one parameter that expects data at execution time (or if you're
passing an array of values for one or more parameters), these functions are
generally used within a loop structure that calls them in sequence. A good
example of this can be found in the Code Example under SQLPutData() in the
ODBC API Help file.

SQLParamData() retrieves the address of the data storage location that holds
the value for the current parameter. On successive calls, it cycles through the
parameters. This is an extension level 2 function; its prototype is:

```
RETCODE SQLParamData(HSTMT hstmt, PTR FAR * prgbValue)
```

prgbValue is a pointer to the location of the next parameter value.

The application should watch the return code closely, because it is more than
just an error indicator in this case. The following are possible return values:

retcode	**Description**
SQL_SUCCESS	The entire operation is complete: the statement has been executed and all iterations of all parameter values have been completed
SQL_SUCCESS_WITH_INFO	The entire operation is complete: the statement has been executed and all iterations of all parameter values have been completed—however, the driver has returned additional information
SQL_NEED_DATA	The SQLExecute() or SQLExecDirect() function running in the background is expecting more parameter values after this one. Call SQLPutData(), then call SQLParamData() again
SQL_STILL_EXECUTING	Running in asynchronous mode. Check again later
SQL_ERROR	Something's not working. The driver may not support this function
SQL_INVALID_HANDLE	The statement handle is unusable. Check your variables and syntax

SQLPutData() is called after each call to SQLParamData(). It actually sends the
data for the current parameter to the currently executing SQLExecute() or
SQLExecDirect() function. The following is the prototype for SQLPutData(),
which is an extension level 1 function:

```
RETCODE SQLPutData(HSTMT hstmt, PTR rgbValue, SDWORD cbValue)
```

rgbValue is a pointer to the location of the value to be sent, usually obtained via SQLParamData(). cbValue is the number of bytes to be found at that location and sent.

> **Note**
>
> SQLPutData() is an extension level 1 function, but SQLParamData() and SQLParamOptions() are only available at extension level 2. Why is that? Because SQLPutData() is also used for other purposes, pertaining to cursors. Refer to Chapter 13, "The Cursor Library and Positioned Operations," for details.

SQLPutData() will return one of the following codes:

retcode	**Description**
SQL_SUCCESS	The data was sent successfully
SQL_SUCCESS_WITH_INFO	The data was sent successfully. However, the driver returned supplemental information
SQL_STILL_EXECUTING	You're running in asynchronous mode. Check again later
SQL_ERROR	Something's not working. The driver may not support this function
SQL_INVALID_HANDLE	The statement handle is unusable. Check your variables and syntax

After each call to SQLPutData(), the application should call SQLParamData() again to find out whether more parameter values need to be sent.

Multiple Parameter Values

If you wish, you can go beyond the method shown previously and instead of providing a single value for each parameter, provide an array of values for each. (This was alluded to in the explanations for some of the parameters on SQLParamData() and SQLPutData()). The array of values is still located in the same place: the buffer pointed to by SQLBindParameter()'s rgbValue argument.

Sending multiple instances of each parameter is more complex and requires more steps, but it offers you the advantage of being able to call SQLExecute() once, yet have the statement run many times with different values. This is primarily useful for implementing a batch insert routine. One additional function is required to set this up: SQLParamOptions().

To indicate the number of parameter values in the arrays for the various parameters, call SQLParamOptions(). This is only called once for the entire statement, not once for each parameter, since you must have the same number of values for all parameters. It must be called before SQLExecute() or SQLExecDirect() in the sequence explained in the "Passing Data at Execution Time" section. This is an extension level 2 function, and its prototype looks like this:

```
RETCODE SQLParamOptions(HSTMT hstmt, UDWORD crow, UDWORD FAR * pirow)
```

crow is the number of array values. pirow points to a storage location in which the current array index value will be kept up to date during the processing of the instances of the statement. Although this value isn't required by ODBC, the usefulness of this information will become clear in a moment.

Possible return codes from SQLParamOptions() are as follows:

retcode	**Description**
SQL_SUCCESS	Row count set correctly
SQL_SUCCESS_WITH_INFO	Row count set, but driver has sent more information
SQL_ERROR	Problem: check variables and syntax
SQL_INVALID_HANDLE	Something is wrong with the handle

Once you have run SQLParamOptions(), go ahead and call SQLParamData() and SQLPutData() in the sequence explained in the previous section. Nothing is different except that you'll need to call those functions many more times as you iterate through your parameter value arrays.

Getting Parameter Information

Several different functions are used to obtain various levels of information and statistics about the parameters the application has set up. The following subsections describe these functions in detail, showing you how to:

- Get detailed information about parameters

- Find out the number of parameters

- Get a list of parameters

Getting Detailed Parameter Information

To obtain all the information about a particular parameter, use the
SQLDescribeParam() function. This is essentially the reverse of
the SQLBindParameter() function. SQLDescribeParam() is defined at
the extension level 2 API conformance level. Here is its function prototype:

```
RETCODE SQLDescribeParam(
     HSTMT        hstmt,
     UWORD        ipar,
     SWORD FAR *  pfSqlType,
     UDWORD FAR * pcbColDef,

     SWORD FAR *  pibScale,
     SWORD FAR *  pfNullable
)
```

The arguments have the same functions as their near-namesakes in the
SQLBindParameter() function, except that pfSqlType, pcbColDef, and pibScale
are now output parameters. pfNullable indicates whether the parameter's
column can contain nulls.

Possible return codes from SQLDescribeParam() are as follows:

retcode	Description
SQL_SUCCESS	The parameter information was obtained and all is correct
SQL_SUCCESS_WITH_INFO	The parameter information was obtained, but more information was returned by the driver
SQL_ERROR	The information could not be obtained. Your data source may not support this function
SQL_INVALID_HANDLE	The statement handle was invalid. Check syntax

Getting the Number of Parameters

To find out the number of parameters in a statement, use the SQLNumParams()
function. This is an extension level 2 function (probably because of its limited value rather than its complexity), and its prototype is:

```
RETCODE SQLNumParams(HSTMT hstmt, SWORD FAR * pcpar)
```

pcpar is an output parameter in which the function will place the number of
parameters. Possible return codes are:

retcode	Description
SQL_SUCCESS	Number of parameters is correct in pcpar
SQL_SUCCESS_WITH_INFO	Number of parameters was obtained, but the driver has more information
SQL_ERROR	Could not obtain the number of parameters. This function may not be supported by your data source
SQL_INVALID_HANDLE	The statement handle was invalid. Check syntax

Getting a List of Parameters and Related Columns

SQLProcedureColumns() provides detailed information about the statement parameters associated with calls to DBMS procedures. This is an extension level 2 function, and its prototype is:

```
RETCODE SQLDescribeParam(
        HSTMT          hstmt,
        UWORD          ipar,
        SWORD FAR *    pfSqlType,
        UDWORD FAR *   pcbColDef,
        SWORD FAR *    pibScale,
        SWORD FAR *    pfNullable
)
```

The arguments contain or receive the following information:

Variable	Description
hstmt	Statement handle
szProcQualifier	Points to a string containing the qualifier for the set of procedures you wish to examine. For database engines that support qualifiers. A *qualifier* is typically a database name. A null value or a search pattern is also acceptable. An empty string specifically indicates procedures with no qualifiers
cbProcQualifier	Length of the string at szProcQualifier, or SQL_NTS for a null-terminated string
szProcOwner	Points to a string containing the name of the procedure's owner, if the DBMS supports ownership of procedures. This can be left NULL if you want to return information about procedures without regard for owners. Or, an empty string specifically indicates procedures with no owners. This string can also contain search patterns
cbProcOwner	Length of the string at szProcOwner, or SQL_NTS for a null-terminated string

(continues)

The ODBC API

Variable	Description
szProcName	Points to a string containing the specific name or the search string representing the procedure names that you want to look at. A NULL value indicates all procedures
cbProcName	Length of the string at szProcName, or SQL_NTS for a null-terminated string
szColumnName	Points to a string containing the exact column name or a search string narrowing the column names to be retrieved. A null value indicates all columns
cbColumnName	Length of the string at szColumnName, or SQL_NTS for a null-terminated string

This is obviously a complex call, and it gets even more complicated. Here's what the results look like; they are returned as a standard result set to be obtained with SQLFetch() or SQLExtendedFetch(). Each row consists of information about a column that a back end procedure uses as a parameter, sends back as part of its result set, or returns as a retcode-style value. Below is a list of the result set columns, with explanations:

Result Set Column	Description
PROCEDURE_QUALIFIER	Procedure's qualifier
PROCEDURE_OWNER	Procedure's owner
PROCEDURE_NAME	Procedure's name
PROCEDURE_COLUMN_NAME	Column's name
COLUMN_TYPE	One of these values: SQL_PARAM_INPUT, SQL_PARAM_OUTPUT, SQL_PARAM_INPUT_OUTPUT, SQL_RETURN_VALUE, SQL_RESULT_COL, or SQL_PARAM_TYPE_UNKNOWN. SQL_RETURN_VALUE indicates that the parameter is the value that's returned by the procedure. And SQL_RESULT_COL indicates that this is one of the columns in the result set produced by the procedure. The others are pretty much self-explanatory
DATA_TYPE	The SQL data type of the column
TYPE_NAME	The data type according to the data source's terminology
PRECISION	Column's precision. This is the maximum length or number of digits for the parameter, depending on the data type. A list of precision constants for the various SQL data types is available under the "Precision" entry in the Help file

Result Set Column	Description
LENGTH	Column's length
SCALE	Column's scale, such as the maximum number of digits right of the decimal point. This doesn't apply to non-numeric data types. A list of scale constants for the various SQL data types is given under "Scale" in the Help file
RADIX	This value only applies to numeric columns, and is otherwise returned as null. The two possible values are 2 and 10. If 2 is returned, that means for you to interpret the precision and scale values as indicating the maximum number of *bits* in the column. If radix is 10, this indicates that precision and scale indicate the maximum number of *digits*
NULLABLE	Indicates whether the column is permitted to contain nulls
REMARKS	A column description, if supported by the data source

The possible result codes from the `SQLProcedureColumns()` function are:

retcode	Description
SQL_SUCCESS	All the specified information was gathered correctly
SQL_SUCCESS_WITH_INFO	Information was gathered correctly, but the driver has returned additional information
SQL_STILL_EXECUTING	The statement was executed in asynchronous mode
SQL_ERROR	Could not obtain the information. This function may not be supported by your data source
SQL_INVALID_HANDLE	The statement handle was invalid. Check syntax

Passing and Accepting Procedure Parameters

There are certain issues involving parameters when they're passed to procedures on which you need to focus.

The differences in sending parameter values to procedures revolve around the fact that a procedure can actually return changed values in parameters. In other words, parameters may not be just for input; they also can be used to hold output. Also, a procedure called at the database engine level can directly return a status value, similar to an ODBC function's `retcode`, and that value can be captured and returned to your ODBC application.

> **Note**
>
> `SQLProcedureColumns()` is an ODBC function that can be used to find out the nature of each column/parameter that a procedure uses or returns. For more information about this function, refer to Chapter 7, "Catalog and Statistics Functions."

To bind an input parameter to a statement that calls an SQL procedure, you don't need to do anything unique. Just do it the same way you would for an INSERT or UPDATE statement, as described earlier in this chapter, in the "Binding Parameter Values" section.

To bind an output or input/output parameter to a statement involving a procedure, you need to do a couple of things differently:

- First of all, you may need to mark one of the parameters in a slightly unusual way. Specifically, if you're trapping the return value of the SQL procedure, you should mark it like this in your ODBC SQL command line:

      {? = call MyProc}

- Also, when calling `SQLBindParameter()`, you have to specify `SQL_PARAM_OUTPUT` or `SQL_PARAM_INPUT_OUTPUT` as the `fParamType` argument for the parameter in question.

Once the statement has been executed with `SQLExecute()` or `SQLExecDirect()`, the updated parameter values returned by the procedure will be located in their respective `rgbValue` buffers set up in the parameter bindings.

Clearing Parameters

To "unbind" parameter definitions from a statement, call the `SQLFreeStmt()` function with `fOption` set to `SQL_RESET_PARAMS`. This will reset all parameter buffers at once.

The result will be that the statement exists in the form that it did before any parameters were bound. You'll need to bind them again if you want to reuse the statement.

From Here...

- Chapter 7, "Catalog and Statistics Functions," discusses `SQLProcedureColumns()` in more detail.

- Chapter 13, "The Cursor Library and Positioned Operations," describes other uses for the `SQLPutData()` function.

Chapter 13

The Cursor Library and Positioned Operations

Cursors have already made appearances in previous chapters in order to simplify the functions under discussion. Now that you've got a good understanding of such operations as SQLFetch() and SQLPutData(), cursors can take the spotlight.

What is a cursor? Well, the term is used a little ambiguously in ODBC jargon. In one sense, the term *cursor* refers to a set of rows fetched from a result set. In the other sense, a cursor is a scrollable "pointer" to the current row of a result set. In either case, think of a cursor as a window on the result set. Cursors are used as a relatively convenient and efficient method for working with one piece of a result set at a time, as needed by the application (usually for display and editing purposes).

There are two general cursor attributes: *block* and *scrollable*. You may have heard these terms before and their definitions follow:

- *Block*—The capability to retrieve a set of rows from a result set, and position the cursor on the first row of that set

- *Scrollable*—The capability to retrieve a set of rows from a result set, and position the cursor on a given row in that set, allowing your application to perform some functions directly on that particular row

If you've ever worked with Xbase, you'll recall that every data manipulation command in that language relies on the "current record" motif, where every row has a sequential key to identify it uniquely with greater ease than a true primary key. The difference between Xbase current records and ODBC cursors, however, is that Xbase record numbers are enumerated from the beginning of the table in the order that the records were inserted into the table, whereas cursors are reckoned from the beginning of the result set, based on the WHERE and ORDER BY clauses of the SELECT statement that retrieved the rows.

In this chapter, we'll talk about the concepts behind cursors, and you'll learn about:

- The cursor library and cursor basics

- Handling result sets with cursors

- Saving yourself hassles with positioned UPDATE and DELETE statements

- Checking your driver's support for cursors

- Setting cursor-related connection and statement options

- Releasing a cursor

The Cursor Library and Cursor Basics

The cursor library is a DLL that sits between ODBC's driver manager and the data-source-specific driver. It contains a variety of functions that are used by other ODBC functions, or which can be called directly by the application. This DLL works with drivers at or above the Extension Level 1 API conformance level.

Under Windows 3.1, the cursor DLL is called ODBCCURS.DLL. Under Windows NT, it's ODBCCR32.DLL. ODBC will automatically use the appropriate library based on the OS you're running. The cursor library DLLs may be distributed with your ODBC applications.

There are several different cursor types with which ODBC applications can work. Here are explanations of the different types:

- *Static*—A static cursor is just a picture of a set of rows. It doesn't get refreshed or updated, even if other users make changes to the underlying data tables. Static cursors are simple to implement, but they are inflexible and the cursor library's implementation is read-only.

- *Dynamic*—A dynamic cursor is a set of rows that is kept up-to-date via strategically placed refreshes (re-fetches, to be more precise).

■ *Keyset-driven*—Keyset-driven cursors are a good compromise between static and dynamic cursors. They start out like static cursors, but subsequent fetches register updates to, and deletes from, the database. *Keyset* refers to the unique key value for each row that is generated in memory by ODBC when the result set is retrieved, and retained throughout the life of the result set. ODBC will generally use a primary key column if one is available, or a column on which a unique index exists. If these aren't available, it may have to use all columns in the row, which can result in some rather large key values.

When the cursor is positioned on a given row in a keyset-driven arrangement, updates to that row can be retrieved from the database. If a given row has been deleted from the database, it's referred to as a "hole" in the result set, and this condition is discovered by the application when the cursor is positioned on it. A hole can't be processed any further.

> **Caution**
>
> There is a caveat to a purely keyset-driven cursor that doesn't exist in a true dynamic cursor. If a row is inserted by another user into one of the tables involved in the result set, a keyset-driven cursor won't pick it up, period. However, depending on the ODBC driver, rows inserted by your application may be detected locally. This is discussed in the "Checking Your Driver's Support for Cursors" section later in this chapter.

■ *Mixed*—A mixed cursor is a cross between a dynamic and a keyset-driven cursor. The concept of a keyset is still used, but keys for *all* rows aren't necessarily maintained by the driver at one time. This is useful if you have retrieved a very large result set and don't want to deal with all keys at once.

A mixed cursor maintains a keyset which at any given time contains at least all rows in the current rowset (rowsets are discussed in the next section). When the rowset changes, the keyset changes with it. Holes are eliminated on subsequent fetches of the set of rows that formerly contained the hole(s).

The cursor library by itself supports only read-only static cursors and forward-only implementations of the other types. Forward-only means that the cursor can only be moved forward, and not scrolled freely with such functions as

`SQLSetPos()`. This is not very serviceable for use with, say, a grid that users update in real-time.

If the driver associated with a given statement provides cursor support over and above that which is included in the cursor library, the cursor library will automatically go to the driver when you try to do something outside the library's base capabilities. Alternately, you may choose to disable the cursor library entirely and let the driver use its built-in cursor support functions, assuming it has a full implementation of all the cursor-related functions. This is discussed later in this chapter, in the section on "Setting Cursor Connection Options."

Handling Result Sets with Cursors

Chapter 11, "Queries and Result Sets," dealt with result sets and retrieving the data with `SQLFetch()`. One thing that wasn't mentioned in that discussion was that when a result set is retrieved, a cursor is automatically created. You can assign your own cursor name to a statement handle (this is recommended for your own convenience); however, if you don't assign a name, the ODBC driver will automatically generate one beginning with SQL_CUR (18 characters long or less) as soon as a SELECT command is executed via the statement handle.

> **Note**
>
> Cursors are created for all statements that return result sets—not just SQL SELECT commands that the application prepares directly. ODBC functions like `SQLTables()` and `SQLColumns()` also return result sets, and have associated cursors. The ODBC SDK's cursor demo program (described in Appendix A, "Resources in the SDK") illustrates the use of cursors on a variety of result sets.

Assigning a Cursor Name

To assign a name to the cursor attached to a given statement, use the `SQLSetCursorName()` function. This is a core-level function, and its prototype is as follows:

```
RETCODE SQLSetCursorName (HSTMT hstmt, UCHAR FAR * szCursor,
➥SWORD cbCursor)
```

The arguments are:

Variable	Description
hstmt	The statement handle
szCursor	A pointer to a buffer containing the cursor's name. It's wise to keep the cursor name shorter than 18 characters because all drivers that support cursors allow at least 18-character cursor names. A given driver may allow you to specify a longer name. To find out a given driver's maximum cursor name length, call the SQLGetInfo() function with fInfoType of SQL_MAX_CURSOR_NAME_LEN. See "Checking your Driver's Support for Cursors" later in this chapter
cbCursor	The length of the cursor name in the buffer

The possible result codes that can be returned by this function are:

retcode	Description
SQL_SUCCESS	The cursor name was set correctly
SQL_SUCCESS_WITH_INFO	The cursor name was set, but the driver returned additional information
SQL_ERROR	The cursor name could not be set as specified. For example, the cursor name may have been too long, or a duplicate of another active cursor name
SQL_INVALID_HANDLE	Something is wrong with the statement handle. Check your variables and syntax

The cursor name you assign to a statement takes effect as soon as you specify it (not retroactively to the existing result set, if any). The name is used for each result set generated by the statement until the statement handle is freed. See "Closing a Cursor" later in this chapter for details.

Because a statement can have only one result set open at a time, there is no possibility of confusion between the cursors for two sequential result sets generated by the same statement. However, you do need to take care to give cursors unique names across different statement handles you may have allocated at the same time. There is one crucial exception to this rule—you need to use the same cursor name for two statement handles which will be used to perform positioned UPDATE and DELETE operations, described later in the "Positioned UPDATE and DELETE Operations" section of this chapter.

As mentioned in the text, cursor names are system-generated if you don't specify your own names. To find out the name of the cursor associated with an hstmt (whether or not you specified it), call the SQLGetCursorName() function. The prototype for this core-level function looks like this:

```
RETCODE SQLGetCursorName (
    HSTMT        hstmt,
    UCHAR FAR * szCursor,
    SWORD        cbCursorMax,
    SWORD FAR * pcbCursor
)
```

The parameters are defined as follows:

Variable	Description
hstmt	The statement handle to examine
szCursor	A pointer to a buffer for the function to place the name of the cursor
cbCursorMax	Specify the size of the buffer you've provided for *szCursor*
pcbCursor	The function places the total number of bytes in the cursor name here, minus the null terminator. This may be different from *cbCursorMax* if *szCursor* isn't big enough for the cursor name. Again, 18 characters is a good bet for all cursor names—so allowing for the null termination byte, make the buffer at least 19 bytes long

SQLGetCursorName() can return the following result codes:

retcode	Description
SQL_SUCCESS	The complete cursor name was obtained correctly
SQL_SUCCESS_WITH_INFO	The cursor name (or part of it) was returned correctly, but the driver has sent additional information. This status occurs if the cursor name had to be truncated due to an *szCursor* buffer of insufficient length

retcode	Description
SQL_ERROR	The cursor name wasn't returned correctly. Check your variables and syntax
SQL_INVALID_HANDLE	The statement handle was not valid. Check variables and syntax

The Result Set Cache

When a result set is retrieved, the data for bound columns is placed in a cache. Along with the data, some additional information is also maintained: a buffer storing the length of each data item, and a buffer storing a 16-bit value that indicates the current status of the row. Here are the possible status values, along with their meanings:

retcode	Description
SQL_ROW_UPDATED	The row has been updated with a positioned update statement
SQL_ROW_DELETED	The row has been deleted with a positioned delete statement
SQL_ROW_SUCCESS	The row has been successfully fetched
SQL_ROW_ERROR	The row was not correctly fetched

At any given time, the result set cache is stored partially in memory, and the rest is stored in temporary files. This means that the disk space available on the drive containing your Windows TEMP directory is the ultimate delimiter for result set size. If you run out of disk space, obviously any operations attempting to access the data will fail. However, the fetch operation may not fail because many drivers don't actually retrieve the data until the first function is called that actually uses the data.

In any case, it's wise to watch for an out-of-disk-space condition in your error-trapping routine and to display the appropriate message, because sooner or later it *will* happen to one of your users.

Setting the Cursor Position

When you execute a SELECT statement and return a result set, you can access the data as described in Chapter 11, "Queries and Result Sets," using the

SQLFetch() statement. As you'll recall, SQLFetch() gets only one row at a time, and on subsequent SQLFetch() calls, the rows are fetched in sequence. Now you need to focus on *how* ODBC keeps track of the current row and how you can change the current row explicitly.

The cursor for a given statement points to the current row in a result set. This pointer is maintained internally by the ODBC driver. Each time SQLFetch() is executed, it increments the cursor to point to the new current row. You can set the current row yourself using the SQLSetPos() function, if your driver supports it. SQLSetPos() is an extension level 2 function, and its prototype is as follows:

```
RETCODE SQLSetPos (
      HSTMT      hstmt,
      UWORD      irow,
      UWORD      fOption,
      UWORD      fLock
)
```

The arguments for SQLSetPos() operate as follows:

Variable	**Description**
hstmt	The statement in question
irow	The number of the row in the result set on which to place the cursor
fOption	To set the current row to *irow*, *fOption* should be SQL_POSITION. To set the current row *and* refresh that row from the data source, *fOption* should be SQL_REFRESH. Other *fOption* values are possible; for details, see "Positioned UPDATE and DELETE Statements" later in this chapter
fLock	Tells the driver how to set the lock on the row on which the cursor will be placed, if necessary. This parameter can be set to one of the following values: SQL_LOCK_NO_CHANGE; SQL_LOCK_EXCLUSIVE; or SQL_UNLOCK. SQL_LOCK_NO_CHANGE leaves the lock status of the row alone. This is regularly used in read-only cursor situations—either the entire result set is locked or none of it is. SQL_LOCK_EXCLUSIVE locks the row for the exclusive use of only those statements in the same connection as the hstmt parameter. This is necessary to make a change to the row. SQL_UNLOCK frees the existing lock on the row so that other connections or other users can make changes to it.

Variable	Description
	Some drivers can't support all of these lock types. For more information, see the information about SQLGetInfo() in the "Checking Your Driver's Support for Cursors" section later in this chapter

SQLSetPos() will return one of the following retcodes:

retcode	Description
SQL_SUCCESS	The cursor was positioned correctly, and any other actions associated with a given *fOption* went normally
SQL_SUCCESS_WITH_INFO	The requested actions were performed with general success, but the driver returned more information. See the SDK's API Reference Help file for details. There are several possible reasons for this result code, but most of them have to do with *fOptions* you'll be looking at a little later
SQL_NEED_DATA	As discussed later, this function can also be used to change the data in the database that corresponds to the row indicated with *irow*. SQL_NEED_DATA is returned if a data-at-execution parameter is encountered; you then need to use the parameter-passing techniques covered in Chapter 12, "Setting Parameters with Prepared Statements," to complete the operation
SQL_STILL_EXECUTING	This is returned if the specified *fOption* made changes to the database, and the statement is operating in asynchronous processing mode
SQL_ERROR	Something went wrong, and there are quite a few things that can go wrong with the more complicated *fOptions*. Again, see the API Reference Help file for details
SQL_INVALID_HANDLE	The handle was unusable. Check your syntax

Again, SQLSetPos() can do more than just position the cursor. Later sections in this chapter will discuss these other capabilities.

Fetching Multiple Rows

The `SQLExtendedFetch()` function is used instead of `SQLFetch()` to retrieve multiple rows of data from a result set at a time. `SQLExtendedFetch()` is a much more complex function than `SQLFetch()` because it supports a much greater level of flexibility.

The set of rows returned by each `SQLExtendedFetch()` call is aptly named a *rowset*. The number of rows returned by one call is determined by the value of the `SQL_ROWSET_SIZE` statement option, discussed later in this chapter in the "Setting Cursor Statement Options" section.

> **Note**
>
> If you have set the `SQL_MAX_ROWS` statement option to set a maximum number of rows to be retrieved, bear in mind that the cursor can't go beyond the boundaries of that limit. Cursors work on a cached result set, not directly on the data that's actually in the database.

`SQLExtendedFetch()` is an API conformance extension level 2 function, so you can't count on it being available from most drivers. Here's a look at its function prototype:

```
RETCODE SQLExtendedFetch (
    HSTMT        hstmt,
    UWORD        fFetchType,
    SDWORD       irow,
    UDWORD FAR * pcrow,
    UWORD FAR *  rgfRowStatus
)
```

The parameters for this function are defined as follows:

Variable	Description
hstmt	The statement handle that returned the result set
fFetchType	`SQLExtendedFetch()` is flexible in the way it lets you specify the block of rows to set. These are the possible methods you can choose from: `SQL_FETCH_ABSOLUTE`: Fetch a rowset starting at the result set row number *irow*. `SQL_FETCH_RELATIVE`: Fetch a rowset starting at the row that is *irow* rows beyond the first row of the *present* rowset. Use 0 to refresh the rowset as is. `SQL_FETCH_PRIOR`: Fetch the rowset immediately above the current one.

Variable	Description
	SQL_FETCH_NEXT: Fetch the rowset immediately below the current one. SQL_FETCH_FIRST: Fetch the first rowset in the result set. SQL_FETCH_LAST: Fetch the last rowset in the result set. This counts rows from the bottom rather than the top. For example, if you have a 15-row result set and your rowset size is 10, this returns rows 6 through 15. Also, if you have a 7-row result set and your rowset size is 15, it will return all 7 available rows. SQL_FETCH_BOOKMARK: Fetch a rowset beginning at a bookmark. Bookmarks are explained later in this section. In this case, *irow* is the bookmark value for the desired starting row
irow	Relevant only for the SQL_FETCH_ABSOLUTE, SQL_FETCH_RELATIVE, and SQL_FETCH_BOOKMARK fetch types. It's used as described in the entries on those fetch types, earlier in this table
pcrow	An output parameter that returns the number of rows fetched by the function. This may be less than the number of rows that were supposed to be fetched according to the SQL_ROWSET_SIZE statement option, if fewer rows were available
rgfRowStatus	A pointer to a pre-prepared array that will contain status values for each of the rows fetched into the rowset. This supports keyset-driven cursors by informing the application of any changes to each row since the last time it was fetched. Depending on the context, you may want your application to scan this array after every SQLExtendedFetch() call to find out if any changes will affect the user's access to the data. The following status values may be returned for a given row: SQL_ROW_SUCCESS: No changes have been made to the row since it was fetched. SQL_ROW_DELETED: The row has been deleted, and can therefore not be accessed any longer. SQL_ROW_UPDATED: One or more columns in the row have been updated, and the application may need to make some sort of change in a display control as a result. SQL_ROW_ADDED: This is a new row, which didn't exist the last time you did a fetch. SQL_ROW_ERROR: The row could not be fetched, for whatever reason.

(continues)

Variable	Description
	SQL_ROW_NOROW: Any extra spaces at the end of the status array will be set this way. Some ODBC drivers are incapable of determining row status changes. If this is the case, the status information is irrelevant to your application. You can save a little time by skipping the array scan if your driver doesn't support this.

Note

Some drivers may not support all the above fFetchType values. See the section on SQLGetInfo()—"Checking Your Driver's Support for Cursors"—later in this chapter, which explains how to find out which ones a given driver supports.

The return code of SQLExtendedFetch() is one of the following values:

retcode	Description
SQL_SUCCESS	All column data was obtained correctly
SQL_SUCCESS_WITH_INFO	Some expected data was fetched, but the driver sends a warning message. For example, this code is returned if data had to be truncated due to a mismatch between the data received and the column binding. Or, some of the rows were not fetched correctly
SQL_NO_DATA_FOUND	You have gone past the end of the result set. This would result from executing SQLExtendedFetch() with an fFetchType of SQL_FETCH_LAST and then again with an fFetchType of SQL_FETCH_NEXT
SQL_STILL_EXECUTING	Returned if running in asynchronous mode. Check again in a moment
SQL_ERROR	There's a problem; check your column bindings and syntax and try again
SQL_INVALID_HANDLE	The statement handle was unusable. Check your syntax

> **Note**
>
> `SQLFetch()` and `SQLExtendedFetch()` are mutually exclusive: you can't call them on the same result set. The extended fetch has different internals (structures and positioning information) and once a statement is being accessed by one, you can't use the other because the internals would not be correct.

Depending on how you want your application to access the rows in the result set, you may wish to make use of *bookmarks*. A bookmark is a unique identifier for a row that's generated by ODBC for the application to use. As far as the application is concerned, the bookmark doesn't mean anything in particular—it's just a 32-bit value that can be used with `SQLExtendedFetch()` to go to a particular row. It may actually be the row's key in the keyset. If the key is character-based or otherwise too large to fit in a 32-bit value, ODBC will map a 32-bit bookmark meta-value to the real key value.

Bookmarks can be treated as a column in a result set—specifically, column 0. If you call `SQLBindCol()` with an `icol` value of 0, a column full of bookmarks will be created which can then be retrieved by `SQLExtendedFetch()`. (For more information about binding columns with `SQLBindCol()`, see Chapter 12, "Setting Parameters with Prepared Statements.") This can be convenient if the application uses them frequently for many of the rows in the result set, but it definitely adds to processing and memory overhead. `SQLFetch()` won't recognize column 0 and can't be used for this purpose.

There are two other ways to get a bookmark for the current row in a result set, both of which work even if you choose not to bind column 0. You can call `SQLGetStmtOption()` with the `fOption` `SQL_GET_BOOKMARK` (described under "Getting Cursor Statement Options," later in this chapter). Or, you can call `SQLGetData()` with an `icol` value of 0.

If you won't be using bookmarks at all, it may save resources or processing overhead to turn them off. This is discussed in the "`SQL_USE_BOOKMARKS`" section, later in this chapter.

> **Note**
>
> Bookmarks don't work at all with ODBC 1.0 drivers, because the bookmark concept didn't exist at the time ODBC 1.0 was created.

Positioned Updates and Deletes

Positioned updates and deletes are simply UPDATE and DELETE statements that make use of cursors to make changes to rows in the current result set. Two special pieces of SQL syntax are used to make positioned update and delete operations possible:

- SELECT FOR UPDATE

- WHERE CURRENT OF

The following subsections talk about the appropriate order and usage of this special syntax.

SELECT FOR UPDATE

As discussed earlier, any SQL SELECT command executed through a statement will return a result set with an associated cursor. No changes are required for read-only operations like a call to SQLExtendedFetch() to populate a read-only front-end control. But in order to use a cursor to simplify UPDATE and DELETE statements, you need to use a special SELECT syntax in the statement that brings over the result set: SELECT FOR UPDATE.

Essentially, if you tack the clause FOR UPDATE onto a SELECT command, this tells the ODBC driver that you'll be using the result set for more than just read-only purposes.

WHERE CURRENT OF

A unique syntax is used for the WHERE clause of a positioned update or delete statement: WHERE CURRENT OF.

To update column values in a given row within a result set, first position the cursor attached to the SELECT statement that generated the result set on the target row. Then prepare a new statement, *taking care to associate the same cursor name with the new statement*. (This was the exception alluded to earlier in the "Associating Result Sets with Cursors" section.) The two statements must be on the same database connection.

Here's an example of a positioned UPDATE SQL statement:

```
UPDATE mytable
  SET column1 = 'New Value 1',
      column2 = 'New Value 2'
  WHERE CURRENT OF mycursor
```

This command will change the `column1` and `column2` values in the row to which `mycursor` is pointing in its associated result set. That's pretty effortless when you consider that the alternative is to keep track of the primary key of each row and issue a statement like this instead:

```
UPDATE mytable
  SET column1 = 'New Value 1',
      column2 = 'New Value 2'
  WHERE primarykey = 321
```

Positioned `DELETE` statements are performed in a similar fashion. Allocate a second statement on the same connection, associate the same cursor, and from the new statement, execute a command like the following:

```
DELETE FROM mytable
  WHERE CURRENT OF mycursor
```

When a positioned `DELETE` or `UPDATE` is executed with success, the status information for the affected row is updated in the `rgfRowStatus` array maintained by `SQLExtendedFetch()`. The status is set to one of the values explained earlier in the entry on the `rgfRowStatus` parameter, in the "Fetching Multiple Rows" section. Under certain circumstances, however, ODBC can do some confusing things during this part of the process.

Even though to the application programmer it appears that positioned updates and deletes are as simple as applying the `WHERE CURRENT OF` clause, the data source still needs a normal `WHERE` clause to work with. No data sources— or virtually none—actually understand that special syntax, and in any case, ODBC doesn't send the `WHERE CURRENT OF` clause to the data source. Behind the scenes, the ODBC cursor library builds a real `WHERE` clause that describes the row that's being updated based on the data in the bound columns. The statement actually issued by ODBC to the driver is called a *searched statement*. ODBC uses keys to determine the uniqueness of the rows in the result set.

Can you see a potential problem here? Well, one does exist: uniqueness. The rule of entity integrity (as discussed in Chapter 2, "The Relational Database Model") indicates that each row in a table must be unique, and you'd think that would extend to result sets retrieved from such tables. But remember that the cursor library only deals with *bound* columns in a result set. If your application is negligent and doesn't `SELECT` *and* bind all of the columns in the primary key for each table involved in the result set selection statement, there's a fair chance that eventually you'll run into a situation where the fetched values in all bound columns are the same across two or more rows. While some data sources, like Gupta SQLBase, can cope with this situation properly, others will be confused and multiple rows will be affected.

If this scenario does present itself, ODBC can deal with it if it has to, but not especially gracefully. If the searched statement issued to perform a positioned UPDATE or DELETE operation actually affected more than one row, the results aren't necessarily what you'd expect. First of all, the rgfRowStatus information for the row that's pointed to by the cursor is updated—that much is normal. However, the rgfRowStatus information is not updated for any *additional* rows also affected by the statement. SQLExecute() or SQLExecDirect() will return SQL_SUCCESS_WITH_INFO, and the resulting SQLSTATE (01S04) will indicate that more than one row was affected. Then you can use SQLRowCount() (described in Chapter 11, "Queries and Result Sets") to find how many rows were really changed.

You can choose to handle this possibility through your error-handling routine, but the best way to handle the uniqueness problem is to plan for it, and avoid it completely. This isn't so hard to do. Again, simply make sure that when you retrieve a result set, you retrieve *and* bind all columns that comprise the primary key. If the result set is the result of a join, that goes for all columns in the primary keys of all tables involved in the join.

Like most potential pitfalls, this situation is best handled at the lowest level. It's bad form to design tables with multiple-column primary keys in the first place: the primary key should really always be a single column, upon which uniqueness is ensured. This can be accomplished through an automatic key generation function in a trigger or procedure (if the data source supports it) coupled with a unique index, or at least by generating unique keys at the application level. Besides simplifying the uniqueness question, the obvious fact that single-column primary keys allow you to retrieve only a single column instead of several will reduce the cache space used by your result set, and almost certainly improve performance throughout the system.

Positioned Operations with *SQLSetPos()*

Earlier, in the "Setting the Cursor Position" section, you took a look at SQLSetPos()'s ability to position the cursor on a particular row. Now, let's look into its other capabilities in the context of positioned operations:

- Specifying SQL_UPDATE as SQLSetPos()'s fOption value will update the row in the database that corresponds to the row specified in irow. If you prefer to do it this way, you can manually change the data in the column buffer (SQLBindCol()'s rgbValue) and then use SQLSetPos() to perform the update.

- Similarly, passing `fOption` as `SQL_DELETE` will delete the corresponding row in the database.

- The `SQL_ADD` `fOption` allows you to insert a new row into the database. Depending on your driver, this new row may or may not also be added to the result set. To make this possible, you need to either overwrite a set of column buffers (`rgbValues`) or to allocate an extra instance of column buffers to accommodate it. Basically, you place the data you want inserted into the appropriate buffers, and call `SQLSetPos()` with `SQL_ADD`. Keep in mind that this implies that all required (non-nullable) columns must be bound and you must provide a value for each.

  This is sort of an awkward way to insert a row, and an INSERT statement is generally an easier way to go.

> **Note**
>
> Various macros are available in SQLEXT.H to make `SQLSetPos()` simpler to use. For details, refer to the SDK's API Reference Help File.

Checking Your Driver's Support for Cursors

If your application is designed to work with a specific ODBC driver, you'll certainly learn in advance from the driver's documentation what level of cursor support it offers. However, since you'll usually be writing to a generic driver standard in order to maximize interoperability, you may need to learn about the driver during execution of the application. This information can be used to determine whether you need to disable cursor-related operations in drivers that don't support a certain level of functionality, or, to switch between the different levels of cursor support that you've built into your application.

`SQLGetInfo()` is the function that's used to find out about your driver's cursor control capabilities. There are 12 `fInfoType` values that relate explicitly to cursors, and these are:

- `SQL_CURSOR_COMMIT_BEHAVIOR`

- `SQL_CURSOR_ROLLBACK_BEHAVIOR`

- SQL_BOOKMARK_PERSISTENCE

- SQL_FETCH_DIRECTION

- SQL_LOCK_TYPES

- SQL_MAX_CURSOR_NAME_LEN

- SQL_POS_OPERATIONS

- SQL_POSITIONED_STATEMENTS

- SQL_ROW_UPDATES

- SQL_SCROLL_CONCURRENCY

- SQL_SCROLL_OPTIONS

- SQL_STATIC_SENSITIVITY

> **Note**
>
> The SQLGetInfo() function is discussed in more detail in Chapter 8, "The ODBC Statement: An Introduction."

SQL_CURSOR_COMMIT_BEHAVIOR

This info type tells you what effect a transaction commit operation will have on open cursors. Behavior is data source-dependent and you must be prepared for any of the following possibilities, returned as a 16-bit integer:

Value	Description
SQL_CB_DELETE	Cursors will be closed and prepared statements will be "unprepared." You can't re-execute a prepared statement unless you prepare it again with SQLPrepare()
SQL_CB_CLOSE	Cursors will be closed, but prepared statements will be left alone for reuse
SQL_CB_PRESERVE	Cursors will be left alone by the commit operation. You can fetch more data using the same cursor. To rerun the prepared statement, simply close the cursor and run SQLExecute() again

> **Note**
>
> For information on transactions and the SQLTransact() function, refer to Chapter 10, "Inserting, Updating, and Deleting Rows."

SQL_CURSOR_ROLLBACK_BEHAVIOR

Very similar to SQL_CURSOR_COMMIT_BEHAVIOR, this info type tells you how a transaction rollback will deal with cursors that are open at the time. Here are the possible 16-bit result values:

Value	Description
SQL_CB_DELETE	Cursors will be closed and prepared statements will be "unprepared." You can't re-execute a prepared statement unless you prepare it again with SQLPrepare()
SQL_CB_CLOSE	Cursors will be closed, but prepared statements will be left alone for reuse
SQL_CB_PRESERVE	Cursors will be left alone by the commit operation. You can fetch more data using the same cursor. To rerun the prepared statement, simply close the cursor and run SQLExecute() again

Keep in mind that a driver won't necessarily show the same behavior for commit operations as it will for rollback operations, so you'll need to check both to be sure.

SQL_BOOKMARK_PERSISTENCE

Bookmarks are fairly resilient and may be preserved through a variety of circumstances, depending on the data source. This fInfoType returns a 32-bit bitmask, to which various values can be compared to check support. Here are the possibilities:

Value	Description
SQL_BP_CLOSE	Bookmarks remain the same even after the cursor has been closed through the SQL_CLOSE option of SQLFreeStmt(). This means that once you know the bookmark for a row, you can use it for quite awhile, at least on the same statement

(continues)

Value	Description
SQL_BP_DELETE	Bookmarks are valid even after their associated rows have been deleted
SQL_BP_DROP	Bookmarks remain the same even after the associated statement has been completely freed
SQL_BP_SCROLL	If a driver supports bookmarks at all, this bit will be set. It indicates that bookmarks persist after each SQLExtendedFetch() call. Essentially this tells you whether the driver supports bookmarks at all
SQL_BP_TRANSACTION	Bookmarks persist after a transaction commit or rollback, assuming your data source supports transactions in the first place
SQL_BP_UPDATE	Bookmarks are valid after any kind of update to the associated rows
SQL_BP_OTHER_HSTMT	This indicates that bookmarks are the same between statement handles

SQL_FETCH_DIRECTION

This fInfoType lets you know which fetch directions the driver will allow you to specify for the fFetchType argument to SQLExtendedFetch(). A 32-bit bitmask is returned, to which you can compare the following values:

- SQL_FD_FETCH_NEXT

- SQL_FD_FETCH_FIRST

- SQL_FD_FETCH_LAST

- SQL_FD_FETCH_PRIOR

- SQL_FD_FETCH_ABSOLUTE

- SQL_FD_FETCH_RELATIVE

- SQL_FD_FETCH_BOOKMARK

These are explained in detail in the "Fetching Multiple Rows" section, earlier in this chapter.

SQL_LOCK_TYPES

This info type returns a 32-bit bitmask that indicates the lock types supported by the driver for the fLock argument to the SQLSetPos() function. You can compare the following values to the bitmask to find out the lock types supported:

- SQL_LCK_NO_CHANGE

- SQL_LCK_EXCLUSIVE

- SQL_LCK_UNLOCK

These lock types were discussed earlier in the section on "Setting the Cursor Position."

SQL_MAX_CURSOR_NAME_LEN

This function simply indicates the maximum length of a cursor name for the current data source. This is a 16-bit integer value. Zero indicates that the maximum length is either unlimited or unknown.

SQL_POS_OPERATIONS

This info type returns a 32-bit bitmask indicating the different positioned operations that the data source supports with its implementation of the SQLSetPos() function. Compare the resultant bitmask with the following values to find out whether a given operation is supported:

Value	Description
SQL_POS_POSITION	SQLSetPos() can position the cursor without doing anything else
SQL_POS_REFRESH	SQLSetPos() can position the cursor and refresh the new current row
SQL_POS_UPDATE	SQLSetPos() can perform positioned updates
SQL_POS_DELETE	SQLSetPos() can perform positioned deletes
SQL_POS_ADD	SQLSetPos() can add rows to the database table under the result set

SQL_POSITIONED_STATEMENTS

This info type comes back as a 32-bit bitmask. Compare it to the following values to find out which types of positioned operations are supported by the data source:

Value	Description
SQL_PS_DELETE	Positioned deletes can be performed
SQL_PS_UPDATE	Positioned updates can be done
SQL_PS_SELECT_FOR_UPDATE	The SELECT FOR UPDATE syntax is supported by the driver to facilitate positioned operations. If this bit is not set, positioned operations almost certainly can't be done at all

SQL_ROW_UPDATES

This info type is a character string, Y or N. Y indicates that keyset-driven or mixed cursors are able to recognize when changes have been made to the rows in the rowset.

SQL_SCROLL_CONCURRENCY

The SQL_SCROLL_CONCURRENCY fInfoType lets you find out the types of concurrency locking that your driver supports. rgbInfoValue is returned as a 32-bit bitmask, to which you can compare the following values to check for their support:

- SQL_SCCO_READ_ONLY

- SQL_SCCO_LOCK

- SQL_SCCO_OPT_ROWVER

- SQL_SCCO_OPT_VALUES

The results will determine which of the same types you can specify in the SQL_CONCURRENCY option under SQLSetStmtOption(), discussed in the "Setting Cursor Statement Options" section, later in this chapter. See that section for information on the potential settings listed above.

SQL_SCROLL_OPTIONS

This fInfoType reports on the types of cursors supported by the driver. The value returned is a 32-bit bitmask to which the following values should be compared:

Value	Description
SQL_SO_STATIC	Static cursors are supported
SQL_SO_KEYSET_DRIVEN	Keyset-driven cursors are supported

Value	Description
SQL_SO_DYNAMIC	Dynamic cursors are supported
SQL_SO_MIXED	Mixed cursors are supported
SQL_SO_FORWARD_ONLY	Whichever of the above cursor types are supported, only forward scrolling is possible

SQL_STATIC_SENSITIVITY

When an application makes changes to rows in a static or keyset-driver cursor, the changes may or may not be reflected in the cursor, depending on the driver's implementation. This info type return a 32-bit bitmask to which the following values can be compared:

Value	Description
SQL_SS_ADDITIONS	Rows added to the database are incorporated into the cursor
SQL_SS_DELETIONS	Rows deleted from the database are removed from the cursor, and no holes are left
SQL_SS_UPDATES	Rows updated in the database are also updated in the cursor

This has nothing to do with whether other users' changes to the database are reflected in the cursor. The cursor type and implementation determines how those are handled.

Connection and Statement Options

Selected connection and statement options have been discussed in Chapters 8, "The ODBC Statement: An Introduction," and 10, "Inserting, Updating, and Deleting Rows," where the particular options mentioned were relevant to the topics at hand. Now let's take a look at options that pertain to cursors.

Setting Cursor Connection Options

There are two SQLSetConnectOption() options that involve cursors. They are:

- SQL_ODBC_CURSORS

- SQL_AUTOCOMMIT

The ODBC API

> **Note**
>
> The function prototype and a complete description of the SQLSetConnectOption()
> function are given in Chapter 6, "Creating the ODBC Environment and Connection,"
> in the section "Using `SQLSetConnectOption()`."

SQL_ODBC_CURSORS

The `SQL_ODBC_CURSORS` connection option is the key to controlling your
application's usage of the cursor library versus possibly improved versions of
cursor functions that reside in the data-source-specific driver. There are three
possible `vParam` choices for this connection option:

Value	Description
SQL_CUR_USE_DRIVER	Tells ODBC to use the driver's cursor functions. This is the default setting if you don't change the SQL_ODBC_CURSORS option, presumably because it grants your application's access to the most advanced set of capabilities available at any given time. However, because it can lead your application to rely on functionality beyond the norm, this is the option *least* conducive to interoperability between drivers
SQL_CUR_USE_ODBC	Tells ODBC to use the cursor library, and nothing but the cursor library, even if the driver supports special or improved cursor functionality. This may be desirable for those programmers who are willing to sacrifice advanced driver-specific cursor support to ensure maximum driver interoperability
SQL_CUR_USE_IF_NEEDED	Use the cursor library for functionality that it supports, but go to the driver for additional capabilities

SQL_AUTOCOMMIT

This connection option is relevant to cursors in the sense that autocommit
mode can cause your cursors to be automatically closed by the system at
inappropriate times. In autocommit mode, each statement is considered a
complete transaction, committed immediately after execution.

Some drivers go so far as to close all cursors for all statements under a connection when a statement is committed. In autocommit mode, this means
that all cursors are closed for a whole connection whenever `SQLExecute()` or
`SQLExecDirect()` is called on any of the connection's statements. To avoid

unexpected behavior of this type, you may have to open multiple connections to the data source, which of course is resource-costly.

> **Note**
>
> "Checking Your Driver's Support for Cursors," earlier in this chapter, shows you how to find a given driver's behavior in this regard.

Getting Cursor Connection Options

You can obtain the current value for either of the connection options detailed in the previous section, or for that matter, for any other connection option, by calling the SQLGetConnectOption() function. SQLGetConnectOption() is described in detail, and its prototype is given, in Chapter 6, "Creating the ODBC Environment and Connection," in the "Using SQLGetConnectOption()" section.

Setting Cursor Statement Options

There are quite a few statement options that pertain to cursors. These are placed at the statement level rather than the connection level because you may wish to set them differently for different hstmts under the same connection. The following values for the fOption parameter are used to set cursor-related statement options:

- SQL_CONCURRENCY
- SQL_CURSOR_TYPE
- SQL_KEYSET_SIZE
- SQL_RETRIEVE_DATA
- SQL_ROWSET_SIZE
- SQL_SIMULATE_CURSOR
- SQL_USE_BOOKMARKS

> **Note**
>
> The function prototype and a complete description of the SQLSetStmtOption() function are given in Chapter 8, "The ODBC Statement: An Introduction."

> **Note**
>
> The ODBC 1.0 SQLSetScrollOption() function is made obsolete by the
> SQL_CONCURRENCY, SQL_CURSOR_TYPE, SQL_KEYSET_SIZE, and SQL_ROWSET_SIZE
> statement options. However, for backward compatibility, SQLSetScrollOption() is
> still supported in ODBC 2.0.

SQL_CONCURRENCY

The SQL_CONCURRENCY fOption lets you specify the type of locking to be used by
a particular cursor. This is relevant to positioned update and delete statements. Possible vParam values are:

Value	Description
SQL_CONCUR_READ_ONLY	Specifies that the cursor should be read-only— unusable for positioned update and delete operations. This avoids the overhead associated with locking controls
SQL_CONCUR_LOCK	Allows ODBC to choose the locking method. The lowest locking level that will allow updates is used
SQL_CONCUR_ROWVER	Assuming it's capable, the driver uses an optimistic concurrency control method and compares row versions based on a data-source-specific unique row identifier
SQL_CONCUR_VALUES	The driver uses an optimistic concurrency control method and compares values

Many ODBC drivers support only some of the listed vParam values. You can
call SQLGetInfo() with an hInfoType of SQL_SCROLL_CONCURRENCY to find out
which are supported by a given driver. If you call SQLSetStmtOption() with a
concurrency type that the driver doesn't support, it will choose the closest
concurrency type that it does support and return SQL_SUCCESS_WITH_INFO.

SQL_CURSOR_TYPE

This option specifies the type of cursor that should be associated with the
statement. Here are the possible vParam values:

Value	Description
SQL_CURSOR_STATIC	The cursor should be static
SQL_CURSOR_KEYSET_DRIVEN	The cursor should be keyset-driven or mixed
SQL_CURSOR_DYNAMIC	The cursor should be fully dynamic
SQL_CURSOR_FORWARD_ONLY	Whichever cursor type you're using, the cursor should only scroll in a forward direction

The cursor types that can be set are dependent on the cursor types supported by the driver. You can call SQLGetInfo() with an fInfoType of SQL_SCROLL_OPTIONS to find out which cursor types are possible.

SQL_KEYSET_SIZE

This fOption is used to specify the keyset size. It must be a 32-bit integer. This is used to facilitate mixed cursors. The value given must be either zero, greater than, or equal to the rowset size. Zero (the default) indicates a keyset-driver cursor.

SQL_RETRIEVE_DATA

This fOption lets the application specify whether SQLExtendedFetch() should retrieve data as it moves the cursor to a given row, or whether it should simply position the cursor. The possible vParam values are:

- SQL_RD_ON (the default)

- SQL_RD_OFF

Typically you'll want to leave this on, because SQLExtendedFetch() is usually used to retrieve data. You can change it to off if you just want to find out whether a particular row exists, or if you want to get a row's bookmark.

SQL_ROWSET_SIZE

Use this fOption to specify the number of rows that SQLExtendedFetch() should retrieve at a time. vParam is a 32-bit value in this case. If you don't call SQLSetStmtOption() with fOption of SQL_ROWSET_SIZE, the default rowset size is 1—making SQLExtendedFetch() little more valuable than SQLFetch().

If you're calling SQLExtendedFetch() to populate some sort of scrolling grid or list control in your application, it often makes sense to set the rowset size to the number of rows displayed by the control at one time. That way you don't have to manage rowsets within your application, and if the control supports it, you can use the cursor refresh features to keep your data up to date whenever the user moves up or down in the result set.

SQL_SIMULATE_CURSOR

If a unique key column is not included as one of the bound columns in the result set, there's a chance that the rows may not be unique. This is a problem for positioned operations, because more than one row may be affected by a positioned operation. This fOption helps determine ODBC's behavior in the (easily preventable) event that a row turns out not to be unique. Here are the possible vParam values and their meanings:

Value	Description
SQL_SC_NON_UNIQUE	Positioned UPDATE or DELETE operations may affect more than one row. It's the application's responsibility to prevent this from happening or deal with it if it does. This is the best option to set if you just take care to always bind all primary key columns in a result set, because it requires less overhead work by the ODBC driver
SQL_SC_TRY_UNIQUE	The driver takes care to avoid affecting multiple rows with a positioned operation, but if it fails to avoid this it will still do so anyway, and will return SQL_SUCCESS_WITH_INFO from the SQLExecDirect() or SQLPrepare() function
SQL_SC_UNIQUE	SQLPrepare() or SQLExecDirect() will fail with an SQL_ERROR code if the statement would affect more than one row

Some drivers don't support all these options. If you attempt to set one that it doesn't support, the driver will make a substitution for you and return SQL_SUCCESS_WITH_INFO.

SQL_USE_BOOKMARKS

You can tell ODBC whether to use bookmarks in its cursor operations by setting this fOption. Possible vParam values:

Value	Description
SQL_UB_OFF	Don't use bookmarks. This may save overhead if you won't be requiring them
SQL_UB_ON	Use bookmarks

Note that bookmarks will only be used on cursors opened *after* this option is set to SQL_UB_ON. Any cursors that were opened previously will not use them.

Getting Cursor Statement Options

The current value for any of the statement options, whether described in the previous sections or not, can be obtained with the SQLGetStmtOption() function. In addition, this function can be used to obtain the following types of information that *can't* be set using SQLSetStmtOption(). Both are returned as 32-bit values:

Value	Description
SQL_GET_BOOKMARK	pvParam is returned as the bookmark for the row pointed to by the cursor
SQL_ROW_NUMBER	pvParam is returned as the row number of the row pointed to by the cursor. Rows are numbered from 0 and are reckoned from the beginning of the entire result set, independent of the *rowset* size

> **Note**
>
> SQLGetStmtOption() is explained, and its prototype is provided, in Chapter 8, "The ODBC Statement: An Introduction."

Releasing a Cursor

A cursor is released with a call to the SQLFreeStmt() function. Specifying SQL_CLOSE in the fOption argument will close the cursor and release the result set. Specifying SQL_DROP for fOption will free the entire statement and as a result, the cursor will disappear as well.

> **Note**
>
> For more information about the SQLFreeStmt() function, refer to Chapter 8, "The ODBC Statement: An Introduction."

From Here...

This chapter concludes our discussion of conceptual ODBC topics. The other parts of the book are more specific in their discussions:

■ Part II, *Visual C++*, is intended for the Microsoft Visual C++ developer, and explains how to use VC++'s special ODBC support features to make your job easier.

■ Part III, *Visual Basic*, is for the Microsoft Visual Basic programmer, describing that environment's ODBC data access capabilities in detail.

■ Part IV, *Advanced Topics*, encompasses a variety of topics for the advanced ODBC practitioner, showing you how to get the most out of ODBC and incorporate it into the strategic direction you want your business to take.

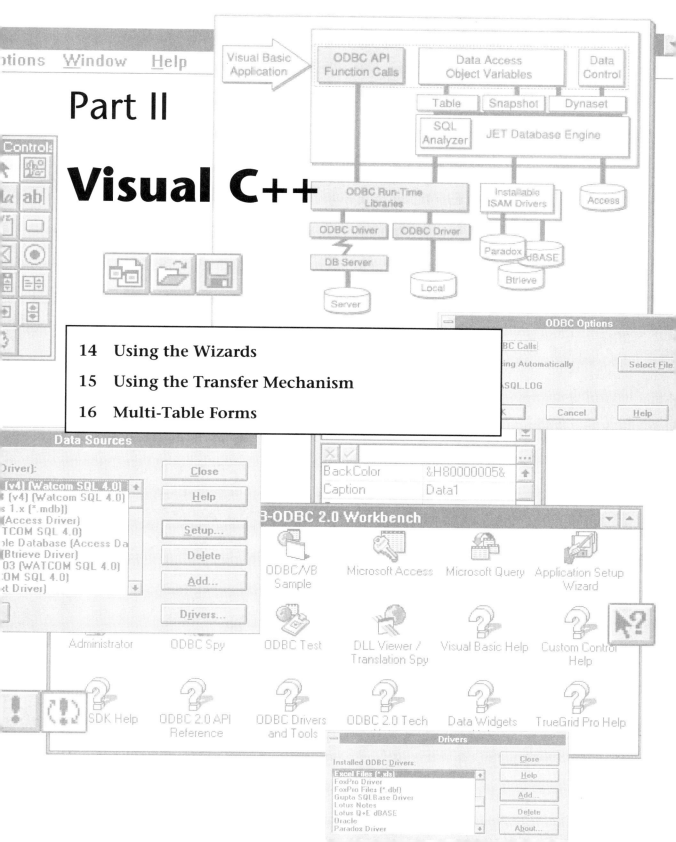

Part II

Visual C++

14   **Using the Wizards**

15   **Using the Transfer Mechanism**

16   **Multi-Table Forms**

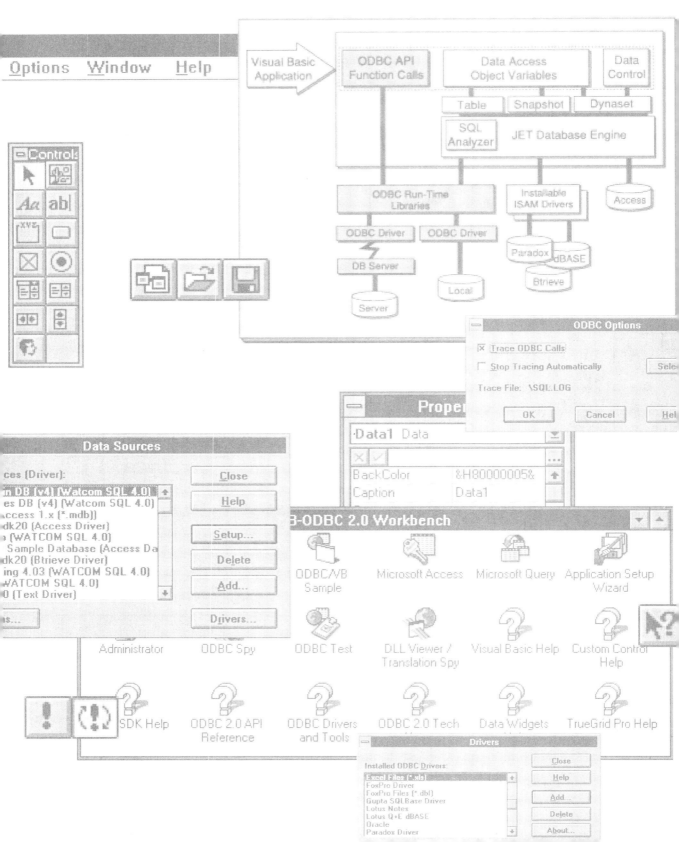

Options **Window** **Help**

Visual Basic Application

ODBC API Function Calls

Data Access Object Variables

Data Control

Table Snapshot Dynaset

SQL Analyzer JET Database Engine

ODBC Run-Time Libraries

Installable ISAM Drivers

Access

ODBC Driver OODBC Driver

DB Server

Paradox dBASE

Btrieve

Local

Server

ODBC Options

☒ Trace ODBC Calls

☐ Stop Tracing Automatically   Sele

Trace File: \SQL.LOG

OK   Cancel   Hel

Proper

·Data1 Data

BackColor   &H80000005&

Caption   Data1

Data Sources

ces (Driver):

n DB [v4] [Watcom SQL 4.0]
es DB [v4] (Watcom SQL 4.0)
access 1.x (*.mdb))
dk20 (Access Driver)
(WATCOM SQL 4.0)
Sample Database (Access Da
dk20 (Btrieve Driver)
ing 4.03 (WATCOM SQL 4.0)
WATCOM SQL 4.0)
0 (Text Driver)

s...

Close
Help
Setup...
Delete
Add...
Drivers...

B-ODBC 2.0 Workbench

ODBC/VB Sample

Microsoft Access

Microsoft Query

Application Setup Wizard

Administrator

ODBC Spy

ODBC Test

DLL Viewer / Translation Spy

Visual Basic Help

Custom Control Help

SDK Help

ODBC 2.0 API Reference

ODBC Drivers and Tools

ODBC 2.0 Tech

Data Widgets

TrueGrid Pro Help

Drivers

Installed ODBC Drivers:

Excel Files (*.xls)
FoxPro Driver
FoxPro Files (*.dbf)
Gupta SQLBase Driver
Lotus Notes
Lotus Q+E dBASE
Oracle
Paradox Driver

Close
Help
Add...
Delete
About...

Chapter 14

Using the Wizards

Many people have avoided using ODBC in their programs because of the level of difficulty involved in learning and using the ODBC Software Development Kit. The complexity of the commands and the technical nature of Microsoft's documentation present even an experienced programmer with a very steep learning curve.

Microsoft Visual C++ 2.0 makes the task of learning and using ODBC much easier. The Visual C++ development environment includes several code generators, called Wizards, that do much of the work for you. These Wizards were introduced in version 1.5 and have been enhanced for version 2.0.

The code generated by the Wizards uses the database extensions of the Microsoft Foundation Classes (MFC), a class library that comes with Visual C++. The database extensions to MFC encapsulate the details of using ODBC datasources, enabling you to concentrate more on what the program needs to do and less on how to do it. The MFC library included with Visual C++ 2.0 has enhancements that support the 32-bit ODBC drivers for Windows NT and Windows 95.

These three Visual C++ chapters show you how to use Visual C++ and MFC to build applications that work with ODBC databases. This chapter gets you started using the Wizards to build an "instant" application. Chapter 15, "Using the Transfer Mechanism," introduces a number of the class functions to add and delete records and navigate through a table. Chapter 16, "Multi-Table Forms," shows how to use the classes to work with multiple tables and databases.

The three chapters follow phases in the construction of a single application. If you want to pick up with an example later in the chapters, you should start with the code from the previous example. The example code for each stage is available on the CD-ROM included with this book. You also need to be sure that the ODBC data sources are set up as indicated later in this chapter. The programs use the data sources to access ODBC databases.

The Application

A good way to learn a new programming skill such as ODBC is to work through code already written by someone else. To this end, the chapters in this part of the book are based on a series of examples that illustrate how ODBC can be used to create a seemingly real-world example. Here is the scenario for these examples; you should find it more interesting than the traditional library book or order processing system.

Merger mania has struck the corporate world, and the nation's railroads are no exception. Three major railroads, the Pennsylvania (PRR), the New York Central (NYC), and the Reading (RDG), have merged to form the new Consolidated Railroad. This new railway system will dominate transportation in the northeastern United States.

This corporate merger has lead to a consolidation of the Information Systems departments of the three former companies. Information about the railroad cars transported by the railroad has been centralized in the Consolidated Railroad database. This includes information about the individual cars and about the many other companies that own the railroad cars that are transported by the railroad.

However, for technical (and political) reasons, the databases that store information about each train, including its name, origin, destination, and other things, must remain in separate databases at each former railroad headquarters. Furthermore, each railroad stores different information about each train and it is likely that other railroads merged with in the future will have still other information.

You have the task of developing the Railroad Management System, a Microsoft Windows application to integrate these separate databases. You must write the program using Visual C++ and ODBC to interface to the different databases. The examples in these three chapters will give you a headstart. After that, you are on your own.

Note

See? Isn't this an interesting scenario? In reality, these companies did merge to form the railroad commonly known as Conrail. However, these mergers occured in the 1960s and 1970s, long before either Windows or ODBC were an issue.

Figure 14.1 shows the general configuration of the databases in the system.

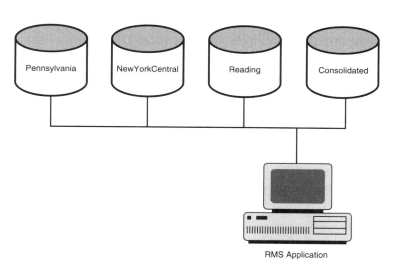

Railroad Management System

Fig. 14.1
An overview of the railroad system database.

RMS Application

The main Consolidated Railroad database—the Central database—includes tables with information that is common to all the railroads. These tables are:

■ *Cars*—information about individual railroad cars including each car's owner, type, and capacity

■ *Owners*—information about the companies that own the railroad cars

Each of the individual railroad databases—the `Railroad` databases—include the same tables, but each contains information for that particular railroad. The tables in these databases are:

■ *Trains*—general information about each train including the train's name, number, origin, and destination

■ *TrainInfo*—supplemental information about each train; the columns in this table are different for each railroad

The entity relationship diagram in figure 14.2 shows the fields in these tables and how the tables are related.

Fig. 14.2
Entity relationship
diagram for the
Railroad database.

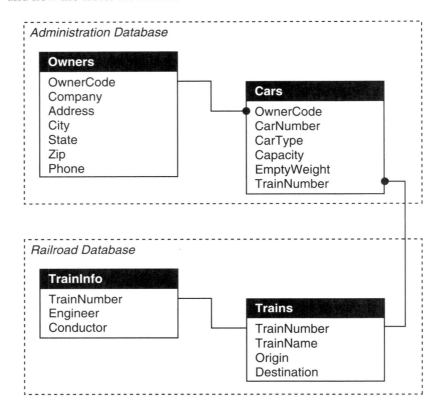

The Central database has an additional table—the RailroadDatabase table. This table contains the names of the railroads that make up the Consolidated Railroad and the name of the data sources for the railroads' tables. Figure 14.3 shows the definition of this table.

Fig. 14.3
The definition
of the
RailroadDatabase
table.

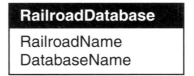

Getting Connected

Before you can use the Wizards in Microsoft Visual C++ to create an ODBC application, you need to set up data sources for the databases you want to use. Visual C++ itself is an ODBC application; AppWizard and ClassWizard use ODBC to get information about your tables that they need to know to generate code. Therefore, the data sources have to be set up so that they can access the information.

The first database you will use is the Consolidated Railroad database. Following are the steps to create a data source for that table, assuming that you already installed ODBC and the Microsoft Access ODBC drivers. If you have not installed these items, you must stop and install them now. The instructions on installing ODBC and the Microsoft Access ODBC drivers are presented in Chapter 5, "Data Sources and Drivers."

1. Copy the databases from the CD-ROM onto your hard drive. The databases for the examples are located in the directory \SAMPLES\VISUALC\DATABASE on the CD-ROM, and the Consolidated Railroad database is called CONRAIL.MDB. Copy this file to an appropriate location on your hard drive. The other databases in this directory are for later examples. You may want to copy these files to your hard drive as well.

2. Start the data source manager. From the Windows Program Manager, open the Control Panel. The data source manager is listed as ODBC; double-click this item to open it.

3. Select the ODBC driver. Choose Add from the Data Sources dialog to see a list of installed ODBC drivers. The sample database included for this section is a Microsoft Access database. If you have successfully installed the Microsoft Access ODBC driver, it will be shown in this list. Select this driver and then choose OK.

4. Finish setting up the data source. Complete the ODBC Microsoft Access Setup dialog box as shown in figure 14.4. Set the data source name to Consolidated and enter the full path for the location where you have installed the database. You should not need to set any other options for the Microsoft Access ODBC driver.

II

Visual C++

Fig. 14.4
Setting up the
data source.

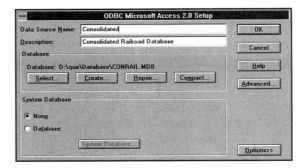

You now have set up the Consolidated Railroad data source. If you plan to follow all the later examples in these chapters, you will have to copy the other databases from this directory on the CD-ROM and set up data sources for them as well. For consistency, you should use the following data source names for the other databases:

Database	Data Source Name
PRR.MDB	Pennsylvania
NYC.MDB	NewYorkCentral
RDG.MDB	Reading

Note

Whenever you install an application that uses ODBC, you must make sure ODBC and the appropriate drivers are installed. At the time of this writing, the REDIST subdirectories on the Microsoft Visual C++ 2.0 installation CD-ROM include the files needed to install ODBC and a number of drivers.

Using AppWizard

Microsoft's AppWizard makes the creation of a basic Windows database application remarkably, and perhaps deceptively, simple. By clicking a few buttons and selecting several items from list boxes, you can cause AppWizard to create all of the source code needed to compile a basic ODBC database browser for an existing table. While the resulting program is unlikely to meet all of your needs and probably won't be the next hot selling software product, it does provide an excellent jumping-off point for creating a complete application.

The following example shows the steps to follow to create a first application with AppWizard. This application is a database viewer that you can use to browse through the Cars table in the Consolidated database. Again, to use these examples, you must have the databases from the CD-ROM set up as data sources on your computer.

The instructions in this example only detail the steps that directly relate to creating an ODBC application. For the other fields, the instructions simply state the values you should use. If you want additional information on AppWizard options, consult the Books Online included with Visual C++ or another book such as Que's *Using Visual C++ 2.0*.

Start AppWizard

In Visual C++ 2.0, AppWizard is activated by creating a new project. Select File, New to open the New dialog box. Select Project from the list and choose OK to begin creating a new project. In the New Project dialog box, enter the information as shown in figure 14.5. Give the appropriate path where you want AppWizard to build the program code and be sure that MFC AppWizard is selected as the project type. Then select Create to cause AppWizard to generate the application.

Fig. 14.5
New Project dialog box.

Complete Step 1

This application is to be a simple Single Document Interface application, so select Single Document for the application type. Choose U.S. English as the resource language. Then select Next to proceed to the next step.

Complete Step 2

Select the type of database support you require. Step 2 requires you to answer two questions:

- What type of database support do you want?

- If you have ODBC support, which data source do you want to use?

Figure 14.6 shows these two options.

Fig. 14.6
Database support
selection.

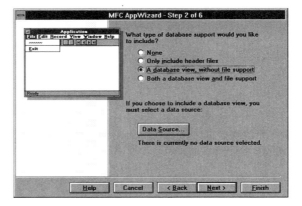

The first question, What kind of database support would you like to include? has the following four choices:

- None—Omits all database support from your application. Select this option if you do not intend to make use of the Visual C++ database features.

- Only include header files—Includes the header files that define the base database classes but does not create database classes or views for specific tables. Select this option if you plan to construct database classes later either manually or through ClassWizard.

- A database view, without file support—Creates a database class and a view class for the table you specify. Select this option if you want to create an application with basic database viewing features. This is the option you want for this application.

- Both a database view and file support—The same as the previous choice, but it also adds the standard file operations (new, open, and so forth). Select this choice if you want to provide both database and file support in your application.

This application is primarily a database viewer and needs ODBC support but not file support. Therefore, you should choose the third option. After you have chosen this option, the Data Source button is available.

Select Data Source and Table

To create a code to access your database table, AppWizard needs to know which columns exist in the table and each column's type. AppWizard learns this information by making requests through ODBC to determine the table definition.

To select the table to use, select Data Source. Choose the Consolidated data source from the list and then select OK. With the Microsoft Access ODBC driver, you are immediately presented with a list of tables in the database. However, with some other database drivers, you may need to give a user name and password to connect to the data source, such as the SQL Server Login shown in figure 14.7. Choose RailCar as the table to use and then se-lect OK. After AppWizard has retrieved the column information for the table, select Next to proceed to the next step.

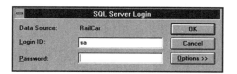

Fig. 14.7
SQL Server Data source selection.

Complete Step 3

This step enables you to include OLE support in your application. OLE is beyond the scope of this book and is not be used in this sample application. Select None for the OLE compound document support and No for OLE automa-tion. Then, select Next to go to the next step.

Complete Step 4

This step gives you options on the look of your base application. Options you can configure are:

- A dockable toolbar

- An initial status bar

- Printing and print preview support

- Context-sensitive help

- The use 3D controls

- The number of files allowed in the Most Recently Used (MRU) file list

- Advanced topics such as the names of the classes to be generated by the Wizard

The default values for this step are acceptable. Select Next to go to the next page.

Complete Step 5

This step enables you to select some compiler and linker options. The default values for this step are fine, so just select Next to go to the next (and final) step.

Complete Step 6

This step enables you to review and change the classes that AppWizard is about to generate. Most of the classes are the same ones that AppWizard generates for any application. The exceptions for a database application are the CRecordset and the CRecordView. These classes are the basis of the MFC's support of ODBC and are explained a little later in this chapter. For now, select Finish to accept these final options.

Approve Project Information

This final dialog summarizes the information AppWizard is to use to generate the program, giving you a final opportunity to change your mind. If anything is not correct, select Cancel to go back to the previous steps and make any needed changes. Otherwise, select OK and AppWizard will generate the program. A Creating Application dialog box shows you each file AppWizard makes.

Build and Run the Application

Select Project, Build to compile and link your new program. Once the compiler has finished, select Project, Execute to start the program. As the program starts, you may need to complete a dialog box to log into your database. Once the program is running, it should appear similar to the one in figure 14.8.

You now have a functional database application. You can scroll through the records in the database either by selecting the arrow-shaped control buttons on the toolbar or by selected items from the Record menu.

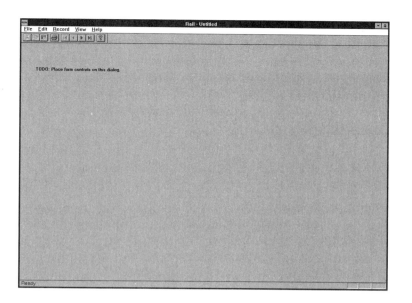

Fig. 14.8
Results of the first
build of RAIL.EXE.

> **Caution**
>
> Unfortunately, the interface between Visual C++ and some ODBC drivers is not per-
> fect. For example, in at least one case, the GetDefaultSQL function created by the
> Wizards returns the full table name with the table owner's name (such as
> "DBA.Table"). However, when the program is run, the record set cannot find the
> table to open it. Removing the "DBA." makes the program work. This is one specific
> case, but other similar problems may appear.

Setting Up a View

As nice as it is, the application created by AppWizard is significantly lacking
in one area: output. Although you can scroll through all of the records in the
table, you cannot see any of the values stored there. AppWizard has created a
class to access the records in the table and has created a form view to display
information; however, it has not placed controls in the view to display the
retrieved information. You must add these controls yourself to see the information from the tables.

Adding the controls to the view involves two parts: creating the controls in
the resource editor and then linking the controls to the records from the
database using ClassWizard. The following sections show how to create a
view for the Car table.

Open *IDD_RAIL_FORM*

Open the IDD_RAIL_FORM dialog in the resource editor. Double-click rail.rc in the project window to open a list of items in your resource file. Then double-click IDD_RAIL_FORM from the list of dialogs. The resource editor shows the current view of the dialog.

Lay Out the New Dialog

You may want to turn on the grid to help you align the controls. Remove the static TODO control from the dialog and add new static text controls and edit boxes to create a dialog which looks similar to the one shown in figure 14.9.

Fig. 14.9
Rail View dialog box.

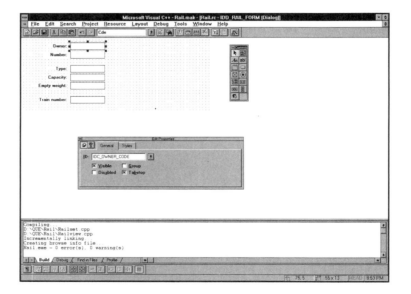

Give the edit boxes the following ids:

Edit Box	Id
Owner	IDC_OWNER_CODE
Number	IDC_CAR_NUMBER
Type	IDC_CAR_TYPE
Capacity	IDC_CAPACITY

Edit Box	Id
Empty weight	IDC_EMPTY_WEIGHT
Train number	IDC_TRAIN_NUMBER

Open ClassWizard

Select Project, ClassWizard to open ClassWizard. Choose CRailView as the Class Name and select Member variables. ClassWizard presents a list of the control ids that you just created in the resource editor.

Link Controls to Fields

Link the controls to the fields in the database. Choose the IDC_CAPACITY control id and then select Add Variables to open the Add Member Variables dialog box. In this dialog box, select *m_pSet->m_Capacity* as the Member Variable Name. The Category and Variable Type fields are completed automatically, so just select OK to return to the main ClassWizard dialog box.

The *m_pSet* variable is a variable in the CRailView. It is a pointer to a record set object that holds the current record from the database. The *m_Capacity* variable is the member variable in that object that receives the value of the Capacity column when a record is retrieved from the database. By assigning the *m_Capacity* variable to the IDC_CAPACITY control, the value for the car number field will be automatically updated and displayed as you retrieve each record from the database.

Repeat this process to bind the other controls to the appropriate member variables. Use the following Member Variable Names:

Control	Variable
IDC_CAR_NUMBER	*m_pSet->m_CarNumber*
IDC_CAR_TYPE	*m_pSet->m_CarType*
IDC_EMPTY_WEIGHT	*m_pSet->m_EmptyWeight*
IDC_OWNER_CODE	*m_pSet->m_OwnerCode*
IDC_TRAIN_NUMBER	*m_pSet->m_TrainNumber*

When you are done, select OK to close ClassWizard.

II

Visual C++

Build and Run the Application

Select Project, Build to rebuild your application with the changes you have just made. Once the compiler is finished, select Project, Execute to start your program. The updated program should look like the one shown in figure 14.10.

Fig. 14.10
Second build of
RAIL.EXE.

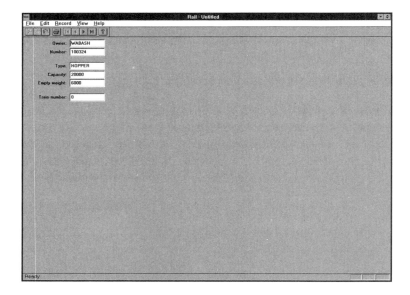

The RAIL program now enables you to scroll through the records in the Car table in the Consolidated database. The VCR-like buttons on the toolbar enable you to move to the first, previous, next, and last records in the database. The buttons automatically are dimmed when you cannot move farther in the database.

An exception to this feature is the first time you reach the last record in the database. When the application runs, it starts retrieving records, beginning with the first one. However, because it has not retrieved all of the records, it does not know which is the last one. Only once the application has attempted to read past the last record does it know which record is the last one and can then gray out the next and last buttons. This process makes sense as there may be a very large number of records in the database and scanning to the last record each time would be very time consuming.

How the Application Works

Much of the RAIL program is like any other program created by AppWizard. The two exceptions are the classes CRailSet (defined in railset.h and railset.cpp) and CRailView (defined in railview.h and railview.cpp).

The class CRailSet is derived from the MFC class CRecordset. The CRecordset class is the key to the support of ODBC by the Microsoft Foundation Classes. It encapsulates the functions needed to work with an ODBC table, including selecting, scrolling, adding, updating, and deleting records.

You generally need to create a new class derived from CRecordset for each database table that you want to use. The derived class should add a member variable of the appropriate type for each column of the table that you want to access. Listing 14.1 shows the declaration of the CRailSet class.

Listing 14.1   Declaration of *CRailSet*

```
class CRailSet : public CRecordset
{
public:
    CRailSet(CDatabase* pDatabase = NULL);
    DECLARE_DYNAMIC(CRailSet)

// Field/Param Data
    //{{AFX_FIELD(CRailSet, CRecordset)
    CString  m_OwnerCode;
    long     m_CarNumber;
    CString  m_CarType;
    long     m_Capacity;
    long     m_EmptyWeight;
    long     m_TrainNumber;
    //}}AFX_FIELD

// Overrides
    // ClassWizard generated virtual function overrides
    //{{AFX_VIRTUAL(CRailSet)
    public:
    virtual CString GetDefaultConnect();           // Default
                                                    // connection
                                                    // string
    virtual CString GetDefaultSQL();               // default SQL
                                                    // for Recordset
    virtual void DoFieldExchange(CFieldExchange* pFX);  // RFX support
    //}}AFX_VIRTUAL
```

(continues)

II

Visual C++

Listing 14.1 Continued

```
// Implementation
#ifdef _DEBUG
    virtual void AssertValid() const;
    virtual void Dump(CDumpContext& dc) const;
#endif

};
```

The member variables for CRailSet are listed in the AFX_FIELD block. You saw these variables when you bound the fields in the view in the previous steps. The Wizards put the AFX_FIELD comments in the code and used them to find the member variables when you make changes to the classes. In general, you should not edit the code within the AFX_... blocks. If you do make changes, you may not be able to use the Wizards to maintain the classes in the future.

The Wizards also generated a number of virtual member functions. The GetDefaultConnect function returns a string with the name of the record set's data source preceded by the characters ODBC; to identify it as an ODBC data source. This is included for future enhancements to the MFC classes. The current version only supports ODBC data sources.

```
CString CRailSet::GetDefaultConnect()
{
    return _T("ODBC;DSN=Consolidated;");
}
```

The GetDefaultSQL function returns the name of the table in the data source to be used by the record set.

```
CString CRailSet::GetDefaultSQL()
{
    return _T("Cars");
}
```

The DoFieldExchange function is used to transfer data between the member variables in the record set and the ODBC driver. When records are retrieved, the RFX_... functions transfer data from the database columns into member variables. When records are added or updated, these same functions transfer data back into the database. These functions work in much the same way as the data exchange functions used in CDialog classes.

```
void CRailSet::DoFieldExchange(CFieldExchange* pFX)
{
```

```
//{{AFX_FIELD_MAP(CRailSet)
pFX->SetFieldType(CFieldExchange::outputColumn);
RFX_Text(pFX, "OwnerCode", m_OwnerCode);
RFX_Long(pFX, "CarNumber", m_CarNumber);
RFX_Text(pFX, "CarType", m_CarType);
RFX_Long(pFX, "Capacity", m_Capacity);
RFX_Long(pFX, "EmptyWeight", m_EmptyWeight);
RFX_Long(pFX, "TrainNumber", m_TrainNumber);
//}}AFX_FIELD_MAP
}
```

The remaining virtual functions in CRailSet are diagnostic functions and simply call the base CRecordset functions. You can add to these functions to provide additional diagnostic information.

```
void CRailSet::AssertValid() const
{
    CRecordset::AssertValid();
}

void CRailSet::Dump(CDumpContext& dc) const
{
    CRecordset::Dump(dc);
}
```

The CRailView class is derived from CRecordView and includes a pointer to a CRailSet object. The CRailSet object itself is a member variable of the CRailDoc document class.

The CRecordView class in turn is derived from the CFormView class. CRecordView adds only four new functions (besides the constructor) to CFormView. The function OnGetRecordset returns a pointer to the CRecordset-based object for the view (for example, CRailView returns a pointer to the CRailSet object). The functions IsOnFirstRecord and IsOnLastRecord return when the current record is the first or last record, respectively, in the recordset. These functions are used to gray out the movement controls on the toolbar. The function OnMove is called when one of the movement controls is selected to go to another record.

When the program runs, it creates a CRailDoc and a CRailView and then calls the OnInitialUpdate function of the CRailView. OnInitialUpdate gets a pointer to the CRailSet object from the CRailDoc and calls CFormView::OnInitialUpdate. This function opens the CRailSet object and copies the values from the first record into the member variables of the CRailSet. The base OnInitialUpdate then calls the virtual DoDataExchange function in the CRailView to place the values on-screen.

II

Visual C++

Each time you move to another record, the CRecordView::OnMove function is called. OnMove causes the CRailSet to move to the appropriate record and to copy the values into its member variables. It then calls the DoDataExchange to update the display.

Creating Recordsets with ClassWizard

You have seen how CRecordset and CRecordView classes created by AppWizard can provide a great deal of functionality when working with a single table. However, most significant programs need to access more than just one table. You need to be able to create CRecordSet-based classes outside of AppWizard. While you certainly could build a CRecordset by hand, it is much easier to allow ClassWizard to create this code for you.

To see how to use ClassWizard to create a CRecordset class, create a class for another table in the Consolidated Railroad database: Owner. The Owner table holds information about the companies that own the railroad cars in your system. This table is referenced by the foreign key OwnerCode in the Car table. In Chapter 16, "Multi-Table Forms," you will use the classes you have created for the tables to perform a join on the two tables.

Because the Owner table is in the same database as the RailCar table, you do not need to set up a new data source for this class. However, if the table were in a different database, you would need to set up the ODBC data source before starting ClassWizard.

The following steps show how to use the ClassWizard to create a CRecordset class for the Owner table.

1. Open ClassWizard. Select Project, ClassWizard in Visual C++ to open the MFC Class Wizard dialog box.

2. Add a new CCarOwner class. Select Add Class to open the Add Class dialog box. To create the new COwnerSet class based on the CRecordset class, complete the dialog box as shown in figure 14.11. Then select Create Class.

Fig. 14.11
Add Class dialog box.

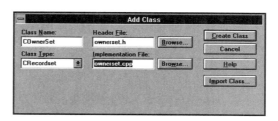

3. Select the data source and table for the class. This step is basically the same step that you performed with AppWizard. Select Consolidated as your data source and complete any dialog boxes needed to log into the database. From the list of tables in the database, select Owners.

After ClassWizard has retrieved the necessary information about the columns in the table, you are returned to the main ClassWizard dialog. Selecting Member Variables shows how ClassWizard has bound the columns in the database table to member variables in the newly created class. The Member Variables dialog box is shown in figure 14.12.

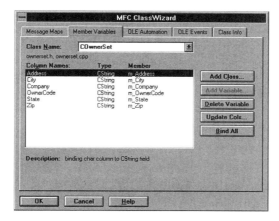

Fig. 14.12
Member variables for the COwnerSet class.

Listings 14.2 and 14.3 show the code generated by ClassWizard for the new COwnerSet class.

**Listing 14.2 Declaration for *COwnerSet (ownerset.h)*

```
// ownerset.h : header file
//


/////////////////////////////////////////////////////////////////////
// COwnerSet recordset

class COwnerSet : public CRecordset
{
public:
    COwnerSet(CDatabase* pDatabase = NULL);
    DECLARE_DYNAMIC(COwnerSet)
```

(continues)

II

Visual C++

Listing 14.2   Continued

```
// Field/Param Data
    //{{AFX_FIELD(COwnerSet, CRecordset)
    CString     m_OwnerCode;
    CString     m_Company;
    CString     m_Address;
    CString     m_City;
    CString     m_State;
    CString     m_Zip;
    //}}AFX_FIELD


// Overrides
    // ClassWizard generated virtual function overrides
    //{{AFX_VIRTUAL(COwnerSet)
    public:
    virtual CString GetDefaultConnect();                // Default
                                                        // connection
                                                        // string
    virtual CString GetDefaultSQL();                    // Default SQL
                                                        // for Recordset
    virtual void DoFieldExchange(CFieldExchange* pFX);  // RFX support
    //}}AFX_VIRTUAL

// Implementation
#ifdef _DEBUG
    virtual void AssertValid() const;
    virtual void Dump(CDumpContext& dc) const;
#endif
};
```

Listing 14.3   Code for *COwnerSet* (ownerset.cpp)

```
// ownerset.cpp : implementation file
//

#include "stdafx.h"
#include "Rail.h"
#include "ownerset.h"

#ifdef _DEBUG
#undef THIS_FILE
static char BASED_CODE THIS_FILE[] = __FILE__;
#endif


/////////////////////////////////////////////////////////////////////
// COwnerSet
```

```
IMPLEMENT_DYNAMIC(COwnerSet, CRecordset)

COwnerSet::COwnerSet(CDatabase* pdb)
    : CRecordset(pdb)
{
    //{{AFX_FIELD_INIT(COwnerSet)
    m_OwnerCode = _T("");
    m_Company = _T("");
    m_Address = _T("");
    m_City = _T("");
    m_State = _T("");
    m_Zip = _T("");
    m_nFields = 6;
    //}}AFX_FIELD_INIT
}


CString COwnerSet::GetDefaultConnect()
{
    return _T("ODBC;DSN=Consolidated;");
}

CString COwnerSet::GetDefaultSQL()
{
    return _T("Owners");
}

void COwnerSet::DoFieldExchange(CFieldExchange* pFX)
{
    //{{AFX_FIELD_MAP(COwnerSet)
    pFX->SetFieldType(CFieldExchange::outputColumn);
    RFX_Text(pFX, "OwnerCode", m_OwnerCode);
    RFX_Text(pFX, "Company", m_Company);
    RFX_Text(pFX, "Address", m_Address);
    RFX_Text(pFX, "City", m_City);
    RFX_Text(pFX, "State", m_State);
    RFX_Text(pFX, "Zip", m_Zip);
    //}}AFX_FIELD_MAP
}

/////////////////////////////////////////////////////////////////////////
// COwnerSet diagnostics

#ifdef _DEBUG
void COwnerSet::AssertValid() const
{
    CRecordset::AssertValid();
}

void COwnerSet::Dump(CDumpContext& dc) const
{
    CRecordset::Dump(dc);
}
#endif //_DEBUG
```

II

Visual C++

That is all that is required to build a new CRecordset-derived class with ClassWizard. As you can see from the dialog box and the generated code shown previously, ClassWizard automatically created member variables for all of the columns in the Owner table with types specified in the original table. It also created methods to exchange data between these variables and the table. In the next chapter, you will see how to use this new class in your own code.

From Here...

This chapter showed how you can use AppWizard to quickly generate basic database applications and ClassWizard to build additional CRecordset-derived classes. For additional information, you may want to see the following:

- Chapter 11, "Queries and Result Sets," goes into detail about result sets and how to retrieve information from them.

- Chapter 13, "The Cursor Library and Positioned Operations," talks about the use of cursors to control the current row in a result set.

Chapter 15

Using the Transfer Mechanism

AppWizard and ClassWizard have performed the tedious, repetitive tasks of building the application framework and other basic classes. However, the creative work of combining these pieces with other code to create a finished application still remains as an exercise for the programmer. In a database application, this work would likely involve scrolling through records in a table, sorting and searching the records, and updates and deletions to the table. This chapter explores how to perform all of these tasks using the CRecordset class.

Navigating Through a Table

Before your application can use a CRecordset object to move through the table, you must call the CRecordset member function Open method to open the table. In the previous chapter's examples, the CDocument and CRecordView classes took care of opening the record sets. In more complex programs, you likely will need to open the record set yourself, either because it is not directly tied to a CRecordView or because you need more control over how the record set is opened.

The CRecordset::Open function is defined as:

```
BOOL Open(UINT nOpenType = snapshot, LPCSTR lpszSql = NULL, DWORD
dwOptions = none)—Open a record set and retrieve the first record
```

The parameters for the CRecordset::Open function enable you to specify which types of operations you will perform on the table, allowing the database engine to perform those operations more efficiently.

The first parameter, *nOpenType*, concerns scrolling and updates. Scrolling refers to moving through the records in a table. Not surprisingly, moving to subsequent records is called forward scrolling and moving to previous records is called backward scrolling. The permitted values for *nOpenType* are:

CRecordset::dynaset—allows forward and backward scrolling. Updates made to the record set are immediately available.

CRecordset::snapshot—allows forward and backward scrolling. Updates made to the record set are not visible until the record set is reopened or requeried. This is the default value.

CRecordset::forwardOnly—allows only forward scrolling. The record set is read-only.

The second parameter, *lpszSql*, is a string containing an SQL statement to be executed when the table is opened. The default value for this parameter is NULL.

The third parameter, *dwOptions*, specifies what types of updates are allowed through the record set. The permitted values for *dwOptions* are:

CRecordset::none—adds, updates, and deletes are allowed. This is the default value.

CRecordset::appendOnly—only adds are allowed. Updates and deletes are not permitted.

CRecordset::readOnly—the record set is read-only. No adds, updates, or deletes are allowed.

A basic call to Open using the default parameters opens the table as an updatable snapshot. This is sufficient to enable you to retrieve the records in the table.

```
CRailSet rsCars;
rsCars.Open();
```

Once the CRecordset is open, the application is free to scroll through the records in the table. The CRecordset class provides five methods for scrolling through a table. These functions are:

- void MoveFirst()—scroll to the first record in the record set

- void MoveLast()—scroll to the last record in the record set

- ■ void MovePrev()—scroll backward one record in the record set

- ■ void MoveNext()—scroll forward one record in the record set

- ■ void Move(long lRows)—if lRows is positive, scroll forward *lRows* records in the record set; otherwise, scroll backward *lRows*

The original definition of SQL only provided for forward scrolling. Therefore, some database engines, and thus some ODBC drivers, only allow forward scrolling. If you attempt to move to a previous record using an ODBC driver that only supports forward scrolling, the CRecordset will throw an exception (see "Exception Handling" later in this chapter).

After each move operation, the member variables in your class that are bound to columns in the table are automatically updated with the values from the new record. To access values from the record, you can read from these bound member variables as you would from any other variable.

While scrolling through the records in a table, it is helpful to know when you have reached the beginning or end of the table. This information is provided through the methods IsBOF and IsEOF.

> BOOL IsBOF()—returns a nonzero value if you have scrolled before the first record in the record set or if the record set has no records; otherwise returns 0

> BOOL IsEOF()—returns a nonzero value if you have scrolled past the last record in the record set or if the record set has no records; otherwise returns 0

As you can see, either of these methods can be used to determine if a record set you have just opened contains any records at all as both return TRUE if there are no records available.

When you are finished with a record set, you must call the Close function to close it. This function closes any open files and frees any resources that were used during the operation. It takes no parameters.

> void Close()—close a record set

Visual C++

II

Following is a quick example of these basic record set functions that count the records in a record set.

```
long CountRecords() {

CRailSet rsCars;
long count;

 rsCars.Open();              // Open the table

 count = 0;
 while (!rsCars.IsEOF()) {   // Until we reach the last record
        count++;             // update the count and
        rsCars.MoveNext();   // move to the next record
        }

 rsCars.Close();             // Close the record set

 return count;
}
```

The following sections use these record set functions to present the user with a list of trains and enable the user to select one. The steps are modifications to the program from the previous chapter. To follow these steps, you must either complete the examples from the previous chapter or load the code for the last example from the CD-ROM.

Set Up the Pennsylvania Railroad Data Source

The previous chapter explained how to set up the data sources. If you have not already set up the Pennsylvania data source, you should do so at this time.

Create a *CTrainSet* Class

These modifications use a different table so you need to create a new record set class called CTrainSet. Open ClassWizard and select Create Class. Complete the Add Class dialog box as shown in figure 15.1 and select Create Class to begin building the new class.

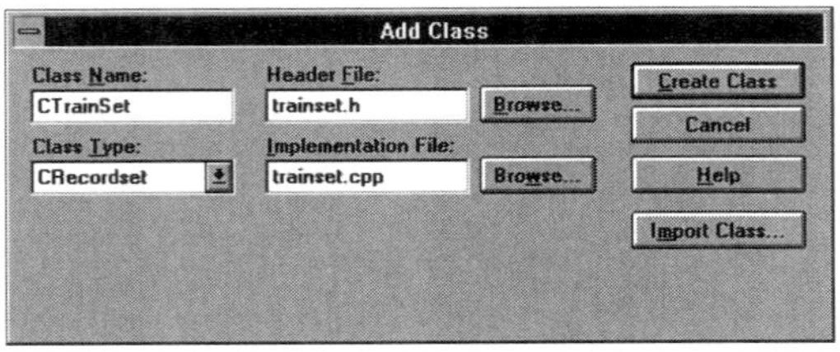

Fig. 15.1
CTrainSet class information in the Add Class dialog box.

Select Pennsylvania as the data source and Trains as the table name. After ClassWizard has built the new class, select OK to close ClassWizard.

Add New Menu Items

Open railcar.rc, expand the list of menus, and open the menu IDR_MAINFRAME. Create a new top-level menu item called &Trains after the Records menu. Create a new item in the Trains menu called &Select. Close the IDR_MAINFRAME menu.

Create a Train List Dialog

Still in railcar.rc, create a new dialog called IDD_TRAIN_LIST with the caption "Select Train." Add a list box with the id IDC_TRAIN_LIST and a button called "All" with the id IDC_ALL. Use the default style for the list box. The finished dialog should look like figure 15.2. Close the dialog and then close railcar.rc.

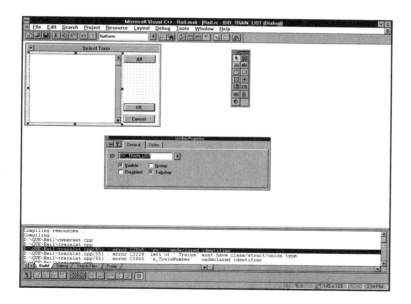

Fig. 15.2
IDD_TRAIN_LIST as it appears in the List Box Properties dialog box.

Create a *CTrainListDialog* Class

Select Project, Class Wizard to open ClassWizard and from there select Add Class. Fill in the Add Class dialog box as shown in figure 15.3, and then select Create Class to build the dialog class.

Fig. 15.3
Information
about the
CTrainListDialog
class.

Add a List Variable

Add a list variable to the dialog. While still working with the
CTrainListDialog class in ClassWizard, add a *m_TrainList* member
variable bound to the IDC_TRAIN_LIST control ID.

Add Member Variables

Add member variables to the dialog. Edit trainlst.h to add the following
member variables to the CTrainListDialog class.

```
CDWordArray          m_TrainNumbers;
LONG                 m_SelectedNumber;
```

The m_TrainNumbers array will store the train numbers in the order they are in
the list. The *m_SelectedNumber* variable will return the number of the selected
train or -1 if all trains are selected.

Add Code to Load the List

Add code to load the list in CTrainListDialog when the dialog is initialized.
Use ClassWizard to add a message handler for WM_INITDIALOG to the
CTrainListDialog class. Edit the code for OnInitDialog to be as follows:

```
BOOL CTrainListDialog::OnInitDialog()
{
    CDialog::OnInitDialog();

    CTrainSet rsTrains;
    char line[80];
    int pos;

    rsTrains.Open();

    m_TrainNumbers.RemoveAll();

    while (!rsTrains.IsEOF()) {

        wsprintf(line, "%s", (const char*) rsTrains.m_TrainName);
        pos = m_TrainList.AddString(line);
        m_TrainNumbers.InsertAt(pos, rsTrains.m_TrainNumber);

        rsTrains.MoveNext();
    }
```

```
    rsTrains.Close();

    return TRUE;  // return TRUE unless you set the focus to a control
                  // EXCEPTION: OCX Property Pages should return FALSE
}
```

The *m_TrainNumbers* array provides an easy way to get the train number for
the item selected in the list box. Each train number is inserted into the
m_TrainNumbers array at the position returned by AddString. The list box is
sorted, so the entries in the list box will end up in alphabetical order by train
name. The train numbers in the array are in the same order as the entries in
the list box so the train number for an item can be selected from the
m_TrainNumber array by index.

You need to add the following to the end of the list of includes in
trainlst.cpp so that the dialog has access to the CTrainSet class.

```
    #include "trainset.h"
```

Add Message Handlers

Add message handlers for the buttons in CTrainListDialog. Use ClassWizard
to add handlers for the BN_CLICKED message for these object IDs: IDC_ALL, IDOK,
and IDCANCEL. Modify the message handler code generated by ClassWizard as
follows:

```
    void CTrainListDialog::OnAll()
    {
        m_SelectedNumber = -1;

        CDialog::OnOK();
    }

    void CTrainListDialog::OnOK()
    {
        int pos = m_TrainList.GetCurSel();

        if (pos < 0) {
            AfxMessageBox("Nothing is selected.");
            return;
            }

        m_SelectedNumber = m_TrainNumbers[pos];

        CDialog::OnOK();
    }

    void CTrainListDialog::OnCancel()
    {
        CDialog::OnCancel();
    }
```

Add a Command Handler

Add a command handler for the Trains, Select menu item. Open ClassWizard and select the CRailDoc class. Select object ID ID_TRAINS_SELECT and message COMMAND and click Add Function to create a message handler. Click Edit Code to go to the message handler function and then change it to appear as follows:

```
void CRailDoc::OnTrainsSelect()
{
    CTrainListDialog dialog;

    if (dialog.DoModal() == IDCANCEL)
        return;

    if (dialog.m_SelectedNumber >= 0) {

        char msg[80];
        wsprintf(msg, "Selected train number %ld",
                dialog.m_SelectedNumber);
        AfxMessageBox(msg);
        }
    else
        AfxMessageBox("Selected ALL");
}
```

You need to add the following to the end of the list of includes in raildoc.cpp to give the message handler access to CTrainListDialog.

```
#include "trainlst.h"
```

Build and Run the Program

Select Project, Build to rebuild the application. Once the project has been rebuilt, select Project, Execute to run the program. Figure 15.4 shows the updated program in action.

In the new program, selecting Trains, Select brings up the Select Train dialog box with the list of train names. You can select one of the trains and then click OK or you can just click All. Once you have made your selection, a message box appears to verify what you have pressed. In the next section, you will use this information to select particular records to view.

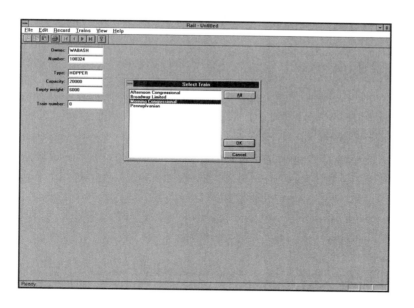

Fig. 15.4
The updated
program showing
the train list.

Filtering and Sorting the Records

When you open a record set, by default you select all of the records in the
table and the records are returned in the order in which they are stored in the
database. The ODBC drivers provide methods to select only the records that
meet certain requirements (filtering) and to return those records in a particular order. The CRecordset class provides easy access to these facilities using
statements like those used in SQL.

If you were using an SQL program instead of ODBC and wanted to retrieve
particular records from the Cars table, you would execute a statement like the
following:

```
SELECT * FROM Cars WHERE TrainNumber = 42
```

This statement retrieves all of the records in the RailCar table for which the
TrainNumber equals 42. To do the same thing using a CRecordset class, you
need to specify a string equivalent to SQL's WHERE clause before you open the
record set. To do this, you place the filter in the *m_strFilter* member variable
of CRecordSet.

```
CRailSet rsCars;
rsCars.m_strFilter = "TrainNumber = 42";
rsCars.Open();
```

> **Note**
>
> When specifying the filter for a CRecordset, do not include the word WHERE from the SQL statement. That is, use TrainNumber = 42 rather than WHERE TrainNumber = 42.

The order in which the record set returns records is specified in a fashion similar to filtering. In SQL, if you want to retrieve all of the RailCar records sorted by car number, you would execute the following statement:

```
SELECT * FROM Cars ORDER BY CarNumber
```

To sort records with a record set, place the contents of the ORDER BY clause in the *m_strSort* member variable of the CRecordset class.

```
CRailSet rsCars;
rsCars.m_strSort = "CarNumber";
rsCars.Open();
```

Again, do not include the words ORDER BY in the sort string; only include the remainder of the sort clause.

Once a record set is opened, the filtering and sorting of the records is fixed as you scroll through the records. To change the filtering or sorting, after assigning new values to the m_strFilter and m_strSort variables, you must either open the record set again or call the Requery method. Typically, requerying is much faster than reopening the table.

The following sections modify the ongoing example so that it only shows the cars in the selected train and so that the cars are presented in order by car number.

Add a Member Variable

Add a member variable to the document to store the selected train. Edit raildoc.h and add the member variable *m_SelectedTrain* to the CRailDoc class.

```
long     m_SelectedTrain;
```

Edit the CRailDoc::OnNewDocument function to initialize this variable to -1 (to indicate that all trains are selected).

```
BOOL CRailDoc::OnNewDocument()
{
    if (!CDocument::OnNewDocument())
        return FALSE;
```

```
            m_SelectedTrain = -1;

            return TRUE;
    }
```

Create a Hint

Create a "hint" to indicate that the selected train has changed. Your program will use the view's OnUpdate function to requery the record set and refresh the view when the selected train is changed. However, many events can cause the OnUpdate function to be called; many of these should not requery the record set. By defining and using a hint, you can indicate which OnUpdate calls need to requery.

Edit raildoc.h and add the following line *outside of the class definition*:

```
        const int HINT_NEW_TRAIN = 1;
```

Modify *OnTrainsSelect*

Modify OnTrainsSelect to set *m_SelectedTrain* and update the view. Whenever a new train is selected, the view needs to be updated to reflect the change. Replace the code for this function in raildoc.cpp with the following code.

```
        void CRailDoc::OnTrainsSelect()
        {
            CTrainListDialog dialog;

            if (dialog.DoModal() == IDCANCEL)
                return;

            m_SelectedTrain = dialog.m_SelectedNumber;

            UpdateAllViews(NULL, HINT_NEW_TRAIN);
        }
```

Add an *OnUpdate* Function

Add an OnUpdate function to CRailView to use the train selection. Select Project, Class Wizard to open ClassWizard. Select CRailView as the object ID and OnUpdate as the message and then click Add Function to create the message handler function. Click Edit Code to go to the source code in railview.cpp and change the OnUpdate function as follows:

```
void CRailView::OnUpdate(CView* pSender, LPARAM lHint, CObject* pHint)
{
        char filter[80];

        if (lHint == HINT_NEW_TRAIN) {

            CRailDoc* doc;
```

```
            doc = GetDocument();

            if (doc->m_SelectedTrain >= 0) {

                wsprintf(filter, "TrainNumber=%ld", doc-
                                ➥>m_SelectedTrain);
                m_pSet->m_strFilter = filter;
                }
            else
                m_pSet->m_strFilter.Empty();

            m_pSet->Requery();
            UpdateData(FALSE);
            }

        else
            CRecordView::OnUpdate(pSender, lHint, pHint);
    }
```

Add a Filter to the Record Set

Modify the view's OnInitialUpdate function as follows. The sort filter must be
set before the OnInitialUpdate so that the initial view of the cars is sorted.

```
    void CRailView::OnInitialUpdate()
    {
        m_pSet = &GetDocument()->m_railSet;

        m_pSet->m_strSort = "CarNumber";

        CRecordView::OnInitialUpdate();

    }
```

Build and Run the Program

Select Project, Build to compile and link the application. Once the project has
been rebuilt, select Project, Execute to run the program.

When you run the revised application, it now displays the records sorted by
their car number. If you choose Trains, Select and pick one of the trains, you
will only see the cars that make up that train. If you choose Trains, Select and
then click All, you will again see all of the cars in the database.

Catching Errors with Exceptions

Exception handling is a method for handling error conditions in a C++ program. When an error occurs, a function can generate, or *throw*, an exception.
Program execution immediately goes to the code that the programmer has set
up to handle, or *catch*, the exception. Using exceptions instead of return
codes for error handling tends to make programs cleaner and faster. Programs

using exceptions do not have to include code to check for error conditions at the return from each function and consequently do not have the overhead of that checking when no error has occurred.

Most of the CRecordset member functions use exceptions to report errors. If your program does not include exception handling to catch exceptions thrown by the class, MFC provides default handlers to catch them. However, the default handlers report exceptions in a rather ungraceful manner. In general, you should provide exception handling for any operation that could throw an exception.

Exception handling is a fairly recent addition to the C++ standard. Through version 1.5, Visual C++ has provided exception handling through a number of macros like TRY, CATCH, and END_CATCH. These macros generally work like standard exception handling but they do have some differences. Version 2.0 of Visual C++ includes true exception handling but retains the exception macros for backward compatibility. This chapter uses the true exception handling of version 2.0.

Exception handling consists of two parts: a try block and one or more catch blocks. A function can generate a number of different types of exceptions and your program may include different catch blocks for each type of exception.

The try block begins simply with the reserved word try. This word is followed by the block that includes the code that might cause an exception to be thrown. The try block may contain more than one statement. If the try block does contain several statements and a statement in the block generates an exception, the remaining statements in the block are skipped and execution immediately proceeds to the catch block.

```
try {
    working_function();
    failing_function(); // this function throws an exception
    another_function(); // this function is skipped
    }
```

The catch block begins with the reserved word catch and the definition of the type of exception that is to be handled by this catch block. The block that follows contains the code to be executed if that particular exception occurs. Additional catch blocks handle other types of exceptions.

```
catch (int i) {
    AfxMessageBox("My function threw an int exception");
    }
catch (CAnException* e) {
    AfxMessageBox("My function threw a different exception");
    }
```

The CRecordset class throws three different types of exceptions. These exception types and their causes are:

- CDBException—an error occurred performing a database operation
- CMemoryException—an error occurred trying to allocate memory
- CFileException—an error occurred trying to access a file

The most common of these exceptions is the CDBException. It is thrown by any problem interacting with the ODBC driver. Some common errors that throw a CDBException are: attempting to access a column which does not exist, incorrect syntax in a filter or sort string, or the inability to connect to the database.

Fortunately, the CDBException class includes member variables to help resolve the problem. The member variable *m_nRetCode* contains the code returned from the ODBC driver. The member variable *m_strError* contains a string that describes what caused the error. The member *m_strStateNativeOrigin* contains a string with the values returned by the ODBC SQLError function.

The following code fragment shows how to catch any CDBException exceptions thrown by the Requery method. If an exception is thrown, the error string is reported in a message box.

```
try {
    m_pSet->Requery();
    }
catch (CDBException* e) {
    AfxMessageBox(e->m_strError);
    }
```

With this exception handler in place, if the Requery method throws an exception, the application presents a window like the one shown in figure 15.5.

Fig. 15.5
A message box
reporting an
exception.

Many of the following examples use exception handling to trap and report errors that occur while accessing and updating the database.

Adding and Updating Records

You have seen how the CRecordset transfer mechanism is used to retrieve records from a table. In different modes, you can use this same mechanism to make additions and updates. When you enter add or update mode, a CRecordset object notes in the record set the initial value of the members variables that are bound to columns in the database. When the Update member function is called, the CRecordset automatically posts the additions and changes to the table. This process is simple to use but it does require considerable processing overhead. Direct SQL statements can be significantly more efficient and may be warranted in time-sensitive applications requiring frequent updates and additions. The next chapter discusses how to directly execute SQL statements using the MFC classes.

Before your application can make additions, updates, or deletions, the record set must be opened in a mode that allows updates. The default parameters for CRecordset::Open do open the record set so that updates may be performed. However, if you used other parameters to open the record set, updates may not be permitted. If you are uncertain if a record set allows updates, you can call the class's CanUpdate method. A similar method, CanAppend, reports if new records can be added to the record set.

> BOOL CanUpdate()—returns nonzero if the record set can be updated; otherwise, returns zero

> BOOL CanAppend()—returns nonzero if records can be added to the record set; otherwise, returns zero

Once you have opened the record set for updating, you begin the process of adding a new record with a call to AddNew. When you call AddNew, the CRecordset marks all of the data fields as Null and unchanged. By setting these values and then seeing when fields change, the record set can store Null in the new record for fields that are not set.

After calling AddNew, place the field values for the new record in the corresponding member variables in the CRecordset object. Then call the Update method to cause the new record to be added to the table. For example:

```
dsCar.Open();

if (!dsCar.CanAppend()) {
    dsCar.Close();
    return;
    }
```

```
dsCar.AddNew();

dsCar.m_OwnerCode = "PRR";
dsCar.m_CarNumber = 12345;
dsCar.m_CarType = "OBSERVATION";
dsCar.m_Capacity = 50;
dsCar.m_EmptyWeight = 25000;

if (!dsCar.Update())
    AfxMessageBox("The update did not succeed.");

dsCar.Close();
```

If you have opened the record set as a dynaset, the records you have added are available as soon as you scroll to them. However, if you have opened the record set as a snapshot, the new records do not show up until the record set is reopened or requeried.

An update to an existing record is similar to the addition of a new one. Once you have opened the database to allow for updates, scroll to the record that is to be changed. Call the Edit member function to indicate that the current record is to be changed. Like AddNew, this function marks all of the fields as unchanged.

Make the changes to the record by setting the member variables to their new values. If you want to set a field to be NULL, call the member function SetFieldNull, passing it a pointer to the member variable for the field that is to be NULL.

> **Note**
>
> The C++ value NULL is not the same as a database NULL. If you want to set a field in a record set to the null value, you must use SetFieldNull rather than assign the value NULL to the member variable.

Once the changes are made, call Update to post the changes to the database. If the record set is open as a snapshot, the changes will not show up in the record set until it is reopened or requeried.

```
dsCar.Open();

if (!dsCar.CanUpdate()) {
    dsCar.Close();
    return;
    }

dsCar.MoveLast();
```

```
dsCar.Edit();

dsCar.m_CarNumber = 0;
dsCar.m_CarType = "DOME";
dsCar.SetNull(&(dsCar.m_OwnerCode));

if (!dsCar.Update())
    AfxMessageBox("The update did not succeed.");

dsCar.Close();
```

The sample program already supports edits through the CRecordView class. If you edit the information in one of the fields and then move to another record, the OnMove function automatically writes the changes to the database. The following sections add a new menu item to the Records menu to add car records to the database.

Create an Add Record Menu Item

Open rail.rc and edit the IDR_MAINFRAME menu. To the top of the Records menu, add the menu item "&Add Record" followed by a separator. Save and close rail.rc.

Create Member Variable *m_InAddMode*

Create member variable *m_InAddMode* and initialize it to FALSE. Edit raildoc.h and add the member variable to CRailDoc as shown. This variable is a flag to indicate if you are in add mode.

```
BOOL m_InAddMode;
```

In the constructor CRailDoc::OnTrainsSelect, add the line:

```
m_InAddMode = FALSE;
```

Create a Handler for *ID_RECORD_ADDRECORD*

Create a handler for ID_RECORD_ADDRECORD. Select Project, Class Wizard to open ClassWizard and select CRailDoc as the class name. Select ID_RECORD_ADDRECORD as the object id and COMMAND as the message and then click Add Function to create the message handler. Click Edit Code and complete the function with the following code:

```
void CRailDoc::OnRecordAddrecord()
{
    POSITION pos;
    CRecordView* view;

    pos = GetFirstViewPosition();
    view = (CRecordView*) GetNextView(pos);
```

```
                        if (m_InAddMode)
                            view->OnMove(ID_RECORD_FIRST);

                        m_railSet.AddNew();

                        m_InAddMode = TRUE;

                        view->UpdateData(FALSE);
                    }
```

The first step in this function is to get the view for the document, as this is where some needed information is kept. Then, if the record set is already in add mode, call `OnMove` to write the current record-in-progress to the database. Call `AddNew` to put the record set into add mode, set the add mode flag to true, and then call view's `UpdateData` function to update the on-screen fields with the same empty values that were just placed into the record set by the call to `AddNew`.

Create an *OnMove* Function for *CRailView*

The `OnMove` function inherited from `CRecordView` nearly does the job in that it automatically calls `Update` to write the new record to the table. However, the function still needs to reset your *m_InAddMode* flag to FALSE and requery the table so the new record is returned in the proper order.

Open ClassWizard again, this time going to the `CRailView` class. Select `CRailView` as the object id and `OnMove` as the message. Click Add Function to create the message handler and then Edit Code to edit the new message handler to look like the following:

```
        BOOL CRailView::OnMove(UINT nIDMoveCommand)
        {
            CRailDoc* doc = GetDocument();

            if (doc->m_InAddMode) {

                UpdateData(TRUE);
                try {
                    m_pSet->Update();
                    }
                catch (CDBException* e) {
                    AfxMessageBox("Could not complete an updated.");
                    AfxMessageBox(e->m_strError);
                    }

                m_pSet->Requery();
                UpdateData(FALSE);
```

```
doc->m_InAddMode = FALSE;
return TRUE;
}

return CRecordView::OnMove(nIDMoveCommand);
}
```

Build and Run the Program

Select Project, Build to compile and link the application. Once the project has been rebuilt, select Project, Execute to run the program.

In the new program, when you select Records, Add Record, you are presented with a blank view to complete for the new record. After you enter the new data and scroll to another record, the program adds the new record to the table and then requeries the table so that the records are in the proper order.

Deleting

Deleting records is even easier than adding or updating records. Open the database in a mode that allows updates, scroll to the record to be removed, and call Delete. You do not need to call Update after calling Delete.

```
dsCar.Open();

if (!dsCar.CanUpdate() && dsRailCar.IsDeleted()) {
    dsCar.Close();
    return;
    }

dsCar.MoveLast();

dsCar.Delete();

dsCar.Close();
```

After calling Delete, you should scroll to another record so that the record set references a record that still exists in the database. To check if the current record has been deleted, call IsDeleted. This member function returns TRUE if the current record has been deleted.

BOOL IsDeleted()—returns nonzero if the current record has been deleted; otherwise, returns zero

Adding a delete function is quite easy, as the following sections illustrate.

Create a Delete Record Menu Item

Open `rail.rc` and edit the `IDR_MAINFRAME` menu. In the Record menu, add the item &Delete Record after the Add Record item. Save and close `rail.rc`.

Create a Handler for *ID_RECORD_DELETERECORD*

Select Project, Class Wizard to open ClassWizard and select `CRailDoc` as the class name. Select `ID_RECORD_DELETERECORD` as the object id and `COMMAND` as the message and then click Add Function to create the message handler. Click Edit Code and complete the function with the following code:

```
void CRailDoc::OnRecordDeleterecord()
{
    POSITION pos;
    CRecordView* view;

    pos = GetFirstViewPosition();
    view = (CRecordView*) GetNextView(pos);

    try {
        m_railSet.Delete();
        }
    catch (CDBException* e) {
            AfxMessageBox("Could not complete a delete.");
            AfxMessageBox(e->m_strError);
            return;
            }

    if (!m_railSet.IsEOF())
        m_railSet.MoveNext();

    if (m_railSet.IsEOF())
        m_railSet.MoveLast();

    view->UpdateData(FALSE);
}
```

This function first gets the view for the document (there is only one because this is an SDI application). It then calls the record set `Delete` method to delete the current record. After the record is deleted, it needs to scroll to a record that is not deleted. If the record set is not past the last record, the set is scrolled to the next record. If the record set is now past the last record, the set is scrolled to the last record. Finally, the view's `UpdateData` function is called to update the display with the new record's data.

Build and Run the Program

Select Project, Build to compile and link the application. Once the project has been rebuilt, select Project, Execute to run the program. To delete a record, select Records, Delete Record. The program deletes the current record and then scrolls to the next record in the record set.

Aggregate Values

So far, all of the functions you have seen work with individual records. However, you may want to know something about an entire column, such as the sum of the values or the largest value. You could retrieve all of the records and compute the value yourself. However, SQL provides a number of functions, called *aggregate functions*, that can perform these calculations for you. Some standard functions are:

- `AVG(expression)`—returns the average of the values

- `COUNT(expression)`—returns the number of non-null values

- `COUNT(*)`—returns the number of selected rows

- `MAX(expression)`—returns the largest value

- `MIN(expression)`—returns the smallest value

- `SUM(expression)`—returns the sum of the values

Using aggregate functions is usually much faster than retrieving the records and computing the result. With the aggregate function, all of the calculations are performed in the SQL engine and only the final result has to be passed back to the application.

To get an aggregate value from a record set, you need to modify the field exchange in the record set `DoFieldExchange` function. For example, to find the heaviest car in the train, you would need to change

```
RFX_Long(pFX, "EmptyWeight", m_EmptyWeight);
```
to
```
RFX_Long(pFX, "MAX(EmptyWeight)", m_EmptyWeight);
```

After you have changed the field exchange function, you only need to open the record set to get the aggregate value. Since there is only one maximum value, the open record set only has one record.

The following sections add a new menu item to determine the total empty weight of a train.

Create a Compute Weight Menu Item
Open `rail.rc` and edit the `IDR_MAINFRAME` menu. Add the menu item &Empty Weight to the end of the Trains menu. Save and close `rail.rc`.

II

Visual C++

Create a New *CRecordset*

Create a new CRecordset to get the aggregate value. You don't want to change the way the rest of the program works, so create a new CRecordset to bind to just the aggregate value. Open ClassWizard and select Create Class. Complete the Add Class dialog box as shown in figure 15.6 and select Create Class to begin building the new class.

Fig. 15.6
CTrainWeightSet
class information.

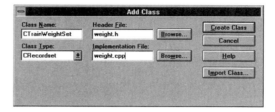

Select Consolidated as the data source and Cars as the table name and build the new class. You still need to make some changes to the class, so don't close ClassWizard yet.

Remove Unnecessary Variables

Remove unnecessary member variables from the class. ClassWizard automatically creates and binds member variables for each column in the table. You are only interested in the empty weight so you can delete the other member variables. While still in ClassWizard, select the Member Variables tab. Use the Delete Variable button to delete all of the variables except *m_EmptyWeight*. Now click OK to close ClassWizard.

Change the Field Exchange

Change the field exchange for the record set to get the sum of the empty weights. The field exchanges function calls created by ClassWizard retrieve the value itself for each column. Open the newly created weight.cpp and edit the OnFieldExchange function as follows:

```
void CTrainWeightSet::DoFieldExchange(CFieldExchange* pFX)
{
    //{{AFX_FIELD_MAP(CTrainWeightSet)
    pFX->SetFieldType(CFieldExchange::outputColumn);
    RFX_Long(pFX, "SUM(EmptyWeight)", m_EmptyWeight);
    //}}AFX_FIELD_MAP
}
```

Create a Handler for *ID_TRAINS_EMPTYWEIGHT*

Select Project, Class Wizard to open ClassWizard and select CRailDoc as the class name. Select ID_TRAINS_EMPTYWEIGHT as the object id and COMMAND as the

message and then click Add Function to create the message handler. Click
Edit Code and complete the function with the following code:

```
void CRailDoc::OnTrainsEmptyweight()
{
    CTrainListDialog dialog;
    CTrainWeightSet weight_set;
    char filter[80];
    char message[80];

    if (dialog.DoModal() == IDCANCEL)
        return;

    if (dialog.m_SelectedNumber >= 0) {
        wsprintf(filter, "TrainNumber = %ld",
                         ➥dialog.m_SelectedNumber);
        weight_set.m_strFilter = filter;
        }

    weight_set.Open();

    if (weight_set.IsEOF()) {

        AfxMessageBox("Could not compute weight.");
        weight_set.Close();
        return;
        }

    if (dialog.m_SelectedNumber >= 0) {
        wsprintf(message, "The empty weight of train %ld is %ld",
          dialog.m_SelectedNumber,
            weight_set.m_EmptyWeight);
        }
    else {
        wsprintf(message, "The empty weight all cars is %ld",
          weight_set.m_EmptyWeight);
        }

    AfxMessageBox(message);

    weight_set.Close();

}
```

You also need to include `weight.h` in `raildoc.h`.

Build and Run the Program

Select Project, Build to compile and link the application. Once the project has
been rebuilt, select Project, Execute to run the program. To compute the
empty weight of a train, choose Trains, Empty Weight and then select a train.
The program shows the total empty weight in a message box.

Dynamic Binding to Columns

ClassWizard is an excellent tool for creating record set classes when you have access to the table you are using. However, this is not always the case. For example, consider creating a database front end in which users can define their own tables. The program uses a pre-existing table to store the definition of the user-defined table. The user-defined table itself is dynamically created. The CRecordSet is still a good place to start, but you need to build your own class and use runtime information for the field exchange.

As a simpler example, consider the remaining table TrainInfo, that exists in the database from each of the three original railroads. Each TrainInfo table includes a column with the train number and additional character array columns with other information. For example, the Pennsylvania Railroad version of the table has columns for the engineer and the conductor, while the New York Central version has columns with the average on-time performance and train length. You could build a record set for each table, but that might be excessive for tables that are only occasionally referenced. An alternative is to build a browser that lets you ask for a particular piece of information for the trains on a railroad. The following sections show how to add this feature.

Create the Browser Dialog

Open rail.rc and create a new dialog called IDD_TRAIN_BROWSER that looks like the dialog in figure 15.7. Give the edit box the id IDC_FIELD_NAME, the list box the id IDC_INFO_LIST, and the Update button the id IDC_UPDATE. Save and close the resource file.

Fig. 15.7
IDD_TRAIN
_BROWSER dialog.

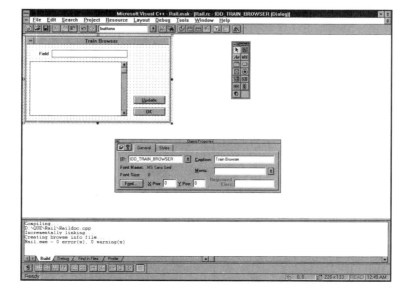

Create a New Record Set Class

You need to build a new class based on CRecordset to perform the dynamic binding. The files traininf.h and traininf.cpp define the new class. Be sure to add traininf.cpp to your project.

```cpp
// traininf.h : header file
//

/////////////////////////////////////////////////////////////////////////
// CTrainInfoSet recordset

class CTrainInfoSet : public CRecordset
{
    public:
    CTrainInfoSet(CDatabase* pDatabase = NULL);
    DECLARE_DYNAMIC(CTrainInfoSet)

// Field/Param Data
    CString m_FieldName;
    long    m_TrainNumber;
    CString    m_DataField;

// Overrides
    public:
    virtual CString GetDefaultConnect();   // Default connection string
    virtual CString GetDefaultSQL();        // Default SQL for Recordset
    virtual void DoFieldExchange(CFieldExchange* pFX);    // RFX support

// Implementation
#ifdef _DEBUG
    virtual void AssertValid() const;
    virtual void Dump(CDumpContext& dc) const;
#endif
};

// traininfo.cpp : implementation file
//

#include "stdafx.h"
#include "Rail.h"
#include "traininf.h"

#ifdef _DEBUG
#undef THIS_FILE
static char BASED_CODE THIS_FILE[] = __FILE__;
#endif

/////////////////////////////////////////////////////////////////////////
// CTrainInfoSet

IMPLEMENT_DYNAMIC(CTrainInfoSet, CRecordset)

CTrainInfoSet::CTrainInfoSet(CDatabase* pdb)
    : CRecordset(pdb)
{
```

```
        m_TrainNumber = 0;
        m_DataField = _T("");
        m_nFields = 2;
}


CString CTrainInfoSet::GetDefaultConnect()
{
        return _T("ODBC;DSN=Pennsylvania;");
}

CString CTrainInfoSet::GetDefaultSQL()
{
        return _T("dbo.TrainInfo");
}

void CTrainInfoSet::DoFieldExchange(CFieldExchange* pFX)
{
        pFX->SetFieldType(CFieldExchange::outputColumn);
        RFX_Long(pFX, "TrainNumber", m_TrainNumber);
        RFX_Text(pFX, m_FieldName, m_DataField);
}

/////////////////////////////////////////////////////////////////////////////
// CTrainSet diagnostics

#ifdef _DEBUG
void CTrainInfoSet::AssertValid() const
{
        CRecordset::AssertValid();
}

void CTrainInfoSet::Dump(CDumpContext& dc) const
{
        CRecordset::Dump(dc);
}
#endif //_DEBUG
```

Build a Dialog Class for the Dialog

Open ClassWizard and select Add Class. Complete the Add Class dialog box as shown in figure 15.8. Select Create Class to build the class.

Fig. 15.8
Defining the
`CBrowserDialog`
class in the Add
Class dialog box.

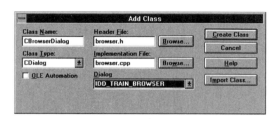

Create Maps and Variables

Create message maps and member variables for the dialog class. While still in ClassWizard, select the Member Variables tab. Create the following member variables:

Control Id	Variable	Category	Type
IDC_FIELD_NAME	*m_Fieldname*	Value	CString
IDC_INFO_LIST	*m_InfoList*	Control	CListBox

Select the Message Maps tab and create a message handler for a BN_CLICKED message for object IDC_UPDATE. Select Edit Code and finish the message handler as follows:

```
void CBrowserDialog::OnUpdate()
{
    CTrainInfoSet train_info;
    char line[80];

    UpdateData(TRUE);

    if (m_FieldName.IsEmpty()) {
        AfxMessageBox("No field specified.");
        return;
        }

    m_InfoList.ResetContent();

    train_info.m_FieldName = m_FieldName;

    try {
        train_info.Open();
        }
    catch (CDBException* e) {
        AfxMessageBox("Could not open train info table.");
        return;
        }

    while (!train_info.IsEOF()) {

        wsprintf(line, "Train %ld: %s", train_info.m_TrainNumber,
            (const char*) train_info.m_DataField);

        m_InfoList.AddString(line);

        train_info.MoveNext();
        }

    train_info.Close();
}
```

Be sure to include traininf.h in browser.cpp.

Create a Browse Info Menu Item

Open `rail.rc` and edit the `IDR_MAINFRAME` menu. Add the menu item "&Browse Info" to the end of the Trains menu. Save and close `rail.rc`.

Create a Handler for *ID_TRAINS_BROWSEINFO*

Select Project, Class Wizard to open ClassWizard and select `CRailDoc` as the class name. Select `ID_TRAINS_BROWSEINFO` as the object id and `COMMAND` as the message and then click Add Function to create the message handler. Click Edit Code and complete the function with the following code:

```
void CRailDoc::OnTrainsBrowseinfo()
{
    CBrowserDialog dialog;

    dialog.DoModal();
}
```

Be sure to include `browser.h` in `raildoc.cpp`.

Build and Run the Program

Select Project, Build to compile and link the application. Once the project has been rebuilt, select Project, Execute to run the program. To access the info browser, select Trains, Info Browser. Enter the name of the field you want to see and then click Update to see the values, if any. When you are done, click OK to close the browser.

From Here...

This chapter shows how to use the `CRecordset` class to retrieve records from a table and how to add and edit records in the table. The next chapter expands on this to explain how to use the `CRecordset` class to access data from multiple tables. For additional information, you may also want to read the following chapters:

- Chapter 3, "The Client/Server Language: SQL," defines the SQL language.

- Chapter 10, "Inserting, Updating, and Deleting Rows," explains how to add, edit, and delete records using ODBC functions.

- Chapter 11, "Queries and Result Sets," shows how to retrieve records with ODBC.

Chapter 16

Multi-Table Forms

The two previous chapters explain how to perform basic operations using ODBC, the Microsoft Foundation Classes included in Visual C++, and one table at a time. There are many cases where you need to perform queries on more than one table. This chapter shows how to query multiple tables with a join, how to parameterize the query for faster access, and how to use the same record set class with multiple tables. The chapter also covers how to directly execute SQL statements for additional improved performance.

Performing Joins

A *join* is a database operation that relates two or more tables by common values in the columns of the tables. An example of a join is the selection of cars by owner name in your sample application. The Cars table has the owner code but not the owner name. The mapping between the owner code and the owner name is stored separately in the Owner table. The OwnerCode column in each table relates the two tables to each other.

Selecting cars by owner could be done by first looking up the owner code by name from the Owner table and then selecting cars by owner code in the Cars table. However, performing this operation with a join can significantly simplify your code and enables the database engine to optimize the search based on its knowledge of that database and its contents. If the relationship involves many records or more tables, doing the operation without using a join can rapidly become too complicated, or memory intensive, to be practical.

In SQL syntax, a join is expressed by selecting more than one table and then specifying the relationship between the tables in the WHERE clause. For example, you could select all of the rail cars from the Pennsylvania railroad with this SQL statement:

```
SELECT * FROM Cars, Owners
WHERE Cars.OwnerCode = Owners.OwnerCode
AND Owners.Company = 'Pennsylvania'
```

You can perform the join with a record set in much the same way by making changes to a basic CRecordset class created by ClassWizard or AppWizard. To build such a class:

- Use ClassWizard to create a new CRecordSet class for one of the tables in the join

- Add the additional table(s) to the list returned by GetDefaultSQL()

- Add member variables for columns needed from the additional tables

- Add field exchange functions for the new member variables

- Construct a new filter string to use the join

After you have built the new class, you can open it and use it like any other record set class.

The following sections show how to modify the sample program to enable you to view cars by owner using a join.

Update the *IDD_RAIL_FORM*

Update the IDD_RAIL_FORM to include a list of owner company names. Open rail.rc and, in that, the IDD_RAIL_FORM dialog. Add a listbox with the id IDC_OWNER_LIST as shown in figure 16.1. Save and close rail.rc.

Fig. 16.1
The updated
IDD_RAIL_FORM
dialog.

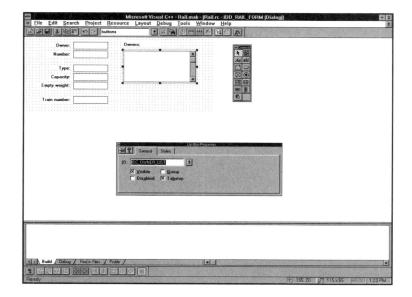

Create a Member Variable

Create a member variable in the view for the list box. Open ClassWizard and select class CRailView. Click the Member Variables table. Create a CListBox control variable for IDC_OWNER_LIST called *m_OwnerList*.

Create a Message Handler

Create a message handler to requery the database when the user selects a different owner. While still in ClassWizard viewing the CRailView, click the Message Maps tab. Add a function OnSelchangeOwnerList for control id IDC_OWNER_LIST, message LBN_SELCHANGE. Select OK to close ClassWizard.

Complete the List Box

Fill the list box in the OnInitialUpdate function. In Chapter 14, "Using the Wizards," you created a record set class for the Owner table. You can use that class here to build the list of owner names by making the following changes to CRailView::OnInitialUpdate():

```
void CRailView::OnInitialUpdate()
{
    COwnerSet owner_set;

    m_pSet = &GetDocument()->m_railSet;
    m_pSet->m_strSort = "CarNumber";

    CRecordView::OnInitialUpdate();

    owner_set.Open();
    m_OwnerList.ResetContent();
    m_OwnerList.AddString("<ALL>");
    while (!owner_set.IsEOF()) {
        m_OwnerList.AddString(owner_set.m_Company);
        owner_set.MoveNext();
        }
    owner_set.Close();
}
```

This function also adds the string "<ALL>" to the list box. Selecting this item will enable the user to view all of the cars regardless of their owners.

Be sure to include ownerset.h in railview.cpp.

Create a Member Variable

Create a member variable to hold the selected owner name. Add the variable *m_SelectedOwner* to the CRailView class definition in railvw.h.

```
CString         m_SelectedOwner;
```

Initialize its value to "<ALL>" in the constructor.

```
CRailView::CRailView()
    : CRecordView(CRailView::IDD)
{
    //{{AFX_DATA_INIT(CRailView)
    m_pSet = NULL;
    //}}AFX_DATA_INIT

    m_SelectedOwner = "<ALL>";
}
```

Next, you need to modify the CRailSet to perform a join.

Modify the *GetDefaultSQL* Method

Modify the GetDefaultSQL method to include both tables. The GetDefaultSQL method returns a string of table names used in the query. By default, it returns the table names specified when the table was created. For a join, this string should include all of the tables included in the join separated by commas.

```
CString CRailSet::GetDefaultSQL()
{
    return _T("dbo.Cars, dbo.Owners");
}
```

> **Note**
>
> This sample was developed using SQL Server, which requires the table owner, in this case "dbo.", prefix on the table names. You should check the notes included with your ODBC driver for similar requirements.

Modify the *DoFieldExchange* Method

Column names used in DoFieldExchange must be unambiguous. If columns with the same name are in more than one table in the join (as is the case with the OwnerCode column), you must add the table name to the column name.

```
void CRailSet::DoFieldExchange(CFieldExchange* pFX)
{
    //{{AFX_FIELD_MAP(CRailSet)
    pFX->SetFieldType(CFieldExchange::outputColumn);
    RFX_Text(pFX, "dbo.Cars.OwnerCode", m_OwnerCode);
    RFX_Long(pFX, "CarNumber", m_CarNumber);
    RFX_Text(pFX, "CarType", m_CarType);
    RFX_Long(pFX, "Capacity", m_Capacity);
    RFX_Long(pFX, "EmptyWeight", m_EmptyWeight);
    RFX_Long(pFX, "TrainNumber", m_TrainNumber);
    //}}AFX_FIELD_MAP
}
```

Create a Function

Create a function to build the new filter string. The filter string for the
CRailSet is now considerably more complicated, since it may include a
phrase for either the car owner and/or the train number. To keep the code
managable, create a new function ConstructFilter that builds the new filter
string. Be sure to add the new function to your CRailView class definition in
railvw.h.

```
void CRailView::ConstructFilter() {

    char filter[80];
    CRailDoc* doc;

    m_pSet->m_strFilter = "dbo.Cars.OwnerCode = dbo.Owners.OwnerCode";

    doc = GetDocument();
    if (doc->m_SelectedTrain >= 0) {

        m_pSet->m_strFilter += " AND ";
        wsprintf(filter, "TrainNumber = %ld", doc->m_SelectedTrain);
        m_pSet->m_strFilter += filter;
        }

    m_pSet->m_strFilter += " AND ";
    m_pSet->m_strFilter += "Company LIKE '";

    if (m_SelectedOwner == "<ALL>")
        m_pSet->m_strFilter += "%";
    else
        m_pSet->m_strFilter += m_SelectedOwner;

    m_pSet->m_strFilter += "'";
}
```

Note that the selected owner part of the filter uses LIKE rather than "=" and
compares the company name to "%" if all owners are selected. The "%" (percent sign) is the SQL wildcard character that matches any string of zero or
more characters. If all owners are selected, the phrase becomes Company LIKE
"%". This expression is true for any company name.

The results of the filter are the same if the owner phrase is left out entirely
when all owners are selected. However, you will need to use the filter in this
format when using parameterized records in the next section.

Now that you have a function to requery the database, the OnUpdate function
needs to be updated accordingly.

```
void CRailView::OnUpdate(CView* pSender, LPARAM lHint, CObject* pHint)
{

    if (lHint == HINT_NEW_TRAIN) {
```

Visual C++

```
                    ConstructFilter();

                    m_pSet->Requery();

                    UpdateData(FALSE);
                    }
              else
                    CRecordView::OnUpdate(pSender, lHint, pHint);
        }
```

You also need to finish the function that is called when the user selects a new company from the owner list.

```
        void CRailView::OnSelchangeOwnerList()
        {
              int index;

              index = m_OwnerList.GetCurSel();
              m_OwnerList.GetText(index, m_SelectedOwner);

              ConstructFilter();

              m_pSet->Requery();

              UpdateData(FALSE);
        }
```

Build and Run the Program

Select Project, Build to build the application and then Project, Execute to run it. The new program should look like figure 16.2. If you select an owner from the list, only the cars belonging to that owner show up in the record set.

Fig. 16.2
A sample run of the updated Rail program.

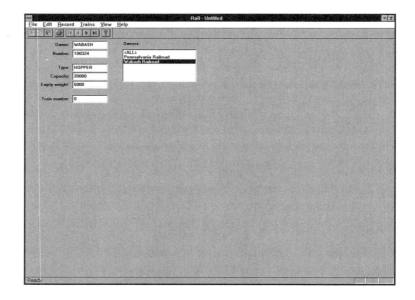

Parameterizing a Record Set

In programs like the one in the last example, every time the user selects a new owner name, the program has to build a new filter string. The ODBC engine then has to parse the new filter string before returning the first record. As a simpler example, consider:

```
LPCSTR owner_name = "Pennsylvania Railroad";

COwnerSet rsOwners;
char filter[80];

wsprintf(filter, "Company = '%s'", owner_name);
rsOwners = filter;
rsOwners.Open();
```

If your application performs this operation many times, it can become relatively time-consuming. You can eliminate these repetitive steps by parameterizing the record set.

A parameterized record set gains efficiency by allowing your application to specify parameters in the filter string and then to update the parameters without rebuilding the filter. The parameters are passed directly to the ODBC engine so it does not have to parse the filter string again.

To parameterize a record set, you add member variables to the record set class to store parameter values. You build the filter string using a "?" (question mark) for each parameter.

```
LPCSTR owner_name = "Pennsylvania Railroad";

COwnerSet rsOwners;

rsOwners.m_strFilter = "Company = ?";
rsOwners.m_CompanyParam = owner_name;
rsOwners.Open();
```

When you want to query the database with new parameters, you simply update the parameters and call `Requery`.

```
rsOwners.m_CompanyParam = "Wabash Railroad";
rsOwners.Requery();
```

The following sections show how to parameterize the `CRailSet` class in the example to more efficiently select cars by car owner.

Add a New Member Variable to the *CRailSet* Class

Modify the definition of `CRailSet` in the `railcset.h` file to add the new member variable *m_CompanyParam*. Place it outside the `AFX_FIELD` section of the class.

II

Visual C++

This new member variable is used to store the company name parameter for the filter.

```
// Field/Param Data
    //{{AFX_FIELD(CRailSet, CRecordset)
    CString  m_OwnerCode;
    long     m_CarNumber;
    CString  m_CarType;
    long     m_Capacity;
    long     m_EmptyWeight;
    long     m_TrainNumber;
    //}}AFX_FIELD
    CString  m_CompanyParam;
```

Add Initialization

Add initialization to the constructor for the CRailSet. Edit the CRailSet constructor in the railset.cpp file to initialize the new member variable and to set the *m_nParams* member variable to the number of parameterized values in the record set.

```
CRailSet::CRailSet(CDatabase* pdb)
    : CRecordset(pdb)
{
    //{{AFX_FIELD_INIT(CRailSet)
    m_OwnerCode = "";
    m_CarNumber = 0;
    m_CarType = "";
    m_Capacity = 0;
    m_EmptyWeight = 0;
    m_TrainNumber = 0;
    m_nFields = 6;
    //}}AFX_FIELD_INIT
    m_CompanyParam = "";
    m_nParams = 1;
}
```

Note

Be sure to initialize *m_nParams* to the number of parameterized values. Omitting this initialization introduces a bug that is difficult to find.

Add the New Member Variable

Add the new member variable to the DoFieldExchange method. The parameterized values are passed to the database driver through the DoFieldExchange method. After the AFX_FIELD_MAP section, add the lines shown. The new call to SetFieldType indicates that the field exchanges that follow are parameterized values.

```
void CRailSet::DoFieldExchange(CFieldExchange* pFX)
{
    //{{AFX_FIELD_MAP(CRailSet)
    pFX->SetFieldType(CFieldExchange::outputColumn);
    RFX_Text(pFX, "dbo.Cars.OwnerCode", m_OwnerCode);
    RFX_Long(pFX, "CarNumber", m_CarNumber);
    RFX_Text(pFX, "CarType", m_CarType);
    RFX_Long(pFX, "Capacity", m_Capacity);
    RFX_Long(pFX, "EmptyWeight", m_EmptyWeight);
    RFX_Long(pFX, "TrainNumber", m_TrainNumber);
    //}}AFX_FIELD_MAP
    pFX->SetFieldType(CFieldExchange::param);
    RFX_Text(pFX, "Company", m_CompanyParam);
}
```

Set Up the Filter

Set up the filter in the OnInitialUpdate function. As the program stands, an
owner could be selected before the filter is set up to use the parameter. Edit
the OnInitialUpdate function to call ConstructFilter and initialize the parameter to "%" (which, as you remember, will match all company names).

```
void CRailView::OnInitialUpdate()
{
    COwnerSet owner_set;

    m_pSet = &GetDocument()->m_railSet;
    m_pSet->m_strSort = "CarNumber";

    ConstructFilter();
    m_pSet->m_CompanyParam = "%";

    CRecordView::OnInitialUpdate();

    owner_set.Open();
    m_OwnerList.ResetContent();
    m_OwnerList.AddString("<ALL>");
    while (!owner_set.IsEOF()) {
        m_OwnerList.AddString(owner_set.m_Company);
        owner_set.MoveNext();
        }
    owner_set.Close();
    m_OwnerList.SetCurSel(0);
}
```

Build the Parameterized Filter String

Edit ConstructFilter to build the filter string with "?" for the parameterized
values.

```
void CRailView::ConstructFilter() {

    char filter[80];
    CRailDoc* doc;
```

```
m_pSet->m_strFilter = "dbo.Cars.OwnerCode =
➡dbo.Owners.OwnerCode";

doc = GetDocument();
if (doc->m_SelectedTrain >= 0) {

    m_pSet->m_strFilter += " AND ";
    wsprintf(filter, "TrainNumber = %ld", doc-
    ➡>m_SelectedTrain);
    m_pSet->m_strFilter += filter;
    }

m_pSet->m_strFilter += " AND Company LIKE ?";
}
```

Update the Parameterized Value

Update the parameterized value when the owner is selected. Edit `OnSelchangeOwnerList` to set the parameterized value rather than to rebuild the filter string.

```
void CRailView::OnSelchangeOwnerList()
{
    int index;

    index = m_OwnerList.GetCurSel();
    m_OwnerList.GetText(index, m_SelectedOwner);

    if (m_SelectedOwner == "<ALL>")
        m_pSet->m_CompanyParam = "%";
    else
        m_pSet->m_CompanyParam = m_SelectedOwner;

    m_pSet->Requery();

    UpdateData(FALSE);
}
```

Build and Run the Program

Select Project, Build to recompile and relink the application and then Project, Execute to run it. The new program runs as before, but selecting a different owner is now somewhat faster.

Working with Multiple Data Sources

In the sample application from the previous chapters, each record set is used with the data source for which it was built. The `GetDefaultConnect` function for the record set specifies the data source to be used. However, as the function name implies, the record set does not have to connect to the data source specified in `GetDefaultConnect`.

In the process of establishing a connection to an ODBC data source, a CRecordset object automatically creates a CDatabase object. This CDatabase object represents the actual connection to the data source. The CDatabase object makes the connection when the CRecordset is opened and then breaks the connection when the CRecordset is closed.

To connect to a different database, you can create your own CDatabase object and have your CRecordset objects use it to connect to the data source. You then can control when to connect to the data source and when to disconnect from it.

You establish the connection between the CDatabase object and the datasource by calling CDatabase::Open. This Open function enables you to specify a complete connect string for connecting to the database. The connect string can include the user id and password to log on to the database, the name of the database, the name of the host where the database resides, and a variety of other options defined by the ODBC driver. By providing all the needed information in the connect string, you allow the application to establish the connection without operator intervention. If all the necessary information is not provided, the user might have to enter one or more values in a connect dialog each time a table is opened.

> **Note**
>
> Standard options for the connect string include DSN= for database name, UID= for user id, and PWD= for the password. However, the recognized connect string options vary between different database engines. Check the help (.HLP) file for your ODBC driver to find out which options it supports. The help file should be installed in the same directory as the ODBC driver.

The CDatabase::Open function has the following declaration:

```
virtual BOOL Open( LPCSTR lpszDSN,
    BOOL bExclusive = FALSE,
    BOOL bReadOnly = FALSE,
    LPCSTR lpszConnect = "ODBC;",
    BOOL bUseCursorLib = TRUE );
```

The parameters for Open are:

■ *lpszDSN*—The *lpszDSN* parameter is the name of the datasource. If you include the datasource name in *lpszConnect* or if you want to user to be prompted to select the datasource name, *lpszDSN* should be NULL.

II

Visual C++

- *bExclusive*—The *bExclusive* parameter is currently not used by the class. You should always pass FALSE for this parameter in order for the *Open* operation to succeed.

- *bReadOnly*—The *bReadOnly* parameter specifies if the connection is to be read-only. If the value is TRUE, you cannot make changes to the datasource.

- *lpszConnect*—The *lpszConnect* parameter is the connect string. The ODBC driver defines the format of this string. Typically, it contains information blocks in the format *tag=information* separated by semi-colons. For example, a Microsoft SQL Server connect string could look like:

  ```
  "ODBC;DSN=Consolidated;UID=user;PWD=password;
  ➥DATABASE=Consolidated"
  ```

- The connect string must begin with "ODBC;". This provides compatibility with future versions of the class that may support data sources other than ODBC.

- *bUseCursorLib*—The *bUseCursorLib* parameter indicates if the ODBC Cursor Library should be loaded. The library provides cursor operations for level 1 ODBC drivers (level 2 drivers have internal cursor support) and support for snapshots. However, the library prevents the use of dynasets. Therefore, the value for *bUseCursorLib* should be TRUE if you want to use snapshots or FALSE if you want to use dynasets. If you need to use both snapshots and dynasets for the same database, you must create two separate CDatabase objects.

After the CDatabase object is open, you can use it to create CRecordset-based objects. To do so, pass a pointer to the CDatabase object as the parameter to the constructor for the CRecordset object. You then can use the record set as you normally would.

The following sections show how to modify the sample application to use a CDatabase to work with different data sources. The changes add a new field to the train info browser that enables the user to select the data source to use.

Add a Control

Add a control to the Browser dialog to select the data source. Open rail.rc and edit IDD_TRAIN_BROWSER. Add the dropdown list called "Railroad," as shown in figure 16.3. Assign the listbox the id IDC_RAILROAD. Close the dialog and save the resource file rail.rc.

```
RailroadDatabase
RailroadName
DatabaseName
```

Fig. 16.3
The updated
IDD_TRAIN_BROWSER
dialog box.

Create a Member Variable for the Control

Open ClassWizard and select class CBrowserDialog. Click Member Variables and add a CComboBox control variable for IDC_RAILROAD called *m_RailroadList*.

Create a *CRecordSet* for the *RailroadDatabases* Table

The RailroadDatabases table has a list of the member railroads and the data source to use to access their tables. While still in ClassWizard, select Add Class. Complete the Add Class dialog box as shown in figure 16.4. Select Create Class and select Consolidated as the data source and RailroadDatabases as the table name.

Fig. 16.4
CRailroadDBSet
class definition.

Add an *OnInitDialog* Function

Add an OnInitDialog function to the browser dialog. While still in ClassWizard, select class CBrowserDialog and click Message Maps. Add the function for class object id CBrowserDialog, message WM_INITDIALOG.

Complete the Control

Fill the control with a list of possible data sources. To keep things easy, fill the list box with the data source names rather than a list of railroad names. This way you won't have to relate the railroad name to the table name when the user makes a selection. While still in ClassWizard, select Member Function OnInitDialog and click Edit Code. Add the following code to the function:

```
BOOL CBrowserDialog::OnInitDialog()
{
    CDialog::OnInitDialog();

    CRailroadDBSet railroad_set;

    m_RailroadList.ResetContent();
```

```
                    railroad_set.Open();

                    while (!railroad_set.IsEOF()) {

                        m_RailroadList.AddString(railroad_set.m_DatabaseName);

                        railroad_set.MoveNext();
                        }

                    railroad_set.Close();

                    m_RailroadList.SetCurSel(0);

                    return TRUE;
                }
```

Be sure raildb.h is included in browser.cpp.

Modify the *OnUpdate* Message

Modify the OnUpdate message handler to use the selected data source. The
existing OnUpdate function uses the data source specified in the record set.
The revised function below opens a CDatabase for the selected data source
and then uses it to create the CTrainInfoSet record set class.

```
        void CBrowserDialog::OnUpdate()
        {
            int index;
            CString datasource;
            CString connect;
            CDatabase database;
            char line[80];
            int pos;

            UpdateData(TRUE);

            if (m_FieldName.IsEmpty()) {
                AfxMessageBox("No field specified.");
                return;
                }

            index = m_RailroadList.GetCurSel();
            m_RailroadList.GetLBText(index, datasource);

            // Strip trailing spaces from the datasource name
            pos = datasource.Find(' ');
            if (pos >= 0)
                datasource = datasource.Left(pos);

            connect = "ODBC;DSN=";
            connect += datasource;
            connect += ";";

            try {
                database.Open(NULL, FALSE, FALSE, connect);
                }
```

```
catch (CDBException* e) {
    AfxMessageBox(e->m_strError);
    return;
    }

CTrainInfoSet train_info(&database);

m_InfoList.ResetContent();

train_info.m_FieldName = m_FieldName;

try {
    train_info.Open();
    }
catch (CDBException* e) {
    AfxMessageBox("Could not open train info table.");
    return;
    }

while (!train_info.IsEOF()) {

    wsprintf(line, "Train %ld: %s", train_info.m_TrainNumber,
        (const char*) train_info.m_DataField);

    m_InfoList.AddString(line);

    train_info.MoveNext();
    }

train_info.Close();
}
```

Build and Run the Program

Select Project, Build to build the application. Once the project has been re-built, select Project, Execute to run the program. Select Trains, Browse Info to use the new information browser as that supports multiple data sources. The browser is shown in figure 16.5.

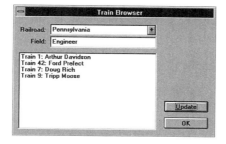

Fig. 16.5
Updating Train
Browser in action.

The CDatabase class has use beyond working with multiple data sources. Every time you open a record set, it has to open a CDatabase object to re-establish its connection to the data source. If your program opens and closes record sets many times, these reconnections can become very time consuming. The operation can be performed more quickly by opening a CDatabase and keeping it open for the duration of the process. If you create each CRecordset using the open CDatabase, the CRecordsets never have to reconnect to the data source. You then can close the CDatabase when all of the database operations are complete.

Using SQL Statements

This chapter has shown how to use the CDatabase class and has given a number of ways to improve database performance through the CRecordset class. However, there are some operations for which a CRecordset is not particularly well suited, such as for updates and deletes that affect many records. While you can perform these processes using a CRecordset, the overhead of scrolling to each record and then updating or deleting it is likely to be prohibitive.

In these cases, it may be more efficient to build an SQL statement and execute it directly using the ExecuteSQL method in the CDatabase class. This method also can be used to perform operations not supported by the CRecordset class. To use ExecuteSQL, simply pass a string containing the SQL statement to the method. For example, if all of the rail cars belonging to owner number 17 are transferred to owner number 23, you can update the database with the following code:

```
dbRailCar.ExecuteSQL("UPDATE RailCar SET OwnerNumber = 23 "
    "WHERE OwnerNumber = 17");
```

Note that ExecuteSQL cannot return data from records. If you need to get data from records in a table, you must use a CRecordset.

From Here...

Chapter 16 showed a number of ways you can work with multiple tables and some techniques for improving program performance. You may want to read the following chapters for additional information:

- Chapter 3, "The Client/Server Language: SQL," defines the SQL language.

- Chapter 12, "Setting Parameters with Prepared Statements," explains how to use parameterized values with ODBC.

- Chapter 20, "Optimizing ODBC," gives further information on how to improve the performance of ODBC operations.

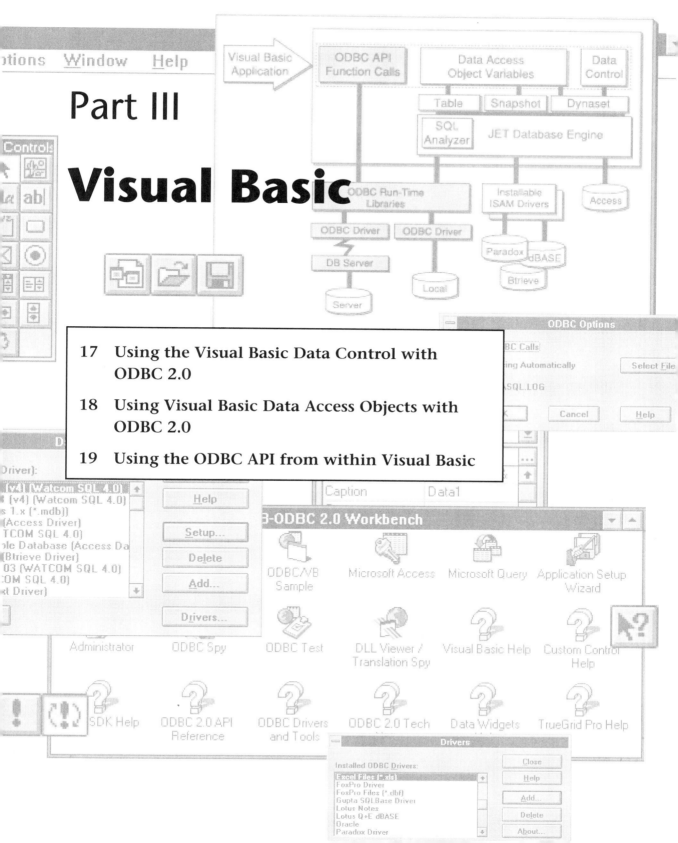

Part III

Visual Basic

17 Using the Visual Basic Data Control with ODBC 2.0

18 Using Visual Basic Data Access Objects with ODBC 2.0

19 Using the ODBC API from within Visual Basic

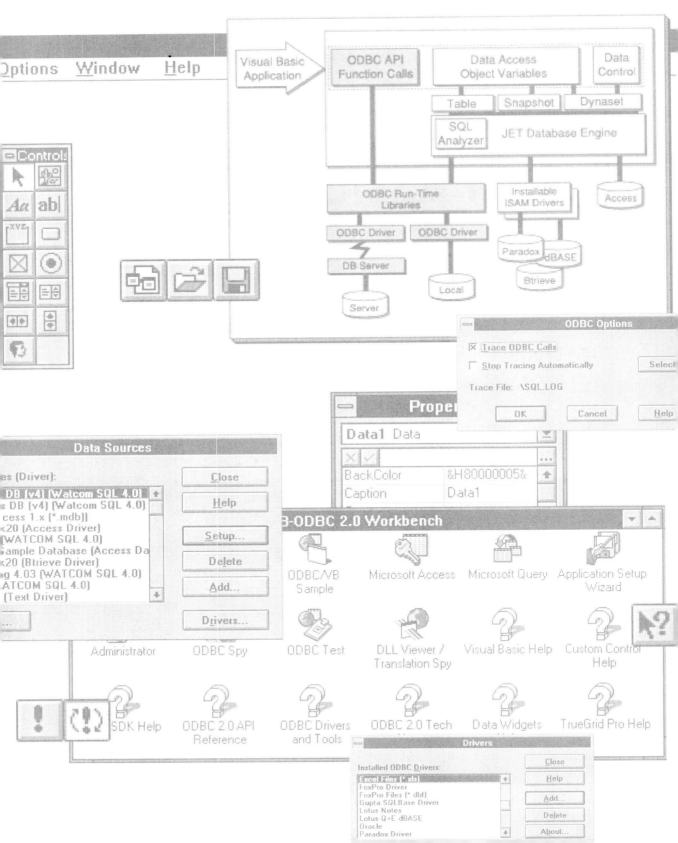

Visual Basic
Application

| ODBC API Function Calls | Data Access Object Variables | Data Control |

| Table | Snapshot | Dynaset |

| SQL Analyzer | JET Database Engine |

Control

ODBC Run-Time Libraries   Installable ISAM Drivers   Access

ODBC Driver   ODBC Driver   Paradox   dBASE

DB Server   Btrieve

Server   Local

ODBC Options

☒ Trace ODBC Calls

☐ Stop Tracing Automatically   Select

Trace File: \SQL.LOG

[OK]   [Cancel]   [Help]

Proper

Data1 Data

✕ ✓	...
BackColor	&H80000005&
Caption	Data1

Data Sources

es (Driver):

DB (v4) (Watcom SQL 4.0)
s DB (v4) (Watcom SQL 4.0)
cess 1.x (*.mdb))
x20 (Access Driver)
(WATCOM SQL 4.0)
ample Database (Access Da
x20 (Btrieve Driver)
g 4.03 (WATCOM SQL 4.0)
ATCOM SQL 4.0)
(Text Driver)

[Close]
[Help]
[Setup...]
[Delete]
[Add...]
[Drivers...]

B-ODBC 2.0 Workbench

ODBC/VB Sample   Microsoft Access   Microsoft Query   Application Setup Wizard

Administrator   ODBC Spy   ODBC Test   DLL Viewer / Translation Spy   Visual Basic Help   Custom Control Help

SDK Help   ODBC 2.0 API Reference   ODBC Drivers and Tools   ODBC 2.0 Tech   Data Widgets   TrueGrid Pro Help

Drivers

Installed ODBC Drivers:

Excel Files (*.xls)
FoxPro Driver
FoxPro Files (*.dbf)
Gupta SQLBase Driver
Lotus Notes
Lotus Q+E dBASE
Oracle
Paradox Driver

[Close]
[Help]
[Add...]
[Delete]
[About...]

Chapter 17

Using the Visual Basic Data Control with ODBC 2.0

Possible Visual Basic mechanisms for using ODBC 2.0 fall into three general categories, which are listed below in order of increasing programming difficulty:

- Using the Data Control and bound controls

- Programming with database object variables

- Invoking the ODBC 2.0 API directly

These three approaches aren't mutually exclusive and often can be effectively combined. This chapter proposes some criteria for making design decisions and also looks in some detail at Visual Basic ODBC 2.0 programming techniques using the Data Control. In this chapter, you explore:

- How to choose among the three basic design approaches

- How to assemble a Visual Basic ODBC 2.0 workbench

- The relationship between Visual Basic and ODBC 2.0

- Incorporating ODBC Administrative dialog boxes

- Executing an SQL query with the Data Control

- Using the Data Control's Recordset

- Capabilities of data-aware custom controls

- Evaluating ODBC 2.0 run-time errors

III

Visual Basic

Choosing Possible Design Approaches

When using ODBC 2.0 with Visual Basic, you have a number of fundamental design approaches available to you. Usually the first design decision you make is selecting one of three basic approaches to your database application. These options and suggested decision criteria are compared in the following sections.

Defining Three Possible Design Strategies

The most direct and least complex approach to using Visual Basic with ODBC 2.0 is to use the Data Control. This control is included as a part of both the Visual Basic Standard and Professional Editions, and is shown in the toolbox in figure 17.1. Using the Data Control offers these advantages:

- Requires the least amount of code of the three methods

- Demands no awareness of the ODBC 2.0 API details

- Enables use of standard and third-party bound controls

- Simplifies error handling

- Automatically manages memory to contain result sets

- Supports all Dynaset methods and properties

Fig. 17.1
Visual Basic
Toolbox showing
the Data Control.

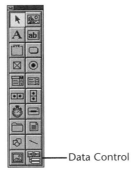

—————Data Control

The Dynaset, automatically created and managed by the Data Control, is a sophisticated and updateable memory Recordset object reflecting the results of an SQL query. You explore its behavior and uses later in this and subsequent chapters.

However, for all of its advantages, using only the Data Control presents some programming limitations that the other two methods do not. Some of these limitations are:

- No access to `Snapshot` or `Table Recordset` objects

- No access to database collections such as `TableDefs`, `Fields`, `Indexes`, and `QueryDefs`

- Limited access to ODBC 2.0 Administrative functions

- No access to true transaction processing methods

- Limited error recovery and diagnostic capabilities

Data Access Object variables offer a major improvement in flexibility and sophistication when creating Visual Basic applications that use ODBC 2.0. Data Access Object variables are available only in the Professional Edition of Visual Basic. The advantages gained in using this more complex approach are:

- Programmed access to ODBC 2.0 Administrative functions

- Control over a wider variety of `Recordset` types: `Dynaset`, `Snapshot`, and `Table Recordset` objects

- Access to stored procedures and action queries

- Access to database collection objects such as the `TableDefs`, `Fields`, `Indexes`, and `QueryDefs` collections

- Ability to use true `transaction` processing facilities including `BeginTrans`, `CommitTrans`, and `Rollback`

Some limitations still present when using Data Access Object variables in comparison to using the ODBC 2.0 API directly or alternatively using the Data Control are:

- Demands more coding than using the Data Control

- Indirect error handling and error recovery

- No fine-grained control over each database action

- Limited manipulation of the result set and associated memory resources used to contain the results set

- Possibly lower performance when compared to using the ODBC 2.0 API functions directly

Finally, using direct calls to the ODBC 2.0 API functions offers the greatest degree of direct control over database operations. Essentially any of the

III

Visual Basic

programming techniques described elsewhere in this book in the context of C/C++ programming using the ODBC 2.0 API functions can also be employed from within Visual Basic. Some of the most attractive advantages of using the ODBC 2.0 API directly are:

- Direct participation in developing, managing, and formatting the result set

- More control over the result set cursor, and a greater variety of cursor types and behaviors

- Maximum access to detailed ODBC 2.0 error information, enabling sophisticated error handling and recovery

- Ability to determine ODBC driver and SQL conformance levels to influence program execution

- Better control over Windows execution scheduling and resource utilization

- All other things being equal, this approach is likely to provide the best performance

Such greater flexibility comes at the price of incurring the following disadvantages:

- Requires significantly more coding than either of the other two alternative approaches

- Coding required is much more complex and demands experience in making API calls

- Less of a safety net is provided by Visual Basic run-time library error handling, and the consequences of coding or run-time errors can be severe

Again, don't forget that it is often advantageous to combine portions of all of these three basic approaches to achieve the specific advantages of each while mitigating the limitations. For example, you might be developing an application that only needs a `Dynaset Recordset` type but could benefit from more detailed error-handling information. Perhaps your best bet might be to combine the basic Data Control techniques with a few ODBC 2.0 API function declarations and calls to achieve your purpose.

Some specific guidelines and decision criteria are presented in the next section to assist you in making this basic design approach determination.

Determining When to Use Each Approach

Another way to evaluate the pros and cons of the three approaches outlined in the previous section is to associate them with broad classes of typical database applications. If your planned database application closely resembles one of the listed classes, then the associated implementation approach usually will work effectively.

Typical Data Control Applications

Typical database applications that might be implemented using only the Visual Basic Data Control are:

- Simple read-only database browsers for small- to medium-sized tables (usually less than about one thousand records)

- Basic database lookup SQL query applications with modest-sized result sets (usually less than one hundred result set records retrieved from one or two modest-sized tables)

- Minor data-entry applications (usually with up a dozen or so fields involving one or two modest-sized tables and with no relational-integrity constraints)

The general classes of applications that lend themselves well to using just the Data Control often are those that can be accomplished with one or two Data Controls and where most of the data presentation or data entry can be accomplished with Visual Basic's bound or so-called "data-aware" controls.

If your planned application is very much more complex than those outlined above, a commitment to using the more powerful Data Access Object variables usually is wise.

Remember also that the scope of sophistication of Data Control-centered applications often can be extended quite a bit by using specialty custom controls. Such custom controls encapsulate much of the additional complexity as built-in behavior already "programmed into" the control. Several representative custom controls and their applicability in database application designs are explored in later sections of this chapter.

Using Data Access Object Variables

Significantly more sophisticated and demanding database applications usually are implemented best using Data Access Object variables. Typical examples are:

III

Visual Basic

- Applications that dynamically create database tables, fields, or indexes during their execution

- Applications that involve processing complex transactions involving synchronized updates of several tables in a logically consistent fashion

- Applications that employ forms of results sets other than the Dynaset, such as Snapshots or Tables, where performance is a key design consideration

- Applications that use tables (or multiple tables) that are quite large, meaning larger than about one thousand records

- Sophisticated data-entry applications that involve dozens of interrelated fields and include database-referential integrity or consistency rules

- Applications that perform extensive manipulation and post-query processing of the result set, especially those that require highly customized presentation or formatting of the data

- Applications that make intricate use of the ODBC Administrative facilities for choosing, configuring, verifying, and setting up a variety of data sources

- Applications that need to "discover" the underlying structure of the database during execution

- Applications that need to use complex multi-key indexing schemes for retrieving or updating records

In general, other than the somewhat modest requirements that can be addressed by the basic Data Control, almost all other Visual Basic database applications can be accomplished using Data Access Objects.

Using ODBC 2.0 API Function Calls

For the ultimate database application demands in terms of sophistication, complexity, and performance, direct use of the ODBC 2.0 API functions may be in order. Typically, such applications demonstrate one or more of the following characteristics:

- Large-scale client/server multi-user applications where precise determination and resolution of myriad possible system errors and failures must be incorporated into production applications

- Applications that are resource intensive and where direct control over the memory, network, and server resources are primary considerations

■ Applications that use very large-scale databases, such as database tables that contain tens or even hundreds of thousands of records

■ Applications that are transaction-oriented and operate at near real-time update rates, and where absolute performance is crucial

Quite frequently, you may find that using Data Access Object variables accomplishes the majority of what you require, and the selective addition of a few ODBC 2.0 API function calls might solve a particularly knotty problem. This situation is most likely to arise in the area of error handling in a large-scale distributed client-server system.

Combining Several Different Techniques

Combining portions of two or even three of these general categories of techniques often is the most effective way to accomplish your Visual Basic ODBC 2.0 application. Summaries of several examples might give you an idea of the range of possibilities and also suggest combinations you might want to use.

Combining the Data Control and Data Access Object Variables

As you will discover a bit later in this chapter, the Data Control implements a specific type of Visual Basic Data Access Object. Although you can't manipulate the Recordset object (called a `Dynaset`) when it belongs to a Data Control like you can when you create your own Dynasets directly, you can nonetheless manipulate the properties and methods of the Data Control using object-oriented techniques that are the same as those of Chapter 18, "Using Visual Basic Data Access Objects with ODBC 2.0."

Combining the Data Access Object with ODBC 2.0 Function Calls

For demanding projects, a few selected ODBC 2.0 API calls can greatly enhance a Visual Basic ODBC 2.0 application. Among the first that are typically used are the ODBC API functions for error reporting. Techniques and specific examples of using this technique and others are discussed in Chapter 19, "Using the ODBC API from within Visual Basic." At this point it is enough to know that direct ODBC API calls can be mixed with the use of Visual Basic's Data Access Object variables.

Combining All Three Approaches in One Application

In the interests of symmetry, as you have probably guessed, it is possible to combine all three techniques successfully in one Visual Basic application.

By the end of Chapters 18 and 19, you will have gained some insight into how this can be accomplished.

III

Visual Basic

Building a Suitable Development Environment

Before beginning development of a Visual Basic ODBC 2.0 application, you might want to assemble the set of tools you are likely to need so that they are readily at hand. In addition to the tools that come with Visual Basic, there are others that become important during a typical project. Collectively, these tools can be considered a specialized Visual Basic ODBC 2.0 *workbench*. These components and their arrangement are addressed in the following section.

Constructing an ODBC 2.0 Visual Basic Workbench

A suggested set of development tools to assemble for your ODBC 2.0 Visual Basic workbench consists at the very least of the following:

- Microsoft Visual Basic 3.0—Professional Edition
- Microsoft Query—for example, available with Microsoft Excel 5.0
- Microsoft ODBC 2.0 SDK—particularly the debug tools
- Several ODBC 2.0 Test Data sources—see ODBC 2.0 SDK
- Microsoft Access 2.0—for creating test databases
- Microsoft Access 2.0—Application Development Kit
- ODBC 2.0 Drivers—based on your specific data sources
- Visual Basic-compatible third-party custom controls
- Your own test and development data sources

Note that Visual Basic 3.0, Professional Edition, is at the top of the list. The Professional Edition includes the additional capability to use Data Access Object variables and tools for developing custom Help systems.

Microsoft Query is included for a variety of reasons. First, it offers an excellent interactive framework for learning the SQL language and testing your SQL queries. In addition, Microsoft Query itself uses the ODBC 2.0 Administrative and runtime facilities and can be invaluable in independently testing your data sources to assure they are behaving correctly. You also can use it to execute your SQL queries while you trace their execution using ODBC 2.0's Trace log feature or Spy utility. Since Microsoft Query behaves correctly in relationship to ODBC 2.0, much can be learned from the resulting Trace logs and Spy logs that assist you in developing your own applications. Finally,

Microsoft Query supports DDE operations and can consequently be used under control of your Visual Basic application as an interactive ad hoc query- building subsystem, eliminating the need for you to program such a capability from scratch. In this regard, Microsoft Query might be viewed as a software component to be incorporated into your completed application.

Another key component of your workbench should be the Microsoft ODBC 2.0 SDK. In addition to including a useful variety of ODBC 2.0-compliant database drivers, it also provides several driver-matched test databases. Also included with the ODBC 2.0 SDK are the ODBC 2.0 Spy and Test utilities, which are vital to actually understanding and monitoring ODBC 2.0 operations while your program is executing. Finally to round out the list of mandatory needs for the ODBC 2.0 SDK, there is an excellent online Help system and a comprehensive Visual Basic sample program. The Visual Basic sample program can be used to study appropriate programming techniques, as well as a source of BAS code modules, which contain all of the ODBC 2.0 function declarations and associated global symbolic constants already formatted for inclusion in your Visual Basic programs.

Microsoft Access 2.0 appears in the workbench list since it can serve a variety of useful purposes during the lifetime of your project. The design of a database application often begins with the design of the database itself. Microsoft Access incorporates graphical and easy-to-use tools for designing databases, tables, fields, referential-integrity rules, relational fields, and queries. Furthermore, the ability to produce well-formatted documentation of the resultant database design is also included. Additional merits of using Access 2.0 are discussed a bit later under the subject of a suggested design methodology.

In addition to Microsoft Access itself, it is suggested that you obtain a copy of the Microsoft Access 2.0 Application Development Kit. Within the Application Development Kit, in addition to other useful database tools, are three next generation custom controls called *OCXs*. Custom controls of this type are envisioned by Microsoft to constitute the next step in the future of custom controls, ultimately replacing today's familiar VBX controls.

Each OCX consists of a small object library that implements a single programmable object. You look at these specific OCXs later in this chapter under the section heading "Incorporating Custom Controls." You also may want to add some other current generation object libraries, such as those that come with Microsoft Excel 5.0 and Graph 5.0 or other software vendors' object libraries that support OLE 2.x Automation, depending on the needs of the application that you are developing.

III

Visual Basic

In the same vein, you may also wish to purchase additional Visual Basic VBX-style custom controls to make your work easier. A sampling of some of the more popular and useful custom controls for database applications is presented later in this chapter also under the section heading "Incorporating Custom Controls."

Finally, you need to obtain the ODBC 2.0 drivers that match the databases your application accesses. A listing of some of the possible sources for ODBC 2.0 drivers is shown in the following table. Note that in many cases there are several vendors supplying compatible drivers. Not all possible vendors or sources are listed. For additional information you can refer to the "ODBC Drivers and Tools" Help system that is included as part of the ODBC 2.0x SDK.

Database	Sources or Vendors
SQL Server	Ships with VB; Intersolv Software; Sybase Corp.
Oracle	Ver. 6 ships with VB; Oracle; Intersolv Software
Ingress	Ask Group; Intersolv Software
DEC Rdb	Digital Equipment Corp.
DEC RMS	Digital Equipment Corp.
SQL/400	IBM; Intersolv Software
DB2/2	Techgnosis, Inc.; Intersolv Software
DB2	Wall Data; Intersolv Software (requires gateway)
MUMPS	Digital Equipment Corp., Information Builders
Gupta SQLBase	Open Link; Intersolv Software
Informix	Informix Software; Intersolv Software
NetWare SQL	Intersolv Software
Progress	Intersolv Software
SQLBase	Intersolv Software
Teradata	Intersolv Software (requires gateway)
HP ALLBASE	Hewlett-Packard; Intersolv Software
Access 1.X	Ships with Excel 5.0; Microsoft
Access 2.0	Ships with Excel 5.0; Microsoft

Database	Sources or Vendors
Btrieve	Ships with Excel 5.0; Microsoft; Intersolv Software
dBASE X.X	Ships with Excel 5.0; Microsoft; Intersolv Software
FoxPro	Ships with Excel 5.0; Microsoft
Paradox	Ships with Excel 5.0; Microsoft; Intersolv Software
Text (*.csv)	Ships with Excel 5.0; Microsoft; Intersolv Software
Excel (*.xls)	Ships with Excel 5.0; Microsoft; Intersolv Software

Some assembly of this kit of parts into a coherent workbench may be required. At the very least, all of the components should be collected into a specialized Visual Basic Workbench program group similar to that show in figure 17.2.

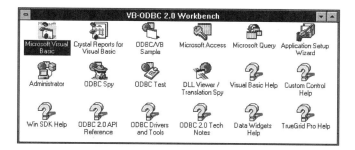

Fig. 17.2
The Visual Basic
ODBC 2.0
Workbench
Program Group.

Adopting a Design Methodology—Some Suggestions

Over time, every programmer develops his or her own personalized style and approach to application design and development. You're not any different, and changing your style may cramp you. But here are some suggestions for your consideration. You should know at the outset that this methodology is based on certain assumptions:

■ It is far more efficient to buy than to build—and usually a lot less costly overall. You can't write and test much code for the current selling price of most third-party custom controls (from $99 to $299).

■ Use the simplest and most direct approach to accomplish the intended job—cleverness at the expense of clarity is usually a foolhardy tradeoff.

■ Attack the design and development steps in small, focused bite-sized functional pieces—this is usually the shortest path to completion.

III

Visual Basic

- Look for paradigms and examples to study before setting out on your journey—it is better to travel new roads well instructed and with a road map.

- Emulate or copy code that accomplishes a similar task—not only is this the sincerest form of flattery, it is usually much more efficient.

- Design your application first; then begin developing the code. Prototype particularly tricky pieces early to gain needed design insights.

As to the suggested methodology based on these foundation principles, follow these steps:

1. Get a sample database you can use locally on your development workstation. If the database is an existing mainframe or client/server database, consider extracting a representative portion of the data as an Access 2.0-formatted database. If the database is an existing single-user local database, make a copy of it for your development use.

    If the database doesn't yet exist, design the database first using Microsoft Access 2.0 with its easy-to-use database design tools and excellent database documentation facilities. You can later easily "cut over" your application to the real client/server production database just by changing the configuration of the data source and driver using the ODBC 2.0 Administrative facilities. Generally, this works without missing a beat.

    Having your own local expendable database copy greatly speeds and simplifies development. It also affords you very tight control over the contents of the database for development testing purposes. In a client/server production environment where there may already be existing production applications using the database server, you will be viewed kindly by existing users for not bogging down the server and the network with your development activities. Without fail some of your coding will result in "goofs" that cause embarrassing server congestion and possibly failure conditions.

2. Design your SQL statements using Microsoft Query and the appropriate ODBC 2.0 drivers and databases. This interactive visual tool provides immediate insight into the effects of any SQL statements you might create. It also gives you a tangible sense of performance early in the design process.

The SQL statements that you design can be saved for later recall, reuse, and modification. Also, using Microsoft Query enables you to test the validity and correctness of the SQL statements. Finally, when used in conjunction with ODBC Spy you can use MS Query to determine the correct sequence of ODBC function calls if you are planning to develop an application that makes direct ODBC API calls.

3. Design and develop Visual Basic code to generate the desired type of result set (that is, `Dynaset`, `Snapshot`, or `Table`) from your SQL statements. Validate the correctness of the result set. This is generally the core of your application.

4. Design and develop user input screen fields or dialog boxes and integrate and test these with the rest of your code.

5. Next, concentrate your design and development efforts on suitably formatting the result set for user consumption. That is, create appropriately formatted grids, tables, graphs, or other presentation interfaces.

6. Finally, add error-handling code to your application. The importance of this step cannot be over-emphasized. The quality and professionalism of your completed application is mostly judged by how well you are able to trap and handle runtime errors. Besides, you really don't like getting those support calls from confused and angry users at 2:00 a.m., do you?

7. Test your application by supplying user inputs with intentional errors, databases with incorrect or inconsistent values, and transactions that are aborted. Check the database state after each test to make sure something undesirable hasn't happened.

8. Use Visual Basic Professional Edition's Setup Wizard to package your compiled application, along with any ODBC drivers, INI files, demo databases, and HELP systems into a neat Windows Setup program for floppy disk distribution.

These steps are admittedly a very brief summary, but they contain the essential sequence of steps to be accomplished.

Beginning Your Visual Basic ODBC 2.0 Application

When you begin developing your Visual Basic ODBC 2.0 application, make sure to decide clearly from among the possible plans of attack outlined above. Are you going to use the Data Control or object variables, or are you going plunge right into using the ODBC 2.0 API?

III

Visual Basic

If you are not sure just where your application development will lead you, then prototype the essential elements using just the Data Control. This gives you a feeling for performance and lets you explore alternative design plans without the need to make major investments in custom code.

Don't become too attached to this first effort—remember, it's just a prototype. You might benefit the most from this prototype in the area of user-interface design. By taking the quickest path to getting your database queries accomplished, you can spend some time concentrating on how the application looks and feels. Get your intended user audience involved at this point, and try to get the user interface pinned down early. If you wait to the very end of your development before involving the users in the screen interface, you may have to redo a lot of work throughout your application to accommodate their needs, prejudices, and sense of artistic interpretation.

Packaging and Distributing Your Application

Regardless of the design strategy you choose for your Visual Basic application, you will most likely want to use the Professional Edition's Setup Wizard to package your finished ODBC 2.0 application into a SETUP floppy-disk set for distribution to your users. However, the techniques needed to distribute a Visual Basic application that includes ODBC 2.0 typically involve some additional considerations. Principal among these considerations are:

- How do you plan to get your end user the needed ODBC 2.0 drivers or, for that matter, the ODBC runtime libraries and ODBC Administrative application?

- Do you plan to distribute a database along with the application if the application is using a workstation local ODBC-compatible database?

- In a client/server environment, how do you get your user's workstation properly configured to access the server, including such items as the data source, network service, and database names and such information?

Responding to these considerations usually can be accomplished by:

- Making appropriate selections in the Setup Wizard's dialog boxes—in steps 2, 3, and 5

- Making modifications to the SETUPWIZ.INI file found in the following directory: C:\VB\SETUPKIT\KITFILES

■ Making modifications to the SETUP1.MAK project found in the following directory: C:\VB\SETUPKIT\SETUP1

Let's briefly look at making the required choices and modifications and the motives for these choices.

Visual Basic ODBC 2.0 Setup Wizard Dialog Box Choices

The ODBC-specific Setup Wizard dialog box choices are made in the step 3 and step 5 dialog boxes. In the step 2 dialog box, you can select an option: Data Access. If you select this option, you are taken to the step 3 dialog box, which lists all of the ODBC drivers that you have installed on your system. Essentially, the Setup Wizard reads and interprets the ODBINST.INI file to determine all of the drivers you have installed.

Be sure to select from the list box in step 3 and choose the ODBC driver your application needs. Also be sure of the license agreements that may be involved in making copies of and distributing any ODBC drivers. Check with you ODBC driver vendor about any per-copy license fees or restrictions that might apply.

After selecting the ODBC driver you need, notice that the Setup Wizard's step 5 dialog box displays another list box showing all of the ODBC driver and ODBC Administrative software that is needed to support your application.

For example, if in step 3 you choose SQL Server as the ODBC database, then your list box in the step 5 dialog box contains the following additional entries:

File Name	Contains
ODBC.DLL	ODBC Runtime library
ODBCINST.DLL	ODBC Installation libraries
ODBCINST.HLP	ODBC Installation Help file
SQLSRVR.DLL	SQL Server Administrative library
DBNMP3.DLL	SQL Server runtime driver library
INSTCAT.SQL	ODBC Installation stored procedures file
CTL3D.DLL	Three-dimensional style dialog box library

Other ODBC drivers you might choose would display their respective libraries and drivers files.

III

Visual Basic

Making Modifications to the SETUPWIZ.INI File

Under several circumstances you might want to make your own custom modifications to the "standard" SETUPWIZ.INI file. Such circumstances might include installing sample databases or installing your own application-specific help files so that they are added to your distribution floppy disks by the Setup Wizard.

Making the needed modifications can be accomplished quite simply by editing in the name of the files into the appropriately named section of the SETUPWIZ.INI file. Follow the style of how the other files are specified in these sections. Again using the example of a SQL Server ODBC database, you add the file names to the [SQL Server] section.

Making Modifications to the SETUP1.MAK Project

Other installation steps you might need to perform can be accommodated by making code modifications to the prototype SETUP program whose source code is contained in the SETUP1.MAK project file. Typically, these additional code procedures are placed in the Form_Load event procedure for SETUP1.FRM file.

Examples of chores you might want to complete during execution of the SETUP program using this technique are:

- Creating additional sections and entries in the ODBC.INI file to cause automatic configuration of an ODBC data source

- Creating an additional SETUP dialog box that requests your users' data source UserID and Password so that these could be automatically configured into your application

Making modifications to ODBC.INI sections during SETUP can be accomplished simply by declaring and invoking the Windows API function WritePrivateProfileString(). Refer to the Windows 3.1 SDK Help system that comes with Visual Basic for information on the WritePrivateProfileString() function.

Summarizing Visual Basic's Database Architecture

Visual Basic has a broad capability to access databases, including direct support for Microsoft Access databases, installable ISAM drivers (supporting Btrieve, Paradox, and dBASE database files), and an interface into the ODBC architecture. All of these mechanisms for database access are managed by the Microsoft JET (Joint Engineering Technology) Engine. The JET Engine's role is essentially to provide:

■ An ANSI SQL standard parser/analyzer

■ Memory management for use by query result sets

■ External interfaces to the supported databases

■ A unified internal interface for application code

Visual Basic's database architecture is shown in figure 17.3.

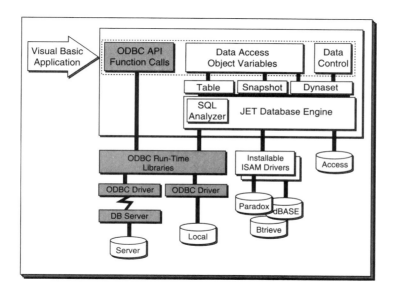

Fig 17.3
The Visual Basic Database Architecture.

Internally, as viewed from the perspective of your application's program code, this architecture provides a unified view of all of these database access facilities. In addition, three types of database result set objects are synthesized—Dynasets, Snapshots, and Tables. These result set objects manage and hide the complexity of memory allocation and deallocation and other difficult chores. As a result, your code is not bogged down in having to implement complex result set memory management algorithms since methods are provided for use with these objects as part of Visual Basic's language syntax to accomplish this easily for you.

In this chapter, you concentrate on understanding and using just the Dynaset object since it is only this result set object type that is manipulated by the

Data Control. In the next chapter, you delve into added details of the Dynaset, as well as the Snapshot and Table objects when we explore Data Access Object variables.

Understanding Visual Basic's Database Engine

At the core of Visual Basic's database architecture is the so-called JET Database Engine, which you often encounter in Microsoft documentation and other literature discussing this architecture.

This engine incorporates several interesting features, many of which can be inferred from figure 17.3. First, notice that the JET Engine acts as a "backplane" facility on one end for plugging in multiple installable ISAM (Indexed Sequential Access Method) database drivers. Drivers for such ISAM databases as Paradox, dBASE (or Xbase), and Btrieve are included in the Visual Basic Professional Edition product. Many additional compatible ISAM drivers are available from aftermarket vendors.

Notice also that the JET Engine provides a similar type of "backplane" interface for accessing the ODBC runtime libraries and Administrative application. In addition, the JET Engine provides direct built-in native support for Microsoft Access-style databases.

Also notice that internal to the JET Engine is an SQL Analyzer. This SQL Analyzer accepts ANSI standard SQL statements, which are submitted by your Visual Basic application code, and provides Visual Basic local parsing, analysis, and error exception handling. In fact, this SQL Analyzer is needed to support the built-in Microsoft Access database library functions but also is available for parsing SQL statements for any of the other support database facilities appended to the JET Engine.

On the inboard side of the JET Engine, notice that there are three types of result set objects which the engine creates and manages for use by your Visual Basic application code. Respectively, these three objects are called the Table, Snapshot, and Dynaset. Collectively, these are often referred to as Recordset objects, but in fact each object has a different set of dynamic behavioral characteristics.

As mentioned earlier, the significance of these Recordset objects is that they are created and managed for you by Visual Basic's JET Engine code, thereby abstracting the detailed complexities of result set-related memory management, cursor management, and exception handling into a highly unified and simplified programming interface for your Visual Basic application code.

This is a great advantage, since from the perspective of your Visual Basic code the whole external architecture of ODBC, ISAM drivers, and Microsoft Access databases is unified into one consistent, single programming interface. That is, the Recordset object view presented to the Visual Basic application programmer appears to be independent of the type and style of database being used. This apparent and real independence can be exploited to your advantage by your Visual Basic applications. For example, representative possibilities might be:

- Designing and developing your application using a workstation local Microsoft Access database and, when completed, putting that application into production using an ORACLE or other ODBC-style database

- Designing and developing your application using a pre-existing dBASE IV database, and then later converting the dBASE IV database into an Informix database accessed via ODBC

- Designing and developing you application using your company's current IBM mainframe DB2 database, and later "porting" the database to a client/server environment with the database on SQL Server

In the examples previously cited, few or no code changes are required to make these transitions from one database type to another. Notice also in the examples given that even databases whose native DDL (Data Definition Language) and DML (Data Manipulation Language) is "non-SQL" (such as, dBASE IV, Paradox, or Btrieve) can be manipulated using SQL language statements and Visual Basic's JET Engine architecture.

Interfacing to ODBC 2.0 Facilities and Databases

As with all other databases in a Visual Basic application context, your application's interface to ODBC 2.0 databases and facilities is via Visual Basic's JET Engine. The JET Engine is the interface target of your SQL statements, and one of the Recordset objects is your interface to the result set. Therefore, ODBC 2.0 databases are treated like any other databases you might access in Visual Basic applications.

Using the Data Control's *Dynaset*

The subsequent focus of this chapter is on accessing ODBC 2.0 databases using Visual Basic's Data Control. Since the Data Control, as shown in figure 17.3, uses only the Dynaset Recordset type, you must take some time at this point to concentrate on the characteristics of the Dynaset and how it can be used in your Visual Basic application.

Dynaset **Characteristics**

A Visual Basic Dynaset embodies a combination of several complex programming chores that in other programming environments are the responsibility of the application programmer. Essentially a Dynaset is an object, with a number of associated properties and methods, that implements the following tasks for a result set:

- Dynamically allocates and deallocates storage in local workstation memory for the purposes of buffering records of a database query result set

- Fetches and buffers the primary index key of the result set in local memory

- Fetches records on demand from the result set based on requests for data from the application

- Monitors and manages result set record updates, deletes, and adds as requested by the application, and writes these changes through to the database tables which are affected

- Automatically manipulates the record set cursor to achieve the other operations outlined above

As a summary, the Dynaset could be described as a dynamic, updateable, memory-resident, and paged "virtual" table because, to the Visual Basic programmer, this is how the Dynaset object appears.

Since a Dynaset is created and modified dynamically, it is appropriate to look at its dynamic behavior a bit more closely to understand how it really works and what it is doing.

The first important concept in this regard is to understand how the primary-index key information of the result set is created and managed by the Dynaset object. Assume that you have just executed an SQL statement to some database source. For purposes of this discussion let's keep this pretty basic, so the SQL statement is

```
SELECT * FROM table-name
```

The result set that is produced within an ODBC 2.0-compliant database server consists of all of the records from the table.

What the Dynaset object does and does not do from this point forward is quite interesting. It does not immediately begin fetching all of the rows in the result set and start buffering them in your workstation's memory. Instead, it begins a process of fetching only the field which contains the primary-index key of the table. Once the code that performs this operation is started, the task is moved into Windows background task queue so that the work required does not interfere with foreground screen painting and user operations. Thus, whenever there is no code stream that needs to be run to service Windows foreground operations, the primary-key fetch operation continues. After some period of time, depending on other work on your computer, a memory-resident "cache" containing the primary-index set is developed.

While this is going on, the Dynaset object also fetches some number of complete records from your result set and buffers these records in your workstation's memory. The exact number of records that are fetched is dependent on the size of a record. The number of whole records fetched is called a *page* and is, by default, set to be 2048 bytes' worth of records. The whole records that are initially fetched (or the initial page) is determined based on primary-index key order. Thus, very quickly, an initial page of records is fetched and buffered. Don't forget that, in the background, the Dynaset continues with its efforts to retrieve the field that contains the primary-index key and "cache" that key set information in memory.

As a Visual Basic programmer using a Dynaset object, your application initially presents you with the first page of result set records in primary-index key order. Having completed this initial flurry of activity, the Dynaset object becomes dormant and awaits your command to see what it is supposed to do next.

The Dynaset object next carries out your programming instructions about what you would like to do with the result set. These instructions are expressed with methods of the Dynaset object such as:

Dynaset **Method**	**Effect of Execution**
MOVEFIRST	Moves to the first record
MOVELAST	Moves to the last record
MOVENEXT	Moves to the next record
MOVEPREVIOUS	Moves to the previous record
FINDFIRST C$	Finds first record matching C$
FINDLAST C$	Finds last record matching C$
FINDNEXT C$	Finds next record matching C$

(continues)

III

Visual Basic

Dynaset **Method**	**Effect of Execution**
FINDPREVIOUS C$	Finds previous record matching C$
ADDNEW	Adds a new record
EDIT	Edits a record
DELETE	Deletes a record
UPDATE	Updates a record
REFRESH	Refreshes the contents of a Dynaset
CLONE	Creates a copy of a Dynaset

In order to implement any of the MOVE or FIND methods, the Dynaset object immediately refers to the "cached" primary-index key set that it created earlier and then evaluates whether the desired record lies within a current memory-resident page of records or not.

If the requested record is within a resident page, all is well. However, if the requested record is not within a current resident page, the Dynaset object automatically performs some more record fetches from the result set, builds an additional page, and adds the new page to the one(s) currently in memory.

Any intervening pages of records (in primary-index key order) that you do not reference are not fetched from the result set. Eventually though, if you were to traverse all of the records, you would find a complete image of the result set buffered in local memory.

Furthermore, the Dynaset object always keeps track of which result set records it currently has buffered as "pages" in memory. If you execute the REFRESH method, the Dynaset object in essence re-executes your original SQL query (actually, it evaluates whether anything has changed in the region of the underlying database's index key tables' rows), automatically fetches any of the affected records, and updates the appropriate pages in memory. This is particularly important when you consider that the underlying ODBC database is likely to be in a client/server configuration supporting numerous users, any of which could be making update or delete changes to the database.

Last but not least, the Dynaset object implements a Least Recently Used (LRU) algorithm as it manages the pages of records in memory. Based on available storage, the Dynaset object abandons the oldest pages in memory as newer records are demanded and fetched. If you later reference the records that have been abandoned, the Dynaset object refetches them.

If you execute any of the Dynaset methods that request a change to the contents of a record in the underlying table(s) represented in the result set (for example, UPDATE, ADDNEW, or DELETE), the Dynaset automatically generates the appropriate commands to the database to modify the contents of the records. In essence, it takes your programming modifications, which have been applied to the memory image, and "writes through" to the underlying tables.

Now, aren't you glad that the Dynaset object does all of these complicated operations so that you don't have to write all of the code required to accomplish this work? I know that I'm grateful.

Visual Basic Application Considerations

As the Visual Basic application programmer in charge of controlling the Dynaset object, it is imperative that you always keep in mind what the internal dynamic behavior of a Dynaset really is. The key considerations from a programming standpoint are:

- The Dynaset represents a "live" connection to the underlying database tables—remember "write through" updates?

- The Dynaset is paged in groups of 2048 bytes worth of records at a time.

- The Dynaset fetches pages in primary-index key order—know which is your primary-index key!

- The Dynaset is the Recordset object type supporting the Visual Basic Data Control and therefore the behavior of the Data Control is influenced by (and influences) the Dynaset behavior described.

Keep these points in mind at all times and the Dynaset can be a Visual Basic ODBC 2.0 programmer's best friend.

Using the ODBC Administrative Dialog Boxes

Now that you have a deeper appreciation for the Dynaset object—the Recordset type attached to the Visual Basic Data Control, you can begin to consider how your Visual Basic ODBC 2.0 application might make use of the Data Control. For this discussion, refer to figure 17.4.

Generally, the first step in programming the use of the Data Control for use with an ODBC data source is to specify the Data Control's related properties. At design time, these are set using the Data Control's Properties window. The Data Control has the following properties:

III

Visual Basic

Property	Purpose
CONNECT	Specify "path" to external data source
DATABASENAME	Specifies the file name of database
RECORDSOURCE	Within a database, the source of records

Fig. 17.4
Visual Basic Data
Control and
Properties
Window.

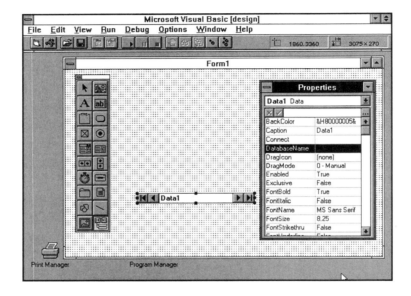

When using ODBC data sources, the CONNECT property is the string that specifies ODBC parameters. A generic example is

```
ODBC;DSN=DataSourceName;UID=UserID;PWD=UserPassword;
```

If the string you provide for the CONNECT property at design time consists only of the string ODBC;, then when your program executes, it automatically invokes the ODBC Administrative dialog boxes, which request selection of a Data Source Name.

If a Data Source Name has already been configured, then your application user makes their selection from this dialog box and chooses a particular Data Source. If the desired Data Source Name hasn't been configured yet, the user must choose the secondary dialog boxes to configure the ODBC driver and related physical database, and then finally dismisses the dialog box. Having completed these actions, the Data Control is thus provided with the CONNECT string that it needs. This process also provides the Data Control with the DATABASENAME that it needs.

Selecting an ODBC 2.0 Data Source

Based on what you need your application to do, you can choose to make only this minimum CONNECT property specification and thereby cause the ODBC Administrative dialog boxes to be displayed for user selection, or you can completely specify the fields in the CONNECT string to control data source access from within your Visual Basic code.

Configuring an ODBC 2.0 Data Source

You also can provide just the portions of the CONNECT string that specify that you want to use an ODBC data source (such as ODBC;) and just the Data Source Name (such as DSN=data-source;). If you take this approach when your program begins execution, the second level ODBC Administrative dialog boxes that deal with configuring the data source (such as UID= , PWD= , and other fields) are obtained after the user provides the needed dialog box information and dismisses the dialog box.

Using Multiple Data Sources

To access multiple ODBC data sources in a Visual Basic application which uses only the Data Control, you must provide and configure the properties of one Data Control for each data source you wish to use. Remember, this is equivalent to creating one Dynaset Recordset object type for each Data Control. Under some circumstances, this could present a limitation which hampers your application design. If this is the case, consult the following chapter on using Visual Basic's Data Access Object variables.

Executing an SQL Query

Once the CONNECT and DATABASENAME properties are set, the remaining task to invoke generation of the Data Controls Dynaset is to specify the RECORDSOURCE property of the Data Control.

When you use the Data Control with an ODBC data source, the RECORDSOURCE property needs to be assigned to a string. This string should contain a suitable SQL query. Any valid SQL SELECT query does nicely.

Once this property is assigned, the Data Control goes about producing its associated Dynaset Recordset object as described earlier.

If at some later point in your program, you want to modify the Data Control's Dynaset, you can do so. All you have to do is assign another properly formed SQL SELECT query to the data Control's RECORDSOURCE property and then invoke the Data Control's REFRESH method.

Setting the RECORDSOURCE to a new SQL statement followed by executing the REFRESH method causes the Data Controls' associated Dynaset to be rebuilt, reflecting the new SQL query.

Preparing the SQL Query

The process of preparing a suitable SQL query for the purposes previously described is left to your imagination, a good SQL syntax reference manual (you know, that big book that came with your ODBC database software, and you can't lay your hands on it right now), or the use of a good tool that creates well-formed SQL statements.

If you are in design mode in Visual Basic and need some intelligent assistance in formulating your SQL query, you should look around the Visual Basic ODBC 2.0 *workbench* outlined earlier in this chapter and lay your hands on Microsoft Query.

Microsoft Query is an interactive "query-by-example" tool that really comes into its own at this point in your programming efforts. You can begin Query and start a new query (open the File menu and choose New Query). You are presented with the usual ODBC Administrator dialog boxes from which you can choose any previously named data source (or configure a new or additional named data source if necessary).

After you select your desired data source, you are presented with a list dialog box (such as, the Add Tables dialog) of the available tables present within the data source. You can choose to add as many tables as you want by selecting them from this list. As you select tables from the Add Tables dialog, they are added to the Tables pane (portion of the screen above the splitter bar) of Query's window.

Once the desired tables are selected, you can dismiss the Add Tables dialog box and begin your work in earnest. You simply drag the fields you want in your SQL query from the tables presented in the Tables pane and drop them in the lower pane of the window, the Result Set pane (see fig. 17.5).

If you need to perform an inner join on two tables, in the Table pane just drag and drop the relational fields from the table with the primary-key side of the join to the table with the foreign-key side. A line appears linking the two joined tables. Some databases catalog such joins internally, and if they do these relational field join lines, will automatically appear linking the tables.

To specify an outer join, click the menu item Table and choose the Joins menu item in the drop-down menu. This action displays the Joins dialog box that enables you to choose which side of the outer join is to be the master table and which the dependent table.

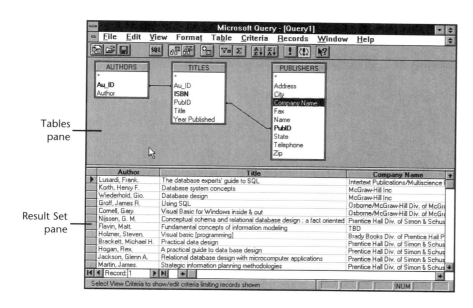

Fig. 17.5
Microsoft Query—
Main Window
Operations.

Tables
pane

Result Set
pane

Beyond the SQL statement's WHERE clause needed to specify any desired joins, you can select the Criteria menu item and choose the Add Criteria drop-down menu item to further develop a more complex WHERE clause. You could also get this same effect by clicking the Show/Hide Criteria button on the toolbar.

When you do this, a third pane (the Criteria pane) is placed in the middle of Microsoft Query's main window. This new pane graphically portrays any other filtering clauses you might need to construct to complete your SQL statement. Remember, you can use the splitter bar handles to resize the three panes.

Here comes the best part. As you are making your choices, the lower pane is constantly being updated to reflect the consequences of your choices in the result set grid.

Once you have the result set you're after, you can click the SQL toolbar button, and a window appears with a well-formed SQL query. The final step is to select the completed SQL query statement from this window and copy it to the clipboard. Then you are ready to paste this SQL query into your Visual Basic code. What could be simpler or more certain?

Using Microsoft Query for Ad Hoc Queries

By now you should be saying something like, "Wow, that was great!" followed by, "I wonder if I could do something like that in my Visual Basic application so that the user could interactively build the query that they want?"

III

Visual Basic

You bet you can—and you don't even have to duplicate all of the code it took to get that result. The way to tackle the problem is to exploit DDE (Dynamic Data Exchange). You can create a DDE link between your Visual Basic code and the MS Query application. There's no need to belabor you with all of the details, but the process is pretty straightforward.

For the necessary information to accomplish this DDE relationship—to answer those questions about the right LINKTOPIC, LINKITEM, and LINKMODE property settings and to find out about the values needed with the LINKEXECUTE method—just refer to the *Microsoft Query User's Guide*. All of your questions are answered there in Chapter 9, "Using Dynamic Data Exchange with Microsoft Query." Don't forget that the object of this exercise is just to get one thing—the well-formed SQL query string you need to assign the Data Control's RECORDSOURCE property.

A minor piece of cautionary advice here is to remember that Microsoft Query is a licensed product from Microsoft. If you are going to distribute your completed application using Microsoft Query, you must make sure that Microsoft Query is already installed on the user's computer, or you are going to have to work out some licensing deal with Microsoft. Since Microsoft Query is included with Microsoft Excel 5.0, you can be sure you're on safe ground if your users have a licensed copy of Excel 5.0. However, don't assume that Query was installed when they set up Excel. Make sure you (or your users) check.

Submitting the SQL Query

As previously described, the act of actually submitting the completed SQL query consists of assigning the SQL query string to the Data Control's RECORDSOURCE property and then invoking the Data Control's REFRESH method to generate (or regenerate) the Dynaset.

Evaluating the Success or Failure of Your SQL Query

Whenever you submit an SQL query, you should always check to see if an error code is returned. In the case you're presently considering, you are using a Data Control, so there is no function-return value to inspect to make this determination.

Instead, what you need to do is write an error trap and handler in the code procedure where you assign the RECORDSOURCE property. If the submitted SQL statement encounters any errors, a runtime error exception is posted by Visual Basic's database runtime library. You need to trap any possible errors, interpret them, and make appropriate recovery provisions in your code to respond to the errors.

For information on the possible error codes and message strings you might need to handle, you can refer to the Visual Basic Help system under the topic of "Trappable Data Access Errors."

Using the Data Control's Result Set

Presuming all has gone well to this point and you've gotten no runtime errors or have successfully recovered from them, you have created the Data Control's Dynaset Recordset object. You then can begin using this result set in your application.

There are two fundamental approaches you can take in using the Recordset. The first approach is the simplest and involves using Visual Basic's (or another third party's custom controls) bound controls. These are also called in the jargon "data-aware controls." The second approach is somewhat more complex and consists of directly accessing fields in the Recordset as properties of the Dynaset object and using the Dynaset's associated methods to maneuver through the results.

These two techniques are described in the following sections, along with some suggestions about which technique might best fit into your Visual Basic ODBC 2.0 application.

Using Visual Basic's Bound Controls

The first programming tactic for using the Data Control's Recordset is to use bound controls. These are Visual Basic controls that have a built-in awareness of the Data Control and can therefore be linked to the contents of the Data Control's Recordset.

Any Visual Basic controls—from Microsoft or third parties—that have the properties, shown in the following table, are bound controls and can be used in the way described shortly.

Property	Purpose
DATASOURCE	Object name of Data Control (Recordset)
DATAFIELD	Named field whose contents are displayed

By setting these two properties, the displayed contents of the bound control shows the field value (DATAFIELD property) of the associated Recordset, as specified by the DATASOURCE property of the control. The DATASOURCE property is the object name of a Data Control object—or in reality the Dynaset that belongs to the Data Control.

The specific record being displayed by one of these bound controls at any given time is determined by the then current position of the Recordset (that is, Dynaset) row pointer.

Of course, at Data Control initialization, recall that the Recordset's row pointer is positioned at the first row or record of the result set. And remember that the first row is first because it is first in primary-index key order.

Your remaining chore as a programmer is to decide how you want to maneuver the row pointer to traverse the rows in the Recordset. Under programming control this movement of the Recordset row pointer is accomplished by using the MOVE (Previous, Next, First, and Last) and FIND (Previous, Next, First, and Last) methods of the Recordset object.

However, the user can participate in this as well. As you know, there are some "video recorder"-style arrow buttons on each end of the Data Control. These buttons, when clicked by the user, invoke the FIND methods as well.

With this in mind, you might decide you do not want your application to enable row pointer movement by means of the Data Control buttons. In this case you have several choices to prevent user interaction. Your first choice is to set the VISIBLE property of the Data Control to False—the Data Control disappears from the screen. This provides you with the Dynaset that you need, without all of that random interference from the user clicking buttons.

The second alternative to consider is to set the ENABLED property to False. This grays out the Data Control signifying to the user, by Windows conventions, that the Data Control does not respond to clicking the button.

Of course, the choice is up to you, but there is an additional consideration that may tip the balance in one direction or the other. You should note that if the user performs the following procedures:

- changes focus, for example to a text-edit control that is bound to the Data Control in question; and,

- if that user then modifies the value by entering something different; and,

- the user (or your program code for that matter) moves the Recordset's row pointer to any other location; then, the modified value is written through to the underlying database tables from which the Recordset was synthesized. In effect, an update operation has just taken place.

The other Visual Basic standard and custom controls that can be bound to a Data Control are:

Control	From	Displayed As
TEXTBOX	Standard Edition	Text property
LABEL	Standard Edition	Caption property
CHECKBOX	Standard Edition	Value property
PICTUREBOX	Standard Edition	Picture property
IMAGE	Standard Edition	Picture property
SSCHECK	Pro Edition	Value property
SSPANEL	Pro Edition	Caption property
MASKEDBOX	Pro Edition	Text property

If you delve a bit deeper into ways to exploit the Data Control's Dynaset, you immediately become involved in discussing programming techniques.

Programming Techniques to Use the Result Set

As just noted in the previous section, you don't have to have a visible Data Control to use the Recordset that it creates. In fact, as noted, having the Data Control visible and its buttons accessible to the user can even present some problems.

Instead, you can take advantage of the Dynaset and implement all of your application's control over it by using the Recordset object's methods. Another bit of information to keep in mind when manipulating this Recordset object under program control is that it is an updateable "virtual table" image. Any modifications made to the fields of a row in the Recordset with any subsequent movement of the row pointer causes an immediate write-through update to the underlying database tables—just as discussed in the preceding section where the user might manipulate the Data Control's buttons. Recall also that the source of this field editing operation can be a user type-in of a bound control or a modification accomplished by your code.

III

Visual Basic

In addition to the Data Controls methods discussed earlier, you need to use one of the syntax forms shown in the following table to modify the value of the field of a Data Control's `Recordset`.

Fields Argument	Example Code Syntax
`index;SELECT order`	`Data1.recordset.Fields(1).Value`

`name;field name`	`Data1.recordset.Fields("name").Value`
	or alternatively
	`Data1.recordset("name").Value;`
	or `Data1.recordset("name")`

In addition, you can use the `ADDNEW` method to insert a new record at the current row-pointer position. Invoking this method on the `Recordset` object of a Data Control presents you with a blank record to which you can assign the desired values using the syntax in the previous table.

Finally, you can invoke the `CLONE` method on the `Recordset`. This does not create a whole new set of memory allocations and a whole new set of "cached" primary-index key lists. Instead, it simply offers you an additional and independent row pointer for navigating through the same `Recordset` object. This can be handy for performing more complex programming techniques while accessing the `Recordset` because there is essentially no cost in terms of memory resources used. It also affords the advantage that any time you might execute the `REFRESH` method of the Data Control, that all `CLONE`d `Recordset` references also are updated.

Incorporating Custom Controls

Many third-party Visual Basic custom controls that are compatible with the `Recordset` of the Data Control are available and can be used as bound controls. Many of these have been cleverly designed to accomplish some of the usual things that Visual Basic ODBC 2.0 programmers might need to do to format a query result set for user interface consumption. Usually your total effort is limited to setting a few properties of these custom controls and then enjoying the squeals of delight and amazement coming from your users.

You take a look at some of these custom controls. The objective here is not to endorse some control by inclusion or to imply rejection due to lack of inclusion. The problem here is one of too much wealth. There are just too many custom controls to even begin to do justice to them, even in a large book dedicated to the subject. So here goes—these custom controls have proven their usability by market popularity.

Browsing the Query Result Set

Sure, with several days of intense work you could get the Visual Basic Grid control to perform spectacular service as a spreadsheet-like result set browser. But for those of you with more important challenges to grapple with, it is usually expedient to purchase the available smart browser custom controls.

One of the more popular custom controls of this type is Apex Software's True Grid Pro Version 2.1. This handy product includes a variety of data-aware custom controls. But to the subject at hand, it includes a data-aware grid control (see fig. 17.6).

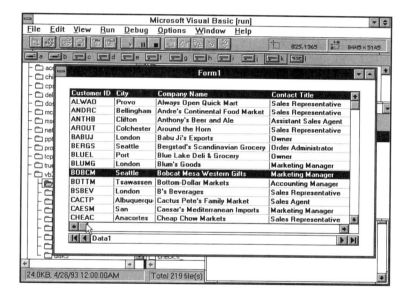

Fig. 17.6

Apex Software's True Grid Pro Grid Control.

In addition to the usual properties and the DATASOURCE property (you may ask, "What about the DATAFIELD property?"), there are 60 additional properties that enable you to customize just about everything about this grid. Also included are splitter bars and other sophisticated characteristics.

Back to your question about the DATAFIELD property. You really don't need to worry too much about that because the True Grid Pro grid's built-in behavior is to create a grid which is populated automatically with the fields it finds in your Recordset. Additionally, as you manipulate the vertical scrollbar on the grid, it takes care of all the work of executing the appropriate Recordset MOVE methods to get enough rows to display in the grid windows. This versatile custom control has many more features, too numerous to mention here. Suffice it to say that you can use True Grid Pro's grid control and easily create a database result set browser capability.

Another custom control in this same camp is Sheridan Software's Data Widgets Version 1.0. Again, this product consists of a number of other bound controls beside the grid that is included. As you can see from figure 17.7, the appearance of Sheridan's grid closely resembles the browser grid found in the Microsoft Access product. It also has similar behavioral characteristics.

Fig. 17.7
Sheridan Software's Data Widgets Grid Control.

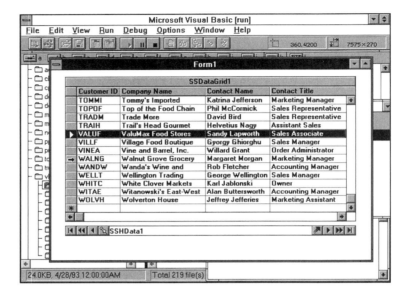

Again, don't limit your search for the perfect bound grid custom control just to these two products. The best thing perhaps is to buy several of them—they are fairly inexpensive—and evaluate them to see if they contain what you need to implement the user interface you had in mind.

Finally, don't overlook the other bound controls that are included in these two product packages and those from other custom control vendors. Some of the more useful controls for database applications are bound combo boxes that can be positioned within a grid cell for displaying drop-down many-to-one relationships and even enhanced Data Controls that include more user selectable buttons, such as buttons for setting bookmarks and similar capabilities.

Preparing the Query Result Set for Printing

Another knotty problem that usually arises in database applications is the seemingly unquenchable desire for printed reports. Even though users can browse the result set to their heart's content, they always seem to want the hard copy.

Formatting and preparing printed reports is usually a real personal and programming trial. First, it seems no matter how brilliantly and beautifully you designed the report format, there always seems to be a large committee formed to discuss how this is just not quite what they had in mind.

The second difficulty is that you can spend more of your programming time trying to fiddle with just the right fonts, organizing the strings for the print lines, managing the printer settings dialog boxes, and then finally managing the paper as it runs through the printer. Then of course there is the inevitable request for a print preview capability because all of the big-time commercial Windows applications have this feature. Sometimes it seems that 80 percent (or more) of your effort goes into printing reports.

Well, there are several custom controls on the market that can do most of the truly ugly work for you without requiring that you write bucketloads of Visual Basic code.

Again, with the same proviso that not all products can be covered here, a sample of such a custom control designed specifically for designing and printing reports from Visual Basic Recordset objects is offered.

The product is from Crystal Computer Services and is called Crystal Reports Pro V3.0. A typical screen from this product is shown in figure 17.8.

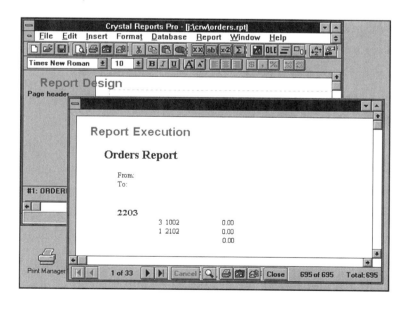

Fig. 17.8
Crystal Computer Services' Crystal Reports Pro V3.0.

This product consists of two fundamental components. The first component is designed to be used during the design and layout phase of developing the report. A specialized editor application enables placement of result set fields, fixed test labels and headings, and a variety of summarization functions. The idea is to do the layout and formatting activities prior to execution. All of the formatting and layout information is stored in a specially formatted file that is opened during execution of your Visual Basic application to retrieve this information.

In addition, there is a custom control VBX library. This is added to your Visual Basic project. This VBX contains the code to link to the layout and formatting files and control report execution and presentation during run time.

Some of the capabilities of the VBX library are to prepare the report and route it to the screen, a file for later output, or the printer directly. Using these features, you can implement a "print preview" type of capability. Almost all of the really complicated formatting and printer control operations are handled by the VBX.

Again, there are other similar products available in the custom control marketplace. Evaluate as many as you can and choose the one(s) that best meet your report printing and formatting needs.

Evaluating Data-Aware Custom Controls

A bit of generalized advice might be in order at this point concerning third-party custom controls with the data-aware features that have just been discussed. First, get as much information about the capabilities of the control before you set your heart on a particular control offering you programmer salvation. If possible, try to get a demo version of the control to play with before you buy it. Also, many vendors have 30-day money-back guarantees. They seem pretty confident that once you've tried their control you'll be hooked—usually a good sign. Finally, due to the usually low cost of these aftermarket controls, you should probably plan on purchasing two or three of them to see which ones best fit the problem you are trying to solve, rather than trying the more difficult approach of jumping up and down on your application to make it fit a particular ill-suited control.

Using Microsoft OCX Controls

As you may or may not have guessed at this point in your life, the whole programming world is going to object-oriented programming. Nowhere is this more evident than in the context of Visual Basic or Visual C++.

One of the signposts along the path leading in that direction can be found in Microsoft's Access Developer's Toolkit. Included with this toolkit are three new generation controls called OCXs or object controls. The three controls in the Toolkit are:

OCX Control	Functionality
Calendar control	Implements an interactive calendar
Data outline control	Implements an outline control
Scroll bar control	Implements a scroll bar control

These OCX controls, as you might guess by virtue of being included in the Access Developer's Toolkit, are controls that are typically used with database applications.

To use these controls, you need to have installed the Access Developers Toolkit. These OCX-type controls are designed to be used as mini-object libraries in the context of OLE 2.x Automation. The controls, when used in a Visual Basic application, require a client-object frame (also known as the Visual Basic OLE 2.x client control).

Once these controls have been installed on your computer, their object libraries are incorporated into the Registry file used by Windows (REG.DAT). As registered objects, you then can specify the CLASS property of the OLE 2.x client control to the class name of the object. Thereafter, you can manipulate the properties and methods of the object. Give these OCX controls a try—you'll be seeing more of them in the following months since they are intended to be Microsoft's successors to the current-day VBX custom control files.

For the additional information you need to incorporate these OCX objects into your Visual Basic ODBC 2.0 application, refer to the corresponding OCX's Help file. The methods and properties of these objects don't bear repeating here.

Capitalizing on OLE 2.x Automation

Now that you're on the subject of OLE 2.x Automation, be sure you don't overlook the great-granddaddy of all object libraries—Excel 5.0's object library. If you need a spreadsheet in your database application, why not get a *spreadsheet*? Also, if you need any of the other sophisticated objects that are in the Excel 5.0 object library, such as Pivot Tables, Charts, and so forth, why not use those available in Excel's object libraries?

The essential steps in "borrowing" these objects from their home object libraries consist of Visual Basic code as shown in this excerpt:

III

Visual Basic

```
Dim myobj as Object                'Declare an object variable
Set myobj = CreateObject("Object.Class.Name")
➥   'Invoke  object constructor; return object variable
myobj.property = VBVariable1       'Set object property
VBVariable2 = myobj.property       'Get object property
myobj.method                       'Invoke an objects methods
Set myobj = Nothing                'Set the object variable to NULL
```

You can find the `Object.Class.Name` you need for Visual Basic's `CreateObject()` function call by using the Windows utility application REGEDIT.EXE. Starting REGEDIT.EXE displays a dialog within which is a list box showing all of the registered class names that are present on you machine. If you really want to be overwhelmed, there is a command-line option switch for REGEDIT (the switch is /v), which puts it into so-called Verbose mode. This mode displays a ton of detailed information about each object in each object library.

Again, make sure that you understand the object library licensing conditions before packaging the object library DLLs with your completed Visual Basic application.

Anticipating Future Visual Basic Directions

By way of summary of this object-oriented discussion, you should keep your eyes and ears open for Windows applications that support OLE 2.x Automation or for more OCX controls. Clearly this is the direction that Microsoft is heading, and numerous other vendors will follow suit. Using appropriate objects from such object libraries is popularly known as *component coding* and for good reason. Why write some complicated Visual Basic source code when you can instead borrow the necessary components from an object library?

Trapping and Processing Errors

In a previous section, writing error traps and error handlers to take care of the inevitable errors that will occur in your Visual Basic ODBC 2.0 application was briefly discussed. There are some considerations that merit further attention in the endeavor and are specific to using the Data Control in an ODBC 2.0 application.

Dealing with ODBC 2.0 Errors

When using Visual Basic's incredible JET Database Engine, there are some translations and conversions made between the extensive error information typically available from the ODBC run-time library, ODBC driver, and the database engine of the ODBC data source.

As you saw earlier, all of the error return codes provided by the JET Engine are listed in the Visual Basic Help system under the topic of "Trappable Data Access Errors." If you look at that list for a minute, you notice that where Visual Basic's trappable data access errors consist of several hundred error returns, only about thirty-nine of these are ODBC-specific error indicators. Of the thirty-nine, many are quite generic or non-specific. This is out of an approximate total of 350 or so error codes.

The remainder of the error codes fall into two rather broad categories which are: JET Engine Access database specific errors and SQL syntax errors. From the earlier discussion of Visual Basic's data access architecture, it should be pretty apparent why this is the case.

If you then turn to the ODBC 2.0 SDK and look through the multitude of error code and condition types, you quickly realize that the Visual Basic ODBC error codes are not providing the whole scoop—something is getting filtered out along the way.

In later chapters, you take a closer look at this phenomenon and identify some different approaches to getting "closer to the source" on error codes. But at the moment, in the interest of keeping it fairly simple when using the Data Control, you look at a couple of techniques that provide more information without having to make ODBC 2.0 API calls.

This investigation centers only on the direct ODBC error returns and sets aside the SQL syntax errors that are well represented in error codes returned by the JET Engine's built-in ANSI SQL parser/analyzer.

Interpreting ODBC Error Return Information

One fairly effective and yet not too complex of a technique is to look not just at the error code, which your error handler retrieves from the run-time environment with the Visual Basic Err function, but involves looking also at the error-message string that is returned by the Visual Basic Error function.

With a bit of string parsing code, you usually can analyze the contents of this error string, and extract additional information about the exact nature of the error.

As an example, take a closer look at error code 602, described in the Visual Basic Help system as follows:

```
602    General ODBC Error: 'item'
```

The 602 error often is used by Visual Basic as a way of passing through an underlying ODBC API error. All that is done is that the source error string from the ODBC API is repackaged as the 'item' part of the 602 error-message string. Parsing and analyzing the string portion identified as 'item' usually yields a wealth of additional error information. The same technique applies equally to the Visual Basic error code 606, described as

```
606     SQL Connect Failure: 'item'
```

So look at all of the ODBC error-message strings in messages that are described in the Visual Basic Help system with the description including 'item'. A comprehensive list of these are the error codes:

```
611, 613, 614, 615, 618, 619, 644, 3151, 3152, 3153, 3154
```

Until you dig deeper in subsequent chapters, that should give you some added insight into ODBC errors you might encounter while programming.

From Here...

To learn more about Visual Basic and ODBC 2.0 refer to the next two chapters.

■ Chapter 18, "Using Visual Basic Data Access Objects with ODBC 2.0," discusses using the more sophisticated Access Objects to implement an ODBC 2.0 application; and,

■ Chapter 19, "Using the ODBC API from within Visual Basic," shows how you can use the ODBC 2.0 API function calls to develop your Visual Basic database application.

Chapter 18

Using Visual Basic Data Access Objects with ODBC 2.0

Visual Basic's Data Access Object (DAO) variables provide a great deal of additional control and flexibility in accessing ODBC 2.0 databases. They offer greatly expanded capabilities over those provided by the Data Control you analyzed in the previous chapter.

The scope and versatility of using these object variables often will provide you with all of the horsepower you need to develop sophisticated database applications. In this chapter you will take a close look at what can be done with these object variables in the context of programming Visual Basic ODBC 2.0 applications. Specifically in this chapter, the following major topics are covered:

- Capabilities of Data Access Object variables

- How to use these object variables effectively

- How to implement SQL language operations

- How to create new databases using object variables

- Methods for complete transaction processing

- Techniques for managing and updating ODBC.INI

- Criteria for choosing a result set object model

- Areas where ODBC 2.0 API calls might be used

- Pros and cons of using data object variables

III

Visual Basic

Understanding Data Access Object Variables

The very first thing you need to know about Data Access Object variable programming is that it is only supported in the Visual Basic Professional Edition. By the time you've finished this chapter, I believe you'll see the wisdom in sacrificing the extra few dollars to make sure that you get the Professional Edition. No self-respecting Visual Basic database application programmer would want to try to do his or her job without object variables.

If you currently have just the Visual Basic Standard Edition, you might want to consider taking Microsoft up on one of its upgrade offers to the Professional Edition level. Again, Data Access Object variable capability is only available in the Professional Edition.

So just what are these "you can't live without them" object variables, anyway? The broadest explanation of the Data Access Object variables is that they provide a unified model—and therefore programming interface—of a database. By "model" I mean that the internal structures and operations of a database can be represented by an abstraction that hides much of the database's complexity—including both static and dynamic operations complexity. With a bit of study of Data Access Object variables, it becomes clear that Visual Basic's object variables offer an additional layer of consistency and simplification on top of the highly unified database interface presented by ODBC 2.0. The two capabilities—Visual Basic and ODBC 2.0—seem like well-suited natural partners in making a database application programmer's life easier and more productive.

In the world of Visual Basic's Data Access Object variables, all databases—I repeat—*all* databases appear to be a large sack full of well-structured, uniform objects. The objects can be inspected, manipulated, created, and destroyed using the properties and methods of the objects. These objects, and their hierarchical relationship to each other, are shown in figure 18.1.

Let's take a brief look at each of the objects that make up the Data Access Object variables of Visual Basic's Professional Edition before you look at how they are used in detail to accomplish specific programming chores.

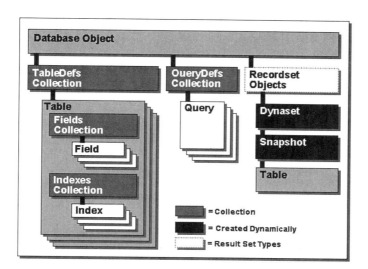

Fig. 18.1
The Visual Basic Data Access Object (DAO) hierarchy.

Programming with Database Object Variables

As you'll notice in figure 18.1, the database object variables are organized into a structured hierarchy. Some of the objects are "persistent" objects; they are "remembered" by the disk drive that contains the object's data structures. Some of the objects are "transient" objects; their data structures are constructed dynamically, on-demand as they are needed. Still other objects are what are called "collection" objects; they enumerate all objects within the hierarchy of a particular object type. The "persistent" objects of this model are, in hierarchical order:

- *TableDefs Collection*—an object that enumerates all table objects within the database object

- *QueryDefs Collection*—an object that enumerates all stored query objects (such as stored SQL statements, or stored procedures, often with replaceable parameters)

> **Note**
>
> The QueryDefs collection object pertains *only* to Microsoft Access-style databases used directly via the JET database engine built into Visual Basic. The QueryDefs collection object is *not supported* by ODBC database access.

> **Warning**
>
> If you try to use the QueryDefs collection with ODBC 2.0, even though you are working with an Access 1.0-, 1.1-, or 2.0- style database, you will get a run-time error.

- *Query Objects*—SQL statements that are stored in the database. They can be invoked for later execution, and often are described with replaceable parameters which are provided prior to execution.

- *Table Objects*—objects that contain Fields and Indexes collections, as well as the Field and Index objects themselves

- *Fields Collection*—within each Table object is a Fields Collection that enumerates all Field objects within the Table

- *Indexes Collection*—within each Table object is an Indexes Collection that enumerates all the Index objects within the Table

The "transient" objects of this hierarchy are the following:

- `Recordset` *Objects*—there are several types of `Recordset` Objects, each with a different behavioral characteristic. One category of `Recordset` Object is the Table Object. We already know that Table Objects are "persistent" objects. The other two types of recordset objects are created dynamically on demand. These are, in essence, different types of result sets.

- `Dynaset` *Objects*—at any given instant there can be from zero to many `Dynaset` Objects associated with a database. These are created on demand, and can be thought of as result sets that *are* updateable "virtual table" images with specific types of sophisticated cursor behaviors.

- `Snapshot` *Objects*—at any given instant there can be from zero to many `Snapshot` Objects associated with a database. These too are created on demand, and can be thought of as result sets that *are not* updateable, but also with sophisticated cursor behaviors.

The remainder of this chapter is devoted to gaining a better understanding of the characteristics of these database component objects. This involves the exploration of the properties and methods of these objects, as well as various functions that are used to open, close, create, and destroy them.

Using the Database Object

To begin using a particular database object, you first must OPEN the database so you can access its object contents. The act of opening the database establishes your connection with the database and with its *engine*—the drivers and algorithms that enable you to access and manipulate the database.

In the context of ODBC 2.0, this opening of the database involves providing the typical ODBC connect string, or invoking the corresponding ODBC Administrative dialog boxes to request the connect information from the user.

To OPEN an ODBC 2.0 database, you invoke the Visual Basic OpenDatabase function. An example of doing this is:

```
Dim db As Database
Set db = OpenDatabase("", FALSE, FALSE, "ODBC;")
```

In the preceding example, the code opens an ODBC database, using the usual ODBC connect string. In this case, since the only part of the connect string that is supplied is ODBC;, the ODBC Manager run time software automatically invokes Select A Data Source and any other necessary dialog boxes (such as Data File, User ID, and Password), and any other dialog boxes as may be required to connect to the data source.

Using the *TableDefs* Object

Once you have opened a database object, you can conveniently discover everything about the tables that it contains by using the TableDefs object. As briefly mentioned earlier, the TableDefs object is a "collection" object. Just what does that mean, anyway? You will soon better understand Collections because you will be using the concepts involved heavily throughout the rest of this chapter.

If you have done very much Visual Basic programming, you are probably familiar with several other "collection" objects that exist within Visual Basic that have nothing at all to do with databases. For example, there are the following two collection types:

- *Forms Collection Object*—This collection is an array of object variables that is automatically managed within Visual Basic. It enumerates all of the Forms Objects within your application.

- *Controls Collection Objects*—I use the plural here because there are many Controls Collection Objects in a typical Visual Basic program. There is a Controls Collection object variable array produced automatically for each Form object within your application. For each Form, its corresponding Controls Collection enumerates all of the Controls Objects (of any class or type) that are part of the Form.

A database's `TableDefs` object—a Collection Object, or an object variable array—is just another one of these collection objects like the Forms and Controls collections.

You're getting a bit closer. It's easy enough to understand arrays of variables, but just what are these object variables within these arrays (or as you now know them—Collections)? I'll try to roll together several different methods to illustrate this key concept.

Defining Objects

First, let's try the academic programming approach. Here's a sort of formal textbook definition:

> An *object variable* is a variable that contains the memory address of the root (or base address) of an object's data structure.

Objects are created by taking a class definition (such as a template data structure) and making a NEW copy (or instance) of the template's data structure somewhere in a newly allocated and unused area of free memory.

How to Create an Object from a Class

The familiar Visual Basic toolbox essentially can be thought of as a rack full of "rubber stamps," each of which has pasted on its face a template for "stamping" out identical replica data structures in memory (or, in proper terms, it's a Class definition).

Each time you grab one of these stamps with your mouse in the Visual Basic editor, and draw a control on a Visual Basic Form, you are creating a new instance of an Object of the Class (in techno-talk, you are performing *instantiation*).

The code execution machinery that is set in motion behind the scenes of this seemingly effortless act is known as invoking the "constructor" of the Class. That is to say, you are executing the Class' "constructor" code to get one of the Object data structures replicated in memory.

Understanding Objects and Object Variables

You just invoked the Class constructor and now have a NEW Object. What is the most important thing you absolutely must know about your NEW Object? I'll give away the answer—you have to know where in memory the constructor has built this NEW Object instance.

Without the memory address of the object's data structure's root, how will you ever find it again, or how will you refer to it when you need to use it? It is at this point that the compiler comes to your rescue. It assigns a *symbol*—a named variable—that it associates with the root address of the object's data structure. You probably know this symbol better as the NAME property of the object. Here is a quick review of the steps involved in creating an object:

1. Select the correct Class definition (or template) for the kind of object you want (such as a toolbox control widget, or the Add New Form button on the toolbar, or the corresponding menu commands).

   This invokes and runs a special set of computer program code that is associated with the Class definition—it's called the *constructor function*.

2. The constructor function executes, and, as a final kindness to the compiler, returns the memory address location of where it has just built the Object you requested using the Class template.

3. The Visual Basic compiler automatically makes up a default name symbol (something like Form1, Text1, or Picture1) and assigns the address returned by the Class constructor to the contents of the symbol (for instance, variable).

4. In the case of all objects for which there are Collections, the compiler automatically adds this symbol and the root address of the Object itself to an array of object variables.

Figure 18.2 recaps the essential steps in this process in a graphical flowchart of what occurs.

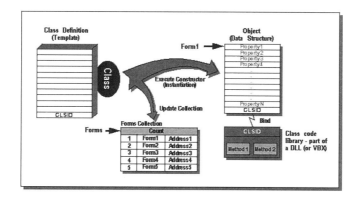

Fig. 18.2
Essential steps in creating an object from a class template.

Object Variables as C/C++ Pointers

Those of you who have some C++ experience will recognize the process; exactly the same steps and concepts are used in C++ programming. So if you do have some C or C++ experience (or know someone who does whom you can cross-examine on the subject), what do you call one of these variables that contains a memory address? That's right, it's called a *pointer*—a symbolic variable—that itself is just a compiler stand-in for a memory address, with the value stored at that address being itself an address. In C/C++ language syntax statements you would have:

```
int * ObjectNameSymbol;        // Declare pointer variable
ObjectNameSymbol = &Object; ·   // Assign address of Object to pointer
```

This can be read one bit at a time, as follows:

> `int * ObjectNameSymbol` means the variable `ObjectNameSymbol` is declared as a variable that can be used to contain an address.

> = means assign the contents of the variable symbol's memory address location that appears on the right-hand side to the contents of the variable symbol's memory address location that appears on the left-hand side.

> & means take the "reference," or obtain the address of the storage location referenced by the variable symbol `Object`, instead of actually retrieving the value stored in that memory location as you usually would do if this were an "ordinary" variable.

There you have it: the pointer variable `*ObjectNameSymbol` has the reference (read address) of the memory storage location `Object` assigned as its value—or the contents of the variable's memory address location.

It's pretty easy to know how much memory to allocate when you declare an object variable such as `ObjectNameSymbol`—you'll always allocate 4 bytes, so you can store those 32 address bits in it.

Understanding Object Variable Arrays

Prior to the previous subsection, you were focused on Collections, and not just simple object variables. So how do you get from object variables to Collections? Let's just take this one step at a time.

Jumping off from the example given above, what if we declared that the variable *ObjectNameSymbol was not just a single variable, but rather an array? The mixed metaphor syntax of the next example line of code is awful, but bear with me—such an array would be declared in pseudo-Visual Basic and mixed C/C++ syntax, something like:

```
Dim *ObjectNameSymbol(10) As Object*
```

What have you achieved with this declaration? You have just declared an array of Object Variables, haven't you? Think for a moment about the storage that is allocated to contain the values of these variables. Assuming the array starts with a lowest subscript of one (OPTION BASE 1 has been specified), you have just allocated 10 storage locations in memory, where each element of the array requires 4 bytes of storage. Each of the elements of this object variable array can be accessed just by using the subscript as you would with any array.

We have arrived (drum roll, please!) at Object Variable arrays. The reason for taking the time is that in the process of making this long journey, you should now understand the following concepts on which you will rely very heavily throughout the remainder of this chapter:

- *The concept of Class definitions*—data structure master templates, and associated constructor code

- *The concept of creating an instance of a Class* (also known as an Object of the Class)

- *The concept of how instances of Objects of a Class are created*—by invocation of the constructor of the Class

- *The concept of an Object Variable*—a variable that contains an address "pointing" to the root of the object's data structure

- *The concept of an Object Variable array*—just an ordinary subscripted variable array, except all of the elements of the array are used to store addresses (or pointers) to Objects located elsewhere in memory

A pictorial representation of an Object Variable array is shown in figure 18.3.

Fig. 18.3

Members of an
initialized Object
Variable array,
pointing to
Objects.

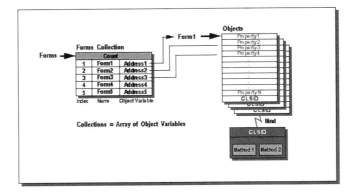

You already know that the Properties of Visual Basic Objects are stored in the
Object data structures. There is a storage variable (such as VISIBLE, CAPTION,
TEXT, and so forth) to contain the value of each of these variables. You can see
how important it is to know where the root address (or base address) of each
Object is at all times.

In fact, Collections are themselves Objects. Of course, there is that array of
object variables—obviously a key component of a Collection object's data
structure. However, there are other elements of a Collection object's data
structure—that is, there also are other Properties.

All Collection objects have a COUNT property so that the current size of the
object variable array is known at all times. Collection objects that are customized to serve a specialized purpose also have some additional properties.

Understanding the *TableDefs* Collection

At this point, the Data Access Object and the TableDefs Collection should be
pretty easy to understand. First, since it resides in and is stored in a "persistent" object—a Database Object—it will always be there when you need it.

Second, since you now understand a Collection as an enumerator and an
object variable array that "points" to other objects, it acts as a sort of telephone directory that you can reference to locate specific types of objects.

In fact, the TableDefs Collection serves just such a purpose. Once you have
opened a database, you can inquire about the contents of the TableDefs Collection, and with it you can ascertain the whereabouts of other objects within
the database. In the case of the TableDefs Collection, you can use it to find
out about all of the Table Objects that are present within a database.

At this point you might want to refer again to figure 18.1 to get yourself oriented to the hierarchical layout of a database and its constituent objects. You will notice that the `TableDefs` Collection is near the top of the hierarchy. The `TableDefs` Collection is in line with such other objects as Tables, and two other Collections, the Fields Collection and the Indexes Collection. Finally, you should be aware that each Table Object contains its own Fields and Indexes Collection objects.

Now for a bit of example code to give you an idea of how powerful these object variable arrays (Collections) are:

```
Dim db As Database                          ' Declare Database
                                            ' Object Variable
Dim intCount As Integer                     ' Declare an Integer
                                            ' Variable
Set db = OpenDatabase("", FALSE, FALSE, "ODBC;")  ' Open Database - pick
                                            ' any data source
For intCount = 0 to (db.TableDefs.Count - 1)  ' Loop: 0 to Count-1
                                            ' through TableDefs
    List1.AddItem db.TableDefs(intCount).Name  ' Use AddItem method to
                                            ' List all Table names
Next intCount                               ' End of For Loop
```

In the preceding example, other than declaring a few variables, there is very little code—just four lines. Yet, with this bit of code you can find out all of the table names within the database. Notice that you don't have to have any prior knowledge about the database at all. Pick any data source at all using the ODBC Data Source dialog boxes that result from the above execution of the `OpenDatabase` function, and you will discover all of the tables within that database.

Allow me one final parting shot here before we move on. Study the line of code above that reads:

```
Set db = OpenDatabase("", FALSE, FALSE, "ODBC;")
```

Ever wonder what the SET keyword does out there in front? Now that you know about object variables, I can tell you. It basically provides the same service as the * operator/symbol does in C/C++. Read the line of code to understand that it is doing the following:

- Invokes the `OpenDatabase` function. As you already know, the `OpenDatabase` function connects to an ODBC data source.

- The `OpenDatabase` function returns an Object—that is to say, it returns a memory address. If you've already read other portions of this book, including Chapter 19, "Using the ODBC API from within Visual Basic," you can think of this address as the `hdbc`—the connection handle to an ODBC

III

Visual Basic

database. The object the `hdbc` points to is an object created by a "constructor" function that resides somewhere deep within the combination of the ODBC Manager and the associated driver it is using. The "constructor" is invoked by the act of opening a connection to a data source, thereby causing the "constructor's" code stream to be run by the ODBC Manager. Obviously, this is an important data structure (object) to keep track of.

■ The keyword `SET` basically says that the resultant Object address that is returned from the OpenDatabase call should be assigned as an address to the Object variable (pointer) `db`.

Caution

Remember, when you no longer need the Object variable—actually, when you run the corresponding "destructor" of a Class to free the memory previously allocated to an object's data structures—then you also need to dispose of the Object variable. It is not a good idea to have variables that contain "pointers" lingering around in memory pointing to vast areas of unallocated memory. To accomplish this use: SET Object Variable = NOTHING. NOTHING is a VOID or NULL pointer (such as an address consisting of four bytes of zeros). More on this subject later.

Using Table Objects

To use a Table Object, it is usually important to know what Fields (Columns) are in a table, and also what Indexes are present within the table. Remember database structure first, and then worry about the contents (such as table rows or records).

If you look back at the organization chart of a database object as depicted in figure 18.1, you will notice the two Collections present in a Table Object. These two Collections will enable you to discover what Field Objects and what Index Objects make up the structure of the Table Object.

Using the Table's Fields Collection

First off, let's look more closely at an individual `TableDef` Object—also known as a Table Object. It would obviously be a member of the `TableDefs` Collection, and it would be the object describing a database table. Within a particular Table you would find the Fields Collection Object. Exactly what can you do with a particular Table Object's Fields Collection?

For example, you can add a few lines of code to your previous example and easily find out all of the Field Objects and all of the Index Objects that reside in a particular Table Object. Let's say you were interested in this information about the first table within a database. You could then write the following code:

```
Dim db As Database                                      ' Declare Database
                                                        ' Object Variable
Dim td As TableDef                                      ' Declare TableDef
                                                        ' Object Variable
Dim intCount As Integer                                 ' Loop counter variable
Set db = OpenDatabase("", FALSE, FALSE, "ODBC;")        ' Open Database - pick
                                                        ' any data source
Set td = db.TableDefs(1)                                ' TableDefs is a method
                                                        ' returns TableDef(1)
                                                        ' object
For intCount = 0 to (td.Fields.Count - 1)               ' Loop: 0 to Count-1
                                                        ' through TableDefs
    List1.AddItem "Name = " & td.Fields(intCount).Name  ' Use AddItem to
                                                        ' List all Field
                                                        ' names
    List1.AddItem "Type = " & td.Fields(intCount).Type  ' To List data
                                                        ' type of Field
    List1.AddItem "Size = " & td.Fields(intCount).Size  ' To List data
                                                        ' field size -
                                                        ' bytes
Next intCount                                           ' End of For Loop
```

The few lines added to the preceding code use the TableDefs Collection and a method of the TableDefs Collection called the TableDefs method—unforgettable, the method has the same name as the Collection!

The TableDefs method, as you will notice, has a calling argument. As with all Collection objects, this argument can be either the subscript of the Collection's Object Variable array, or the argument can be the name of the object in the Collection.

Back to the telephone book lookup example—you can look up someone's address in at least two possible ways:

- You can look up their address by using their name, or, if you have one of those Police Department reverse directories, then

- You can look up the person's address if you know their telephone number.

> **Note**
>
> Actually, there's (at least) a third strategy for locating the correct address. You could start at one corner of town and cruise down all the streets, ringing each doorbell in turn until you found the party in which you were interested. If you used this equivalent approach here, you would experience a General Protection Fault (GPF). Windows doesn't like it when you paw through memory, ringing doorbells uninvited! Besides, it could take a very long time to find what you are looking for, so a more organized approach is better.

It's exactly the same concept here. All Collection objects maintain and use two kinds of indexes—a subscript type of numerical index, and a "locate-by-name" index.

Using either type of argument with the like-named method of a collection instructs the method (also known in C++ circles as a member function of the Class) to look in the object variable array and find the object you want.

So, what's going on here? The `TableDefs` method of the `TableDefs` Collection Object is searching the `TableDefs` object variable array (also known in C++ circles as a member variable of the Class) to locate the object you want. It can search by the index of the array, or by object name lookup. When the `TableDefs` method locates the correct object variable array entry, it returns it to you as—you guessed it—an object (for example, a pointer or address).

The observation then from the code example is that in a few more lines of code you can find out everything you need to know about the Field Objects within a Table Object. You can find out the data TYPE of each field, the NAME of each field, and the SIZE (in bytes) of each field. Of course, you can find out in total how many fields there are by evaluating the `Fields.COUNT` property. Remember, all Collection objects have a COUNT property.

Using the Table's Indexes Collection

By now it should be boringly clear that there is a great deal of regularity to these Data Access Object variable techniques. In the pursuit of the computer programming profession, a bit of regularity and boredom is good news indeed. Who needs more irregular and inscrutable complexity to keep the old adrenaline level just over panic threshold at all times?

The regularity of Visual Basic's database objects is really driven home when we look at another Collection object that resides in a Table Object—the Indexes Collection.

If you have been following along this far you can probably guess what is coming next. That's right—the Indexes Collection enumerates all of a Table's indexes. And you also guessed correctly that the code required to get information about these indexes is quite similar to the code used to discover the characteristics of all Fields in the Fields Collection. To verify this suspicion, I have duplicated the code used in the previous example concerning the Fields Collection, and have simply replaced all of the references to "Fields" with the word "Indexes." This code looks like this:

```
Dim db As Database                                ' Declare Database
                                                  ' Object Variable
Dim td As TableDef                                ' Declare TableDef
                                                  ' Object Variable
Dim intCount As Integer                           ' Loop counter variable
Set db = OpenDatabase("", FALSE, FALSE, "ODBC;")  ' Open Database - pick
                                                  ' any data source
Set td = db.TableDefs(1)                          ' TableDefs is a method
                                                  ' returns TableDef(1)
                                                  ' object
For intCount = 0 to (td.Indexes.Count - 1)        ' Loop:  0 to Count-1
                                                  ' through Indexes
    List1.AddItem "Name = " & td.Indexes(intCount).Name    ' Use AddItem
                                                  ' to List all
                                                  ' Index names
    List1.AddItem "Type = " & td.Indexes(intCount).Fields  ' List fields
                                                  ' used in
                                                  ' Index
    List1.AddItem "Size = " & td.Indexes(intCount).Unique  ' List data
                                                  ' index unique
                                                  ' T/F
Next intCount                                     ' End of For
                                                  ' Loop
```

Go back and check that previous code example just to make sure that I am an honest man. I have been true to my word—I only changed all occurrences of "Fields" to "Indexes"—right? Well, not quite true, but you get the idea. An Index Object of the Indexes Collection has a Name property all right, but it has a Fields property that identifies the fields that make up the index, and a Unique property that tells if the index is unique (TRUE) or not (FALSE).

Using Snapshot Objects

So far we have looked at the "persistent" objects associated with a database—those that are permanently stored on the disk drive. We next will look at Data Access Object Variables that are created dynamically. These created on-demand objects are the Snapshot and the Dynaset. First, let's look at the simplest type of what are called generically "recordset" objects—the Snapshot object.

III

Visual Basic

Snapshot objects are created during the execution of your Visual Basic program. You can think of a Snapshot object as a result set created in response to an SQL query submitted by code in your program. A Snapshot object is an object that is constructed in memory that contains your SQL statement's result set records (rows) and fields (columns).

Creating a *Snapshot* Object

The way you create a Snapshot object is the same as you previously learned—you invoke the object's "constructor." In the case of a Snapshot object, this function is the CreateSnapshot function, and the function returns an object. A code example illustrating this is:

```
Dim db As Database
Dim sn As Snapshot
Dim strSQLQuery As String
strSQLQuery = "SELECT * FROM Customer"
Set db = OpenDatabase("", FALSE, FALSE, "ODBC;DSN=Access_2.0;
➥DBQ=C:\ODBCSDK\SMPLDATA\ACCESS\SAMPLE.MDB;FIL=RedISAM;")
Set sn = db.CreateSnapshot(strSQLQuery)
```

In the previous example, sn is a Snapshot object variable, or a "pointer" to the area in memory where the CreateSnapshot "constructor" has created and placed the Snapshot object. The sample ODBC database used in this example is one that comes with the ODBC 2.0 SDK, and happens to be an Access 2.0-style database.

The Snapshot object appears to be like a memory resident table that contains all of the fields (columns) and records (rows) requested by the SQL statement that is the argument of the CreateSnapshot function. You also could call the CreateSnapshot function a method (remember—member function of a Class) of the database object. Notice in the previous example the syntax db.CreateSnapshot("SQL"). In fact, the CreateSnapshot function is a member function or method of the database Class.

A Snapshot object, as a virtual memory resident Table, also has a Fields Collection object which enumerates all of the Fields that are present in this "virtual" Table Object. Again, as you saw previously you can use the "call-by-name" or "call-by-index" approach to identify the Fields in the Snapshot object. Following on then from the above example, you access the Fields as:

```
Dim varArray() As Variant
Dim intFlds As Integer
Dim intCnt As Integer
intFlds = sn.Fields.Count
ReDim varArray(intFlds)
For intCnt = 0 to (intCnt - 1)
➥varArray(intCnt) = sn.Fields(intCnt).Value
Next intCnt
```

This example declares an undimensioned array of variants—varArray. It then uses the Fields Collection object of the Snapshot object and the Count property of the Fields Collection object to redimension the variant array varArray to the number of Fields present in the Snapshot object sn.

In a loop, all of the values (notice a Field has a Value property) of each Field are assigned to successive elements of the variant array. A variant array is used because the data types of the several fields might be of different data types such as integer, long, double, string, and so forth. A variant can contain any of these data types. The value assigned to the elements of the array are those that comprise the first record or row of the Snapshot object.

Here are a few more facts about the Snapshot object. First, it is a "static" or non-updateable "virtual" memory resident Table image. Second, it is produced all at once. That is, every row that is returned as a member of the result set of your SQL statement is populated into the Snapshot object at the time you create the object. You cannot update the fields or rows in the Snapshot object.

From a performance standpoint, a Snapshot object is the fastest object to create. It can be created in almost the same time that would be required if you used the ODBC 2.0 API calls directly (see Chapter 19, "Using the ODBC API from within Visual Basic," for more discussion on this subject).

If you need a result set consisting of a few dozen to several hundred rows, and you don't need to do transaction processing to effect updates through the fetched rows, then the Snapshot object is for you.

Moving the Row Pointer within a *Snapshot* Object

As you noticed earlier, when you first access a Snapshot object immediately after it has been constructed, you will be looking at the first row of the Snapshot. How then do you maneuver away from that first row, and access other rows in the Snapshot?

The answer to this lies in a series of methods of the Snapshot object; incidentally, these also are methods of a Dynaset object that are discussed in the next section. Methods—remember, member functions of the Class? The methods of the Snapshot (or the other recordset type, the Dynaset) class are:

Method	Action Provided
MOVEFIRST	Move to the First row of the recordset
MOVELAST	Move to the Last row of the recordset
MOVENEXT	Move to the Next row of the recordset
MOVEPREVIOUS	Move to the Previous row of the recordset
FINDFIRST C$	Find the First row matching criteria C$
FINDLAST C$	Find the Last row matching criteria C$
FINDNEXT C$	Find the Next row matching criteria C$
FINDPREVIOUS C$	Find the Previous row matching criteria C$

Note

In the preceding table, you will notice that the FIND… Methods each have a string argument, denoted as C$. This is the FIND criteria, and is what the FIND search is looking for in the recordset. This C$ string can be any valid SQL WHERE clause that pertains to the fields present in the recordset.

In the previous example code, if you want to move through the Snapshot object, and look at each row in it, use:

```
Dim varArray() As Variant
Dim intFlds As Integer
Dim intCnt As Integer
Dim intRows As Integer
intFlds = sn.Fields.Count
ReDim varArray(intFlds)
Do Until sn.EOF                     ' Loop until the Snapshots
                                    ' EOF Property is FALSE
    intRows = intRows + 1
        For intCnt = 0 to (intCnt - 1)
            varArray(intCnt) = sn.Fields(intCnt).Value
        Next intCnt
    sn.MoveNext
Loop
MsgBox "Number of Rows = " & Str$(intRows)
```

The preceding example shows the use of the EOF property of a Snapshot object. When maneuvering through a Snapshot, you will eventually encounter a pair of "specially" formatted rows known as the EOF (End of File) and the BOF (Beginning of File) rows. These rows signify that you have just left the domain of valid rows, and are now either in the EOF or BOF row. In the previous example, until the EOF property becomes TRUE, you will continue to do MOVENEXT operations, moving the Snapshot's row pointer to successive rows.

Using *Dynaset* Objects

Unlike Snapshot objects that are Recordset objects which are fairly simple "static" memory images of an SQL statement result set, Dynasets are much more complex, more versatile, and also are more intensive resource users.

Dynasets are "updateable" virtual memory images of an SQL statement result set. As such they maintain a "live" linkage all the way back to the underlying database Tables that served as the source of the result set.

For a detailed discussion of how these Dynaset objects are constructed and how they operate, please refer to Chapter 17, "Using the Visual Basic Data Control with ODBC 2.0," where these topics are treated. The pertinent section in Chapter 17 is "Using the Data Control's Dynaset," and subsequent subsections.

For additional information about the behavior of the "keyset-driven" and "block-scrollable" types of result set cursors implemented by the Dynaset object, please see Chapter 19, "Using the ODBC API from within Visual Basic," especially the section titled "Addressing Application Performance," and related subsections.

Dynaset Object Methods

Due to the "live link" nature of a Dynaset object through to the underlying database tables, modifications made to the Dynaset are reflected in the underlying tables. That is, a transaction is processed against the database tables that were affected by the modification.

The methods discussed earlier concerning the Snapshot object also work the same way with a Dynaset object. However, there are additional methods that pertain only to Dynaset objects; these are:

Method	Action Provided
ADDNEW	Adds a new record to the Dynaset
DELETE	Deletes a record from the Dynaset
UPDATE	Updates a record in the Dynaset
EDIT	Places the Dynaset in Edit Mode
REFRESH	Refreshes the Dynaset contents

Dynaset **Dynamic Behavior**

Since the Dynaset implements a "keyset-driven," "block-scrollable," "dynamic" cursor model, the underlying database tables that formed the basis of the Dynaset might be shifting and changing while your Dynaset exists. This typically happens in a busy multi-user database environment.

For the Dynaset to reflect these changes, it uses a series of techniques to attempt to reflect the most current information possible—even though the source database is constantly in motion beneath its feet.

It automatically implements several techniques that are just inherent to the behavior of a Dynaset. Briefly summarized, these are:

- Unlike the Snapshot object, the Dynaset object only fetches rows of the result set as it needs them, and not all at once. It fetches "pages" of result set rows. A "page" is as many result set rows as will fit into a 2048-byte buffer segment. Since the Dynaset "waits" until your program actually moves through the result set before it populates the Dynaset buffers, it automatically gets the most current information from the database at the time the "page" is actually developed.

- At any time you can invoke the REFRESH method of the Dynaset object. When you do, the Dynaset's REFRESH method will identify only those pages in the Dynaset that have experienced changes in the underlying database tables since they were originally populated. It will then re-fetch and rebuild only those pages that may have changed. As a result, the Dynaset will contain rows that reflect the most current state of the database.

■ Only those "pages" of rows to which you actually request access will be populated. That is, the Dynaset is built one page at a time. If you are moving the row pointer through the rows of the populated "page" and you move off of the end of a currently populated "page," then and only then will the Dynaset fetch rows and populate an additional adjoining "page." For example, when the Dynaset is first constructed, it automatically populates the first "page" of result set rows. If you were to immediately execute a method like MOVELAST, the Dynaset would jump past any intervening "pages" of rows in the result set, and would only populate the additional "page" containing the last row of the result set.

Now that you are more familiar with the almost "magical" characteristics of a Dynaset's behavior, you need to understand how you can obtain one of these very "smart" objects.

Suggested Dynaset Exercise

For your enlightenment, amusement, and amazement—and to gain a real gut-level intuition about Dynaset behavior—you can conduct the following experiment:

Write some sample Visual Basic code that opens a database, and then creates a Dynaset from it. Pick a simple SQL statement like SELECT * FROM SomeTable as your CreateDynaset method argument.

Place a single Command Button on a Form that just executes the MOVENEXT method of the Dynaset object. However, before you execute your program, start up ODBC Spy, and "Spy" on the data source you will be using for your experiment.

Watch what happens in the ODBC Spy trace window when you first create the Dynaset, and subsequently when you MOVENEXT through it. You should notice that when you first create the Dynaset, a stream of SQLFetch and SQLGetData operations happens. These operations populate the initial "page" of the Dynaset. After a while everything settles down, and ODBC Spy shows no more SQLFetches.

Now, move through the Dynaset until you move off the initially constructed "page," and watch the SQLFetch operations start up again. Then, just as abruptly, they will cease as the next "page" has been constructed. You should really try this—it's very instructive. Keep this demo program because you might want also to experiment with the UPDATE, EDIT, DELETE, ADDNEW, and REFRESH methods as well to watch what they do.

You might also be intrigued to find out what happens when you perform the same experiment, but this time create a Snapshot object, and use the same SQL statement as before.

III

Visual Basic

Creating a *Dynaset* Object

To create a `Dynaset` object, you invoke the `CreateDynaset` method of a database object. This is all quite similar to the previous section where you investigated the `Snapshot` object. As you would suspect, the basic code to do this is also quite similar:

```
Dim db As Database
Dim ds As Dynaset
Dim strSQLQuery As String
strSQLQuery = "SELECT * FROM Customer"
Set db = OpenDatabase("", FALSE, FALSE, "ODBC;DSN=Access_2.0;
➥DBQ=C:\ODBCSDK\SMPLDATA\ACCESS\SAMPLE.MDB;FIL=RedISAM;")
Set ds = db.CreateDynaset(strSQLQuery)
```

You also can create a `Dynaset` from another `Recordset` object; for example, you can create a `Dynaset` from a `Snapshot` object. The fundamentals of the code would be:

```
Dim db As Database
Dim sn As Snapshot
Dim ds As Dynaset
Dim strSQLQuery As String
strSQLQuery = "SELECT * FROM Customer"
Set db = OpenDatabase("", FALSE, FALSE, "ODBC;DSN=Access_2.0;
➥DBQ=C:\ODBCSDK\SMPLDATA\ACCESS\SAMPLE.MDB;FIL=RedISAM;")
Set sn = db.CreateSnapshot(strSQLQuery)
Set ds = sn.CreateDynaset()
```

On the surface, this operation, creating a `Dynaset` object from a `Snapshot` object, would appear to be somewhat foolish—after all, you may ask, "Aren't both objects just the same?" Well, no; they are not the same. The `Snapshot` object is "static" and not updateable, while the `Dynaset` object is "dynamic."

Once you have created a `Dynaset` object, in addition to invoking the MOVEXXXX and FINDXXXX methods, you also can use the ADDNEW, EDIT, DELETE, and UPDATE methods. These methods are discussed in the section "Designing Transaction-Processing Applications" later in this chapter.

For the moment, however, you should note that if you set the value of any Field within a `Dynaset`, and then execute any method that moves the row pointer away from the row you were just looking at, the modification to the Field is "written through" to the underlying Table(s) from which the `Dynaset` was constructed. For example:

```
Dim db As Database
Dim ds As Dynaset
Dim strSQLQuery As String
strSQLQuery = "SELECT * FROM Customer"
```

```
Set db = OpenDatabase("", FALSE, FALSE, "ODBC;DSN=Access_2.0;
➥DBQ=C:\ODBCSDK\SMPLDATA\ACCESS\SAMPLE.MDB;FIL=RedISAM;")
Set ds = db.CreateDynaset(strSQLQuery)
ds.Field(1).Value = "The Changed Name of a Customer"
ds.MoveNext
```

In the example you will notice that in the second-to-last line you have assigned a new value to `Field(1)` of the `Dynaset` `ds`. In the last line of the example you execute the `MoveNext` method of the `Dynaset` that moves the row pointer down one row in the `Dynaset`. After the last line executes, the new value `"The Changed Name of a Customer"` will have been written through to the contents of `Field(1)`—which is the `"Company"` field of the underlying `CUSTOMER` Table within the `Access_2.0` database.

Designing Database-Generating Applications

Not only can you exploit the Tables, Fields, Indexes, and your choice of `Recordset` objects within an existing database, but you also can use Visual Basic object variables to create a brand-new database from scratch. Fortunately, or unfortunately, using the `CreateDatabase` function only enables you to create Microsoft Access-type databases. This capability is not presently generalized for other types of databases.

However, once you have created an Access-style database from within Visual Basic, you later can use the database through ODBC 2.0 facilities. This is also true if you create a non-Access database using the database creation procedures or functions of that particular ODBC 2.0 supported database. All you need to do, at a minimum, is to create the database "shell" itself. You later can use SQL statements such as `CREATE TABLE` and `CREATE INDEX` to "flesh out" the actual internal structures of the database.

Creating a New Database

To create a new Access-style database using Visual Basic, you use the `CreateDatabase` function, as shown in this example:

```
Dim db As Database
Set db = CreateDatabase("c:\dbdir\MyNewDB.mdb")
```

The database object variable `db` automatically has the Exclusive access attributes set, so only your application has access to it. Of course, this easily can be changed when you `CLOSE` the database, and use the `OpenDatabase` function to `OPEN` it again later.

III

Visual Basic

Creating the Database's Structure

Once you've created a new empty database object, you can proceed to create its internal structures—Tables and Indexes, the corresponding `TableDefs` Collections, Indexes Collections, and Fields Collections will be "Appended" to using code similar to the following example:

```
Dim db As Database                               ' Declare database
                                                 ' object variable
Set db = CreateDatabase("c:\dbdir\MyNewDB.mdb")  ' Create NEW blank
                                                 ' or empty database
Dim td As New TableDef                           ' Key word NEW - creates
                                                 ' NEW TableDef object
Dim fld As New Field                             ' Key word NEW - creates
                                                 ' NEW Field object
Dim inx As New Index                             ' Key word NEW - creates
                                                 ' NEW Index object
    td.Name = "MyNewTable"                       ' Set NAME property of
                                                 ' NEW Table
    fld.Name = "ATableField"                     ' Set NAME property of
                                                 ' NEW Field
    fld.Type = 10                                ' Set TYPE property of
                                                 ' NEW Field - Text
    fld.Size = 25                                ' Set SIZE property of
                                                 ' NEW Field - 25
                                                 ' characters
    td.Fields.Append fld                         ' Use APPEND method of
                                                 ' Fields collection
    inx.Name = "PrimaryKey"                      ' Set NAME property of
                                                 ' NEW Index
    inx.Fields = "ATableField"                   ' Set FIELDS property of
                                                 ' NEW Index
    inx.Primary = TRUE                           ' Set PRIMARY property of
                                                 ' NEW Index
    inx.Unique = TRUE                            ' Set UNIQUE property of
                                                 ' NEW Index
    td.Indexes.Append inx                        ' Use APPEND method of
                                                 ' Indexes collection
    db.TableDefs.Append td                       ' Use APPEND method of
                                                 ' TableDefs collection
db.Close                                         ' Close NEW database
```

Key Concepts in Using *NEW*

Obviously, the crucial ideas here are the NEW keyword, which creates a NEW instance of an object of a Class (or invokes the "constructor" of the Class), and the APPEND method that attaches an object to a collection.

1. You APPEND the NEW Field object to the Fields Collection.

2. You APPEND the NEW Index object to the Indexes Collection.

3. You APPEND the NEW TableDef object to the new blank database object you created.

The preceding example is highly simplified since it only creates one index, one table, and one field within the table, but you easily can repeat these steps to create and append as many indexes, tables, and fields as you desire.

Cloning an Existing Database

Sometimes the most direct way to accomplish a task is to plagiarize something almost like what you need, and then make a few crucial modifications. We of the professional programming trade prefer to use the turn of phrase "leveraging" prior practice, instead of the harsher and more legalistic sounding "plagiarizing." I'll leave the choice of the semantics up to you.

In any case, the Clone method enables you to use the OpenTable method of a database object, and create another "Cloned" object just like it as a separate object. You then could use the Append method with the cloned Table object, adding it to a brand-new database that you just created.

Subsequently, you could use the NEW operator to create a few more NEW Field and Index objects to the cloned table, thereby leveraging the structures of an existing database table that were just about right, but needed a bit of modification.

Designing Query Result Applications

Many Visual Basic database applications are of the type that just read an existing database and provide a particular result set as an "answer" to an SQL query. You will look at this category of applications exclusively in this section, and then turn your attention to database applications that interact with the database (such as read and write) in a later section titled "Designing Transaction-Processing Applications."

Preparing and Executing Your SQL Statements

In so-called read-only types of database applications, there are basically four primary considerations:

- Writing the SQL statement(s) that you need to get the desired result set

- Deciding on what type of Recordset object you want to use for the result set (as in Snapshot, Dynaset, or Table)

- Figuring how you need to navigate or maneuver your way around within the result set (for example, manipulate the row pointer or cursor)

III

Visual Basic

■ Determining how you can get the specific values you want from the result set

Let's take each of these subjects in turn, starting with the SQL statement.

Not all SQL statements are created equal. The SQL language model honored by Visual Basic is the SQL syntax conventions of the SQL parser/analyzer built into the JET engine. In most cases, if the JET engine analyzer will recognize and accept an SQL statement, then so will an ODBC data source. There are exceptions to this, and if you are trapping and tracing errors and notice what appear to be SQL analysis errors, you might rightfully suspect that the ODBC data source has a little different spin on the SQL statement than does Visual Basic's JET engine.

Caution

If you are having trouble getting past the JET engine's SQL analyzer/parser because your ODBC database uses a slightly different dialect of SQL, you can always set the DB_SQL_PASSTHRU option when submitting your query to the database. Recall, however, that if you do use the DB_SQL_PASSTHRU option flag, Visual Basic will only create a Snapshot object as the result set—regardless of whether you used the CreateDynaset method of the Database object to submit your query.

The exact syntax of Visual Basic's JET engine SQL parser/analyzer is well documented in the Visual Basic online Help system. If you are going to bypass this analyzer and go directly to an ODBC database, you will need to either get the manufacturer's documentation, or use the techniques for determining SQL conformance levels discussed in Chapter 19, "Using the ODBC API from within Visual Basic," to determine what flavor of SQL your database will accept.

Submitting your SQL statements is accomplished by using either the CreateSnapshot or the CreateDynaset methods of the Database object. Your next chore, then, is to see how to interact with this result set.

Interacting with the Result Set

Interacting with the result set, regardless of whether it is a Dynaset or Snapshot object, is the same—use the various MOVE and FIND methods to maneuver the row pointer to the row you want. There are a few additional concepts that merit discussion at this point, and these are related to another property of the Dynaset or Snapshot, called the Bookmark.

The Bookmark is a particularly useful property when using any of the FIND methods. A simple scenario easily illustrates the use of this Bookmark property:

■ Let's say you have a Recordset object and you want to locate a particular record within it. Naturally, you want your recordset's row pointer positioned at the desired row when it is located.

■ You decide that the best way to accomplish this is to use one of the FIND methods with an appropriate search criteria string (any valid SQL "WHERE" clause).

■ But what happens if no record matching the criteria is found when you execute one of the FIND methods? The row pointer will either be positioned at the EOF or the BOF of the result set. How then do you find your way back to the row where you just were without repeating all of the steps that got you there before you went on the wild goose chase with a non-matching FIND criteria?

The answer to the scenario just outlined makes use of the recordset's Bookmark property. The idea is that before you go moving the row pointer from the current row, and if you might want to come back easily to that row, then you assign the Bookmark property of the recordset object to a Variant-type variable.

If you later want to return to the aforementioned row, you then assign the recordset's Bookmark property to the value of the Variant-type variable. The row pointer will then immediately return to the point where you captured the Bookmark.

Obtaining the Values in the Result Set

Having positioned yourself to the appropriate record of interest in your SQL query result set (Recordset), you can retrieve the values associated with the Fields in that row by evaluating the Value property of the Field object of the Fields Collection of the Recordset. The code would look like this:

```
Dim curBalance As Currency
Dim db as Database
Dim ds as Dynaset
db = OpenDatabase("", FALSE, FALSE, FALSE, "ODBC;") ' Open database
                                                    ' containing Passbook
ds = db.CreateDynaset("SELECT * FROM Passbook")      ' Get all fields of
                                                     ' Passbook table
ds.FindNext "Date = " &
➥ Format$((Now - 1#), "MM/DD/YY")                    ' Find Yesterday's Date
curBalance = ds.Fields("AcctBalance").Value          ' Yesterday's Balance
```

III

Visual Basic

Programming of this sort can be generalized quite a bit, since Field objects (such as members of the Fields Collection) also have TYPE and SIZE properties so you can "discover" the nature of the Field you are using.

Designing Transaction-Processing Applications

So far, you've looked at the simple, "read-only" type of SQL statement and query. All that is desired in such applications is to retrieve a value from a record or records in a database that was placed there by some other process.

In this section you'll explore the more complex database operations that can be generally characterized as "transaction" applications. Typically, transaction-oriented applications are those that are placing new rows in database tables, or modifying or deleting rows in one or more tables.

A whole host of new considerations must be dealt with in transaction-processing applications. Among these considerations are:

- How do you get the contents of rows in a table or tables updated (or rows deleted, or added)?

- What if more than one table is involved to reflect a particular update; for example, tables that have to be synchronized to be consistent with each other?

  Typical examples are tables that are inner-joined where there must always be a primary key for a matching foreign key instance.

- What if in the middle of one of these consistent updates (or deletions or additions) you find, due to some circumstance, that you need to abandon the transaction and it has already been partially completed?

- What if the update that you are about to do to a particular row or set of rows in the database has already been modified by some other user (remember multi-user databases?)? How do you prevent the other user from stepping all over your modifications while you're in the middle of doing yours?

These and a host of other vexing issues are some of the complexities that you encounter when you venture into the world of database transaction-processing applications.

To get a focus on this assortment of issues, let's break the problem down into a few simpler constituent parts.

Using SQL Statements to Accomplish Your Transactions

One course of action that can be undertaken is to use specially constructed SQL statements that are designed for updating, deleting, and adding information in databases. These SQL statements generally only work with Table objects.

The following SQL statement clause types can be used to accomplish this; again, check with your ODBC database vendor and his documentation to find out if these are available:

■ DELETE FROM table-name WHERE...

■ INSERT INTO table-name.column-id VALUES...

■ UPDATE table-name SET column-id = Value WHERE...

If you want to manipulate Table objects within the database, you can use SQL statements. This is usually the most difficult mechanization to accomplish the results you desire.

Usually, a much easier way to accomplish the same transaction is to use some of the other methods of a Recordset object that have not yet been discussed.

Using *Recordset* Methods for Transaction Processing

As was noted in a previous section of this chapter, the Dynaset recordset object has the following additional methods that can be used to manipulate the result set, and since the Dynaset maintains a "live" write-through connection to the underlying database tables, modifications made to the Dynaset using these methods will be posted through to the database table (or tables) involved:

Method	Action Provided
ADDNEW	Adds a new record to the Dynaset
DELETE	Deletes a record from the Dynaset
UPDATE	Updates a record in the Dynaset
EDIT	Places the Dynaset in Edit Mode
REFRESH	Refreshes the Dynaset contents

Some examples of how these would be used in an interactive "transaction" processing type of application serves to illustrate how this method might simplify your work.

The *Dynaset*'s *REFRESH* Method

The REFRESH method is very useful in interactive multi-user database environments because by executing the REFRESH method of the Dynaset object, all changes that may have been made to the underlying database since you created the Dynaset are automatically reflected as updates to the Dynaset. Therefore, you are always assured that you have the most current information upon which to base your programming decisions. An example might look like this:

```
Dim db As Database
Dim ds As Dynaset
Dim strSQLQuery As String
strSQLQuery = "SELECT * FROM Customer"
Set db = OpenDatabase("", FALSE, FALSE, "ODBC;DSN=Access_2.0;
➥DBQ=C:\ODBCSDK\SMPLDATA\ACCESS\SAMPLE.MDB;FIL=RedISAM;")
Set ds = db.CreateDynaset(strSQLQuery)
            .
            .                              ' Some period of time goes
                                           ' by .....
            .
            .
ds.Refresh                                 ' Refreshes the Dynaset ds
                                           ' to reflect current state of db
```

Now that you've gotten the latest and greatest state of the database, what's next?

Using the Dynaset's *EDIT* and *UPDATE* Methods

An instant ago you had the lastest state of the database; if you wait for a bit it might change again. Why not guarantee that the the recordset row you have your sights set on doesn't get a chance to change again before you make some modification? Why not indeed—you can grab the recordset row, and in so doing grab all the way through to the underlying database table (or tables) involved just by executing the EDIT method of the Dynaset.

Once you execute the EDIT method of a Dynaset, the row in the Dynaset where your row pointer is currently positioned will go out to the database and "lock" the records involved so that no other application or user can access them for modification until you get your modifications made.

To be accurate, not just the row or rows you intend to update are locked. What is locked is a "page" worth of records in the tables. Again, this is 2048 bytes worth of Dynaset page and that translates into some number of actual table records, depending on the record size.

Now's your chance to make those modifications—go for it! Change the fields within the record that need modification and there you are.

But how about those locked records? How do you release them? Sooner or later—usually sooner—some other user or application will want to access the same record or records in the same locked page.

To get out of this locked state, you execute another method of the Dynaset— the UPDATE method. Executing the UPDATE method actually writes your changes through to the underlying database tables, and in the process re- leases the edit lock. Remember, with a Dynaset, executing any of the MOVE or FIND methods that move the recordset row pointer will also write through to the database. This would also release the edit lock.

Deleting and Adding New Records

The remaining two methods of the Dynaset, the DELETE method and the ADDNEW method, are fairly straightforward. The DELETE method removes the row from the Dynaset, and after executing the REFRESH method also removes the record(s) from the underlying database table(s) involved.

The ADDNEW method opens up a new blank row in the Dynaset that you can populate with appropriate field values. Execute the REFRESH method, or any of the MOVE or FIND methods, and the new record is posted through to the under- lying database table(s).

In all of these EDIT, DELETE, ADDNEW, and UPDATE operations, what if something prevents your completing what could be a number of interrelated modifica- tion operations? How can you back off, clear up the partially completed mess, and perhaps try again? This type of "I've changed my mind, and I would like to go back to square one" capability is provided by the BeginTrans, CommitTrans, and Rollback statements.

Managing Transaction Consistency

It is quite usual for several tables and often several Dynasets to be involved in complex transactions. This is especially true for databases that consist of mul- tiple highly normalized tables where a typical transaction usually will include some sort of JOIN operation among several tables. In such cases, the interrela- tionships among the tables is of paramount importance. The tables thus JOINed must be updated or modified in a harmonious, consistent way.

III

Visual Basic

What if the updates to one of the tables involved in a transaction can be modified, but something prevents synchronized, compatible modifications of the other tables? This frequently can happen when you lock one table and begin making modifications to it, and then cannot lock the necessary corresponding page in a related table to complete a consistent update.

Under these circumstances, if you were to make the updates to the first table, and then were unable to complete the corresponding updates to the second or successive tables, your database would be in an inconsistent state. Correcting this type of scrambled update would take considerable effort—if in fact you were ever able to recover the transaction's series of operations correctly. Remember, particularly in a multi-user environment, the world of transactions moves on and doesn't wait for you to fix your mistakes.

To come to your assistance in solving this type of problem, there are three crucial statments in the Visual Basic langauge, which are:

- `BeginTrans`—Marks the start of a series of modifications

- `CommitTrans`—Marks the end of a series of modifications

- `Rollback`—Aborts all modifications since `BeginTrans`

You can immediately see how handy these statements might be. They are used as follows, as illustrated by this sort of pseudo code:

```
Sub MyTrans()
    On Error GoTo AbortTrans
        BeginTrans
            ds1.Edit
            ds1.Field(1).Value = "New Value"   ' Modification to ds1
            ds1.Update
            ds2.Edit                            ' *** Get Lock edits
                                                ' error - can't edit ds2
                                                ' [other lock]
            ds2.Field(7).Value = "New Value"    ' Synchronized
                                                ' modification to ds2
            ds2.Update
        CommitTrans                             ' All has gone well.
                                                ' Commit the transaction
NotNow:
Exit Sub
AbortTrans:                                     ' Error handler executes
                                                ' Rollback - backs out

    Rollback
    Resume NotNow
End Sub
```

Using BeginTrans, CommitTrans, and Rollback, you can follow through on a series of modification steps, or roll back the mess that would otherwise have been made.

From Here...

To learn more about some of the objects discussed in this chapter, you should refer to the following materials elsewhere in this book:

- Chapter 17, "Using the Visual Basic Data Control with ODBC 2.0," in the section "Using the Data Control's Result Set," where you find additional information concerning the behavior of the Dynaset.

- Chapter 19, "Using the ODBC API from within Visual Basic," under the subsection "Retrieving the Result Set," where you find additional information about connecting to data sources.

- Chapter 19, "Using the ODBC API from within Visual Basic," under the subsection "Manipulating the Result Set Cursor," where you find additional details about the behavior of result set cursors.

- Chapter 19, "Using the ODBC API from within Visual Basic," under the subsection "Debugging and Testing with the ODBC 2.0 Development Tools," where you get some information on techniques that will help you in debugging any ODBC 2.0 database application.

In these chapters, you explore additional specific details and more in-depth materials about the inner workings of the all-important result set (such as the Recordset object).

III

Visual Basic

Chapter 19

Using the ODBC API from within Visual Basic

Of the three general approaches to incorporating ODBC 2.0 support in your Visual Basic application, the direct use of the ODBC 2.0 API is both the most sophisticated and at the same time the most complex. This chapter explores the motivating factors and the techniques for directly using the ODBC 2.0 API. By way of a road map to this chapter, we cover the following major subjects:

- How to decide when it is best to use the API

- General strategies for laying out your application

- How to declare the ODBC 2.0 API functions

- How to declare the data structures and constants

- Techniques for organizing your Visual Basic code

- How to choose a cursor model for the result set

- Management and manipulation of the result set

- Debugging and testing techniques

- Runtime error trapping and handling

Deciding When to Use the ODBC 2.0 API Approach

As you explored in the previous two chapters, the decision to directly use the ODBC 2.0 API approach in your Visual Basic application generally would be motivated by one or more of the following factors:

■ Fine-grained control of exact program operations executed against your database could not be accomplished by using the simpler Data Access Object variables

■ More exact and detailed error codes and messages are critical to the operation of your application

■ Absolute maximum performance may be such a significant consideration in your application that only recourse to direct use of the ODBC 2.0 API function calls can satisfy you needs—this one can be tricky!

Once again, remember that direct use of the ODBC 2.0 API is not an "all-or-nothing" affair. You easily can mix in a few critical API calls with the use of Data Access Object variables (or even the Data Control) to accomplish some particularly complex programming task without the need to use only API calls.

In the next few sections you will delve a bit further into the nature of using ODBC 2.0 API techniques and what you can expect to accomplish.

Considering the Need for API-Level Control

First, let's revisit the general categories of the API function calls and for what they are intended to be used. A bit of comparison between these related groups of API calls and how these also might be accomplished by simpler Visual Basic techniques can afford you a more specific basis for making your design decisions.

The general ODBC 2.0 API function categories are:

■ *ODBC Administrative functions*—used for installation, setup, and configuration of the ODBC environment in which your application must run

■ *ODBC Driver manager functions*—responsible for "housekeeping" tasks like obtaining the necessary resources, initialization, and termination of ODBC operations

■ *ODBC Catalog functions*—return information about the data source's catalog of tables, fields, indexes, stored procedures, and access permissions

■ *ODBC SQL statement submission and execution control functions*—control analysis and execution of your SQL statements

■ *ODBC Result Set functions*—determine the characteristics of the result set and fetch portions of the result set providing several different types of result set cursor behaviors

■ *ODBC Error retrieval and analysis functions*—obtain error information from throughout the ODBC runtime environment from drivers, data sources, the ODBC Driver manager, SQL execution, and the result set

The category of ODBC 2.0 API functions that is most likely to be first employed in a Visual Basic program is the group of error retrieval functions. As discussed in Chapter 17, "Using the Visual Basic Data Control with ODBC 2.0," error information provided directly by the Visual Basic runtime libraries is, of necessity, transformed into pretty generic error codes and messages. Techniques were also described in Chapter 17 to help you squeeze more "juice" out of these Spartan error codes, but ultimately the best approach might be to use the API functions to get direct error information.

The next most likely group of ODBC functions that is investigated is the ODBC Catalog functions. However, before you run off and make major coding investments in using this group of functions, you should make sure that you've exhausted the possibilities of the Data Access Object variable techniques described in Chapter 18, "Using Visual Basic Data Access Objects with ODBC 2.0."

The purpose of the ODBC Catalog functions group is to enable you to discover information about the structure of a database. Typically, these functions are used when the only information known about the database is that a data source was selected.

The ODBC Catalog group of functions enables you to "discover," without any pre-knowledge, the complete structure of a database, including such information as:

■ The number and names of all the database's tables

■ The characteristics of all the fields within a particular table—field names, data types, lengths, and so forth

■ The number of indexes for each table, and the characteristics of these indexes—primary key, foreign key, and so forth

■ The number of stored procedures within a database, and the replaceable parameter fields within each of these stored procedures

However, this is not to say that you always need to use the ODBC API Catalog functions to discover this information. Don't forget that the collections objects of the Data Access Object variables discussed in Chapter 18, "Using Visual Basic Data Access Objects with ODBC 2.0," also provide this type of

III

Visual Basic

information. In particular, you might want to review the TableDefs, Fields, QueryDefs, and Indexes collections objects to see if these will handle the job for you before you plunge into direct use of the ODBC API.

Two other categories of ODBC 2.0 API functions—the SQL Submission functions and the Result Set control functions—are best evaluated in the context of the general subject of application performance.

Addressing Application Performance

All other conditions being equal—same database design, same computer, same network, same server, all tuned to their peak levels—performance of your ODBC 2.0 Visual Basic application usually is determined by four primary factors, which are:

- How efficiently you design the structure of your database in terms of table design, index design, and so forth

- How well you write your SQL statements—there are efficient and inefficient ways to get the same SQL result set

- How your SQL statements are processed

- How you choose and manage result set cursors and the associated memory allocated to receive the result set

I will defer the subjects of the performance effects of SQL statement and database design, and the efficiencies attendant thereto to the numerous specialized texts on the subject. Also, nothing substitutes for actual measured performance tests, so make sure to instrument and run some to determine the most efficient SQL statement design methodology. As a first-cut tool to assist you in this, don't forget about using Microsoft Query, and always make sure that you have a sample database that remains the same throughout your testing efforts. That leaves us with two major performance subjects to be investigated more closely.

Performance Effects of SQL Statement Processing

In the world of Visual Basic ODBC 2.0 database applications, using Data Access Object variables, or even the Data Control, you can choose to specify that either:

- The Visual Basic JET engine first syntax analyzes your SQL statements, and then passes the "error free" SQL statement onward into the ODBC architecture; or,

- The Visual Basic JET engine doesn't touch your SQL statement syntax, and just passes the SQL statement onward into ODBC

This choice of behaviors is determined by setting the Data Control's OPTION property to the constant DB_SQLPASSTHRU. Likewise, when using Data Access Object variables, you can achieve this effect by setting the OPTION argument of the Database objects' Execute method to DB_SQLPASSTHRU.

By setting the DB_SQLOPASSTHRU option, thus bypassing the Visual Basic JET engine's SQL analyzer/parser, you eliminate a lot of potentially redundant work. Remember, once an ODBC base driver gets an SQL statement it will first try to optimize it and do an extensive syntax check on it too. After all, how much syntax checking and analyzing does an SQL statement need? One parsing and analysis is usually enough. By using DB_SQLPASSTHRU you typically can speed things up a bit. The disadvantage, of course, is that your SQL statement has traversed its way quite a distance into the innards of ODBC before you might find out it's "bad." By contrast, JET engine SQL pre-processing has the advantage of being local to the execution environment of your Visual Basic program and interacts with you quite a bit more quickly if there is an error.

Presuming that you are attempting to execute "tried-and-true" SQL statements, then by all means use DB_SQLPASSTHRU, since there would be absolutely nothing at all to be gained by local JET engine SQL analysis.

As a very rough rule of thumb, using DB_SQLPASSTHRU and Data Access Object variable techniques will offer performance approaching that of using the direct ODBC API calls. For typical database operations, this means performance in the range from parity with to twice the time required for the same operation using the API calls. Of course, each particular case is dependent on factors such as the SQL you are processing, the size of the result set, and the type of result set manipulation you need to do.

III

Note

Using DB_SQLPASSTHRU causes the JET engine to create a Snapshot recordset object, even though your code uses the CreateDynaset function. This is due to the fact that the JET engine is not able to directly use the keyset to create a Dynaset object. As a result of this Snapshot creation, you cannot update the recordset object as you would be able to with a Dynaset. However, using DB_SQLPASSTHRU is still faster than using the CreateSnapshot function without using DB_SQLPASSTHRU. The exact performance enhancement varies depending on the SQL statement, but is in the approximate general range of 2 to 20 times faster.

Visual Basic

By using the ODBC API directly to submit and manage your SQL statements, you won't get any interference with Visual Basic's JET engine SQL analyzer. You are going direct from your code to the API function calls. This is one performance-related issue—although as you can see, there are equivalent non-API techniques to accomplish a similar task.

A second but potentially much more important performance advantage that can be obtained by using the ODBC 2.0 API SQL statement processing functions is the ability to cause your SQL statements to be "pre-analyzed" and then executed. To understand what is going on here you need to realize that there are two fundamental tactical approaches to using the ODBC API SQL-related functions. These two methods are the:

- *Prepared method*—using the SQLPrepare, SQLSetParam, and SQLExecute function calls; and the

- *Direct method*—using the SQLSetParam and SQLExecDirect functions

In the Prepared method, you have an application that needs to execute an SQL statement repeatedly. You can make parametric changes in the SQL statement (using the SQLSetParam function), but between successive executions of the SQL statement, the basic structure of the SQL statement doesn't need to change.

The process of invoking the SQLPrepare function causes the data source to "compile" the SQL statement as a first step. This compilation produces an intermediate form of your SQL statement known as an access plan. A unique internal (to the data source and driver) identifier is assigned to this access plan, so that subsequent repeated executions of the same basic access plan proceed very quickly—a few parameter values are passed and associated with the access plan, and away goes execution.

In this scheme, the actual invocation of the access plan to cause SQL statement execution is handled by a call to the SQLExecute function. The other added advantage of the Prepared method, in a two-tiered data source/data driver environment, is that the amount of network traffic is cut down significantly.

Notice that only SQL statement parameters that change have to transit the network upon each SQLSetParam and SQLExecute invocation pair, and not the whole SQL statement. What with the loading on most real world networks, this also has the effect of enhancing performance while conserving network bandwidth resources.

By way of comparison, the Direct method accomplishes both of the steps—developing an access plan and submitting it for execution—all in one function call invocation. This method, using the SQLExecDirect function, might be appropriate if you will be executing a given SQL statement only once.

The Visual Basic data control employs the SQLExecDirect function call approach. Similarly, when using the Data Access Object variable approach, for example, with the Visual Basic OpenDatabase and CreateDynaset functions, the SQLExecDirect method is also used.

In both cases a single SQL statement is submitted using the Direct method outlined above. It is pretty easy to conclude why you might be able to get better performance by taking matters into your own hands and making the ODBC 2.0 API calls, rather than use the Visual Basic data control or even the Data Access Object variables if you have an SQL statement that you want to execute repeatedly with only parametric changes.

Performance Effects of Cursor Management

Perhaps one of the most profound performance effects in using an ODBC 2.0 data source is related to the type of result set cursor chosen. It is in this area that choosing to make direct ODBC 2.0 API calls in Visual Basic might provide the greatest performance payback.

In the dim dark past, SQL result set cursors could only be tasked to scroll forward through a result set. One row or record of the data from the result set could be accessed and returned at a time. This behavior might be just fine for batch-oriented applications—however, even in batch applications such cursor behavior often presents problems.

The real difficulty with "scroll-forward-only" cursors quickly becomes apparent in more interactive types of applications. In interactive applications it is highly desirable that the result set cursor can be moved both forward and backward in the result set, and the capability for both absolute and relative offset cursor motions is also usually required. Finally, there are applications where it clearly would be advantageous to have cursor behavior that allowed positioning to blocks of result set rows.

ODBC 2.0 includes cursors which can provide:

- Block cursor behavior—cursors for rowsets

- Cursors that allow forward and backward scrolling

- Cursors that can move in both absolute and relative offsets through the result set

■ Cursors with both types of behavior, both block and multi-directional scrolling capabilities

Types of Cursor Models

Block cursors enable your application to fetch a rowset at a time, and not just a single row. This can be accomplished with a couple of function calls—one to SQLSetStmtOption to specify the rowset size, and a second to SQLExtendedFetch that actually fetches the rowset.

Scrollable cursor concepts are somewhat more complex to understand. There are many varieties and variations of scollable cursor behavior. First let's look at the extreme ends of the spectrum and investigate static and dynamic cursors.

Forms of Cursor Behavior

Static cursors are those which give the appearance that the underlying result set is completely static—nothing changes. Once you open a static cursor for use with a result set, the effects of updated rows, deleted rows, or inserted rows which may result from other users' modifications of the database are not noticed. The effect is that the result set appears to be a snapshot frozen in time, or a set of records that have been locked to prevent changes.

At the opposite pole are *dynamic cursors*. These give the appearance that the data in the result set is dynamically changing and shifting. As rows are added, deleted, or modified by other database users' actions, the result set reflects the changes. As you might guess, this completely dynamic scrollable cursor appears to be the ideal thing for many applications, but don't be too quick to make that judgment. Completely dynamic cursors can be very tricky to use and manage, because you never know quite what to expect from the result set from moment to moment.

Fortunately for all concerned, there are *scrollable cursors* available in ODBC 2.0 that incorporate some features from both ends of the spectrum—a bit of static behavior blended with dynamic behavior. One of these hybrid cursors is called the *Keyset-Driven cursor*, and is explained in the following section.

Keyset-Driven Cursor Behavior

Keyset-driven cursors embody both dynamic and static cursor features blended together. Like dynamic cursors, the result set provides visibility into any underlying changes that may have resulted from database modification operations performed by other users. At the same time, however, keyset-driven cursors also exhibit static cursor characteristics in that the ordering and membership of the result set appear to be fixed at the time the cursor is opened.

Such keyset-driven cursors are implemented by the ODBC driver and are created when the cursor is opened. The ODBC driver saves what appears to be a static keyset for the entire result set when the cursor is opened. As the cursor scrolls through the result set, the driver then uses the keys to retrieve the then-current values for each row referenced in the result set. Therefore, since data values only are retrieved at the time that the scrollable cursor actually scrolls to any given row, then any intervening modifications that may have taken place since the result set was created are automatically reflected in the fetched row (or rowset). This gives the distinct appearance of what would be expected from a dynamic cursor.

If you think back for a moment to the discussions of Chapters 17, "Using the Visual Basic Data Control with ODBC 2.0," and 18, "Using Visual Basic Data Access Objects with ODBC 2.0," where you focused on the behavior of the Visual Basic Dynaset record set object, this keyset-driven cursor behavior will sound quite familiar. Visual Basic's Dynaset object is constructed by the JET engine to implement a form of keyset-driven cursor.

Mixed Cursors Behavior

Another variation of the keyset-driven cursor is the so-called *mixed cursors*—cursors that have both keyset-driven and dynamic behaviors mixed. Such cursors are motivated by the observation that if a result set becomes large, the effort required to produce the keyset-driven cursor's static keyset also could be very large. In mixed cursors, therefore, the keyset that is produced is artificially limited in size. It is sized so that it is smaller than the size of the result set, but it is larger in scope than a rowset. That is to say, the keyset that is generated is only large enough to cover several rowsets.

In this scheme, as the scrollable cursor is moved it will eventually run off one end or the other of the "static" keyset. When that happens, a new segment of the keyset is built to span the new rowsets being traversed. This process repeats as often as needed to provide keyset information as the cursor is scrolled. In other respects, the mixed cursor behavior is like that of the previously described dynamic cursor—that is, data changes that may have taken place are visible in the result set.

You explore these cursor options and their operations in more detail later in this chapter. For the moment, though, you can summarize the performance considerations in using the ODBC 2.0 API with Visual Basic as follows:

III

Visual Basic

■ Before plunging off and using the ODBC 2.0 API, you should see if using techniques like DB_SQLPASSTHRU might get you acceptable performance

■ Under all circumstances, using the ODBC 2.0 API will provide you with better performance than using Visual Basic's JET engine techniques

■ If your application is one that could use Prepared queries, you most likely will want to use the ODBC 2.0 API to exploit the performance advantages of this over using Direct query execution (as Visual Basic's JET engine does)

■ Choosing an appropriate cursor model for your application is about the most important performance-affecting decision you must make

Getting More Detailed Operations and Error Information

Using the ODBC 2.0 API functions to obtain exact error information is sometimes required to enable your program to make intelligent error handling and recovery decisions. As previously noted, the error information Visual Basic provides about ODBC errors is somewhat limited.

You will later see how to use the SQLError function of the ODBC 2.0 API to achieve a variety of important programming chores, including:

■ Using SQLError to determine what's happening in the result set

■ Using SQLError to determine the capabilities of a particular ODBC driver and data source

■ Using SQLError to monitor other ODBC 2.0 API function operations

Using the detailed information returned by the SQLError function, you can determine precisely what ODBC 2.0 is doing at all times.

Taking Direct Control with ODBC 2.0 API Calls

Using the ODBC 2.0 API calls within Visual Basic involves the same considerations required to use any other Windows dynamic link library (DLL) function calls. In fact, unlike some DLLs, the ODBC 2.0 library does not require the use of complex programming concepts like callback functions that you might encounter using other database-oriented DLLs, like those in SQL-Server's DB-Library. To use the ODBC 2.0 API, the general considerations are:

- Declare the DLL functions you will be using

- Define the special user-defined TYPE structures that are used by the ODBC 2.0 library

- Make the appropriate series of API function calls

In preparing to use the ODBC 2.0 API, you need to become familiar with the function calls involved. Many of the other chapters of this book can offer you assistance in developing the needed expertise. In addition, don't forget about the Microsoft ODBC 2.0 API Reference that is provided with ODBC 2.0 SDK in the form of a Help file.

You will take a look at some of the general and specific uses of the ODBC 2.0 API library in the subsequent sections.

Understanding the Sequence of API Function Calls

As with any plan of attack on a complex subject, the best starting point is usually a general outline. That approach is presented here so that you can see a generic plan for the steps involved in using the ODBC 2.0 API with Visual Basic. In time sequence, the steps you will go through to use the ODBC 2.0 API are:

- Initialize the ODBC subsystem to ready it for use

- Connect to an ODBC data source that you need

- Optionally, obtain information about the data source's system tables to discover the database's structure

- Obtain information about the data source's driver and about the data source itself

- Retrieve and set up various driver options you want to use

- Prepare and submit your SQL statements

- Retrieve information about the result set, and retrieve the result set itself

- Terminate SQL statement processing

- Terminate the ODBC data source connection established earlier

- Shut down your program's relationship with the ODBC subsystem

- Process error information throughout the above period

III

Visual Basic

Relating ODBC Function Calls to Your Application

The ODBC 2.0 API functions involved in each of these steps, and what they are used for in your application, are shown in the appropriate function group (see table 19.1):

Table 19.1   ODBC 2.0 API Function Summary

Function	Result
Initialize ODBC	
SQLAllocEnv	Obtains ODBC environment handle
Connect to Data Source	
SQLAllocConnect	Obtains Source connection handle
SQLConnect	Connects Driver by DSN, UserID, Password
SQLDriverConnect	Connects to Driver by connection string
SQLBrowseConnect	Connects attributes and values
Database Catalog	
SQLColumnPrivileges	Obtains list of columns and privileges
SQLColumns	Obtains column names in tables
SQLForeignKeys	Obtains list of foreign keys for table
SQLPrimaryKeys	Obtains list of primary keys for table
SQLProcedureColumns	Obtains input and output parameters
SQLProcedures	Obtains list of stored procedure names
SQLSpecialColumns	Obtains list of auto-updated columns
SQLStatistics	Obtains table and index statistics
SQLTablePrivileges	Obtains list of tables and privileges
SQLTables	Obtains list of database tables

Function	Result
Driver and Data Source Information	
SQLDataSources	Returns list of data sources
SQLDrivers	Returns list of drivers and attributes
SQLGetInfo	Returns info about driver and source
SQLGetFunctions	Returns supported driver functions
SQLGetTypeInfo	Returns info about supported data types
Retrieve and Set Up Driver Options	
SQLSetConnectOption	Sets connection option
SQLGetConnectOption	Returns value of connection option
SQLSetStmtOption	Sets statement option
SQLGetStmtOption	Returns value of a statement option
Prepare SQL Statements	
SQLAllocStmt	Allocates statement handle
SQLPrepare	Prepares SQL statement for later use
SQLBindParameter	Assigns storage for parameters in SQL
SQLParamOptions	Specifies values for parameters
SQLGetCursorName	Returns cursor name of statement handle
SQLSetCursorName	Sets cursor name of statement handle
SQLSetScrollOptions	Sets options controlling cursors
Submit SQL Statements	
SQLExecute	Executes prepared statement
SQLExecDirect	Executes statement directly
SQLNativeSql	Returns SQL text translated by driver
SQLDescribeParam	Returns description of parameter
SQLNumParams	Returns number of SQL parameters

III

Visual Basic

(continues)

Table 19.1 Continued

Function	Result
Submit SQL Statements	
SQLParamData	Sets SQL parameter data values
SQLPutData	Sends part or all of SQL parameter value
Retrieve Information About Results and Results	
SQLRowCount	Returns count of rows from updates
SQLNumResultCols	Returns number of columns in result set
SQLDescribeCol	Describes column in result set
SQLColAttributes	Describes column attributes in results
SQLBindCol	Assigns storage for results column
SQLFetch	Returns result row
SQLExtendedFetch	Returns multiple result rows
SQLGetData	Returns part of column of one row
SQLSetPos	Positions cursor within fetched block
SQLMoreResults	Determines if more results are present
SQLError	Returns error or status information
Terminate SQL Statement Processing	
SQLFreeStmt	Ends statement processing; frees cursor
SQLCancel	Cancels SQL statement
SQLTransact	Commits or rolls back a transaction
Terminate ODBC Relationship	
SQLDisconnect	Closes connection
SQLFreeConnect	Releases connection handle
SQLFreeEnv	Releases environment handle

You will be using these function calls later in this chapter as you follow the steps involved in a typical Visual Basic ODBC 2.0 application.

Managing the Data Structures and Handles

When using the ODBC 2.0 API function calls, several handles are used, either as return values or as arguments of the function calls. These handles are:

Handle	Purpose	VB Data Type
henv	ODBC environment handle	Long
hdbc	Database connection handle	Long
hstmt	SQL statement handle	Long
hlib	Driver library handle	Long
hwnd	Window handle	Integer

For the purposes of managing and keeping all connection related information together, the following user-defined TYPE can be defined:

```
Type ConnectionInfo

    hdbc As Long         ' Connection handle
    hstmt As Long        ' Statement handle
    Status As Integer    ' Active or Inactive
    Tag As String        ' A string of the form "DataSource <number>"
                         ' uniquely identifying a connection
End Type
```

This user-defined type will be used in later examples in this chapter.

Declaring ODBC 2.0 API Functions, Constants, and Variables

As a first step in developing a Visual Basic ODBC 2.0 application, you need to declare the ODBC 2.0 API functions, symbolic constants, and general variables you want to use. This process is the same as you would use to declare any functions that are referenced in any external library.

Using the ODBC 2.0 SDK Visual Basic Sample Program

Included with the ODBC 2.0 SDK is a sample Visual Basic program called VBDEMO.

III

Visual Basic

> **Note**
>
> There is also a sample program called VIZDATA that is provided with the Visual Basic Professional Edition that uses a number of ODBC API calls. You might want to study the techniques used in this program as well.

The VBDEMO program can be used as a source of already-coded declarations for the ODBC 2.0 API function and constants you will need to use in your Visual Basic application. The constants and function declarations are already in the correct Visual Basic format. The specific modules you will need are:

Module Name	Contents
ODBCOR_G.BI	Constants used by core ODBC 2.0 functions
ODBCOR_M.BI	Declarations for core ODBC 2.0 functions
ODBEXT_G.BI	Constants used by extended ODBC 2.0 functions
ODBEXT_M.BI	Declarations for extended ODBC 2.0 functions
ODBC.BAS	Declarations for some Windows API functions

The use of ODBC.BAS is optional, depending on the specific needs of your application.

> **Note**
>
> If you have not used Dynamic Link Library (DLL) functions before in a Visual Basic program, you might want to give the subject some study. A definitive book on the matter is *Visual Basic Programmer's Guide to the Windows API*, by Daniel Appleman, published by PC Magazine Press, ISBN: 1-56276-073-4.

Choosing the ODBC Conformance Level You Need

An early choice in developing your Visual Basic ODBC 2.0 API application is deciding on the ODBC conformance level that you need to (or want to) support. As you can tell from the preceding section, the functions that you need in the ODBC API library are related to the choice of ODBC conformance level. Choosing a conformance level is a matter related both to the functionality of the ODBC driver, and also the grammar features of SQL language support.

ODBC Core-Level Functionality

Each ODBC driver vendor determines what level of ODBC functionality his driver will support. However, all ODBC drivers are required to support the Core-level functions.

The basic—or Core—level conformance to the ODBC 2.0 specification provides the following capabilities:

- Allocate and free environment, connection, and statement handles

- Connect to data sources, with multiple statements on a connection

- Prepare and execute SQL statements, or execute SQL statements directly

- Assign storage for parameters in SQL statements and in result set columns

- Retrieve data from and about a result set

- Commit or roll back transactions

- Retrieve error and status information

For many applications the Core level capabilities are adequate to accomplish your objectives. The added advantage of being able to stay within the Core level functions is that any ODBC data source you connect to will work with your application.

ODBC Extended Functionality—Levels 1 and 2

There are two levels of extended ODBC 2.0 functionality—Level 1 and Level 2. Each level adds extended features to the Core level capabilities. The Level 1 extensions enable you to:

- Connect to data sources with driver-specific dialogs

- Set and inquire about values of statement and connection options

- Send part or all of a parameter value—useful for long data types

- Retrieve part or all of a result set column value—useful for long data types

- Retrieve catalog information (columns, special columns, statistics, and tables)

- Retrieve information about drivers and data source capabilities such as supported data types, scalar functions, and ODBC functions

III

Visual Basic

Level 1 conformance is especially important if you need to determine the structure of your data source by means of the catalog functions, or if you need to invoke driver-specific dialogs.

The Level 2 extensions provide the capabilities of the Core and Level 1 extensions plus the capability to:

- Browse connection information and list available data sources

- Send arrays of parameter values, and retrieve arrays of result set columns

- Retrieve the number of parameters and describe individual parameters

- Use a scrollable cursor

- Retrieve the native form of an SQL statement

- Retrieve additional catalog information such as privileges, primary and foreign keys, and stored procedures

- Invoke a result set translation DLL

Usually the key capabilities of the Level 2 extensions are the availability of a scrollable cursor, and the ability to retrieve added catalog information.

SQL Conformance Levels

In addition to driver functional capabilities that differ with conformance level, there are differing levels of SQL language grammar support. Table 19.2 summarizes the language features supported at each level:

Table 19.2	SQL Grammar Level Feature Summary
Level	**Feature**
Minimum SQL Grammar	
DDL	CREATE TABLE and DROP TABLE
DML	SELECT, INSERT, UPDATE SEARCHED, and DELETE SEARCHED
Expressions	Simple types such as A > B + C
Data types	CHAR, VARCHAR, or LONG VARCHAR

Level	Feature
Core SQL Grammar	
DDL	ALTER TABLE, CREATE INDEX, DROP INDEX, CREATE VIEW, DROP VIEW, GRANT, and REVOKE
DML	Full SELECT syntax
Expressions	SUBQUERY, aggregation functions such as SUM, MIN, MAX, AVG, and so forth
Data types	DECIMAL, NUMERIC, SMALLINT, INTEGER, REAL, FLOAT, and DOUBLE PRECISION
Extended SQL Grammar	
DML	OUTER JOINS, positioned UPDATES, positioned DELETE, SELECT FOR UPDATE, and UNIONS
Expressions	Scalar functions such as SUBSTRING, and ABS; and DATE, TIME, and TIMESTAMP literals
Data types	BIT, TINYINT, BIGINT, BINARY, VARBINARY, LONG VARBINARY, DATE, TIME, and TIMESTAMP. Support for Batch SQL statements and procedure calls

To make the decision about the SQL grammar conformance level you need, you will have to understand the SQL statements that you will be using in your application.

Both the ODBC API function conformance levels supported and the SQL grammar conformance levels supported are usually very closely related to the capabilities of the underlying data source. It is therefore usually wise to get the database vendor's documentation to determine what features and capabilities you can expect to have available to you.

In very general terms, you will have to analyze your application's needs to determine what level of ODBC conformance is required.

Determining ODBC Conformance Level—API and SQL

Determining the API and SQL grammar conformance levels of the whole chain of components that comprise your Visual Basic application's ODBC environment is usually your first programming chore. Typically, quite a bit of the structure and logic of your application depends on making this determination early in the program's execution.

III

Visual Basic

> **Note**
>
> In this section, and those that follow, the symbolic constants used are defined in the ODBC 2.0 SDK and associated documentation, and are declared in the previously mentioned code modules of the VBDEMO application.

You can determine the API ODBC conformance level from within your Visual Basic program, provided that the ODBC driver you will be using supports the SQLGetInfo and the SQLGetTypeInfo functions. Although these functions are defined as part of the Extended Level 1 capabilities, many ODBC driver vendors support these functions, even though they may not support the complete Level 1 functionality. If the ODBC driver you want to use does not support these two functions, you will have to refer to the driver documentation.

Additionally, you can call the SQLGetFunctions function to get conformance level information. Since this function is part of the ODBC Driver Manager, it can be called for any driver regardless of its level. To determine if a driver supports a particular function, you would call the SQLGetFunctions function with the appropriate flag associated with the function you are interested in.

Presuming, however, that the first two functions are supported, you can call SQLGetInfo with the SQL_ODBC_API_CONFORMANCE flag to get information about the API compliance levels. The return value indicates the API compliance level as follows:

Return Value	Indicates
SQL_OAC_NONE	No extended function support (Core level)
SQL_OAC_LEVEL1	Level 1 API extensions supported
SQL_OAC_LEVEL2	Level 2 API extensions supported

Likewise, you can get information on SQL level compliance by calling SQLGetInfo with the SQL_ODBC_SQL_CONFORMANCE flag. The return value indicates the SQL compliance level as follows:

Return Value	Indicates
SQL_OSC_MINIMUM	Minimum grammar supported
SQL_OSC_CORE	Core grammar supported
SQL_OSC_EXTENDED	Extended grammar supported

Structuring Your Visual Basic Code

In this section you will go through the basics of putting together your Visual Basic ODBC 2.0 API application. Although an infinite number of variations are clearly possible, the steps discussed here are fundamental to all applications. The steps will be covered in the approximate order in which you would develop the code.

The basic steps are these:

1. Connect to your data source

2. Prepare and execute your SQL statements

3. Retrieve your result set

4. Evaluate the status and error information

5. Release or disconnect your data source

Connecting to Data Sources

The process of connecting to an ODBC data source is the first order of business in most Visual Basic ODBC 2.0 API applications. This process actually consists of a number of specific programming actions.

Initializing ODBC

As a first step, your Visual Basic program must initialize the ODBC interface and associate a handle with the environment. This process causes the driver to initialize the ODBC environment, and allocate memory to store information. An application only needs to do this once, regardless of how many connections it uses. This is accomplished by calling the SQLAllocEnv function as follows:

```
Global henv As Long
Dim rc As integer
rc = SQLAllocEnv(henv)
```

The return value of the SQLAllocEnv function needs to be tested to see if it was successful.

Connecting to a Data Source

Next, you will have to get a connection handle before you can connect to a driver or data source. The connection associated with the connection handle allocates memory for use by the driver. Getting a connection and handle is done by calling the SQLAllocConnect function as follows:

III

Visual Basic

```
Global hdbc As Long
rc = SQLAllocConnect(henv, hdbc)
```

Again, you will need to test the return value from `SQLAllocConnect` to make sure it was successful.

Now you are ready to make a connection to a specific driver and data source. A data source in combination with its associated driver must provide certain information in order that a connection can be made. Usually, information such as the name of the data source, user ID, and password must be provided. Some data sources require additional information such as network addresses or additional special passwords to gain access to the network or to the host computer where the data source resides.

The necessary connection information for each available data source is stored in the ODBC.INI file that was created during installation of the ODBC system, and which has been subsequently maintained by the ODBC Administrator program as additional drivers and data sources are installed and configured.

Later in this chapter you will learn how you can register additional data sources under program control.

A typical call to the `SQLConnect` function to connect to a data source that required just a user ID and password would be:

```
rc = SQLConnect(hdbc,"MyDataBase", 10, "ImAUser", 7, "MyPassword", 10)
```

In this example, `"MyDataBase"` is the Data Source Name (DSN), `"ImAUser"` is the user ID, and `"MyPassword"` is the user's password. Using `SQLConnect` is the simplest way to establish a connection to a data source. Some more complex data sources cannot be connected using just `SQLConnect`.

Alternatively, if the arguments are literals (as shown in the preceding example), or are Visual Basic string variables, it is possible to omit actual string length argument values. Recall for a moment that the Visual Basic compiler performs a conversion on BSTR formatted strings (Basic Strings), and automatically recasts them into CSTR formatted strings (C-Strings) which are null terminated. This is performed automatically, if the Visual Basic string arguments are passed *ByVal*, as specified either in the API function declaration, or in the function invocation.

To use this alternative form of invocation, you code the following equivalent call to `SQLConnect`:

```
rc = SQLConnect(hdbc,"MyDataBase", SQL_NTS, "ImAUser",
➥SQL_NTS, "MyPassword", SQL_NTS)
```

Notice that in place of all of the string parameter length arguments you would specify SQL_NTS, which is a symbolic constant indicating that the corresponding string arguments are null terminated strings.

Other Connection Possibilities

Other data source connection scenarios are also possible, and can be created using the SQLDriverConnect function. This function allows an application to request that the driver and the ODBC Manager obtain login information from the user prior to establishing the connection. Additionally, this function is useful if the data source requires more information than can be supplied by the simple SQLConnect function. SQLDriverConnect uses a connection string to connect a driver with a data source. The connection string contains the following information:

- The data source name

- Zero or more user IDs

- Zero or more passwords

- Zero or more data source parameter values

There are several ways in which the SQLDriverConnect function can be used to obtain a variety of different types of user interactive connection dialogs. These are:

- *Specify a connection string that allows the driver to connect to the data source*—no user interaction needed

- *Specify a connection string without a data source*—this causes the ODBC Manager to display a dialog box enabling the user to select an available data source

- *Specify a connection string with just a partial connection string*—this causes the ODBC Manager to prompt the user to select a data source from the data sources dialog, and can also allow the driver to display a standard login dialog box to the user

A typical use of SQLDriverConnect might be something like:

```
Dim strConn As String*255
Dim intLenOut As Integer
Const intDialogFlags = SQL_DRIVER_PROMPT
rc = SQLDriverConnect(hdbc, MyApp.hWnd,
➥"", 0, strConn, 255, intLenOut, intDialogFlags)
```

Tip

To determine the correct connection string for a data source, call SQLDriverConnect with no connection string, respond to all data source and login dialogs, and examine the connection string buffer's contents.

III

Visual Basic

This example initially provides a NULL connect string, and thus the ODBC Manager and driver will provide the necessary dialogs to develop the connection string by interaction with the user. The dialogs are associated with the Visual Basic Form identified by the MyApp windows handle. Once the dialogs are completed, the finished connection string will be available in the string variable strConn. Figure 19.1 illustrates the dialogs that result from this code example.

Fig. 19.1
Using the ODBC dialogs for interactive data source selection.

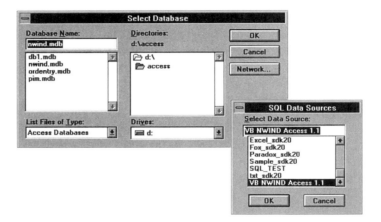

Obviously, numerous other possibilities exist for getting the desired connection established. Again, don't forget to evaluate the return code of these function calls to determine whether they were successful or not.

Preparing Your SQL Statements

The next step in the process of implementing a Visual Basic program using the ODBC 2.0 API is to prepare the SQL statements you want to execute. As mentioned earlier in this chapter, there are two fundamental alternatives to consider at this point. The first alternative is to use the Direct mode of SQL execution. This method is appropriate if you only will be executing your SQL statement once.

Alternatively, you may choose to use the Prepared method. Recall that in using the Prepared method, you are in a situation where you will be executing your SQL statement repeatedly, with parameter value variations. Also recall that the Prepared method is faster in such circumstances than repeated execution using the Direct method.

Regardless of which method you will be using, the next programming step would be to get a statement handle. This statement handle (hstmt) identifies a particular SQL statement, and associates it with a specific data source connection. An example of a typical call to the SQLAllocStmt function would look like:

```
Dim rc As integer          ' Variable for return value
Global hstmt As Long       ' Statement handle
rc = SQLAllocStmt(hdbc, hstmt)   ' Invoke SQLAllocStmt
```

Direct Method SQL Statements

Using the Direct method, you would develop a string variable that contains the desired SQL statement you plan to execute. You then would invoke the SQLExecDirect function to submit and execute your statement using the statement handle you just obtained from the SQLAllocStmt function. A typical code segment to do this would be something like:

```
Dim MySQL As String                ' Desired SQL statement
Global hstmt As Long               ' Statement handle
Dim rc As Integer                  ' Variable for return value
MySQL = "SELECT * FROM orders"     ' Your SQL statement
rc = SQLExecDirect(hstmt, MySQL, Len(MySQL))   ' Invoke SQLExecDirect
```

Prepared Method SQL Statements

If you choose to use the Prepared method, you also would develop a string variable which contains the desired SQL statement you want to execute. However, this SQL statement differs from the one prepared for the Direct method. The SQL statement for using the Prepared method contains fields that are replaceable parameters you would change with successive executions of the SQL statement. Replaceable parameters in your SQL statement are indicated by a "?" in the appropriate positions.

When you submit an SQL statement using the Prepared method, the ODBC driver and the data source create an access plan. The data source provides the driver with an access plan identifier. This access plan, from your perspective, is associated with the statement handle (hstmt). The advantage here is one of enhanced performance, since the driver only needs to refer to the access plan identifier instead of requesting the data source to re-analyze the SQL statement each time it is submitted.

Another benefit is that the driver can return information about the access plan and its anticipated result set before actually executing the SQL statement.

Expanding a bit on the previous sample code, we can develop an SQL statement which has replaceable parameters, and invoke the SQLPrepare function to create an access plan:

```
Dim MySQL As String                    ' Desired SQL statement
Global hstmt As Long                   ' Statement handle
Dim rc As Integer                      ' Variable for return value
MySQL = "SELECT * FROM employees
➥WHERE (Extension) > (?)"              ' Your SQL statement
rc = SQLPrepare(hstmt, MySQL, Len(MySQL))  ' Invoke SQLPrepare
```

At some later point in your code you would supply the values of the replaceable parameters using the SQLBindParameters function. This function "binds" a memory storage location containing the parameter value with the column associated with the value. Continuing the above example then would result in:

```
Dim rc As Integer
Dim strExtID As String
strExtID = "'3447'"
rc = SQLBindParameter(hstmt, 1, SQL_PARAM_INPUT,
➥SQL_C_CHAR, SQL_CHAR, 4, 4, ByVal strExtID, 4, 4&)
```

This causes SQLBindParameter to "bind" the value of the variable *strCustID* to the first (and in this case, only) replaceable parameter in the Prepared access plan. You then can later provide values for the parameter and execute the Prepared access plan with the desired parameter value.

Caution

When passing string parameters to ODBC 2.0 API calls, make sure you pass them ByVal. If you look at the function templates in the declarations, you often will find that some arguments can take various types of parameters. These will be declared like "SomeParam As Any," which essentially disables the Visual Basic compiler's type checking. If you look in the API on-line reference you will notice that these parameters are looking for an address as the argument. Visual Basic strings are automatically recast by the compiler into C-style null terminated strings, and the address of the C-style string is passed if you make sure to pass them ByVal. I know this sounds contradictory, but that's what the compiler does.

Submitting Your SQL Statements

After you have developed your Direct or Prepared SQL statements, you can submit them for execution. As you have done earlier, if you use the Direct method you invoke the SQLExecDirect function to submit and execute your SQL statement.

On the other hand, if you have used the Prepared method, and already have executed your `SQLBindParameter` function call to provide the values for the parameters, you can submit your SQL statement using the `SQLExecute` function. Continuing with the example of the previous section, this would be:

```
Dim rc As Integer          ' Execute prepared SQL statement --
rc = SQLExecute(hstmt)     ' access plan + parameter values
```

The steps of invoking `SQLBindParameter` with different parameter values can be repeated as often as desired, using the same access plan submitted with the `SQLPrepare` function, with subsequent calls to the `SQLExecute` function.

It should be noted here that since the parameter is specified by the calling arguments of the `SQLBindParameter` function as an address (or pointer) to the parameter variable value, that you only need to assign a new value to the parameter variable, and then make successive `SQLExecute` invocations. It is not necessary to continually invoke the `SQLBindParameter` function if only the value of the parameter is being changed.

Retrieving the Result Set

At this juncture, you have submitted your SQL statement and if all has gone well you have developed a result set. The next step is to obtain the values you need from this result set. To do this, there are a variety of techniques ranging from the simple to the complex. I will defer the complex techniques to a subsequent section—see "Programming the Result Set with the ODBC 2.0 API." In that section you will concentrate on such subjects as selecting and using various cursor models, and memory allocation.

For the moment, you will explore the simplest and most direct method of retrieving values from the columns of your result set. The simplest method of retrieving values from the result set involves the use of the functions `SQLFetch`, `SQLGetData`, and `SQLBindCol`.

The `SQLFetch` function advances the row pointer of the result set to successive rows. The cursor model used here is the basic "move forward" cursor discussed earlier. All that `SQLFetch` does is move the row pointer to the next row. It does not actually transfer any data to your application unless you do one of two things—call the `SQLGetData` function, or call the `SQLBindCol` function. These two functions serve similar purposes, but accomplish their results in different ways.

SQLGetData Function Retrieval Operations

The SQLGetData function retrieves a single column value from the current location of the row pointer in the result set. That means that if you have ten columns in your result set and you want to retrieve all of the column values, then you have to invoke the SQLGetData function ten times for each SQLFetch operation.

An example of just retrieving a single column from a result set for all rows of the result set follows:

```
Dim strEmpName As String*20           ' Buffer for EmpName
strEmpName = String$(20,0)            ' Initialize to NULLS
Dim lngNameLen As Long                ' Column width - CHARS
Dim fc As Integer                     ' Fetch return code
Dim gc As Integer                     ' GetData return code
fc = SQLFetch(hstmt)                  ' Fetch a row
gc = SQLGetData(hstmt, 2, SQL_C_CHAR,
➥strEmpName, 21, lngNameLen)          'Get data
Form1.Print "Last Name = " & strEmpName   ' Print on Form
```

You can execute the SQLFetch and SQLGetData functions repeatedly in a loop until the return value of the SQLFetch function is SQL_ERROR. At this point you have reached the end of the result set.

It also is possible to retrieve additional information about the result set, such as the number of columns, by invoking the SQLNumResultCols. Code for doing this would be:

```
Dim rc As Integer                     ' Return code variable
Dim intCols As Integer                ' Buffer for Num Cols
rc = SQLNumResultCols(hstmt, intCols) ' Inquire about Cols
Form1.Print "Number of Result Set Columns = "
➥& Str$(intCols)                      ' Print on Form
```

SQLBindCol Function Retrieval Operations

An alternate way to retrieve your result set is to use the SQLBindCol function. This technique is particularly useful if you wish to retrieve multiple fields (columns) from each row of the result set with each move of the result set cursor. For most applications, you will typically want to retrieve multiple columns with each SQLFetch operation, so the approach using the SQLBindCol function is the most frequently used approach.

It should be noted here that this approach is more efficient than invoking the SQLGetData function for each column value you want to retrieve within each row of the result set.

To use this approach, you make as many invocations of the SQLBindCol function as necessary to bind the desired result set columns to memory buffers. For example, if you wanted to retrieve six columns from each row of the result set, you would invoke the SQLBindCol function six times—once for each column desired before you started retrieving result set rows using the SQLFetch function. Typical code might look something like the following, after you declare the appropriate Visual Basic string variables, and assuming all of the columns are strings, denoted by the string variables ColX:

```
Dim rc As Integer                   ' Variable for return code
rc = SQLBindCol(hstmt, 1, SQL_C_CHAR, ByVal Col1, Len(Col1), SQL_NULL_DATA)
rc = SQLBindCol(hstmt, 2, SQL_C_CHAR, ByVal Col2, Len(Col2), SQL_NULL_DATA)
rc = SQLBindCol(hstmt, 3, SQL_C_CHAR, ByVal Col3, Len(Col3), SQL_NULL_DATA)
rc = SQLBindCol(hstmt, 4, SQL_C_CHAR, ByVal Col4, Len(Col4), SQL_NULL_DATA)
rc = SQLBindCol(hstmt, 5, SQL_C_CHAR, ByVal Col5, Len(Col5), SQL_NULL_DATA)
rc = SQLBindCol(hstmt, 6, SQL_C_CHAR, ByVal Col6, Len(Col6), SQL_NULL_DATA)
```

This simple example would bind six columns, comprising result set column positions 1 through 6, numbering from the leftmost column of the result set, to similarly named string variables. These string variables provide the buffer storage for the result set values for each bound column. It is also possible to bind columns of other data types in the result set to appropriately typed Visual Basic variables, even though only string variables are shown in the preceding example code.

Again, as in the code examples dealing with the SQLGetData function, you would make repeated calls to the SQLFetch function to retrieve successive rows of the result set. Likewise, when you encountered a SQL_ERROR value as the function return code, you will have traversed all of the rows of the result set. However, this time, each call to the SQLFetch function would simultaneously return a value for each of the result set columns which were previously bound to buffers using the SQLBindCol function calls.

Using Status and Error Information

Your application will need to process return code information from each function call you make to control the various operations described previously. Some of the possible return codes provided as the return value of function execution will be error codes. These can be expanded upon by making a call to the SQLError function.

A great deal of information is available by invoking the SQLError function. One of the standardized error codes that all functions can return is the SQL_ERROR code. To obtain additional information about the specific error

III

Visual Basic

encountered you can invoke the `SQLError` function immediately. A typical call to the `SQLError` function would be:

```
Dim rc As Integer
Dim strBuff1 As String * 16
Dim strBuff2 As String * 256
Dim intOutLen As Integer
Dim lngNative As Long
strBuff1 = String$(16, 0)
strBuff2 = String$(256, 0)
Do
      rc = SQLError (henv, hdbc, hstmt, strBuff1,
      ➥lngNative, strBuff2, 256, intOutLen)
      If (rc = SQL_SUCCESS Or rc = SQL_SUCCESS_WITH_INFO)
      ➥And intOutLen = 0 Then
            MsgBox "Error with no information available"
      Else
            MsgBox Left$(strBuff2, intOutLen)
      End If
Loop Until rc <> SQL_SUCCESS
```

You will notice that a single error return code from a function can result in several `SQLError` errors to decode. That is the purpose of the loop construct in the preceding example. The loop will continue until there are no further errors to be decoded for the path henv-hdbc-hstmt.

`SQLError` retrieves the following information:

- *SQLSTATE*—an ODBC standardized error identifier found in `strBuff1` in the preceding example

- *Native Error Code*—found in `lngNative` in the preceding example which is provided by the data source

- *Error message string*—found in `strBuff2` in the preceding example

`SQLError` returns information on errors at a variety of levels. In the previous example it reports on errors from henv-hdbc-hstmt, or a specific statement handle. However, `SQLError` can be used to retrieve error information in other ways. In general it returns error information concerning the rightmost non-null handle in its argument list. Therefore, to retrieve information about:

- The environment (henv), set the appropriate environment handle, and set hdbc to `SQL_NULL_HDBC` and set hstmt to `SQL_NULL_HSTMT`

- The connection (hdbc), set the appropriate connection handle, and set hstmt to `SQL_NULL_HSTMT`

- The statement (hstmt), just ignore the other handles, or set them to 0& (long NULL pointer)

In repeated invocations of SQLError, when no additional information
is found concerning the rightmost non-null handle, it will return
SQL_NO_DATA_FOUND.

Terminating Statements, Connections, and the Environment

After you complete your database operations, you need to deallocate the
resources that were allocated earlier. The resources allocated are: Statement
handles, Connection handles, and Environment handles.

First, when you are finished with an SQL statement execution, your application can call SQLFreeStmt to free the resources associated with the statement
handle. Four possible options can be used in the SQLFreeStmt call, which are:

■ *SQL_CLOSE*—closes the cursor and discards pending results. The statement handle can be reused later if desired

■ *SQL_DROP*—closes the cursor, discards pending results, and frees all resources associated with the statement handle. The statement handle
cannot be reused later

■ *SQL_UNBIND*—releases the return buffers bound with the SQLBindCol function to the statement handle (more on this later)

■ *SQL_RESET_PARAMS*—releases all parameter buffers used by SQLSetParam for
a statement handle

Additionally, you can decide to cancel an SQL statement operation that is
currently underway—perhaps it is taking too long, or causing some other
problem. To accomplish this you can call the SQLCancel function.

Finally you can release other resources as follows:

■ *Close a connection*—call SQLDisconnect(hdbc) to close a connection. The
application then can reuse the hdbc to connect to another data source

■ *Free a connection*—call SQLFreeConnect(hdbc) to release the connection
handle and free all resources associated with it

■ *Free the environment*—call SQLFreeEnv(henv) to release the environment
handle and cease ODBC operations

You should always free these resources before terminating your Visual Basic
application.

III

Visual Basic

Programming the Result Set with the ODBC 2.0 API

In the previous section, "Retrieving the Result Set," you looked at the most direct and simple form of getting values from a result set. In this section you will investigate more sophisticated methods for interfacing with the result set.

One general concept in this area is using the SQLSetConnectOption function. Using this function call, you can establish the behavioral characteristics of a connection as a whole. You can set up such features as read-only or read-write processing, time-out periods for logins, execution tracing options, language translation, and most importantly, you can establish the behavior of transactions and cursors on a connection. Once these options are set, they apply to all statements that are associated with the connection. An example of this might be:

```
Dim rc As Integer
rc = SQLSetConnectOption(hdbc, SQL_ODBC_CURSORS, SQL_CUR_USE_ODBC)
```

This code establishes that the hdbc identified will use the ODBC cursor library instead of the native cursor of the driver.

Another general concept is that of setting statement-specific options for each statement. This is accomplished using the SQLSetStmtOption function. By using this function, your application can select options for such things as asynchronous processing, parameter binding, query timeouts, maximum number of rows and columns, and other options.

An example of using the SQLSetStmtOption function call would be:

```
Dim rc As Integer
rc = SQLSetStmtOption(hstmt, SQL_CURSOR_TYPE,
➥SQL_CURSOR_KEYSET_DRIVEN)
```

This code sets up the type of cursor behavior you want the result set to exhibit for a given statement. Refer to the earlier section titled "Performance Effects of Cursor Management" for more information on cursor types and behaviors, especially keyset-driven cursors.

Additionally, you can use the SQLSetStmtOption function to set up the number of rows in the range of the keyset-driven cursor. This would implement the mixed cursor behavior discussed earlier in this chapter, and would be particularly appropriate for very large result sets. This would be achieved by:

```
Dim rc As Integer
rc = SQLSetStmtOption(hstmt, SQL_KEYSET_SIZE, 100&)
```

The preceding code further refines a keyset-driven cursor to span a specified number of rows in the range of the keyset—in this case, 100 rows are specified. Remember that in mixed cursor operations such as this, as the row pointer moves out of the range of the current keyset, another 100 rows worth of keyset information would be developed.

Another use of this function that you will frequently find useful is in setting up asynchronous processing. In asynchronous processing mode, the statement is submitted and execution proceeds while the SQLExecute or SQLExecDirect function (or other statement-related functions) returns and your subsequent code then can continue execution. There is a distinct advantage to asynchronous processing when the time required to complete the statement could be quite large. To establish asynchronous processing you would make the following call:

```
Dim rc As Integer
rc = SQLSetStmtOption(hstmt, SQL_ASYNC_ENABLE, SQL_ASYNC_ENABLE_ON)
```

The code example given above turns on the asynchronous processing mode. While processing in asynchronous mode, no other functions can be called on the same hstmt or the hdbc associated with the asynchronous function until processing is completed. To detect if the synchronous operation is completed, make some other function call for the same hstmt or hdbc and check the return code. If the return code is SQL_STILL_EXECUTING, asynchronous operations are not yet completed. When the return code is SQL_SUCCESS or SQL_ERROR, or some other return code, then processing is completed.

Working with Result Set Data Structures

In preparation for manipulating the result set's cursor using SQLFetch or SQLExtendedFetch in a more efficient manner, you will need to create an application data structure to act as a buffer for the rows of the result set. After creating the buffer data structure, the SQLBindCol function is called to bind a buffer variable with a specific column in the result set row. For example:

```
Dim rc As Integer
Dim strColThree As String
rc = SQLBindCol(hstmt, 3, SQL_C_CHAR, ByVal strColThree, 31&)
```

This code binds column 3 of the hstmt result set to the string variable *strColThree*, which is sized to be a maximum of 31 characters in length (including the terminating NULL).

Subsequent calls to SQLFetch will have the effect of placing the value found in column 3 into the string variable *strColThree*.

SQLExtendedFetch also can be called to return result set rows (such as a rowset) more than one at a time. In that case, the bound columns variables would have to be arrays large enough to buffer the number of rows in the rowset, since that is how the rowset is returned.

Manipulating the Result Set Cursor

In addition to the previously discussed use of the SQLSetConnectOption and SQLSetStmtOption functions to select a particular type of cursor and its behavior, you can use the SQLsetScrollOptions function to define the scrolling behavior of the cursor. Cursor scrolling behavior such as concurrency control, sensitivity to changes in the result set made by other transactions, and rowset size can be set using this function.

Concurrency control determines what happens to the result set in the event of concurrent access requests to modify data that is within the rows of the result set. That is, your application is in the process of editing or modifying a row in the result set, and someone else is attempting to perform a similar operation. Selecting a specific form of concurrency control needs to be considered carefully, especially in a heavily loaded multi-user database server environment. A typical call to set up scrolling options might be:

```
Dim rc As Integer
rc = SQLSetScrollOptions(hstmt, SQL_CONCUR_LOCK, 25&, 10%)
```

This invocation of SQLSetScrollOptions would use the lowest level of locking to ensure that a row being edited can be updated. In addition, it specifies that 25 rows of keys should be buffered, and that there are 10 rows in a rowset— related to using SQLExtendedFetch that retrieves a rowset each time it is invoked.

Debugging and Testing with ODBC 2.0 Development Tools

I don't know about you, but I know that I spend much of my programming time debugging—or sometimes just trying to understand—my program code and the operations of the ODBC 2.0 API calls. Having good debugging tools is a great asset in this effort.

While you are developing your Visual Basic ODBC 2.0 application, you should use a variety of tracing, debugging, and development tools to assist you. Usually the initial chore with your first ODBC 2.0 API application is to become familiar with just what ODBC is doing as you call the various functions. Some of the tools available to help you are discussed in the following sections.

Using ODBC Trace to Log Data Source Operations

The ODBC Manager has a built-in tracing option you can turn on for any data source. This tracing facility writes ODBC operations to a log file for later analysis. The trace facility can be turned on using the ODBC Administrator dialog under the Options sub-dialog when configuring an ODBC data source. See figure 19.2 for these dialogs.

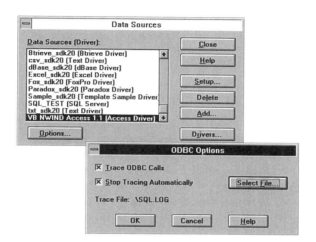

Fig. 19.2
ODBC Administrator log trace dialogs.

The ODBC Trace log also can be controlled from inside your Visual Basic code by using the SQLSetConnectOption function with the SQL_OPT_TRACE parameter thus:

```
rc = SQLSetConnectOption(hdbc, SQL_OPT_TRACE, SQL_OPT_TRACE_ON)
```

By default this causes tracing to be recorded in the file SQL.LOG in the root directory of the Windows drive. You can specify a different file of your choice by the following additional call to SQLSetConnectOption:

```
Dim rc As Integer
Dim strFileName As String
strFileName = "c:\temp\myfile.log"
rc = SQLSetConnectOption(hdbc, SQL_OPT_TRACEFILE, ByVal
➥strFileName)
```

Tip
Clean-up of these trace logs is not performed automatically. Be sure to clean them up when you're through looking at them.

> **Note**
>
> Turning on tracing by any of these methods greatly increases execution time for all of your ODBC operations, and also creates a fair amount of disk activity. Don't forget to turn off tracing when you are finished with it.

Invoking ODBC Spy To Monitor ODBC Transactions

Another excellent tool for debugging and also for identifying what is happening when your application makes ODBC function calls is the ODBC Spy utility that comes with the ODBC 2.0 SDK.

ODBC Spy can be configured to spy on any data source, and it will intercept and decode all function calls that are made from the driver to the data source. This intercepted information can be displayed as your program executes so you can watch each function call execute. The information can also be logged to an ASCII file for later review and analysis. A typical session with ODBC Spy displaying the intercepted function calls is shown in figure 19.3.

Fig. 19.3
ODBC Spy offers live tracing of ODBC data source function calls.

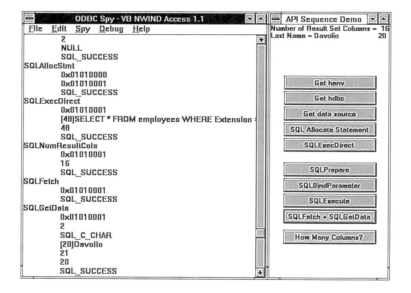

Again, as was the case with the ODBC Log facility, all of this useful information comes at the price of significantly reduced real-time performance. Realize that during ODBC Spy operations both ODBC Spy's logging window and optionally a log file must be updated on a constant basis.

From Here...

To learn more about using the ODBC 2.0 API, you should refer to the following materials elsewhere in this book:

- Chapter 10, "Inserting, Updating, and Deleting Rows"

- Chapter 11, "Queries and Result Sets"

- Chapter 12, "Setting Parameters with Prepared Statements"

- Chapter 13, "The Cursor Library and Positioned Operations"

In these other chapters, you explore additional specific details in using the programming techniques involving the ODBC 2.0 API functions covered in this chapter. All the techniques of these other chapters are equally applicable to developing programs in Visual Basic when using the ODBC 2.0 API functions.

III

Visual Basic

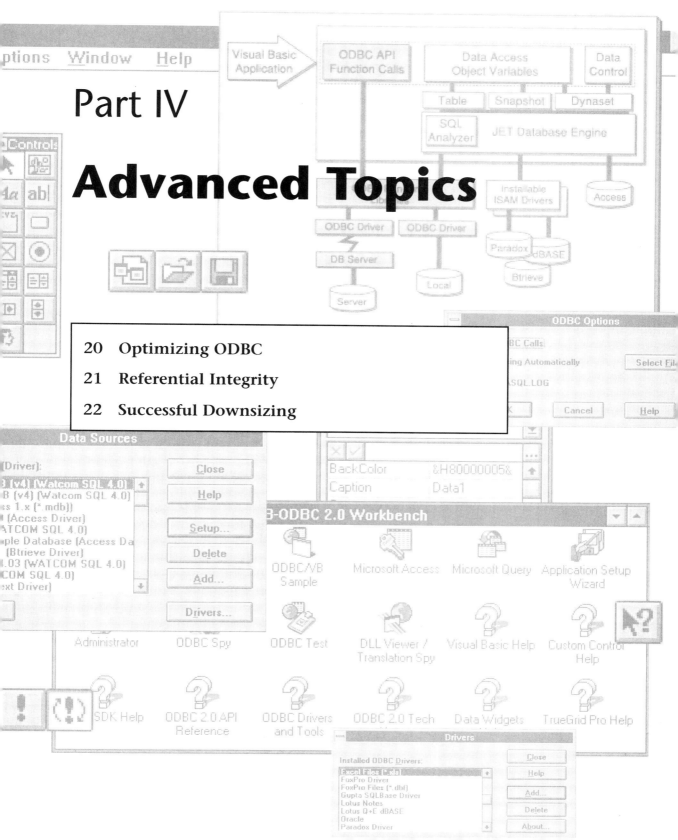

Part IV

Advanced Topics

20 Optimizing ODBC

21 Referential Integrity

22 Successful Downsizing

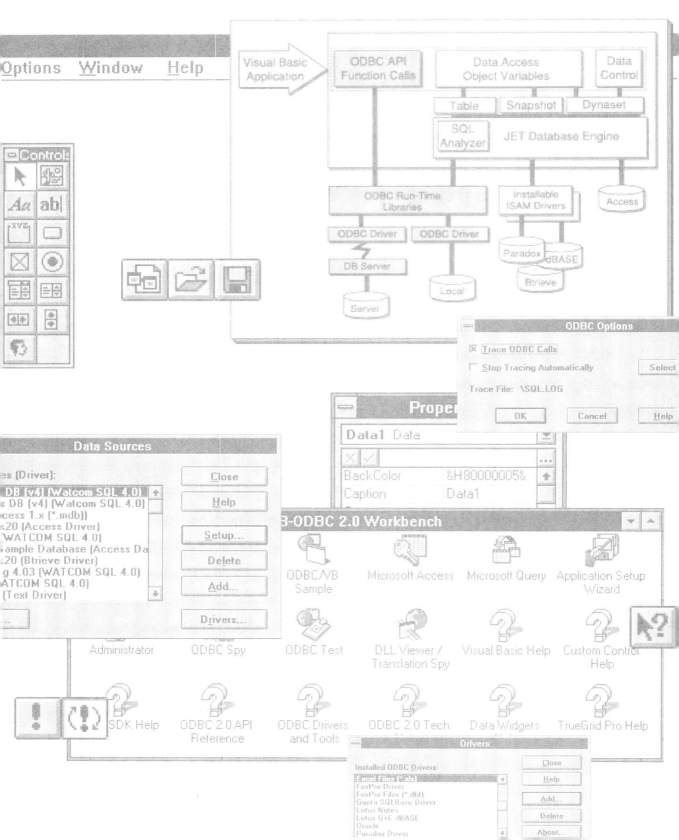

Chapter 20

Optimizing ODBC

IV

Advanced Topics

I've heard many rationalizations from developers attempting to explain why they don't work with ODBC, but the most significant and credible one is that the extra functionality carries with it a performance hit. There is some truth in this: translation between ODBC standard syntax and the unique commands expected by the database engine takes time, and almost every ODBC operation involves some translation. This still isn't enough to dissuade a lot of people from realizing the benefits of ODBC in their applications, but optimization is a serious issue that merits careful consideration.

This chapter discusses the following ways that you can improve the speed of your ODBC-enabled application:

- Reduce all kinds of problems by designing your database right in the first place

- Make yourself look good by choosing optimized drivers

- Minimize overhead by checking each driver capability only once

- Trim down application and feature initialization times by disconnecting/reconnecting as little as possible

- Make judicious use of synchronous/asynchronous modes

- Minimize execution preparation times by choosing between `SQLExecute()` and `SQLExecDirect()`

- Make your queries efficient by retrieving results judiciously

- Streamline your cursor operations by always binding the primary key column

- Avoid extra work by turning off bookmarks if not needed

■ Tailor the application to your load expectations by selecting the lowest usable transaction isolation level

■ Look for inefficiencies by testing your code with the tracing facility

Design Your Database Right in the First Place

The key to any good database application is a solid foundation—the database itself. Designing a database is a science, not a hit-and-miss affair. Chapter 2, "The Relational Database Model," discusses the concepts and techniques behind proper database design, and I encourage you to take them to heart. If you don't follow the tips given here, your database search times will suffer, and users will perceive it as the application's fault.

Proper normalization—the placement of fields within the tables—is the main key to a successful data model. This may not mean full normalization of *all* tables in your database. I don't recommend going below third normal form under most circumstances, but in the case of relatively unimportant (and frequently used) lookup tables, it may be the fastest way to get from database table to screen control: you can read one table instead of two or more.

Using single-column primary keys throughout your database is a no-brainer way to speed things up on the database engine side, which is the ODBC driver itself in the case of a single-tier driver (see Chapter 5, "Data Sources and Drivers," for more information). Search times are reduced, the possibility of redundant rows is eliminated, and indexes tend to be smaller.

The tools that you choose to use for the *enforcement* of referential integrity (and other rules for the data in your tables) will depend on how important interoperability is to your application. For example, if you're developing an application that is intended to work with most or all ODBC drivers, you must include any enforcement mechanisms you need within your front-end application itself. The danger here is that users may be able to get into the tables outside your application and mess things up. Unfortunately, this can't be avoided if maximum interoperability is your goal.

If, on the other hand, your application is designed to work with a few specific high-powered platforms like Oracle and SQL Server, it often is best to rely on the referential integrity features. Unique indexes, triggers, rules, stored procedures, and such can take the onus of bounds-checking completely off the application's shoulders and hand it to the database engine, which is supposed to be good at that sort of thing. One tradeoff in this scenario is the requirement for the application to make sure a given driver supports the required features. This is dealt with in the later section entitled "Check Each Driver Capability Only Once."

Choose Optimized Drivers

This piece of optimization advice is so obvious that it might be overlooked if not emphasized. Probably the single most important factor in the speed of an ODBC connection is the driver itself. Your selection of the right driver for your needs is key to your application's performance—and it's an easy way to get a speed boost with no programming involved.

While most modern PC DBMSs come with ODBC drivers included, third-party companies often develop alternative drivers for the same database engines which in many cases are faster than the standard ones. For example, Intersolv (the company that sells Q+E) also sells ODBC drivers for several common data sources. These drivers are in most cases faster than the standard ones, in some cases have additional features, and don't cost very much on a per-desktop basis.

You may not be able to determine which drivers your users use, but if you're shipping ODBC drivers with your application you definitely have some control over this facet of optimization.

Check Each Driver Capability Only Once

You can save quite a bit of time in the long run if you spend some time learning about the driver's capabilites immediately after you connect to a data source. There are quite a few types of information your application needs to learn about a driver, so that it can decide:

- Whether any special configuration changes are needed based on the driver's default settings

- Whether to withhold certain features of the program if the driver doesn't support required functions

- Whether to accept a given driver at all, based on supported functions

Most of the types of checks I'm talking about are done with the SQLGetInfo() function, which gets many different types of information about a driver that can directly influence the operation or success of your program—although `SQLGetFunctions()` may also be needed for some drivers. Here are some key examples:

- SQL and API conformance levels supported by the driver

- Degree of support for transaction processing

- Degree of additional support for cursors

- Numbers of concurrent connections and statements supported

- Numeric functions supported by the driver

- Maximum length of various types of objects (such as cursor names)

- Maximum number of columns allowed in tables, GROUP BY clauses, ORDER BY clauses, and so on

The least efficient way to handle your driver examination needs is simply to call `SQLGetInfo()` every time you need a particular piece of information. This is likely to result in a tremendous number of function calls that always return the same fixed information.

A major improvement is to perform the checks you need, then store the information you've discovered in variables that can be referred to in the future instead of calling the function again. There are several approaches to this basic idea.

You may find it easiest to place your driver examination routine right after (or even within) your connection routine, so that all the checks you could possibly need to perform are done immediately upon connection. Except for the fact that it increases the perceived login time to the user, this is not a bad way to go because it's quite tidy to program. This doesn't work well at all if you're not doing a lot of connecting and reconnecting, however.

The most efficient, realistic way to perform driver capability checks is also the most cumbersome, but if you're an optimization fanatic it may be for you. Incorporate the following steps into your application if you're willing to put in the time to save your users' time:

1. When you first create a connection to a given data source, query it for any information you absolutely need up front.

2. Store all results in such a way that they can be accessed by all parts of your program—for example, in global variables.

3. The next time you need to connect to the same data source, don't bother to run your checks again—simply refer to the information already in memory.

4. As you need more information about the driver, gather it and store it in a publicly accessible fashion. Never check the driver for the same information more than once.

An alternate, *extremely* efficient way to handle questions about a driver's capability is to support only certain specific ODBC drivers and therefore to know in advance of what the data source is capable. This is a classic example of effectiveness being sacrificed for efficiency, and unless your application only supports a couple of specific drivers for other reasons, it is not a good idea.

Avoid Disconnecting/Reconnecting

When you possibly can avoid it, do not free and then reallocate database connections. The connection process can be quite time-consuming when you consider login requirements and the potential for errors. Instead, allocate one connection to each DBMS your application needs to work with, and add new ones as needed during execution, freeing them only when you're sure they'll no longer be needed.

There is one consideration that may preclude this approach, however. ODBC connections generally map directly to the proprietary connection mechanism particular to a given database engine. There is often a cost associated with this. For one thing, each connection may grab a great deal of memory on the server. For another, each connection may count against some sort of limit built into the server software, such as a license count.

As an example, back when Microsoft SQL Server was only available under OS/2 1.3, servers were limited to 16M of RAM—yet database connections ate up almost 50K each on the server. One hundred connections to a database would take up five precious megabytes of server memory. Large-scale SQL Server developers in those days actually went the other direction and built on-the-fly connect/disconnect logic into their programs to be as conservative of server resources as possible. Windows NT has opened the door to virtually unlimited RAM, and connect/disconnect apps are rare now. However, licensing considerations can still drive development in a similar direction.

Under such circumstances, conserving connections may be critical to the success of your application, and may override speed optimization concerns.

Although allocating and freeing statement handles does not take as much time as the similar operations on connections, it still makes sense to avoid these processes in excess. A statement handle can be used and reused, and unless you're frantic to preserve resources, it doesn't make sense to kill and recreate them all the time. This is particularly true if you have bound parameters to or set options for a statement that will apply if the statement is reused, and that's likely. If you believe you may need to run the same statement again, leave it alone and allocate a new statement handle to work with. Obviously, you shouldn't keep more than a few statements active at a time, so balance the goals of speed optimization and resource preservation.

Make Judicious Use of Synchronous/ Asynchronous Modes

Synchronous mode or asynchronous mode? That is the question. This is another example of optimization leading to a whole new level of complexity in your application.

Although intuitively this may not sound right, synchronous mode is very frequently the faster of the two. This is because of the overhead required to support an asynchronous execution model: the application needs to execute the statement, then keep returning to check on its status while trying to get other work done in the meantime. Synchronous mode is great if your queries or database modifications are relatively simple, and return in a couple of seconds or less, an acceptable wait time for most users under most circumstances. Also, there's no reason to trouble with asynchronous mode if the application can't go on without the result set anyway.

However, under certain circumstances asynchronous mode makes a whole lot of sense. Complex queries, and especially complex multi-row database UPDATE or DELETE operations, can take literally hours to complete, and in many such cases it's possible to let the user continue working in other parts of the program in the meantime.

Very few professional ODBC-enabled applications execute exclusively in one mode or the other. If you're willing to spend the time to get asynchronous mode to work in the first place, mix the modes as appropriate to meet your users' needs.

Choose between *SQLExecute()* and *SQLExecDirect()*

As discussed in Chapter 8, "The ODBC Statement: An Introduction," there are two functions that can be used to execute SQL statements: SQLExecute() and SQLExecDirect(). SQLExecute() requires that you first prepare the statement using the SQLPrepare() function, which checks the validity of the SQL command before it's actually executed. SQLExecDirect() just goes for it, checking the statement's validity on the fly. From an optimization standpoint, both have their charms.

When to Use *SQLExecDirect()*

Using SQLExecDirect() is the fastest way to execute a statement. It's only a single function call, and therefore requires less work for both the application and the driver. SQLExecDirect() is great for operations that are done only rarely by your application.

When to Use *SQLExecute()*

The SQLExecute()/SQLPrepare() combination should usually be used for any operation that needs to be repeated frequently, especially if the calls are in proximity to one another. For example, if the user is working in a data entry form and certain lookup tables associated with the form need to be refreshed often, it makes a lot of sense to leave the statement that retrieves the lookup table data prepared, at least while the form is being displayed, and use SQLExecute() to run it whenever a refresh is needed. As usual, it's up to you to balance users' resource conservation requirements with their optimization needs.

> **Caution**
>
> This method can cause additional problems under certain circumstances. Having too many active *hstmt*s can cause a resource hogging problem at some point, and the driver may only support a limited number of them in the first place.

Retrieve Results Judiciously

The most time-consuming aspect of most database applications is the time spent retrieving result sets, especially large ones. All layers of the system are involved in such operations: the application, the database engine, and the pipeline between them.

This being the case, it's important to retrieve only the rows and columns you need at any given time. Even if it is expedient, resist the temptation to retrieve the same result set more than once except when you need to refresh the entire set.

Making use of the cursor library and additional cursor functions supported by ODBC drivers is almost always the most efficient way to retrieve results. This is true for nearly all data retrieval purposes, with the possible exception of small result sets retrieved for read-only purposes. Refer to Chapter 13, "The Cursor Library and Positioned Operations," for details on the different types of cursors and appropriate methods for using them.

Large-scale database applications can become quite complex, and at some point, you may lose control over the ODBC communications being issued by yours. To make sure this does not happen, use the ODBC tracing facility (discussed in a later section of this chapter) to monitor the functions being called and the statements being executed by your app. If you see an operation being repeated unnecessarily, take measures to break it out into a separate process and run it as infrequently as possible.

Always Bind the Primary Key Column

If your application makes extensive use of cursors, following one simple rule can substantially reduce result set parsing times. Binding the primary key column ensures that every row in a result set remains unique. This benefits your application in two ways:

- ODBC will recognize the uniqueness of the single-column field value and use it as the exclusive differentiator between rows. This is more efficient than a multiple-column key, and totally prevents the possibility of indistinct result set rows.

- You won't have to waste time after the fact dealing with the consequences of multiple rows inadvertently being affected by a positioned operation, in the event that two rows in the result set turn out to be the same.

This, of course, assumes that you followed the advice given in the first section of this chapter and designed your database properly to begin with. If you do not provide a unique primary key for each column *and* bind it as part of every result set from a given table (or include it in every result set that's the result of two or more tables joined), you'll have to face the consequences. This is an exception to the general rule of retrieving only result set columns that will be displayed or manipulated by the front-end application.

Turn Off Bookmarks If Not Needed

If you're using cursors but you will not be using bookmarks to position the cursor and read or manipulate specific rows, you can turn them off using the SQLSetStmtOption() function. This will, of course, only work on a single statement at a time. The following line of code will turn off bookmarks for statement *hstmt*:

```
retcode = SQLSetStmtOption (hstmt, SQL_USE_BOOKMARKS, SQL_UB_OFF);
```

Since this is the default, you don't need to issue it unless you have previously turned on bookmarks for the statement.

Disabling bookmarks slightly reduces the amount of work ODBC does when fetching each result set.

Select the Lowest Usable Transaction Isolation Level

Transaction processing is an invaluable tool for protecting users from their own mistakes, and from the changes made to the database "behind the scenes" by other users on the network. There is quite a bit of overhead involved in supporting transaction processing features, however, and where possible you may wish to "turn it down." Some ODBC drivers do not allow you to change transaction isolation options, in which case you are "stuck" with the default. If not, you can choose different levels depending on the type of result set processing being done by your application.

Chapter 10, "Inserting, Updating, and Deleting Rows," describes in detail how to change transaction isolation levels for ODBC drivers that permit it. The general rule is, the lower the isolation level, the less overhead that needs to be performed by the driver and the database engine.

Keep in mind that the transaction isolation option setting applies to an entire connection, not just a single statement. If you want to change the setting for a particular operation, you'll have to change it again at the end to allow future operations to work as desired. At some point all the time spent in switching back and forth will exceed the benefits of lower isolation levels, and it won't be worth the effort.

> **Note**
>
> For more information about transaction processing, refer to Chapter 10, "Inserting, Updating, and Deleting Rows."

Test Your Code with the Tracing Facility

You can use ODBC's tracing facility to monitor the ODBC calls made by the application, and examine the output for unexpected results or inefficient use of the various ODBC functions. This is especially useful for watching the tracing.

The tracing facility is activated through the use of a pair of `SQLSetStmtOption()` calls. The relevant `fOption` values for that function are:

    SQL_OPT_TRACEFILE;

    SQL_OPT_TRACE;

SQL_OPT_TRACEFILE

This `fOption` supplies the name of the file to which trace results will be written. `vParam` is specified as a null-terminated string that must be a valid DOS path and filename. The default tracefile name is specified in the ODBC.INI file or registry, under the TraceFile key in the [ODBC] section.

SQL_OPT_TRACE

This option enables you to turn the trace on and off. Possible `vParam` values:

    SQL_OPT_TRACE_ON: Turn on the trace.

    SQL_OPT_TRACE_OFF: Turn off the trace.

To selectively trace sections of code, simply turn on the trace at the beginning of each section and turn it off at the end. This is perhaps your most useful tool for debugging a misbehaving procedure.

Interpreting the Trace Results

Once you have executed the series of operations you want to look over, simply open the trace file in a text editor (such as Notepad). Each ODBC function call appears in the trace file, with the function name and all parameter values sent to the function being shown.

Your more sophisticated users may appreciate it if you build in a switch they can use to turn on tracing for their own use. This can be beneficial in, for example, a reporting application, to enable users to duplicate the various SELECT commands involved in constructing a report (that will show them where each item on the report comes from). It's up to you whether you want to include this option for their use, the down side being that you are revealing—to potential competitors—exactly how your application interacts with ODBC.

From Here...

Please refer to the following chapters and appendixes of this book for additional information about ways to further optimize your OBDC application.

- See Chapter 21, "Referential Integrity," for information about enforcing referential integrity throughout your database.

- Refer to Chapter 22, "Successful Downsizing," for tips on downsizing your database systems.

- Appendix A, "Resources in the SDK," concisely describes the utilities, samples, and help files provided with the SDK.

- Appendix B, "ODBC Function Reference," is a concentrated reference guide giving function prototypes, legal parameter values, and other information about all ODBC function calls.

Chapter 21

Referential Integrity

When countries involve themselves in relationships with each other, they take great pains to ensure that their partners comply with any terms of the relationships. Thus it is that when countries agree to limit nuclear proliferation, they also agree to admit each other's inspectors. Without these inspectors, the countries have no assurance that their partners are playing fairly, and that arms production is within the mandated limits.

Similarly, database designers take great pains to ensure that their data complies with the "terms" set forth in their design. Instead of inspectors, though, they use software tools to enforce the *integrity* of the data. In this chapter, you learn the types of integrity defined in and enforceable in the relational database model; the chapter also describes the three common approaches to enforcing that integrity, and discusses how to use ODBC 2's implementation of one of those approaches.

In this chapter, you explore:

- Integrity in the relational database model

- Methods of enforcing integrity

- ODBC applications and SQL's built-in integrity enforcement keywords

Integrity in the Relational Database Model

The relational model includes the concept of *data integrity*—a set of rules by which the database system and its programmers can ensure that data is valid and conforms to a designed structure. This integrity concept applies in two different scopes: that of the entities, and that of the relationships among entities. We call these scopes *entity integrity* and *referential integrity*, respectively.

Entity Integrity

The entity integrity rules apply to individual instances of entities—to records in your tables. They are the way you enforce primary key validity, restrict the values that can be entered into fields, prevent fields from being left empty, prevent duplicate fields, and define default values for fields. The rules can be combined to fit design goals—a few of the rules are already combinations of the others! As you see later in the chapter, entity integrity is fundamental to referential integrity, for if you can't be sure of the countries, how can you be sure of their treaties?

Enforcing Primary Key Validity

The primary key validity rules exist to ensure that entities can be uniquely identified by values in the fields comprising the primary key. If a table has primary key fields defined, then entries in the table must have valid, non-null, and unique data in the primary key fields. Thus, in your RailCar example later in the chapter, each RailCar entity must have a valid CarNumber assigned. Without this CarNumber, the RailCar entity is invalid, and can't be added to the database. In the following StationStop table (see fig. 21.1), the primary key fields (TrainNumber and ArrivalTime) *together* must be unique. You can have as many entries with TrainNumber 5 as you want, and you can have as many entries as you want with an ArrivalTime of 12:00:01 PM on 01/01/95. You can only have *one* entry, however, that describes TrainNumber 5 arriving on 01/01/95 at 12:00:01 PM.

Fig. 21.1
The StationStop table and its constraints.

StationStop	
TrainNumber	PK
ArrivalTime	PK
DepartureTime	>= ArrivalTime
StationName	NOT NULL
NumPassengers	>= 0

Restricting Field Values

Under the entity integrity rules, you can define constraints on individual fields, or on combinations of fields in an entity. This is your way of ensuring that field values fall within specified ranges, or that they are valid with respect to each other. If, for example, you add the StationStop table in figure 21.1 to your railroad, you will want to ensure that DepartureTime is always equal to or later than ArrivalTime, because a StationStop represents a train's arrival at and eventual departure from a station. In this case, you're constraining a field's value relative to another field's value. You also might decide that you need to know how many passengers are on the train when it arrives at a StationStop. Since you know that it is functionally impossible to have a negative number of passengers on board, you will need to ensure that NumPassengers is always greater than or equal to zero.

Preventing Null Fields

You also can constrain fields so that they *must* be filled. In this way, you can specify that no RailCar goes into the system without your knowing the OwnerNumber, or specify that each StationStop entry has a StationName—it doesn't make sense to stop at a null station.

Preventing Duplicate Values

The uniqueness constraint enables you to specify that a field must contain unique values, or that a combination of fields must contain a unique combination of values. The rules are similar to the primary key rules—data in "unique" fields must be valid and unique—but fields *can* be null, unless explicitly declared otherwise. The uniqueness constraint enables you to specify uniqueness in fields on which the table is *not* dependent—fields which are *not* a part of the primary key. Each employee on your railroad has a unique tax ID number assigned by the government. Since you have your own EmployeeId, you do not use this field to index the employee, and it is not a primary key. It is, however, guaranteed to be unique, so you constrain the field to be unique. It can be null, since it is possible that the employee hasn't yet received a tax ID number.

Specifying Default Values

When you can make assumptions about your data, you might want to implement these assumptions as default value rules. In your RailCar example, you know that almost 70 percent of your cars are "coach" cars—you are, after all, the foremost passenger rail line in the world (to the marketing department, at least). You can enforce this assumption by specifying "coach" as the default value for the `RailCar` entity's `CarType` field, and enjoy the lunches your data entry operators offer as compensation for making their lives easier. They *can* override a default value by specifying some particular `CarType`, but they will most often want to press Enter and move on.

Referential Integrity

The referential integrity rule applies to the relationships defined among tables. It exists to validate the *references* that entities make to one another, and also goes by the name of "foreign key" validation. By this rule, each `RailCar` entity's `OwnerNumber` must refer to the `CompanyNumber` of a valid Company entity, or must be null. Attempts to add or update a `RailCar` record where the `OwnerNumber` refers to a non-existent Company will fail, according to the referential integrity rule.

Methods of Enforcing Integrity

You have thus far seen integrity enforcement almost as though it were a simple fact of relational database life. It is not. In fact, you can choose to enforce the rules in several ways, at several points in the "life" of the data. You can use whatever built-in enforcement services your DBMS provides to enforce integrity as the application commits data to the database, you can use application code to enforce integrity as the user enters, modifies, or deletes data, or you can post-process the data to detect and possibly correct integrity violations.

Enforcing Integrity through DBMS Services at Update Time

As a rule, a database engine can most efficiently manage the integrity rules you've used in your system design. Many of the databases that offer ODBC drivers also offer some method of integrity enforcement, although they vary in scope and method. When your integrity requirements are straightforward and supported by our DBMS engine, you save yourself from writing unnecessary code, and save your users and systems from the overhead that code introduces, by using the built-in services of the database engine to enforce integrity. Your application view of the data is necessarily high-level and often inefficient, so you do well to allow the database to manipulate data internally as often as your design allows.

Enforcing Integrity through Application Code at Entry Time

When your integrity enforcement needs to grow beyond the simple, or your DBMS engine does not support the integrity rules you need enforced, you can validate the data before you ever pass it to the database. You can do so both by querying the database and validating references to existing data, and by validating data against constant values. If you design a dialog box to enter RailCar records, you can ensure that the user enters a valid CarType in the dialog box code, without asking the database to validate the entry. You also can choose to validate data in your own code if you plan on manipulating the data in ways your DBMS engine might not understand. If you had a circular relationship between entities, for instance, a limited DBMS engine might not allow you to delete related entries, since doing so would violate the integrity of the reference.

After you've finished cursing yourself for designing that circular relationship, and verified that it *is* in there for a valid, defensible reason, you would turn off the DBMS engine's automatic, internal validation, and go about adding the validation to your own code. Since the validation is in your domain, you can choose to ignore the validation routines when you're attempting to delete one of these circular relationships.

Enforcing Integrity through Post-Processing

There are a few applications in which the above options incur processing overhead that the system cannot handle within the scope of its other responsibilities. These applications typically have extreme loads placed upon them during peak use, and power to spare at other times, or involve particularly expensive operations. When these systems require complex integrity management, *post-processing* may be the solution. In both the update time and entry time enforcement methods, you validate the data before it becomes an active part of the system, able to be queried, edited, and deleted by other users. With the post-processing method, though, you validate the data *after* it becomes an active part of the system. Whether you do this validation seconds, hours, or days after that data enters the system depends entirely on the application constraints. Consider the following examples:

■ *Example 1: The Railroad Alarm System*

Your railroad has decided to improve emergency response by adding an electronic monitoring and alarm system. You will install sensors and annunciators on all of your cars, engines, and track segments, and you will create a software package to manage all of this hardware. Because the alarms rapidly generate data that your system must process in real-time, you cannot immediately validate data modifications the system makes in response to these alarms. Instead, you will postpone all validation and correction until the day shift, when your trains run less frequently, and the alarms generate less data.

■ *Example 2: The Nightly Railroad Data Transfer*

As your railroad expands, you find yourself fiscally devoured by communications charges. The most expensive part of your communications infrastructure is the satellite link between your Blacksburg, VA, North American headquarters and your Cairo, Egypt, Middle East headquarters. You have evaluated your needs, and found that you can redesign the system to bulk upload all of the day's transaction and administration data during the wee hours of the night. Because of the volume of data involved, though, you would more than double your connect time if you had to validate all of the data as you moved it from one system to the other. Instead, you will copy all of the data, validate it off-line during the day, and return a validation report to the Cairo office during the next night's transfer, allowing them to address any discrepancies.

In both cases, post-processing is the most effective solution. You have a period of time during which you can perform the validation without interrupting the operation of the system. You are designing the application, so you can ensure that no other system components depend on the data's validity. If you were not designing the application, you would have to consider the effect of invalid data on the other components—does your alarm processor allow displaying an alarm from a sensor that is not in the database? Does it allow you to sound the annunciator attached to that sensor? If it does not, then you will likely have to find another solution, since lives are at stake, and you must inform the engineers of alarms.

Systems with hard real-time constraints or high-cost operations are excellent candidates for post-processing integrity enforcement. Since post-processing leaves potentially invalid data in the system, accessible to other users and system components, it is best left to systems wherein performance and response are absolutely critical, and the consequences of invalid data's existence are containable.

A Look at SQL's Built-In Integrity Enforcement Keywords

Most database engines offering ODBC drivers support some or all of the SQL standards' integrity enforcement keywords. Since these keywords are a part of the SQL grammar itself, they enable you to enforce integrity in your database systems using commands issued from within your program. Without the SQL support for integrity enforcement, you would have to specify constraints within a database design package designed for use with your chosen engine. While this may seem a minor inconvenience, it severely restricts the application user's ability to change database engines when they need something bigger, faster, or more robust. Since the SQL grammar enables you to create and constrain tables from within your application, and is common to many ODBC drivers and SQL database engines, here is a brief introduction to DBMS integrity enforcement using its keywords (see listing 21.1). All of the explanations refer to the two following SQL code statements, which represent the creation of your StationStop and RailCar examples (integrity-specific statements are bold-faced):

Listing 21.1 SQL Code to Create the *StationStop* and *RailCar* Tables

```
CREATE TABLE StationStop (
     TrainNumber   INT,
     StationName   CHAR(40) NOT NULL,

     ArrivalTime       TIMESTAMP,
     DepartureTime     TIMESTAMP,

     NumPassengers     INT,

     PRIMARY KEY (TrainNumber, ArrivalTime),
     CHECK (DepartureTime >= ArrivalTime),
     CHECK (NumPassengers >= 0),
     FOREIGN KEY TrainNumber REFERENCES Train,
     FOREIGN KEY StationName REFERENCES Station.StationName
)

CREATE TABLE RailCar (
     CarNumber            INT PRIMARY KEY,
     CarType              CHAR(32) NOT NULL,

     OwnerNumber          INT NOT NULL,
     MaxLoad              INT NOT NULL CHECK(MaxLoad >= 0),
     BuildDate            TIMESTAMP NOT NULL,
     NextInspection       TIMESTAMP,

     FOREIGN KEY OwnerNumber REFERENCES Company.CompanyNumber
)
```

Enforcing Primary Key Validity

SQL provides the PRIMARY KEY (*field1*, *field2*, ... *fieldn*) construct to specify the fields that make up a primary key. The database will check each field in the comma-separated list for validity and, if the fields are foreign keys, existence in related tables, and will not allow any update which would produce an invalid primary key. Your StationStop table uses the PRIMARY KEY construct to specify TrainNumber and ArrivalTime as members of the primary key. Your RailCar example uses the PRIMARY KEY construct a bit differently—it refers to only one field, so you append it to the field's declaration. You don't have to specify single-field keys this way, but it's often easier to read and comprehend.

Restricting Field Values

The CHECK (*condition*) construct allows restriction and verification of fields, both against constant data and against each other. The database will evaluate the condition, and will not allow updating the record if any of the conditions are FALSE. Note that the database will evaluate conditions to one of three states: TRUE, FALSE, and UNKNOWN. It will allow update of any record which is either TRUE or UNKNOWN.

In your StationStop example, you've checked two conditions: NumPassengers >= 0, and DepartureTime >= ArrivalTime. The meaning of the NumPassengers condition is straightforward, but the departure/arrival time condition highlights a peculiarity of SQL's evaluation of NULL values, and the differences among TRUE, FALSE, and UNKNOWN. Since ArrivalTime is prevented from being NULL (see the following section), and DepartureTime is not, it is possible to have a StationStop record for a train which has arrived at the station but has not yet departed, in which case ArrivalTime will have a value, but DepartureTime will be NULL. In this case, the database will evaluate the condition and discover it to be UNKNOWN, because one of the elements of the expression is NULL. If the fields are both filled, the database will evaluate the condition as TRUE if DepartureTime is greater than or equal to ArrivalTime, and FALSE if DepartureTime is less than ArrivalTime. Thus, the database *will* allow a StationStop for a train that hasn't departed yet, but will conveniently *not* allow a StationStop for a train that has departed before it has arrived.

Preventing Null Fields

The NOT NULL construct appended to the StationStop table's StationNamefield prevents the field from being updated with a NULL value. This is SQL's way of forcing a field to have a value. In your case, the StationName *must* be entered for a StationStop, since you can't have a StationStop without a train's arrival at a station.

Enforcing Foreign Key Validity (Referential Integrity)

The final SQL integrity-enforcement tool is the FOREIGN KEY (*field*) REFER-
ENCES (*table.field*) construct. With this construct, you define a relationship
between a single field in your table (the related table), and a single field in
another table (the primary table). In your two example statements, you've
used the construct slightly differently—the TrainNumber reference does not
include a specific field name to reference in the Train table. You can do this
because the database assumes that you want all foreign keys to refer to the
primary key of the primary table. If the primary key of the primary table
consists of a single field of the same type as our foreign key field, the database
will assume you intend the relationship to refer to this field. Since the Train
table's primary key only contains the TrainNumber field, the database will
build the relationship based on its assumption. In your StationName reference,
you have arbitrarily elected to explicitly state the field in the Station table to
which StationName maps. There will be other cases in which you will want to
map a foreign key field to a non-primary key field in the primary table, precisely the explicitness for which the dot ('.') dereference operator exists.

You have seen a broad range of methods and tools for enforcing the integrity
of data in your database systems. Like the countries involved in treaty nego-
tiations, you have to decide which methods and which tools will best enforce
the terms you've set forth in your design. The tools and methods you've seen,
though, do not represent everything available to you. The database driver's
documentation will provide more information about extensions to these
basic integrity enforcement tools.

From Here...

- Chapter 2, "The Relational Database Model," provides more basic information on the relational database model, and outlines a context in
  which to view the integrity concepts presented in this chapter.

- Chapter 3, "The Client/Server Language: SQL," provides more basic
  information on the SQL language.

Chapter 22
Successful Downsizing

If you work for a corporation of any size, chances are you're going to be involved in a downsizing project sooner or later. The trend in the data-processing industry is definitely toward smaller, cheaper, and distributed systems.

Unfortunately, the road down isn't always smooth and fast. It's easy to fail even when everything should go right. Lack of user participation, resistance from corporate information services staff, under-powered platforms, poor project management, and any number of things can cause a "can't miss" project to flop.

First, you're going to look at the process of downsizing and then look specifically at how ODBC can help to make a project a success.

In this chapter, you explore how to

- Choose a downsizing model

- Pick a hardware and software platform

- Use ODBC to increase project options

- Model the downsized system

- Meet performance objectives

- Avoid the common pitfalls

Picking a Downsizing Model

The decision to downsize is often made purely on the basis of cost savings. When managers see large mainframes with a large support staff, they think big dollars. When managers see personal computers with virtually no support staff, they think savings.

You know the real world doesn't work that way. Centralized mainframes with trained personnel can be highly efficient at supporting large numbers of users. The incremental cost of adding a single user to a large system (providing it has some reserve capacity) is almost always smaller than the cost of adding a user to a downsized system. After all, adding a user to a personal computer-based system involves installing a new system. With a mainframe, it often involves little more than connecting a dumb terminal. Ongoing support costs are probably less with the homogeneous hardware and software of a mainframe system versus the dispersed personal-computer system with sometimes idiosyncratic mixtures of hardware and software.

The point being made isn't that downsized systems don't save money. They can and will, but the savings don't always come from running on smaller and cheaper systems. They come from the new capabilities that are opened up with the downsized system.

If you haven't worked in a mainframe environment, it's probably hard for you to realize how inaccessible to the end-user the data is in the typical system. Usually the smallest change to a report requires the involvement of several programmers and may take weeks (even months) to complete as it becomes queued up behind other requests. Just giving users easy-to-use tools that give them access to their data is a tremendous savings. It eliminates the cost of programmer time that would have been required to complete the request. Those easy-to-use tools also give the user access to the required information more quickly.

A redesigned, downsized application has potential for savings in training costs, increased productivity, and reduction of user error. Mainframe applications usually are text-based. They often require users to know arcane codes and quirky keystroke combinations to accomplish their work. A re-engineered downsized application could make use of a GUI interface with help facilities ranging from combo and list boxes to full contextual help.

Then there are the new opportunities for enhancing the system opened up by downsizing it. The most obvious one is the ability to incorporate document- and image-processing capabilities. Most systems could benefit from the addition of an imaging component.

The reason this is brought up is that cost-conscious managers, in choosing the methodology and platforms for downsizing, are often tempted to prove the cost savings up front. They pick the cheapest hardware and software and the shortest path. This decision might diminish some of the secondary benefits of downsizing that could, over time, be the source of real savings.

Depending upon your role in the downsizing effort, you may have little impact on these decisions. You should, however, at least understand the general principles and possible difficulties involved with each approach.

The three main approaches to downsizing are the port, the rewrite, and the new front-end. There are all kinds of different ways to combine them. Seldom is any of them done in a pure form.

The Port

Porting an application refers to the process of taking the source code that runs on one system and making it run on another system. This process may be either as simple as recompiling the source code or as complicated as redesigning and rewriting the application.

The porting of an application is often the path chosen by companies interested in a quick, painless migration to a downsized system. How quick and painless the path is depends on the state of the source being migrated and the quality of the various porting tools and emulators employed to accomplish the migration.

The simple path of recompiling the source code leaves little room for ODBC. Mainframe applications are mostly written in COBOL and have a text-based interface. If they use any relational database technology, they won't be using ODBC protocol. Furthermore, there is no need to introduce ODBC into the process because it requires source code changes.

How prudent is this method of porting an application? If you have the tools to pull it off and the application is fairly well designed, this can be a good method.

What are the problems? First, the tools often aren't all they're cracked up to be. Once the code is ported, it may require significant reworking by programmers. Techniques used on the old platform may not be supported on the new platform. The methods of handling data may not work the same way or they may have a different performance impact on the application.

The bigger problem is what happens after you've ported the code and you've implemented the application on the downsized platform. Most applications are works-in-progress. They have a past and a future. The original designers may have used state-of-the-art technology when the system was written. Today, the system may use technology barely supported even on its current platform. More importantly, if the application has been around for a while, it's accumulated a backlog of change requests. Users just may not like some features of the application. The way the company does business may have changed and the application hasn't kept pace. Lengths of some fields may be too small; other needed fields may be absent.

Once you commit to the recompile method of porting, you bring along the deficiencies of the application along with the source. What's more, you now have to face those deficiencies on a foundation that may not be the most adequate or appropriate one for addressing them. So what do you do?

The most important thing is to convert the application to use relational database technology. But watch out. You may already have some of the work done for you by a software tool. A naive translation of mainframe logic to relational database logic can lead to trouble.

For example, let's say a non-database mainframe application needs to select records having a date earlier than today. In most cases, the only way the mainframe application has to select those records is to start at the beginning of the file and read each record of the database.

To port this same logic to a client/server environment can result in disastrous performance. Every record of the database is read and passed over the network for the client application to choose or reject. A more appropriate porting of the logic is to pass an SQL string that encompasses the selection logic to the server. The database software performs the selection and passes only the records meeting the criteria back to the client application. The workload is placed on the server, not on the client, and the network traffic is reduced.

You should be aware of this sort of consideration even if you're not employing a true client/server database. After all, with ODBC, who's to say you won't be using one eventually?

> **Note**
>
> If your organization is willing to spend a little extra effort in porting the application, here are some things you might want to do:
>
> ■ Convert the application to use relational database technology (hopefully an ODBC-compliant one) if it doesn't use it already.
>
> ■ Review the database structure and modify it to accommodate anticipated future requirements.
>
> ■ Consider integrating end-user tools, such as report writers, to meet some of the requirements.
>
> ■ Evaluate the feasibility of giving the application a new front-end GUI look.

The Rewrite

The rewrite path to downsizing may be the most rewarding path in many cases. That's the good news. The bad news is it has the potential to be the longest, most costly, and hardest to manage path. Rewriting has the most unknowns and possibility for overruns.

Rewriting an application for a downsized platform has all the difficulties of a new development project. In addition, it carries the burden of having to create a completely new application that behaves in many ways similar to the application that it's modeled upon.

A rewritten downsized application must strike a delicate balance between being different and being the same. Users are accustomed to an application behaving in a certain fashion. No matter how idiotic the behavior of an application may be, people are used to it. If you change it too much, you have to consider the retraining issues.

> **Note**
>
> If you're involved in developing a rewritten mainframe application, here are some things you might want to do:
>
> - Take time to understand the existing application. Things which at first appear meaningless might have significance.
>
> - Involve the end-users along the way so they understand how and why the system is changing.
>
> - Don't take as gospel what people say about how a system operates. Even people using the system sometimes have partial understandings of it.
>
> - Watch out for special code, exceptions, and patches in the old system. Try to incorporate them as setup and configuration options rather than through code.

The New Front End

Adding a new front end to an existing application is often the simplest path to downsizing. It can take full advantage of the best features of the downsized hardware and software platform and preserve current investment in mainframe hardware and software if that is desirable.

The abilities of a revamped front end running on a personal computer to offload mainframe processor cycles and increase the accessibility of an existing system shouldn't be minimized. The requirement for using ODBC for the front end is that the application database already uses (or can be converted to use) existing relational database technology that is ODBC-compliant. When you give an application a new front end, you replace the existing text-based interface with a Windows GUI interface. All the back-end operations of the application stay on the mainframe without any change.

This approach probably has the lowest risk of any discussed. You've left the data where it's always resided and much of the system intact. You have easy recovery capabilities if something doesn't work out. Just keep a dumb terminal nearby.

A new front-end can be a variation on the porting method already discussed. The data is moved off the mainframe to a mid-ranged processor (such as an AS400) or UNIX server. You make use of the porting tools to convert the back-end operations to run on the mid-ranged processor or server. The new front-end provides new functionality without the cost of rewriting the whole system.

A new front-end, in addition, can be a technique for expanding access to the application to users who are primarily off-line to the main database. For example, an order-entry application might be given a PC front-end. It holds orders entered for transmission to the main database at the end of the day.

One of the difficulties of off-line front-ends is keeping databases in sync. In the order-entry example, you probably need to establish a system of downloading new items and prices to the front-end personal computers on a regular basis.

What happens if someone forgets to download? You need to develop foolproof procedures to cover every eventuality.

Note

If you're adding a new front-end to an existing application, here are some things you might want to do:

- Study the existing application carefully and make certain you understand how the user interface fits into the overall scheme of the application.

- Try to keep database accesses simple and straightforward.

- Avoid complicated, database-intensive queries in the front-end application. Let the back-end processes handle those sorts of operations.

- Watch for potential deadlocking situations when front-end and back-end processes collide. Try to let the back-end processes run at night while the front-end runs during the day.

Choosing the Hardware and Software Platform

The choice is wide-open for hardware and software if you select ODBC as part of your downsizing strategy. In fact, your choices are so varied and so vast that it is almost impossible to evaluate even a fraction of the combinations in a reasonable time frame.

The key factors that govern your decisions are:

- Cost of the hardware and software

- Cost of implementation of the proposed system

- Desire to allow for future growth of the application

In many cases, you discover the cost of implementation far outweighs the cost of the hardware and software. People cost more than things.

Tip
Start with what you know in picking a platform. Don't assume you need an exotic database technology.

Common Hardware Platforms

The most popular hardware platforms for running downsized systems are:

- Stand-alone personal computers

- File server-based networks

- Client/server-based networks

- Mid-ranged processors, such as the AS400

The stand-alone personal computer carries the tremendous advantage of its simplicity. You don't have any complicated communications software to install. No obscure interrupt conflicts to resolve. Even capacity these days isn't much of a problem.

The problem is the single keyboard. Unless your application is very simple, eventually your application is going to have to connect to other machines.

File server-based networks are the next step up in complexity. Novell, Microsoft LAN Server, IBM LAN Server, and Microsoft Windows NT Advanced Server are a few of the more popular network operating systems. Typically a dedicated machine serves as a repository of database files that are shared by users on the network. You can use many of the same databases you might choose for the stand-alone personal computer. The difference is the data is shared.

Many organizations experience installing and supporting these kinds of networks. They can potentially support quite large databases, maybe up to the several hundred thousand range size. Their drawbacks are more fully discussed when personal computer databases are discussed in the next section.

Client/server based networks are next in complexity. Typically they involve database software running on a UNIX processor and workstations running TCP/IP protocols.

Just to throw an element of confusion into the picture: UNIX processors can function as file servers and most of the client/server databases can run on top of file server network operating systems. So technically there is no real difference in the two hardware platforms. The difference is in the software.

Nevertheless, true client/server technology has traditionally been associated with the UNIX operating system. Most of the high performance databases are optimized for the UNIX platform. Windows NT is the new kid on the block in this arena. It has the promise of offering high performance at a lower price.

Client/server networks using this sort of technology can support databases into the millions of records. They require, however, the most technical expertise to implement and deploy.

The mid-ranged processor is an odd animal in this mix of hardware. Although originally intended as a smaller version of mainframe, the mid-ranged processor now finds itself functioning sometimes more as a server. Although this platform generally doesn't provide as good performance for the price as the UNIX platform, it is usually easier to implement. If you decide to port some or all of your application, you may find the transition easier to a platform offered by your mainframe vendor.

Personal Computer Databases

Personal computer databases have really developed a great deal of sophistication in recent years. They have also made enormous strides in improving performance.

A few of the ODBC-compliant personal computer databases are Access, FoxPro, Paradox, and dBASE. Each of these databases can provide good performance. They all offer sophisticated, user-friendly Windows interfaces. The problem with these databases is their vulnerability.

On a stand-alone personal computer, any user who can find their way into the directory where the tables reside can wipe out the database. It often isn't much better on a network. Since users often must be given significant access rights to the directories where the tables are located, unenlightened (or malicious) users can do severe damage.

What's more, these databases have limited recoverability. If the damage occurs late in the day, you may have to restore from a previous night's backup. An entire day of work can be lost.

True Client/Server Databases

True client/server databases differ from the personal computer databases in that they actually run as separate processes on a server machine. This gives you an ability to distribute the workload of the system over at least two machines: the workstation where your code runs and the back-end server where the database software runs.

Some of the true client/server databases that are ODBC-compliant are ORACLE, Sybase, Informix, Ingres, Guptas SQlBase, and Microsoft SQL Server.

Client/server databases offer the top performance and greatest ability to handle large volumes of data. Client/server databases have some other features that make them attractive as mission-critical platforms. They have integrated security, a high degree of recoverability, and the ability to enforce database integrity at the database level.

If you have a disk drive failure in the afternoon, a properly configured database enables you to restore from the previous backup and replay all the activity that had occurred on the database since then.

This performance and recoverability comes with a cost. True client/server databases are relatively difficult to install. You should definitely get special training in installation and administration of your database if you don't have a lot of experience with it already.

Tip

With a true client/server database, place transaction logs on disk drives separate from your main database tables.

> **Note**
>
> True client/server databases, such as ORACLE, Sybase, and Informix, offer several features you must carefully consider before employing them in your design.
>
> *Procedures*, which are supported by ODBC, offer a capability to write code that is incorporated as part of the database on the server. This code can be executed by a client workstation through the EXECUTE PROCEDURE SQL statement.
>
> *Triggers* provide an automatic capability for the database to take some kind of action when an event occurs. For example, when an order record is deleted, a trigger might activate a procedure to delete all the item records associated with the order.
>
> (continues)

(continued)

Transactions, with `commit` and `rollback` logic, are also supported by ODBC. They allow you to define units of work and easily recover if any step in the task fails.

These capabilities are wonderful, but they may diminish the portability of your application. Not all databases have these capabilities. In some cases, the implementations of them are unique.

Using ODBC to Increase Your Options

ODBC opens up your options in hardware and software. Relational database technology can run on almost any platform from the stand-alone personal computer to the largest mainframe. Most relational databases already are (or soon will be) ODBC compliant. When you write to the ODBC standard, you can pick and choose the hardware and software combinations that meet your present needs without fear that your choices won't meet your future needs.

Here are some of the options ODBC gives you:

- Implement initially with data on your mainframe and later migrate the data to a smaller platform

- Begin development before you've even made all the final decisions about your platform

- Implement a portion of your application as a pilot project on stand-alone personal computers to test the feasibility of the project

- Implement on different platforms at different locations

- Enable painless upgrades to high-end servers if your future requirements should exceed your present anticipated ones

Mix and Match for Cost and Performance

ODBC gives you an unprecedented ability to combine hardware and database platforms to run your application without the software management hassles of multiple versions of your source.

Suppose that your company, a recruiting firm and temporary placement agency, has branch offices throughout the United States. You have offices in New York, Boston, Chicago, and all the major cities. You also have offices in Albany, Georgia and Eugene, Oregon. You once maintained all your employee and candidate information on a mainframe in New York City. Now you've decided to put the information locally on systems in each office.

What system do you run it on? A UNIX system with an ORACLE database might be just right for New York City. It might be complete overkill for Eugene, Oregon, where a small Novell network with dBASE files would work best. Albany, Georgia only has a single personal computer. Write the system one time with ODBC and you can have the best of both solutions.

What if you take over your closest competitor next year and the office in Eugene suddenly triples in size? No problem. Hook up a UNIX processor with ORACLE, migrate your data from dBASE, and you're ready to roll.

Integrate End-User Tools

Once you have selected an ODBC-compliant database and installed the drivers on the personal computer, you now have the ability to access your database from any ODBC-compliant application. The tools a user has been trained to use to access dBASE files can now be used to access ORACLE databases.

Sooner or later, most (if not all) database tools that survive in the market will be ODBC-compliant.

If your end-users already are trained in a report writing or query tool, check it out. It may be ODBC-compliant. If it is, make it a part of your downsizing strategy.

Here's the way to do it:

1. Make the table and field names meaningful. Use the user's terminology. For example, call the date an employee begins work "start_date" instead of "strt_dte."

2. Give indicator, flag, and status fields meaningful alphanumeric values (for example, "Y" for "yes" and "N" for "no"). When a user places them on a report, nobody has to guess what "*" means.

3. Spend time training the user on the structure of the database.

4. Let the users define some or all of the reports used by the system.

Modeling the System

You need to get a feel for how your system behaves before you commit completely to a design and a hardware and software configuration. That's what's meant by modeling the system.

Don't be intimidated by the word "model." This doesn't have to be anything super-sophisticated. Think of all the pieces that must work together to have the system operate successfully.

Draw the hardware, how it's connected, and what software runs on each piece. Get hardware and software from vendors for evaluation purposes. Hook it up and see how it all works.

Identify the Critical Performance Elements

Most systems have a mixture of performance elements. Some operations need a response in seconds. Others in minutes. Still others in hours.

Some elements of a system may be particularly time-critical. Perhaps the printing of all the reports must be completed by a certain time. An inquiry must return in five seconds or customers on the phone begin to hang up.

Whatever elements are critical to your system's success, identify them and understand them. Most systems have a mixture of elements. Acceptability of the system, to a degree, involves catering to the user's expectations.

Regular queries and updates on small groups of related data you expect to happen in seconds if you can specify the exact group of records. You have to achieve this by building appropriate indexes for your tables.

Infrequent, especially unanticipated, queries expect to take a while. You can achieve good performance here through native database performance and fine-tuning of your SQL statements.

Make Sure All the Software Works Together

ODBC is just one software component in a complicated web of many other components. Each of your selected components—driver, communications software, database software—may work wonderfully on their own terms. You need to make certain they work just as well when they're together.

You should review the layers. Your application communicates with the ODBC driver manager, which in turn communicates with the ODBC driver to achieve a database connection or disconnection. Your application calls the ODBC driver to perform other functions.

The ODBC driver calls the native database drivers to execute your SQL statements. In a network environment, the native database driver calls communication software to talk to the server. A bad setup on any piece of software in this path can cause problems. A few things to watch out for are:

- Incompatible versions of software

- Out-of-date DLLs floating around the machine

- Incorrect software installation

- Lack of memory

- Bad software at one or more layers

There can be significant performance differences on the same database with different combinations of communications software. Not all problems show up as failures to connect. The insidious problems—such as poor performance and occasional failures—can arise from this same cluster of software.

Use the drivers and software combinations recommended and tested by your database vendor.

Simulate the System

Put your hardware and software together. Create your database and its tables. Take each of your critical performance elements and design a test for it. Write a simple program with a minimal interface. Use various query tools.

You're trying to get answers to how this system is going to perform:

- How long does it take to retrieve one row with a query on an indexed field?

- How long does it take to retrieve one hundred rows on non-indexed fields?

- How long does it take to load one hundred thousand records to the database? How long does it take to retrieve every row?

These are the sorts of questions you need to ask. If you don't like the answers you get, you need to read on.

Getting the Performance You Need

Poor performance is the downsizer's nightmare. Your mainframe application has been tuned and tweaked over time. Its tasks and jobs have well-known performance characteristics. Job scheduling and other work-arounds have gotten everyone used to a certain level of performance. Now you move the application off the mainframe and everything changes. Things that used to run fast now run slowly. Maybe some of the things that used to be slow now are fast. Probably nobody notices that.

Worse case: An order has already been placed for one hundred units of XYZ hardware so don't expect faster processors or more memory to bail you out.

If you've modeled your system, you hope not to find yourself in this situation. However, models can be wrong. Transactions and processes sometimes cannot be completed the way you believed they might when you designed the system. Users can be wrong about database sizes. Sometimes even good news—the addition of a new large account—can throw the original estimates out the window. You always need to strive for optimum performance.

ODBC and Performance

Having told you to strive for optimum performance, I'm now going to tell you ODBC never gives you optimum performance. There's no way it can. ODBC is another layer of software over the native database calls. It can never be as fast as native calls. (There is one exception. The Microsoft SQL Server is able to emit the database protocol directly with no translation layer.)

How much impact do these additional layers have on performance? Not much compared to the impact that other factors have on performance. In other words, application and database design, communications software, network traffic, and native database performance have a greater effect on the overall performance of a system than the selection of ODBC as a database access technique.

It's not a free lunch with ODBC. The advantages weigh very much in ODBC's favor unless you require the absolute optimum in performance and never need to support more than one database.

Database Design

You can't possibly go into all the considerations of good database design. That would be a book in itself. You can at best touch a few of the things that might affect performance that you need to consider in designing your database.

The first rule is know your database (or databases). What might be good design for high performance with one database might not give you good performance with a different database. So everything said here must be tempered by the fact that it may not be true for your particular database.

To get good performance, you usually strive for fewer and smaller row-sized tables. One of the main performance bottlenecks is the speed that data moves from one part of the system to another. To access data, first, it must be retrieved from disk. Then it must be passed through various software layers, possibly broken into pieces and sent over a network before it reaches your application. Obviously, the less data being passed at each stage, the better the performance.

Even small changes in row size can make a big difference in performance because of buffering. If the read buffer of your database is 4,096 bytes, you can read four 1,024-byte rows with one disk access. However, if your rows are 1,025 bytes, you can only read three.

If you can represent a field with an integer instead of a floating point value, use an integer. If you can represent a field with ten bytes instead of fifteen bytes, use ten bytes. This may seem commonsensical, but sometimes in defining tables, it's easy to fall into the habit of padding the fields "just in case." Sometimes you need to allow for future growth, but you shouldn't do it indiscriminately.

> **Note**
>
> Normalization encourages breaking complex tables into multiple simpler ones and eliminating redundant data fields. In an ideal normalized database, each group of data that logically belongs together has its own table. The only overlap of data fields from one table to another is the relational hooks to tie the tables together.

For performance reasons, you want fewer rather than more tables. Can you achieve all the functionality intended for the application with fewer tables?

If you adhere strictly to the design philosophy of normalization, however, you have little control over the number of tables in your application and the data that is contained within them. The data in your application can be represented in only one way. That way dictates the number of tables.

For example, say you have an application that keeps track of employee information. You want to keep information about who should be contacted in case of emergency. You have an employee table. Do you have a contact table?

Probably no if the user says you never want to keep track of more than one contact. Breaking the data into separate tables gives you flexibility to change your mind later. It also gives you a smaller row size in your employee table and possibly reduces your I/O if you need to access the emergency contact information infrequently in your application. Otherwise, the most straightforward implementation is no contact table. The contact information is placed in the employee table.

Definitely yes if the user says you must track a potentially unlimited number of contacts. The only way to track an unlimited number is a separate table. Whatever performance costs are involved, you must pay them.

Maybe if the user says you only need to track two contacts. Strict normalization dictates a separate contact table. On the other hand, if every time you display employee information you also must display the two contacts, you're committed to at least two I/Os instead of one.

Breaking your data up into many tables has other ramifications. You end up with additional complexity in your application with more tables. Your end-users also face a more complicated structure to navigate when they try to do things for themselves.

Should you ignore the rules of normalization? Sometimes. But you do so at your own risk and with the knowledge you may regret the decision later.

The judicious use of indexes is where to look next for performance gains. Naturally you're going to index the relational keys of your tables and the fields that make records unique. Where do you go from there?

You'll probably want to index any fields requiring quick access to meet the needs of the application. What if the field is a free-form character field? Let's say it's a name field. For the same person, some users might enter "John Smith;" others "J. Smith;" and others "John W. Smith, Sr." Nobody can be certain exactly how it was entered. An index with any of these entries in it won't do you a bit of good if you try to query on the name "Smith." If you look for an exact match, you won't get it. If you use any of the wildcard operators, you'll find "Smith," but it might not be in the timely fashion you need.

Tip

Don't over-index your tables. Index the main access keys of the application and secondary fields where essential for real-time look-ups. Let the database do the work by itself.

You're probably going to have to take the name apart in your application, place the last name in a separate field, and index on it.

Do you want to index on a field with a small number of possible values—for example, a sex field? No. The costs of maintaining the duplicates in the index outweigh any gains you could possibly make on queries.

Indexes are wonderful for retrieval, but you don't want indexes when you're loading a table. If your application requires the periodic reloading of a table, the fastest way to do this is to drop the table, create the table, load the table, and then create the index.

The Power of SQL

SQL is a two-edged sword. It can enable you to do the most stupid things imaginable and get away with them. It also can enable you to completely harness the power of your back-end database and the hardware it runs on to get amazing performance.

If you are running in a true client/server environment (or expect you eventually will), you want to make the maximum use of the back-end engine. Every operation you place in your client workstation must be repeated on every other workstation performing the same operation. The data to complete it must pass over the same network. Your performance is limited by network and workstation processor speed.

When you move the operation to the back-end database, you remove the network as a limiting factor. Plus, you've added the power of the database and processor it runs on. This processor might have a large enough memory that it can cache large parts of the database.

This can be overdone. If your application is driven by complex SQL statements, look for ways to simplify them or make certain your database design provides you with good performance for them.

Any qualification you can place on your query of the database can have a cascading effect if the database technology is well optimized.

> **Note**
>
> One of the most powerful techniques discovered for moving processing to the back-end database is the use of EXISTS and NOT EXISTS conditions.
>
> EXISTS enables you to select a record from one table when a certain condition exists in a related table.
>
> Say you want to select orders that have a certain item in them. One approach is to query the item table for the item you're looking for and use the order number as a parameter to query the order table.
>
> The operation can be done in a single query with the work done by the back-end database with a query like this:
>
> ```
> select orderno from order where EXISTS (select * from items where itemno
> = "1234" and items.orderno = order.orderno)
> ```
>
> The above query returns the order numbers of all orders that have item number "1234" in the order.

The Superstation

Just about every system is faced with the problem of long-running processes. These may be certain reporting functions, data import-export operations, file maintenance, or other operations that require the application to look at a large number of records. One technique for getting good performance on these operations is to separate them from the mainstream application and run them on a dedicated processor—the superstation.

The superstation is a machine with the fastest processor and most memory you can afford. You may want to closely evaluate the option of running Windows NT with a 32-bit driver for the operating system. The idea is to load the machine for as much performance as possible and then design the application to make use of this machine for long-running processes.

Get this machine in-house as soon as possible in the design and development cycle. Begin running your tests with it and use the machine as the benchmark for your best performance. If you can't meet the performance objectives with this machine, you need to change your design or your code.

The Bottlenecks

Every system has bottlenecks—components that confine the performance of your system. If you alleviate one of them, another appears. That's the way it is. You need to find what yours are and decide if you can live with them.

Here are some ways to move around the bottlenecks:

- Allocate non-critical work to slow workstations and time-critical work to faster machines and those with more memory.

- Migrate some processes to the server if they are creating too much of a load on the network.

- Move processes that make high demands on the server or the network to non-peak hours.

- Add indexes to maximize performance for certain functions, and then drop them for normal operations.

- Upgrade line speed if you have a remote connection to a mainframe database.

- Move some of the data—small static tables and work tables—to the workstation.

- Update servers and workstations.

- Swap out your database and your server.

> **Troubleshooting**
>
> *Performance is poor throughout the system. All workstations and all operations are affected.*
>
> Your server may be under-powered or your network overloaded. Your workstations may be under-powered or lack memory. Cabling problems can also occasionally cause this behavior. If high-end workstations show the problem and your server doesn't show high CPU usage, you may want to reevaluate your database design.
>
> *Performance is good throughout the system, but some workstations get poor performance.*
>
> Make certain the users at the poorly performing workstation aren't doing something different from the other users. If the workstation isn't different in processor speed or memory from the other workstations with good performance, look for more subtle differences: different network boards, different versions of communications software, or incorrect software setup and installation.
>
> *Performance is good on most operations, but some operations perform poorly.*
>
> Look at your code, particularly at the SQL being passed during the poorly performing operations. Try to run the SQL statement by itself using Microsoft Query or another tool. If it runs with good performance by itself, you have some problem in your code independent of the database. If it runs poorly, try reworking the SQL statement until it gets good performance. You may need to change your database design or add additional indexes to improve the performance.
>
> *Performance is good most of the time but sporadically degrades.*
>
> If the degradation occurs with heavy user activity, your hardware is probably under-powered or your network overloaded. If the degradation is more random, try to find some activity occurring on some workstation that seems to be associated with the degradation. Look especially at any locking that may be occurring. Some operation may be locking other users out of the database.

Avoiding Common Pitfalls

Downsizing projects can and do fail. There's no boilerplate technique that works for every application or every organization. ODBC, as you've seen from this section, can be a valuable tool to assist you in downsizing an application. The ultimate success of the project, however, is more likely to depend on other factors, not ODBC.

The following sections discuss some solutions for a few common mistakes.

Don't Mistake Small for Simple

When you mistake small for simple, you underestimate the scope of the project. Project timelines are too short and the project is understaffed. This can lead to a rushed project with a disastrous implementation or a project that exceeds its budget and is dropped.

A rule of thumb: take your best estimate, multiply by twenty, and divide by your number of years of experience in the data-processing industry. My many erroneous time estimates on projects over the years have confirmed this rule. There's also the 80/20 rule. Eighty percent of the project can be completed in twenty percent of the time required to complete the entire project.

Just because the application runs on relatively small, cheap machines doesn't mean it is cheap to implement. No matter how you cut it, every bit of the logic (and probably more) that was in the old system must run in some way in the new system. The years that may have been spent in refining the mainframe application must be compressed into the development cycle of the new downsized application.

Be realistic about the time required for the project and its complexity.

Involve the Users

The end-users must be involved throughout the process of design and implementation. They must understand how the new downsized system works—its new capabilities as well as its deficiencies.

You need to find appropriate means of channeling this involvement.

Here are some ideas:

- Begin the project with a kickoff meeting to build enthusiasm.

- Keep long meetings with large groups of people to a minimum.

- Work with small groups on specific tasks.

- Identify incremental milestones, and celebrate them when they are reached.

- Involve the users in the database design.

Understand the System

Make certain you look closely at the system you are downsizing. Most systems carry a shiny layer of simplicity over a body of complexity. What usually kills you are the exceptions.

Develop System Deployment Techniques

After you develop the system, you must implement it and support it.

What's involved here? You must install hardware and software. Sometimes you must train people to install hardware and software. You must maintain tight control and standards over how software is installed. You can't have the software installed differently on every machine. You'll never be able to support it even if you can make it work.

You must write documentation and, hopefully, help files for the system.

You must train users on the system. Users may have to learn tasks that computer operators used to do on mainframes, such as backing up the system.

When you fix bugs in the system, you must have a way of distributing them without disrupting operations.

From Here...

From here you may want to review the following chapters of this book:

- For further information on generating tables using ODBC, see Chapter 9, "Creating Tables with the DDL."

- For assistance in optimixing ODBC when you begin your downsizing project, see Chapter 20, "Optimizing ODBC."

For general information about downsizing, you may want to look at the following books:

- *Downsizing: Strategies for Success in the Modern Computer World* by Dan Trimmer, Addison-Wesley Publishing Company, 1993, ISBN 0-201-62409-5.

- *Downsizing: How to Get Big Gains from Smaller Computer Systems* by Richard H. Baker, McGraw-Hill, 1992, ISBN 0-070004563-1.

Both of the above books discuss not only the technological issues of downsizing but also the organizational ones.

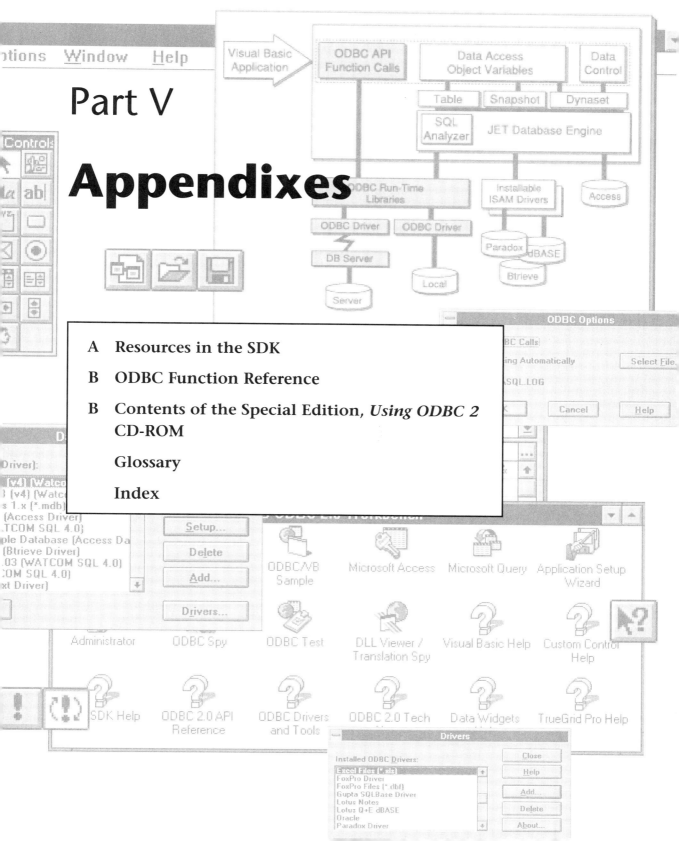

Part V

Appendixes

A   Resources in the SDK

B   ODBC Function Reference

B   Contents of the Special Edition, *Using ODBC 2* CD-ROM

Glossary

Index

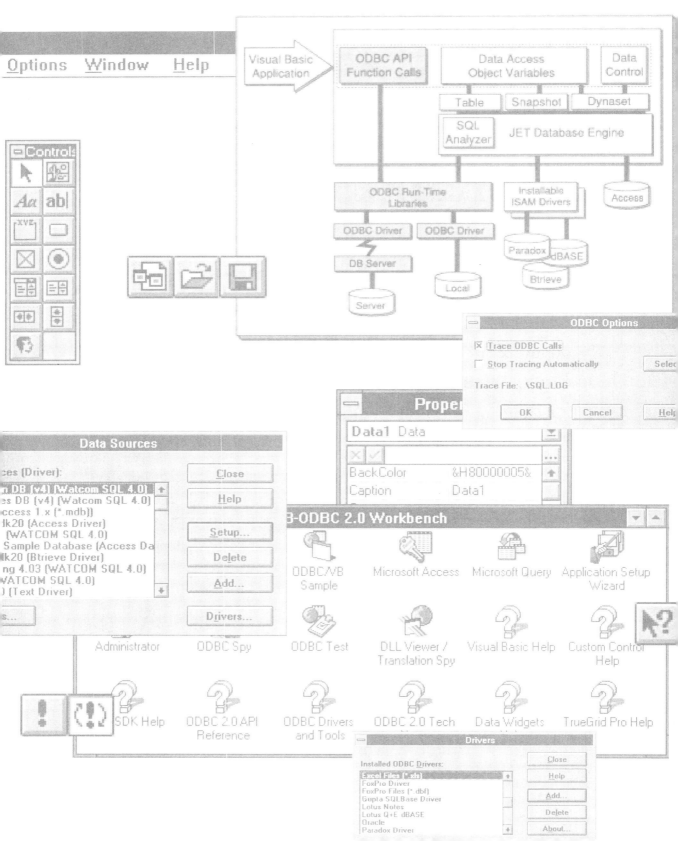

Options   Window   Help

Visual Basic Application

ODBC API Function Calls

Data Access Object Variables

Data Control

Table   Snapshot   Dynaset

SQL Analyzer   JET Database Engine

ODBC Run-Time Libraries

Installable ISAM Drivers

Access

ODBC Driver   ODBC Driver

DB Server

Paradox   dBASE

Btrieve

Local

Server

ODBC Options

☒ Trace ODBC Calls

☐ Stop Tracing Automatically   Selec

Trace File: \SQL.LOG

OK   Cancel   Help

Proper

Data1 Data

BackColor   &H80000005&
Caption   Data1

Data Sources

ces (Driver):

n DB (v4) (Watcom SQL 4.0)
es DB (v4) (Watcom SQL 4.0)
ccess 1.x (*.mdb))
lk20 (Access Driver)
(WATCOM SQL 4.0)
Sample Database (Access Da
lk20 (Btrieve Driver)
ng 4.03 (WATCOM SQL 4.0)
WATCOM SQL 4.0)
) (Text Driver)

s...

Close
Help
Setup...
Delete
Add...
Drivers...

B-ODBC 2.0 Workbench

ODBC/VB Sample   Microsoft Access   Microsoft Query   Application Setup Wizard

Administrator   ODBC Spy   ODBC Test   DLL Viewer / Translation Spy   Visual Basic Help   Custom Control Help

SDK Help   ODBC 2.0 API Reference   ODBC Drivers and Tools   ODBC 2.0 Tech   Data Widgets   TrueGrid Pro Help

Drivers

Installed ODBC Drivers:

Excel Files (*.xls)
FoxPro Driver
FoxPro Files (*.dbf)
Gupta SQLBase Driver
Lotus Notes
Lotus Q+E dBASE
Oracle
Paradox Driver

Close
Help
Add...
Delete
About...

Appendix A

Resources in the SDK

The ODBC 2.0 Software Development Kit includes the standard things you'd expect from an SDK: the API itself, auxiliary DLLs (like the cursor library), and ODBC administration utilities. But it also comes with some pleasant surprises—truly useful programs that go beyond the call of duty and can really help reduce your ramp-up and development time.

In this appendix, I want to highlight a few of the interesting bonuses that are shipped with the ODBC SDK. You can use these as learning tools or as reference materials to trigger your memory when you're doing the actual development:

- The ODBC Test Program

- The ODBC Spy Program

- The ODBC Help Files

- The Sample ODBC Applications

The ODBC Test Program

In this author's humble opinion, this is the best accessory in the SDK. This program is a shell that enables you to try out ODBC functions and execute statements without having to go through the trouble of writing, debugging, and compiling your own example application. The various statements are listed under the Connect, Statement, Results, Catalog, and Misc menu options, organized into appropriate categories.

ODBC Test enables you to type in values for parameters where appropriate, such as the rgbValue in SQLExecDirect() (see fig. A.1). For parameters where pointers are required, the system generates them automatically, and often lets you choose whether to specify a valid pointer or a null pointer. Figure A.2 shows an example of a pre-execution dialog, in this case from the `SQLSetStmtOption()` function.

Fig. A.1
ODBC Test lets you experiment with ODBC commands.

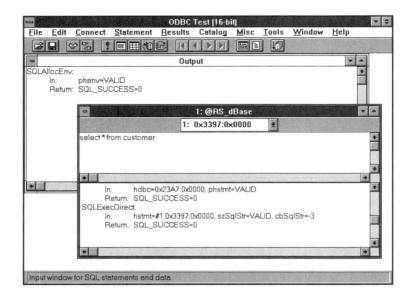

Fig. A.2
ODBC Test's pre-execution dialog boxes enable you to specify function arguments in the most convenient way possible.

I found several uses for ODBC Test. For one thing, when you're just getting started, you can use it to experiment with the various ODBC functions as you're learning them. For example, you can allocate an ODBC environment, make a connection to a data source, allocate a statement, and execute it, monitoring the results in the bottom half of the connection window. If you want, you can type the text of a SQL command into the top half of the connection window, and then press one of the toolbar buttons to run it immediately with `SQLExecDirect()`. This program is also especially excellent for exploring and working with the various possible constant values that are passed to various functions (such as `fOption` in `SQLSetStmtOption()`).

Another use for the program (and probably its real intended use) is to find out in a reasonably graphical way what the capabilities of a given driver are. Any API functions that are not available will be disabled in the pull-down menus. You also can type in SQL syntax and `SQLExecDirect()` it, then watch what the driver has to say about it.

The ODBC Spy Program

ODBC Spy lets you debug the link between the front end app and the database engine. It watches the ODBC code that flows between the ODBC application and the ODBC driver.

ODBC Spy is sort of like a tape recorder for ODBC commands. It can monitor a data source for ODBC requests, and as they are executed, record them to a file and/or display them on-screen. Figure A.3 shows the main ODBC Spy window, which displays the last few items in the log created by the program.

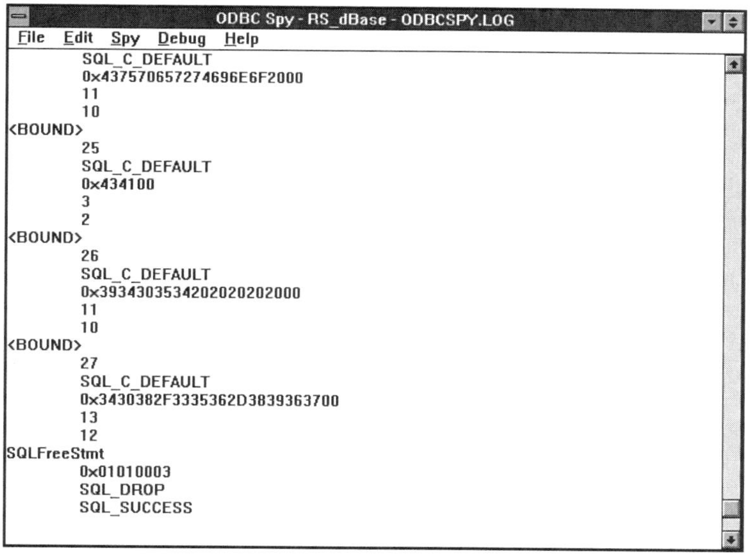

Fig. A.3
ODBC Spy lets you record and play back strings of ODBC commands.

Once you've recorded a sequence of commands to a log file, there are two things you can do with them to help debug an ODBC problem. Your approach will depend on where you think your problem is: in the application or in the driver.

If you believe the trouble is with the driver, you can set up ODBC Spy to emulate the application, and play back the sequence of commands while the driver processes them. That way, you can watch the results and see where the error occurs.

If you think the application is at fault, use ODBC Spy to emulate the driver instead. You need to use an automated script (or a very good memory) to replay the commands to ODCB Spy, because all it can do is play back the responses in order—and they need to line up exactly with the resent commands.

To learn about using ODBC Spy, you can make it work in conjunction with ODBC Test and watch both sides of the drama develop. ODBC Spy's Help file talks about how to set this up.

The ODBC Help Files

The ODBC 2.0 SDK comes with five general-purpose help files (in addition to special ones for the utilities). Most of them are good for answering occasional questions about specific topics (or for hopeful consultation in desperate information searches). However, you'll probably spend almost as much time perusing the API Reference Help entries as you will actually programming, at least on your first ODBC project. The Help files included are:

- The API Reference
- The Release Notes
- The Tech Notes
- The Sample ODBC Applications
- The ODBC Drivers and Tools

The API Reference
ODBCAPI.HLP, the main SDK Help file, is the ultimate reference for all ODBC functions. It is presented in Microsoft's typical API reference layout: one entry per function, plus quite a few entries on data types and other auxiliary topics.

The function call reference entries are quite complete. Each provides the following information about the function under scrutiny:

- The API conformance level under which this function is supported

- The version of ODBC (1.0 or 2.0) in which this function first appeared

- The function prototype

- An explanation of each of the parameters

- Possible return codes

- Explanations for the possible error conditions. Unfortunately, this does not always explain the contextual meaning of the return codes other than SQL_ERROR.

- Detailed comments on the purpose and proper usage of the function. The comments are sometimes very clear and in other places a little mystifying.

The one major flaw in this Help file is that its organization is not conducive to learning the way functions work *together*. For example, the various entries dealing with statement parameters are very confusing. However, many of the functions are linked to code samples that illustrate functions in the proper sequence, and this is of great value to the novice ODBC developer.

In this book we've tried to clear up some of the questions you might have after referring to the API Reference. However, we have not duplicated all the information in the Help file. After Special Edition, *Using ODBC 2* helps you learn the principles of a given operation and introduces the functions and methods involved, you'll want to refer to the API Reference for the ultimate details regarding each function.

The Release Notes

This short and sweet Help file (RELNOTES.HLP) explains what's in the SDK, and provides the latest change information and usage tips.

The Tech Notes

This file does more than provide answers to the fifteen-or-so most important technical questions asked of Microsoft Product Support Services. It also fills in a lot of the gaps left by the API Reference Help file. If you're confused about a concept that was glossed over in the other documentation, there's a fair chance you'll find it in ODBCKNWL.HLP (though you're also likely to find your answer right here in Special Edition, *Using ODBC 2*).

Appendixes

The ODBC Drivers and Tools

This rather odd little Help file is a catalog of available-at-publication Microsoft and third-party ODBC drivers and programmers' tools. The name of this file is ODBCINFO.HLP.

The Sample ODBC Applications

This is a reference/usage guide for the various sample and demonstration applications provided with the SDK. It explains which aspects of ODBC they are intended to demonstrate, what they do, and how to build, run, and use them.

The samples covered in this particular Help file are:

- The Admin Demo
- The C++ Demo
- The Cursor Demo
- The Query Demo
- The Sample Driver
- The DLL Viewer/Translation Spy
- The Visual Basic Demo

These sample applications are discussed in the following section.

The Sample ODBC Applications

The SDK comes with the source and object code for several fairly complex sample applications. They're prebuilt so you can play with them right away, but you can modify them if you want, and instructions are included in case you want to build your altered versions.

The Visual Basic Sample

As with most of the SDK's sample apps, the Visual Basic sample is more than just an illustration of ODBC techniques: it's also a useful program in its own right (see fig A.4). This sample application works as a basic querying tool.

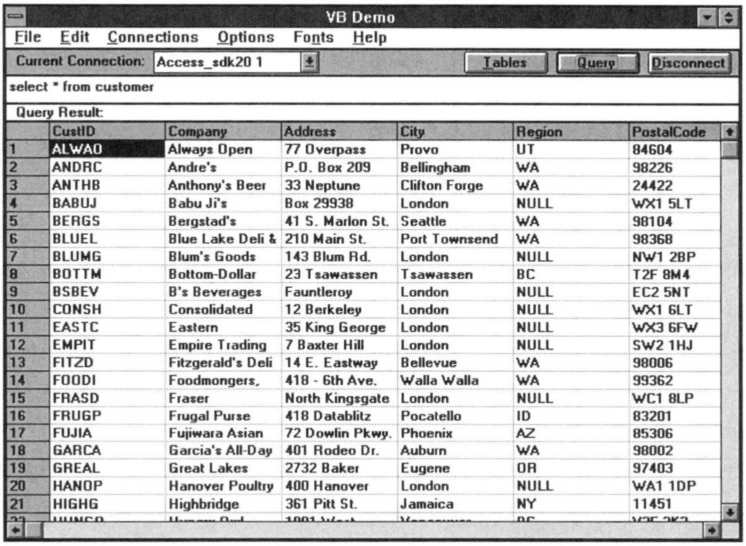

Fig. A.4
The VB sample is
a simple query
utility.

You can connect to multiple data sources and switch between them during a session. Once you've established a connection, you can input single- or multiple-line queries and retrieve the results in a grid. You also can get a list (also in a grid) of the tables available in the database to which you've connected. Grid results can be copied to the Clipboard for you to paste into other applications.

> **Note**
>
> VBDEMO.BAS and ODBC.BAS provide good examples of constants and ODBC-related declarations for your own Visual Basic programs, but the most interesting module in the Visual Basic demo is MISCPROC.BAS. It contains `BeginConnection()` and `EndConnection()`, which show the essentials of connecting and disconnecting. Also, `FillForm()` is a good example of placing result set data into a grid control.

The C++ Sample

In one sense, the C++ demo program goes a little beyond the VB sample (see fig. A.5). You can use it to define a new data source. To do this, it calls certain parts of the ODBC Administrator program, bringing up the usual *Add Data Source* and *Setup* dialogs.

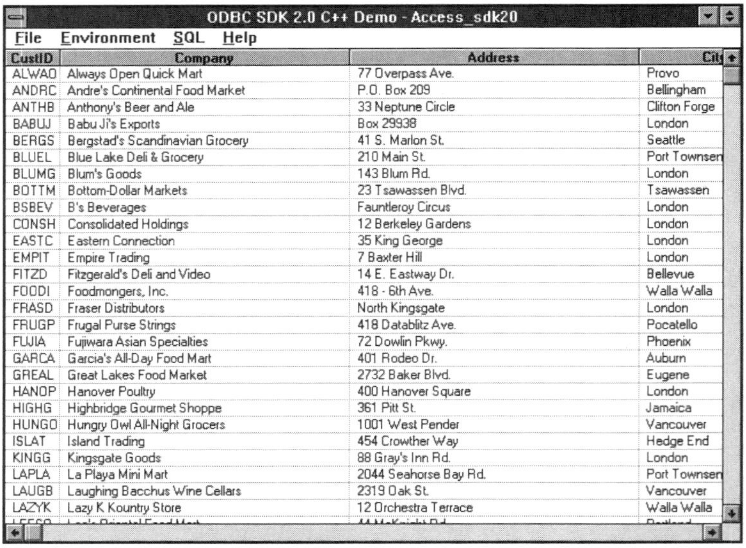

Fig. A.5
The C++ sample enables you to query the database as well as create a new data source.

Like the VB sample, you also can retrieve data in a grid. This grid doesn't support Clipboard functions, but it does serve to illustrate a method for the retrieval of a limited number of rows at a time. After the first 100 rows are retrieved, you need to choose Fetch Next Rowset from the SQL menu to get the next 100.

> **Note**
>
> Interestingly enough, although included in the Microsoft SDK, this sample is done in Borland C++ rather than Microsoft's Visual C++.

> **Note**
>
> The most interesting module in the C++ sample is the main one, CPPDEMO.CPP. It is fairly long and contains numerous functions, many of which are irrelevant and non-ODBC-related. However, there are a couple you might want to examine. vDoSQL() illustrates many aspects of statement preparation, execution, and result set handling, as well as error-trapping. fODBCError() is an interesting example of an error-trapping routine.

The QueryDemo Sample

The QueryDemo program is a fancier querying tool, written in Microsoft C (see fig. A.6). In QueryDemo, connections can be opened in two different ways: through the standard dialogs, or through dialogs designed especially for the application (thus illustrating both techniques for developers to imitate). You can open connections to multiple data sources at the same time. Each connection initially opens a single MDI child window, to be used to query that data source.

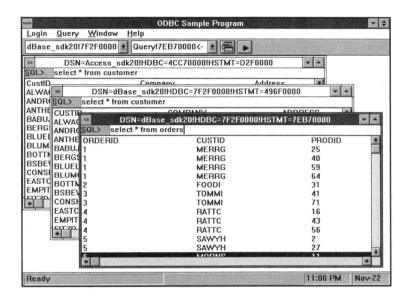

Fig. A.6
QueryDemo is a more sophisticated querying utility that supports the MDI model.

Once you've opened a connection, pressing Ctrl+N will open a second window to that same connection. This illustrates ODBC's ability to manage multiple statements on a single data source link.

Note

The file MAIN.C contains mostly ODBC-unrelated functions, with a couple of exceptions like `ConnectDlgProc()` and `DisconnectDlgProc()`. The real action is in QUERY.C—this file is rife with interesting functions. `ConnectDatabase()` and `DriverConnectDatabase()` show the initial data source connection process, and `FreeConnect()` shows the disconnection procedure. `ExecuteQuery()` takes a query and sends it to the database, similar to what any ODBC program has to do.

The Cursors Sample

The cursor demo is actually a fairly complex little app with a lot of function-ality packed in (see fig. A.7). This one also is written in C, and some pretty sophisticated cursor management techniques are illustrated herein.

Fig. A.7

The cursor demo program illustrates virtually all aspects of cursor usage.

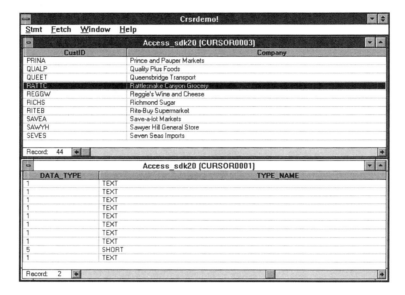

With this program, you can bring several different types of information into MDI-style child windows. For one thing, you can execute a free-form SQL statement. Alternately, you can request various types of information about the tables in the database, such as tables themselves, columns, procedures, statistics, or privileges. Finally, you can retrieve a list of the data types supported by your data source. The purpose of all this is to show you how to use cursors with the result sets returned by different ODBC function calls.

The result sets are placed in grids, *n* records at a time (defaulting to a rowset size of ten). The records are numbered based on the order in which the data source has sent them, and the current "record number" is displayed in the lower left corner of each MDI child window.

You can retrieve the first, last, prior, or next set of records at any given time, using the simple Home, End, PgUp, and PgDn keystrokes, respectively. As you move from one rowset to another, the current record number changes; al-though you may only see ten records at a time, the record number of a given row could easily be in the hundreds or thousands.

Arguably the best thing about this application is the flexibility of the options you can set—and therefore the variety of coding techniques available in the source. For example, you can run your queries in asynchronous mode. You also can experiment with different binding styles and configure the concurrency settings of the driver.

> **Note**
>
> In this sample, CHILD.C is the key file for students of ODBC. It contains cursor-related routines that merit close attention, including DeleteRow(), ProcessResults(), and Fetch().

The Admin Sample

In case you need to build a customized ODBC administration program, the SDK includes a sample that shows you how to do it. The administration sample (see fig. A.8), written in Microsoft C, shows off all manner of administration functionality, much of it well beyond the capabilities of the actual ODBC Administrator program.

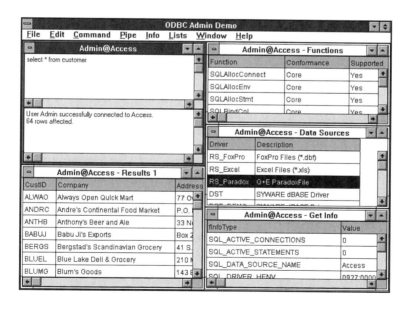

Fig. A.8

The Admin Sample is useful as an ODBC administration control center.

The administration sample will enable you to manage ODBC data sources: create new ones, modify old ones, or even delete them. It does this by calling the standard ODBC Administrator dialogs. But there are several administration utility functions that operate within the program. You can bring up a list of the data sources installed on your system, a list of data types, a list of system constants and their values with respect to the current data source, and (I think this is the most interesting of all) a list of the ODBC functions supported by the data source. All of these lists appear in scrollable grids.

You can bring up grids full of several different types of data source information, such as tables, columns, statistics, keys, privileges, and procedures. You also can set up and experiment with "pipes," which let you take results from one statement and turn them around to be used as the parameters for another.

The ODBC Admin Sample does more than just administration: it's also yet another MDI-capable querying utility. This one can even save and load SQL scripts, something you probably won't do too often in your applications. It's neat functionality, nonetheless.

> **Note**
>
> In the admin sample, the source file to scrutinize is INFO.C. Some functions to look at are `DisplayODBCDataSources()` and `DisplayODBCDataTypes()`, which illustrate some atypical examples of result sets.

The DLL Viewer/Translation Spy Sample

This rather unique pair of programs serves to demonstrate translation DLL functionality. A translation DLL is required when your application stores data very differently from the data source, perhaps using a different character set. It serves as an interpreter for the data passed between the two, by providing special functions that the application can call to transfer data either way.

The DLL Viewer program enables you to examine the various DLLs in memory, whether or not they are translation DLLs (see fig. A.9). Statistical information, such as module size and the load count, is displayed for each and for the system as a whole. You also can use the program to remove a DLL from memory, although this can be hazardous to system stability if other active applications are using the DLL's functions.

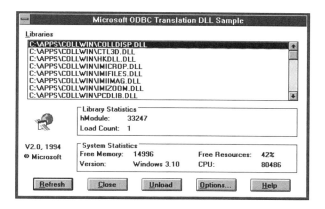

Fig. A.9
Among other things, DLL Viewer lets you unload a DLL from memory.

The DLL Viewer's Options dialog serves as an administration program for Translation Spy settings. TRNSLCHK.DLL, the Translation Spy, is a sample translation DLL, but it doesn't really translate data. Instead, when one of the translation functions is called by an application, it pops up a dialog box and displays values for all parameters to the functions. It also can maintain a log of calls to translation functions.

> **Note**
>
> In the TRNSLCHK.C file, SQLDriverToDataSource() and SQLDataSourceToDriver() are the functions that show the key translation functionality.

The Sample ODBC Driver

Building ODBC drivers is a highly complex task that's beyond the scope of this book, but in case you'd like to get a taste of what it's like, take a look at the sample ODBC driver. This is really just a template for driver developers to use, and its functionality is extremely limited, but the source code does offer a useful look at the innards of one of the key rungs in the ODBC ladder.

> **Note**
>
> The entire sample application is of general interest, but not of too much use to the programmer who simply wants to include ODBC connectivity in his programs.

Appendixes

The Quick Test

One last ODBC sample program is provided. Very little information is given about the Quick Test utility, and it does not come pre-built, but what it does is run down the list of ODBC functions and test a driver to see whether it performs them correctly. Again, this is mostly useful for a driver developer.

> **Note**
>
> The Quick Test sample is of interest in the sense that it calls quite a variety of ODBC functions.

In Summation

When you install the SDK, you might have the intention to ignore all the frippery and just start coding. But I'd like to recommend that you take an hour or two and look at the extras included in the package. Run the samples and root through their source code; you're sure to get some good ideas. Spend a few minutes playing with each of the utilities; in the end, they might end up saving you a lot of time.

Appendix B

ODBC Function Reference

When you're experimenting with a particular function for the first time, it's often the basic things, like argument types, that get you. As your ODBC applications grow and become more complex, you may find yourself forgetting the details of some of the functions. This appendix is a quick reference to the key components of all ODBC functions.

The tables in this appendix provide three pieces of information about each ODBC function:

- The function prototype, including the function's name and its parameters

- A brief description of the function's purpose

- Possible *retcode* returns

Table B.1 lists these values for the ODBC functions that are defined as part of the Core API conformance level.

> **Note**
>
> All ODBC functions can return a status of SQL_SUCCESS or SQL_ERROR. To avoid unnecessary duplication of information, only result codes other than these are listed in the Unique Returns column in the following tables.

Table B.1 Core-Level Functions

Function Prototype	Purpose	Unique Returns

SQLAllocConnect(
  HENV henv,
  HDBC FAR * phdbc)
	Allocates a connection	SQL_SUCCESS_WITH_INFO
		SQL_INVALID_HANDLE

SQLAllocEnv(HENV FAR * phenv)	Allocates an ODBC environment	

SQLAllocStmt(
  HDBC hdbc,
  HSTMT FAR * hstmt)
	Allocates a statement	SQL_SUCCESS_WITH_INFO
		SQL_INVALID_HANDLE

SQLBindCol(
  HSTMT hstmt,
  UWORD icol,
  SWORD fCType,
  PTR rgbValue,
  SDWORD cbValueMax,
  SDWORD FAR * pcbValue)
	Binds a column to a
	statement
		SQL_SUCCESS_WITH_INFO
		SQL_INVALID_HANDLE

SQLCancel(HSTMT hstmt)	Cancels an asynchronously executing statement	SQL_SUCCESS_WITH_INFO SQL_INVALID_HANDLE

SQLColAttributes(
  HSTMT hstmt,
  UWORD icol,
  UWORD fDescType,
  PTR rgbDesc,
  SWORD cbDescMax,
  SWORD FAR * pcbDesc,
  SDWORD FAR * pfDesc)
	Returns one piece of
	information about a
	column in a result set
		SQL_SUCCESS_WITH_INFO
		SQL_STILL_EXECUTING
		SQL_INVALID_HANDLE

SQLConnect(
  HDBC hdbc,
  UCHAR FAR * szDSN,
  SWORD cbDSN,
  UCHAR FAR * szUID,
  SWORD cbUID,
  UCHAR FAR * szAuthStr,
  SWORD cbAuthStr)
	Connects an allocated
	connection to a data
	source
		SQL_SUCCESS_WITH_INFO
		SQL_INVALID_HANDLE

SQLDescribeCol(
  HSTMT hstmt,
  UWORD icol,
  UCHAR FAR * szColName,
  SWORD cbColNameMax,
  SWORD FAR * pcbColName,
  SWORD FAR * pfSqlType,
  UWORD FAR * pcbColDef,
  SWORD FAR * pibScale,
  SWORD FAR * pfNullable)
	Returns several pieces
	of info about a column
	in a result set
		SQL_SUCCESS_WITH_INFO
		SQL_STILL_EXECUTING
		SQL_INVALID_HANDLE

Function Prototype	Purpose	Unique Returns
SQLDisconnect(HDBC hdbc)	Closes a connection without freeing the connection handle	SQL_SUCCESS_WITH_INFO SQL_INVALID_HANDLE

SQLError(
  HENV henv,
  HDBC hdbc,
  HSTMT hstmt,
  UCHAR FAR * szSqlState,
  SDWORD FAR * pfNativeError,
  UCHAR FAR * szErrorMsg,
  SWORD cbErrorMsgMax,
  SWORD FAR * pcbErrorMsg)
	Returns detailed status information for the last ODBC function called	SQL_SUCCESS_WITH_INFO
		SQL_NO_DATA_FOUND
		SQL_INVALID_HANDLE

SQLExecDirect(
  HSTMT hstmt,
  UCHAR FAR * szSqlStr,
  SWORD cbSqlStr)
	Prepares and executes a statement	SQL_SUCCESS_WITH_INFO
		SQL_NEED_DATA
		SQL_STILL_EXECUTING
		SQL_INVALID_HANDLE

SQLExecute(HSTMT hstmt)	Executes a prepared statement	SQL_SUCCESS_WITH_INFO SQL_NEED_DATA SQL_STILL_EXECUTING SQL_INVALID_HANDLE
SQLFetch(HSTMT hstmt)	Gets a row of data from a result set	SQL_SUCCESS_WITH_INFO SQL_NO_DATA_FOUND SQL_STILL_EXECUTING SQL_INVALID_HANDLE
SQLFreeConnect(HDBC hdbc)	Deallocates a connection handle	SQL_SUCCESS_WITH_INFO SQL_INVALID_HANDLE
SQLFreeEnv(HENV henv)	Deallocates an ODBC environment	SQL_SUCCESS_WITH_INFO SQL_INVALID_HANDLE

SQLFreeStmt(
  HSTMT hstmt,
  UWORD fOption)
	Deallocates a statement handle, or releases objects associated with a statement	SQL_SUCCESS_WITH_INFO
		SQL_INVALID_HANDLE

SQLGetCursorName(
  HSTMT hstmt,
  UCHAR FAR * szCursor,
  SWORD cbCursorMax,
  SWORD FAR * pcbCursor)
	Returns the cursor name for a statement	SQL_SUCCESS_WITH_INFO
		SQL_INVALID_HANDLE

SQLNumResultCols(
  HSTMT hstmt,
  SWORD FAR * pccol)
	Returns the number of columns in a result set	SQL_SUCCESS_WITH_INFO
		SQL_STILL_EXECUTING
		SQL_INVALID_HANDLE

SQLPrepare(
  HSTMT hstmt,
  UCHAR FAR * szSqlStr,
  SDWORD cbSqlStr)
	Prepares a statement for execution by SQLExecute()	SQL_SUCCESS_WITH_INFO
		SQL_STILL_EXECUTING
		SQL_INVALID_HANDLE

Appendixes

(continues)

Table B.1 Continued		
Function Prototype	**Purpose**	**Unique Returns**

SQLRowCount(
  HSTMT hstmt,
  SDWORD FAR * pcrow)
	Returns the number of rows affected by an INSERT, UPDATE, or DELETE operation	SQL_SUCCESS_WITH_INFO
		SQL_INVALID_HANDLE

SQLSetCursorName(
  HSTMT hstmt,
  UCHAR FAR * szCursor,
  SWORD cbCursor)
	Names the cursor that belongs to a statement	SQL_SUCCESS_WITH_INFO
		SQL_INVALID_HANDLE

SQLTransact(
  HENV henv,
  HDBC hdbc,
  UWORD fType)
	Commits or rolls back all transactions on a connection or all connections in an ODBC environment	SQL_SUCCESS_WITH_INFO
		SQL_INVALID_HANDLE

Table B.2 includes the ODBC functions that are defined as part of the Extension Level 1 API conformance level. Drivers that include Extension Level 1 functions also generally include all Core-level functions, but there are often exceptions.

Table B.2 Extension Level 1 Functions		
Function Prototype	**Purpose**	**Unique Returns**

SQLBindParameter(
  HSTMT hstmt,
  UWORD ipar,
  SWORD fParamType,
  SWORD fCType,
  SWORD fSqlType,
  UDWORD cbColDef,
  SWORD ibScale,
  PTR rgbValue,
  SDWORD cbValueMax,
  SDWORD FAR * pcbValue)
	Binds a parameter buffer	SQL_SUCCESS_WITH_INFO
		SQL_INVALID_HANDLE

SQLColumns(
  HSTMT hstmt,
  UCHAR FAR *
    szTableQualifier,
  SWORD cbTableQualifier,
  UCHAR FAR *
    szTableOwner,
  SWORD cbTableOwner,
	Returns a result set of columns in one or more tables	SQL_SUCCESS_WITH_INFO
		SQL_STILL_EXECUTING
		SQL_INVALID_HANDLE

Function Prototype	Purpose	Unique Returns
| ```
UCHAR FAR *
  szTableName,
SWORD cbTableName,
UCHAR FAR *
  szColumnName,
SWORD cbColumnName)
``` | | |
| ```
SQLDriverConnect(
  HDBC hdbc,
  HWND hwnd,
  UCHAR FAR * szConnStr,
  SWORD cbConnStr,
  UCHAR FAR * szConnStrOut,
  SWORD cbConnStrOut,
  SWORD FAR *
    pcbConnStrOut,
  UWORD
    fDriverCompletion)
``` | Connects an allocated connection to a data source, providing additional information | SQL_SUCCESS_WITH_INFO SQL_NO_DATA_FOUND SQL_INVALID_HANDLE |
| ```
SQLGetConnectOption(
  HDBC hdbc,
  UWORD fOption,
  PTR pvParam)
``` | Returns a connect option setting | SQL_SUCCESS_WITH_INFO SQL_NO_DATA_FOUND SQL_INVALID_HANDLE |
| ```
SQLGetData(
  HSTMT hstmt,
  UWORD icol,
  SWORD fcType,
  PTR rgbValue,
  SDWORD cbValueMax,
  SDWORD FAR * pcbValue)
``` | Returns data for an unbound column | SQL_SUCCESS_WITH_INFO SQL_NO_DATA_FOUND SQL_STILL_EXECUTING SQL_INVALID_HANDLE |
| ```
SQLGetFunctions(
  HDBC hdbc,
  UWORD fFunction,
  UWORD FAR * pfExists)
``` | Indicates whether a driver supports a specific ODBC function | SQL_SUCCESS_WITH_INFO SQL_INVALID_HANDLE |
| ```
SQLGetInfo(
  HDBC hdbc,
  UWORD fInfoType,
  PTR rgbInfoValue,
  SWORD cbInfoValueMax,
  SWORD FAR * pcbInfoValue)
``` | Returns one of many pieces of information about an ODBC driver | SQL_SUCCESS_WITH_INFO SQL_INVALID_HANDLE |
| ```
SQLGetStmtOption(
  HSTMT hstmt,
  UWORD fOption,
  PTR pvParam)
``` | Returns a statement option setting | SQL_SUCCESS_WITH_INFO SQL_INVALID_HANDLE |
| ```
SQLGetTypeInfo(
  HSTMT hstmt,
  fSqlType)
``` | Returns a result set of data types supported by a data source | SQL_SUCCESS_WITH_INFO SQL_STILL_EXECUTING SQL_INVALID_HANDLE |

Appendixes

(continues)

Table B.2 Continued

Function Prototype	Purpose	Unique Returns

SQLParamData(
  HSTMT hstmt,
  PTR FAR * prgbValue)
	Part of the data-at-execution process	SQL_SUCCESS_WITH_INFO
		SQL_NEED_DATA
		SQL_STILL_EXECUTING
		SQL_INVALID_HANDLE

SQLPutData(
  HSTMT hstmt,
  PTR rgbValue,
  SDWORD cbValue)
	Part of the data-at-execution process	SQL_SUCCESS_WITH_INFO
		SQL_STILL_EXECUTING
		SQL_INVALID_HANDLE

SQLSetConnectOption(
  HDBC hdbc,
  UWORD fOption,
  UDWORD vParam)
	Sets a connection option	SQL_SUCCESS_WITH_INFO
		SQL_INVALID_HANDLE

SQLSetStmtOption(
  HSTMT hstmt,
  UWORD fOption,
  UDWORD vParam)
	Sets a statement option	SQL_SUCCESS_WITH_INFO
		SQL_INVALID_HANDLE

SQLSpecialColumns(
  HSTMT hstmt,
  UWORD fColType,
  UCHAR FAR *
    szTableQualifier,
  SWORD cbTableQualifier,
  UCHAR FAR *
    szTableOwner,
  SWORD cbTableOwner,
  UCHAR FAR *
    szTableName,
  SWORD cbTableName,
  UWORD fScope,
  UWORD fNullable)
	Retrieves information about uniquely identifying and auto-update columns in a table	SQL_SUCCESS_WITH_INFO
		SQL_STILL_EXECUTING
		SQL_INVALID_HANDLE

SQLStatistics(
  HSTMT hstmt,
  UCHAR FAR *
    szTableQualifier,
  SWORD cbTableQualifier,
  UCHAR FAR *
    szTableOwner,
  SWORD cbTableOwner,
  UCHAR FAR *
    szTableName,
  SWORD cbTableName,
  UWORD fUnique,
  UWORD fAccuracy)
	Returns a result set of statistics and index information about a table	SQL_SUCCESS_WITH_INFO
		SQL_STILL_EXECUTING
		SQL_INVALID_HANDLE

SQLTables(
  HSTMT hstmt,
  UCHAR FAR *
    szTableQualifier,
	Returns a result set of tables in a data source	SQL_SUCCESS_WITH_INFO
		SQL_STILL_EXECUTING
		SQL_INVALID_HANDLE

Function Prototype	Purpose	Unique Returns

```
    SWORD cbTableQualifier,
    UCHAR FAR *
      szTableOwner,
    SWORD cbTableOwner,
    UCHAR FAR *
      szTableName,
    SWORD cbTableName,
    UCHAR FAR *
      szTableType,
    SWORD cbTableType)
```

Finally, table B.3 includes the ODBC functions defined as part of the Extension Level 2 API conformance level. Again, drivers that include Extension Level 2 functions generally include most Extension Level 1 functions as well.

Table B.3   Extension Level 2 Functions

Function Prototype	Purpose	Unique Returns

`SQLBrowseConnect(`
`  HDBC hdbc,`
`  UCHAR FAR *`
`    szConnStrIn,`
`  SWORD cbConnStrIn,`
`  UCHAR FAR *`
`    szConnStrOut,`
`  SWORD cbConnStrOutMax,`
`  SWORD FAR *`
`    pcbConnStrOut)`
	Connects to a data source step by step	SQL_SUCCESS_WITH_INFO
		SQL_NEED_DATA
		SQL_INVALID_HANDLE

`SQLColumnPrivileges(`
`  HSTMT hstmt,`
`  UCHAR FAR *`
`    szTableQualifier,`
`  SWORD cbTableQualifier,`
`  UCHAR FAR *`
`    szTableOwner,`
`  SWORD cbTableOwner,`
`  UCHAR FAR *`
`    szTableName,`
`  SWORD cbTableName,`
`  UCHAR FAR *`
`    szColumnName,`
`  SWORD cbColumnName)`
	Returns a result set of column privileges for a table	SQL_SUCCESS_WITH_INFO
		SQL_STILL_EXECUTING
		SQL_INVALID_HANDLE

`SQLDataSources(`
`  HENV henv,`
`  UWORD fDirection,`
`  UCHAR FAR * szDSN,`
	Lists the names of available data sources	SQL_SUCCESS_WITH_INFO
		SQL_NO_DATA_FOUND
		SQL_INVALID_HANDLE

(continues)

Appendixes

Table B.3 Continued		
Function Prototype	**Purpose**	**Unique Returns**

SWORD cbDSNMax,
SWORD FAR * pcbDSN,
UCHAR FAR *
  szDescription,
SWORD cbDescriptionMax,
SWORD FAR *
  pcbDescription)		

SQLDescribeParam(HSTMT hstmt, UWORD ipar, SWORD FAR * pfSqlType, UDWORD FAR * pcbColDef, SWORD FAR * pibScale, SWORD FAR * pfNullable)	Returns various pieces of information about a statement parameter	SQL_SUCCESS_WITH_INFO SQL_STILL_EXECUTING SQL_INVALID_HANDLE

SQLDrivers(
HENV henv,
UWORD fDirection,
UCHAR FAR *
  szDriverDesc,
SWORD cbDriverDescMax,
SWORD FAR *
  pcbDriverDesc,
UCHAR FAR *
  szDriverAttributes,
SWORD cbDrvrAttrMax,
SWORD FAR *
  pcbDrvrAttr)
	Lists information about
	available drivers
		SQL_SUCCESS_WITH_INFO
		SQL_NO_DATA_FOUND
		SQL_INVALID_HANDLE

SQLExtendedFetch(HSTMT hstmt, UWORD fFetchType, SDWORD irow, UDWORD FAR * pcrow, UWORD FAR * rgfRowStatus)	Retrieves several rows from a result set	SQL_SUCCESS_WITH_INFO SQL_NO_DATA_FOUND SQL_STILL_EXECUTING SQL_INVALID_HANDLE

SQLForeignKeys(
HSTMT hstmt,
UCHAR FAR *
  szPkTableQualifier,
SWORD
  cbPkTableQualifier,
UCHAR FAR *
  szPkTableOwner,
SWORD
  cbPkTableOwner,
UCHAR FAR *
  szPkTableName,
SWORD
  cbPkTableName,
	Returns a list of
	foreign keys for a
	table or its related
	tables
		SQL_SUCCESS_WITH_INFO
		SQL_STILL_EXECUTING
		SQL_INVALID_HANDLE

Function Prototype	Purpose	Unique Returns

UCHAR FAR *
  szFkTableQualifier,
SWORD
  cbFkTableQualifier,
UCHAR FAR *
  szFkTableOwner,
SWORD
  cbFkTableOwner,
UCHAR FAR *
  szFkTableName,
SWORD
  cbFkTableName)		

SQLMoreResults(HSTMT hstmt)	Indicates whether an additional result set has been returned	SQL_SUCCESS_WITH_INFO SQL_STILL_EXECUTING SQL_NO_DATA_FOUND SQL_INVALID_HANDLE

SQLNativeSQL(
  HDBC hdbc,
  UCHAR FAR *
    szSqlStrIn,
  SDWORD cbSqlStrIn,
  UCHAR FAR * szSqlStr,
  SDWORD cbSqlStrMax,
  SDWORD FAR * pcbSqlStr)
	Accepts a SQL statement in ODBC syntax; returns it in a driver's syntax	SQL_SUCCESS_WITH_INFO
		SQL_INVALID_HANDLE

SQLNumParams(
  HSTMT hstmt,
  SWORD FAR * pcPar)
	Returns the number of parameters for a statement	SQL_SUCCESS_WITH_INFO
		SQL_STILL_EXECUTING
		SQL_INVALID_HANDLE

SQLParamOptions(
  HSTMT hstmt,
  UDWORD crow,
  UDWORD FAR * pirow)
	Part of the data-at-execution process	SQL_SUCCESS_WITH_INFO
		SQL_INVALID_HANDLE

SQLPrimaryKeys(
  HSTMT hstmt,
  UCHAR FAR *
    szTableQualifier,
  SWORD cbTableQualifier,
  UCHAR FAR *
    szTableOwner,
  SWORD cbTableOwner,
  UCHAR FAR *
    szTableName,
  SWORD cbTableName)
	Returns a result set of the columns in a table's primary key	SQL_SUCCESS_WITH_INFO
		SQL_STILL_EXECUTING
		SQL_INVALID_HANDLE

SQLProcedureColumns(
  HSTMT hstmt,
  UCHAR FAR *
    szProcQualifier,
  SWORD cbProcQualifier,
  UCHAR FAR *
    szProcOwner,
	Returns a result set of input, output, and result set columns for a database/stored procedure	SQL_SUCCESS_WITH_INFO
		SQL_INVALID_HANDLE

Appendixes

(continues)

Table B.3 Continued

Function Prototype	Purpose	Unique Returns

SWORD cbProcOwner,
UCHAR FAR *
  szProcName,
SWORD cbProcName,
UCHAR FAR *
  szColumnName,
SWORD cbColumnName,		

SQLSetPos(
  HSTMT hstmt,
  UWORD irow,
  UWORD fOption,
  UWORD fLock)
	Positions a cursor,
	and optionally performs
	a positioned operation
		SQL_SUCCESS_WITH_INFO
		SQL_SQL_NEED_DATA
		SQL_STILL_EXECUTING
		SQL_INVALID_HANDLE

SQLTablePrivileges(
  HSTMT hstmt,
  UCHAR FAR *
    szTableQualifier,
  SWORD cbTableQualifier,
  UCHAR FAR *
    szTableOwner,
  SWORD cbTableOwner,
  UCHAR FAR *
    szTableName,
  SWORD cbTableName)
	Returns a result set of
	privileges for one or
	more tables
		SQL_SUCCESS_WITH_INFO
		SQL_STILL_EXECUTING
		SQL_INVALID_HANDLE

Note

Use the SQLGetFunctions() function to find out whether a driver supports a particular function. This is necessary in case a driver claims a higher API conformance level than it fully supports, or supports additional functions beyond its "official" conformance level.

Appendix C

Contents of the Special Edition, *Using ODBC 2* CD-ROM

This appendix explains the contents of the CD-ROM that is included with your copy of Special Edition, *Using ODBC 2*.

Sample Code Used in the Book

The code samples are located in the \CODE directory of the CD-ROM. Some subdirectories under \CODE have README.TXT files that contain additional information.

A List of Databases

This list is located in the USEODBC.HLP file in the root directory of the CD-ROM. There are certain databases that are not in the list included on the CD-ROM. A call to one of the larger vendors (Intersolv, perhaps) might supply some information about your particular database.

A List of Vendors

This list is located in the USEODBC.HLP file in the root directory of the CD-ROM. The market for ODBC products is constantly evolving; new vendors are continuously entering the field. If you don't find the company or product that you are looking for in the list, perhaps contacting Microsoft can help.

The Demos on This CD-ROM

Following are instructions for using the demonstration databases for various software packages.

Paradox for Windows

This is a DOS-based presentation located in the \DEMOS\PARADOX directory.

Following are the steps for using this demo:

1. Connect to the CD-ROM drive.

2. Switch to the \DEMOS\PARADOX directory.

3. Run the **demo** batch file.

dBASE for Windows 5.0

This software is a full working version, good for 30 days.

Following are the steps for using this demo:

1. From the Windows Program Manager, use the **F**ile **R**un menu option to run the **setup** program in the root directory of the CD-ROM.

2. Follow the on-screen instructions to install dBASE for Windows.

Jet Inspector v2.0

This is a full working version of the program, and is usable for 30 days.

Following are the steps for using this demo:

1. From the Windows Program Manager, use the **F**ile, **R**un menu option to run the **setup** program in the \DEMOS\JETINSP directory of the CD-ROM.

2. Follow the on-screen instructions to install Jet Inspector.

ODBC Inspector v2.0

This is a full working version of the program, and is usable for 30 days.

Following are the steps for using this demo:

1. From the Windows Program Manager, use the **F**ile, **R**un menu option to run the **setup** program in the \DEMOS\ODBCINSP directory of the CD-ROM.

2. Follow the on-screen instructions to install ODBC Inspector.

SQL Inspector v2.0

This is a full working version of the program, and is usable for 30 days.

Following are the steps for using this demo:

1. From the Windows Program Manager, use the **F**ile, **R**un menu option to run the **setup** program in the \DEMOS\SQLINSP directory of the CD-ROM.

2. Follow the on-screen instructions to install SQL Inspector.

Help Files from South Wind Design

These help files are located in the root directory of the CD-ROM. ODBCPP.HLP contains the Basics of ODBC Application Development. You also can find this help file by looking in the South Wind Design help topic.

SWDIINFO.HLP, located in the root directory of the CD-ROM, contains ODBC/ClassLib v2.0 product information.

REFHELP.HLP, also located in the root directory of the CD-ROM, describes the classes and their data and function members of ODBC/ClassLib, along with the typedefs, macros, and data structures that support them. It is not intended to be a replacement for the Microsoft ODBC Software Developers Kit manuals. Where a member function relies on an ODBC API function, that fact is noted, but no attempt was made to reproduce the extensive listing of error returns, status information, and side effects that result from such a function.

Products

Crystal Reports v3.0 Standard Edition is a full working version of the software. Please remember to register!

Following are the steps for installing this product:

1. Connect to the CD-ROM drive.

2. Switch to the \PRODUCTS\CRYSTAL directory.

3. Run the **CREATDSK** batch file to create installation diskettes. Remember to label the diskettes as they are created.

4. From the Windows Program Manager, use the **F**ile **R**un menu option to run the **setup** program in the root directory of disk 1.

5. Follow the on-screen instructions to install Crystal Reports.

Appendixes

Shareware

The *Analyst's Tool Kit* helps build and maintain DFDs (data flow diagrams). An analysis package and data dictionary also are included. Display is supported for CGA, EGA, VGA, and SuperVGA cards; printing is supported for Epson, HP, and PostScript printers; a mouse is supported if present, but a mouse is not required. Windows import filters are provided. The product supports eight levels of decomposition, and is easy and intuitive to use. This package gives you a 90-day trial period. Printed manuals and inexpensive updates also are available.

Following are the steps for using this demo:

1. Connect to the CD-ROM drive.

2. Switch to the \SHARWARE\ATK19 directory.

3. Read all of the files with a TXT extension.

4. You can run the DOS-based programs directly from the CD-ROM. The Windows-based programs need to be installed using the **setup** program.

MDS PowerBase is a powerful client server development tool used to quickly create, manage, and edit the data and server-based objects (such as tables, procedures, views, and the like) on your SQL Server/SYBASE databases. MDS PowerBase provides database maintenance facilities, which separates MDS PowerBase from all other products on the market.

Following are the steps for installing this application:

1. From the Windows Program Manager, use the **F**ile **R**un menu option to run the **setup** program in the \SHARWARE\PBASE20 directory of the CD-ROM.

2. Follow the on-screen instructions to install MDS PowerBase.

Caution

The MDS PowerBase installation process will add the file VBRUN300.DLL to your \WINDOWS\SYSTEM directory. If you already have this file installed on your system in the \WINDOWS\SYSTEM directory, the PowerBase installation program will give you an error and will not install properly. To avoid this problem, simply delete the DLL file or move it to another directory *before* you install PowerBase.

If you do not have the VBRUN300.DLL file in your \WINDOWS\SYSTEM directory, PowerBase should install without error.

X-Ray/ODBC traces function calls of the ODBC API.

Following are the steps for installing this product:

1. From the Windows Program Manager, use the **File Run** menu option to run the **xrayodbc** program in the \SHARWARE\XRAY directory of the CD-ROM.

2. The INSTALL.TXT in the \SHARWARE\XRAY directory gives further instructions on installing the software.

White Papers

The ODBC White Paper "ODBC: Getting Connected" is located in the USEODBC.HLP file in the root directory of the CD-ROM.

The ODBC White Paper "Designing ODBC Databases with S-Designer" is located in the USEODBC.HLP file in the root directory of the CD-ROM.

The ODBC White Paper "INTERSOLV Data Direct Developer's Toolkit" is located in the USEODBC.HLP file in the root directory of the CD-ROM.

Glossary of Terms

The glossary contains some terms used in ODBC circles.

Appendixes

Glossary

ANSI   The American National Standards Institute. An organization that gathers and defines technical standards of all kinds. Among many others, and ANSI standard specification exists for SQL.

Attribute   Another term for *column*.

Binding   The process of associating attributes with an ODBC construct such as a statement—for example, parameters or relevant columns.

Bookmark   A 32-bit "key" for a given result set row, provided to the application by ODBC as a convenient method for accessing the row.

Client/Server   Describes a DBMS model wherein most database processing is performed at the back end, or database engine, on the server computer, and most display and user interaction is performed at the front end, or database application, on the workstation (also known as the "client"). All ODBC operations are based on a segmented client/server model, even if the "server" portion is actually built into the ODBC driver (in which case it's known as a "single-tier driver").

Column   In ODBC terminology, a field within a table. The term "column" can be used to refer to the column as a whole or to the value of the column within a particular row.

Commit   The process of authorizing and finalizing all commands that comprise a transaction. The opposite of *rollback*.

Concurrency   Refers to the care that is taken by the database engine (and/or the ODBC driver) to manage changes made to the database by different users and keep data in each user's workstation's memory in sync.

Conformance Level   The degree to which a given ODBC driver fulfills certain requirements. There are two types of conformance levels: API and SQL. The API conformance level of a driver indicates the set of ODBC functions it supports. The SQL conformance level of a driver indicates the set of SQL commands it supports. Conformance levels are not etched in stone, and some drivers support most requirements for a given conformance level but neglect others. Such drivers may or may not claim the higher conformance level, although technically they're not supposed to.

Connection   A construct in workstation memory that allows communication between the ODBC application and a particular data source. In the case of most data sources, each connection can have multiple statements associated with it.

Cursor   A "pointer" to the "current row" of a result set (not a pointer as defined by C).

Cursor Library, The   A pair of DLLs, one for 16-bit Windows and one for 32-bit Windows NT, that provide basic cursor functionality for all ODBC drivers. Some drivers offer additional cursor capabilities on top of the basic ones provided by the cursor library.

Data Definition Language (DDL)   A set of commands that enable database administrators and developers to create and modify database objects. Most SQL implementations contain a DDL as a subset of their syntax.

Data Source   A source of data; that is, a client/server database engine or a set of local database files.

DELETE   The SQL command that eliminates a row from a table.

Driver (ODBC)   A module containing ODBC functions that work in a fashion specific to a particular data source.

Environment   A construct in memory on the workstation which allows an ODBC-enabled application to perform ODBC operations.

Execution   The process of sending a SQL command through ODBC to the database engine, where it will be run and results returned if applicable.

Extensions   Additional features of a particular type that are provided by the driver over and above ODBC's standard features in that category. For example, some drivers provide supplementary cursor management capabilities.

Fetching   The process of bringing a result set from the database engine, through ODBC, to the ODBC application running on the workstation.

Foreign Key   A column in a given table that links the table in a parent relationship with another table, in which the same value is referred to as the *primary key*.

INSERT   The SQL command that adds a new row to a table. In fact, the row is under most circumstances appended to the table rather than physically inserted.

Keyset   A subset of the rows in a result set that are currently being used by the application. The term refers to unique key values which are generated by ODBC in memory to uniquely identify each row.

Local   Describes a DBMS model wherein all database processing (except perhaps the storage of raw data blocks) is performed on the workstation, by the application.

Multiple-Tier Driver   An ODBC driver that serves as a translator and negotiator between the application and the separately existing database engine (which usually runs on a different computer).

ODBC   Open Database Connectivity. Microsoft's specification for universal communication between database engines from different vendors. A given DBMS can be used with ODBC-capable applications if an ODBC driver exists for that platform.

Parameter   Although the term also means the same as function arguments, in ODBC jargon a parameter is a value that exists outside a statement but is associated with it for the purpose of passing variable values to the same basic statement syntax.

Positioned Operation   An UPDATE or DELETE statement that uses a WHERE CURRENT OF clause to make a change to the row in a result set on which the cursor is positioned.

Prepared Statement   A statement that has been validity-checked in advance, before presentation to the driver for execution.

Primary Key   A column that uniquely identifies each row within a table, at the database level itself. Some DBMSs can generate unique keys internally, but otherwise the application must handle this, and there are a variety of techniques for achieving it. Also referred to as a *unique key*.

Query   In the context of this book, a query is a SQL SELECT command that's executed through the SQLExecDirect() or SQLExecute () function.

Referential Integrity   The concept of designing a database with as little as possible overlap and duplication of data between tables.

Relational Database Management System (RDBMS)   A database management system that enforces good database design principles to the point where violating them is virtually impossible at any level. Almost all true RDBMSs are client/server in nature.

Result Set   The set of rows that's sent back by the data source in response to a SQL SELECT command.

Rollback   The process of undoing the successful operations within a transaction in which some component commands have failed. The opposite of *commit*.

Row   In SQL terminology, a record in a table.

Rowset   The part of a result set that is fetched using the SQLExtendedFetch() function.

SDK   Software Development Kit. A set of tools that allows the programmer to use a particular library of functions in custom applications.

SELECT   The SQL command that performs all types of queries.

Single-Tier Driver   An ODBC driver that, in addition to interacting with the application, also performs the work of the database engine, querying and manipulating data directly.

SQL   Structured Query Language. Often pronounced as "sequel." An industry standard language for querying and manipulating relational databases. ANSI has come out with a "true" SQL standard, which ODBC follows. However, most SQL DBMSs vary a little on their implementation of SQL syntax, often for the purpose of offering special functionality (such as database procedures or transaction processing commands) on top of that specified in the ANSI standard.

Statement   This term has two definitions in ODBC terminology. You'll have to consider the context to understand which meaning is being used. The "proper" usage of the term refers to a statement handle (hstmt) that's used to send SQL commands to the driver. Among other things, a statement includes a SQL command. However, *statement* is also used to refer to the SQL command itself.

Table   In SQL terminology, a single entity within a database, consisting of rows and columns.

Transaction   A set of SQL commands that are designated as a unit. All commands within a transaction must succeed or the whole thing rolls back.

Transaction Processing   Refers to the features and techniques of a particular data source that allow it to organize statements into transactions.

Tuple   Another term for *row*.

UPDATE   The SQL command that makes changes to column values within existing rows in a table.

Index

Symbols

16-bit drivers, 104-105
1NF (first normal form), 40
2NF (second normal form), 41
32-bit drivers, 104-105
3NF (third normal form), 41

A

Access, 15, 341
access mode (connections),
  135
ADDNEW method (dynasets),
  403
addresses (data storage), 223
administration sample,
  503-504
Administrator, *see* ODBC
  Administrator
aggregate functions, 86-88,
  307-309
allocating
  connections, 128
    connecting data sources,
      511
    data sources, 508
    environments, 508
    statements, 508
ALTER TABLE command, 59,
  176-177
alternate keys, 22
Analyst's Tool Kit, 520-521
ANSI (American National
  Standards Institute), 523
answer sets, 74
APIs, 10
  conformance, 113-114, 524
  disadvantages, 13

help reference, 496-497
ODBC 2.0 API, 407
  applicability, 407-416
  declaring functions,
    421-426
  function categories, 408
  performance issues,
    410-416
ODBC conformance levels,
  425-426
online help, 113
appending record sets,
  301-314
Apple Macintosh systems, 10
applications
  book disc, 517-521
  creating tables, 169
  debugging, 495-496
  designing with Wizards,
    266-275
  diagnostic functions, 281
  distributing (Visual Basic),
    346-347
  downsizing
    client/server model,
      477-478
    end-user tools, 479
    hardware platforms,
      475-479
    implementation, 489
    modeling systems,
      479-481
    PC databases, 476-477
    performance issues,
      481-487
    precautions, 487-489
    user involvement, 488

front-end changes
  (downsizing), 473-474
logical data independence,
  20
MFC, 14
multiple data sources, 105
multiple driver support,
  118-119
multiple-tier drivers, 525
parameterizing record sets,
  321-324
  filters, 323-324
  member variables,
    321-323
  updates, 324
porting, 471-472
rewriting, 473
security, 63-64
single driver support, 119
single-tier drivers, 526
Translation Spy, 505
see also design issues
Approach, 99
AppWizard, 270-275
  building applications,
    274-275
  class generation, 274
  data source selection, 273
  database support, 272
  IDD_RAIL_FORM dialog, 276
  linking controls, 277
  opening ClassWizard, 277
  program generation, 274
  starting, 271
  table selection, 273
  views, 275-278
arrays, *see* object variable
  arrays

ascending key indexes, 61
ASCII delimited files, 15
asynchronous execution
  (statements), 159-160
asynchronous mode, 452
asynchronous processing, 439
atomic column values, 20
attributes, 21, 523
  binding, 523
  columns, 202, 205-207
  cursors, 233
  defining, 39-44
  derived attributes, 43
  history tables, 46-48
auto-commit mode
  (connections), 193, 256-257
auto-update columns, 512
AUTOCOMMIT mode
  (transactions), 167
autocommit option, 135
AVG function, 307

B

backward scrolling, 288
beginning of table function,
  289
BeginTrans statement, 404
BETWEEN predicate, 76
bExclusive parameter, 326
binding, 523
  buffer variables, 439
  column-wise, 209-210
  columns, 208-211
  dynamic binding (columns),
    310-314
  parameter values, 219-222
  parameters, 230, 510
  primary key columns,
    454-455
  row-wise, 210-211
  statements to columns, 508
block cursors, 233, 414
BN_CLICKED message
  handler, 293
book disc, 517-521
bookmarks, 245, 523
  cursors, 251-252, 260-261
  turning off, 455
  Visual Basic, 399
BOOL CanAppend() function,
  301
BOOL CanUpdate() function,
  301

BOOL IsBOF() function, 289
BOOL IsDeleted() function,
  305
BOOL IsEOF() function, 289
bottlenecks, 486-487
bound controls (Visual Basic),
  361-363
bReadOnly parameter, 326
browsing result sets
  (Visual Basic), 365-366
browsing command, 314
buffer variables, binding, 439
building applications
  (AppWizard), 274-275
bUseCursorLib parameter, 326

C

C++ sample application,
  499-500
cabling problems, 487
caches (result sets), 239
calling SQLError() function,
  125-127
calling procedures, 91-92
canceling statements, 508
candidate keys, 22
capability checks (drivers),
  449-451
Cartesian product operator, 27
CASCADE statements, 60
cascades, 189
cascading deletes, 187
catalog and statistics
  functions, 106
catalog functions, 137-138
  classes, 150-152
  result sets, 152
catch blocks, 299
CDatabase objects, 325
CDatabase::Open function,
  325
CDBExceptions, 300
CFileExceptions, 300
checking
  connection options, 134-135
  cursor options, 261
class generation (AppWizard),
  274
classes
  catalog functions, 150-152
  member variables, 308
  MFC, 14

ClassWizard
  creating recordsets, 282-286
  opening, 277
clearing parameters, 230
client/server model, 523
  database interfaces, 96-99
  databases, 477-478
  downsizing, 476
  drivers, 12, 104
  Extension Level 2
    (API conformance), 114
  permissions, 116
  porting, 472
  privileges, 148-150
  simulation, 13
  Watcom SQL, 13
closing
  connections, 509
  record sets, 289
closing connections (Visual
  Basic), 437
clustered indexes, 60, 174
CMemoryExceptions, 300
Codd, Dr. E.F., 19
column-level privileges,
  149-150
column-wise binding, 209-210
columns, 21, 523
  adding table names to
    columns, 318
  alternate keys, 22
  atomic column values, 20
  attributes, 202
  auto-update columns, 512
  binding, 208-211
    primary key columns,
      454-455
    statements, 508
  candidate keys, 22
  deleting, 59
  derived attributes, 43
  dynamic binding, 310-314
  extracting values, 162
  foreign keys, 23-24, 144, 525
  naming, 70, 83
  null values, 91
  primary keys, 21-24,
    143-144, 525
  result sets, 508-510
    attributes, 205-207
    counting, 201-204
    descriptions, 204-205
    privileges, 513
  retrieving names from tables,
    140

returning subsets, 24
special columns, 141-143
updating in result sets, 246
views, 65
combining tables, 26
command handlers, 294
commands
ALTER TABLE, 59, 176, 177
COMMIT, 165
committing, 523
CREATE CLUSTERED
INDEX, 174
CREATE INDEX, 61, 174
CREATE TABLE, 57, 171
CREATE VIEW, 64
creating
appending records, 303
browsing, 314
deleting records, 306
table navigation, 291
DDL, 524
DELETE, 69, 186, 524
DROP INDEX, 175
DROP TABLE, 59, 172
executing, 524
GRANT, 66
INSERT, 70-71, 183, 525
REVOKE, 68
ROLLBACK, 165, 168
SELECT, 71-72, 526
statements, 526
transactions, 527
UPDATE, 90, 184, 527
COMMIT command, 165
committing transactions,
510, 523
CommitTrans statement, 404
concatenating rows, 27
concurrency, 523
cursors, 258
concurrency locking, 254
result sets, 440
configuring
data sources, 357
statement options
retrieval, 158
setting, 159
conformance level, 524
conformance levels
APIs, 425-426
core level, 423
extended, 423-424
SQL, 424-426
CONNECT property (Data
Control), 356

connection handles, 509
connections, 524
access mode, 135
allocating, 128, 508
autocommit option, 135
behavioral characteristics,
438
CDatabase object, 325
closing, 509
cursor options, 255-257
data sources, 427-430
handles, 427-429
initializing, 427
optional, 131-134
specific, 129-131
freeing, 437
initializing, 128-129
login timeout, 135
ODBC 2.0 API functions, 418
options
checking, 134-135
setting, 134
setting options, 512
terminating (Visual Basic),
437
constructs, 20
controls
bound controls, 361-363
Crystal Reports Pro v3.0, 367
custom controls, 364-370
Data Widgets Version 1.0,
366
data-aware custom controls,
368
linking (AppWizard), 277
OCX, 368-369
OCXs, 341
True Grid Pro Version 2.1,
365
VBX library, 368
VBX-style custom controls,
342
Controls Collection objects,
377
core, 12
Core API conformance, 113
core grammar (drivers), 115
core level functionality, 423
core-level functions, 508-510
cost-based optimizers, 60
COUNT function, 86, 307
count() function, 162
counting
columns, 201-204
parameters, 226-227

queries, 207
rows, 162, 187-188
CRailSet (listing 14.1), 279-280
CREATE CLUSTERED INDEX
command, 174
CREATE INDEX command,
61, 174
CREATE TABLE command,
57, 171
CREATE VIEW command, 64
CRecordset class
applicability, 330
deleting records, 305-306
navigating tables, 287-294
updating record sets,
301-305
Crystal Reports Pro v3.0, 367
Crystal Reports v3.0, 519
CTL3D.DLL, 347
CTrainSet class, 290-291
cursor demo, 502-503
cursor library, 524
cursors, 233, 524
attributes, 233
auto-commit mode, 256-257
behavioral characteristics,
438
block cursors, 414
bookmarks, 251-252,
260-261
caches, 239
checking options, 261
concurrency, 258
concurrency locking, 254
connection options, 255-257
driver support, 244, 249-255
dynamic, 234, 414
extended fetching, 242-245
fetch directions, 252
forward-only
implementations, 235
function usage, 256
keyset size, 259
keyset-driven, 235, 414-415
lock types, 252-253
mixed, 235, 415-416
naming, 236-239, 253
ODBC 2.0 API
behavior, 414
keyset-driven, 414-415
managing, 413-414
mixed, 415-416
models, 414
result sets, 440
open cursors, 250-251

positioned operations
support, 253-254
positioned updates/deletes
SELECT FOR UPDATE
clause, 246
SQLSetPos() function,
248-249
WHERE CURRENT OF
clause, 246-248
positioning, 239-241, 248,
516
releasing, 261
retrieving data, 259
returning names
(statements), 509
rollbacks, 251
rowset retrieval, 259-260
scrolling, 440
setting options, 257-261
simulating, 260
statements, 510
static, 234, 414
static sensitivity, 255
types, 258-259
custom controls, 341
Crystal Reports Pro v3.0, 367
Data Widgets Version 1.0,
366
data-aware, 368
OCX, 368-369
True Grid Pro Version 2.1,
365
VBX library, 368
VBX-style, 342
Visual Basic, 364-370
browsing result sets,
365-366
data-aware, 368
OCX, 368-369
printing result sets,
366-368

D

**Data Access Object variables,
335-339, 374-395**
cloning databases, 397
creating databases, 395-397
dynasets, 354-355
creating, 394-395
dynamic behavior,
392-393
methods, 391-392
NEW keyword, 396-397

programming, 375-376
queries
result sets, 398-400
SQL statements, 397-398
Snapshot objects, 387-391
creating, 388-389
row pointers, 389-391
Table objects
Fields collection, 384-386
Indexes collection,
386-387
TableDefs objects
class definitions, 378
defining, 378
object variable arrays,
380-382
pointers, 380
TableDefs collection,
382-384
transactions
management, 403-405
record sets, 401-403
SQL statements, 401
Data Control
data sources
configuring, 357
multiple, 357
selecting, 357
dynasets, 351-355
properties, 355
result sets, 361-364
bound controls, 361-363
programming strategies,
363-364
**Data Control (Visual Basic),
334-339**
Data Definition Language,
see DDL
data integrity
enforcing
entry time, 463
post-processing, 463-464
SQL, 465-467
update time, 462
entity integrity, 460-462
default values, 461-462
duplicate values, 461
null fields, 461
primary key validity, 460
restricting field values,
461
referential integrity, 24, 448,
462, 526
constraints, 58
dropping tables, 173
foreign key validity, 467

rows, 188-197
transaction processing,
190-196
triggers, 188-197
updating databases, 184
Data Manipulation Language,
see DML
data sources, 524
allocated connections, 508
CDatabase objects, 325
connecting, 427-430
handles, 427-429
initializing, 427
optional, 131-134
specific, 129-131
connecting allocated
connections, 511
creating, 117
data types, 171
disconnecting, 135-136
isolation levels, 192-193
listing available, 513
multiple, 324-330
multiple access, 105
ODBC 2.0 API, 418-419
result sets, 511-512
selecting, 326
selecting with AppWizard,
273
tracing, 441
Visual Basic Data Control,
357
data types (SQL), 54-56
supporting, 171
user defined data types, 56
Data Widgets Version 1.0, 366
**data-aware custom controls,
368**
database engines, 350-351
database-specific interfaces
client/server model, 96-99
local, 94-96
**DATABASENAME property
(Data Control), 356**
databases
cloning, 397
creating, 395-397
data integrity
enforcing, 462-464
entity integrity, 460-462
referential integrity, 462
design issues, 482-484
normalization, 448
relational, 17
advantages, 19
constructs, 20-21

entity definition, 29-33
history, 19-20
integrity, 21-24
join operator, 26
projection operator, 24
referential integrity, 24
relationship definitions,
35-39
selection operator, 24
union operator, 27
supported, 15
table lists, 139
see also columns; rows; tables
Date literals, 79
dBASE, 15, 518
DBNMP3.DLL, 347
DCL (Data Control Language),
66-68
DDL (Data Definition
Language), 57-66, 169, 524
functions, 77-78
IN predicate, 75-76
indexes, 60-61
numeric expressions, 77
ORDER BY clause, 74-75
tables, 57-66
deallocating, 509
debugging, 440-442, 495-496
declaring ODBC 2.0 API
functions, 421-426
decoding function calls, 442
dedicated processors, 486
default values, 461-462
defining objects, 378
DELETE command, 69, 186,
524
DELETE method (dynasets),
403
delete triggers, 189
deleting
columns, 59
records, 305-306
rows, 69, 186-187
views, 65
demonstration applications,
498
dependent entities, 30
derived attributes, 43
descending order indexes, 61
design issues
relational databases, 28-51
attributes, 39-44
entity definition, 29-33
history tables, 46-48
many-to-many
relationships, 38-39

one-to-many
relationships, 37-38
one-to-one relationships,
36-37
recursive relationships,
44-46
relationship definition,
35-39
Visual Basic, 334-339
API function calls,
335-339
Data Access Object
variables, 335-339
Data Control, 334-339,
351-357
data sources, 357
distributing applications,
346-347
guidelines, 343-345
workbench design,
340-343
Desktop Database Driver Set,
15-16
DFDs (data flow diagrams),
520
diagnostic functions, 281
dialog boxes
Drivers, 111
ODBC Options, 111
Setup Wizard, 347
dialog classes, 291
dialogs
command handlers, 294
creating, 291
list variables, 292
loading lists, 292-293
member variables, 292, 303
message handlers, 293,
303-304
message maps, 313
difference operator, 27
direct execution (statements),
156-157
Direct method, 412, 431
dirty reads, 192
disconnecting, 135-136,
451-452
distributing applications,
346-347
DLLs
cursor library, 234-236, 524
ODBC32.DLL, 110
sample application, 504-505
Visual Basic programs, 422
see also APIs; drivers

DML (Data Manipulation
Language), 69-92
DELETE, 69
DISTINCT, 74
INSERT, 70-71
LIKE predicate, 72-73
SELECT, 71-72
documentation, 489
DoFieldExchange method, 318
downsizing, 469
client/server databases,
477-478
client/server module, 476
end-user tools, 479
file server-based networks,
475
front-ends, 473-474
hardware platforms, 475-479
implementation, 489
mid-ranged processors, 476
modeling systems, 479-481
models, 469-474
PC databases, 476-477
performance issues
bottlenecks, 486-487
database design, 482-484
dedicated processors, 486
SQL, 485
porting, 471-472
precautions, 487-489
rewriting applications, 473
transactions, 478
user involvement, 488
driver manager, 12
drivers, 12, 112
16-bit, 104-105
32-bit, 104-105
adding, 111
API Conformance, 113-114
asynchronous execution,
160
capability checks, 449-451
client/server, 12
conformance level, 524
core, 12
cursor library, 524
cursor support, 236, 244,
249-255
Desktop Database Driver Set,
15-16
extensions, 524
function support, 113, 511,
516
help files, 498
information queries, 511
ISAM drivers, 348

listing, 514
lock types, 252-253
MFC (Microsoft Foundation
Classes), 14
multiple-tier, 102-104, 117,
525
ODBC 2.0 functions, 419
ODBC Administrator
installation, 109-111
logging, 111-112
ODBC support, 423
optimized, 449
PowerKeys, 99-100
read-only mode, 197
sample drivers, 505
searched statements, 247
single-tier, 100-101, 116,
196, 526
SQL conformance level,
114-116
support
multiple, 118-119
single, 119
thunking, 104
writing, 112
Drivers dialog box, 111
DROP INDEX command, 175
**DROP TABLE command, 59,
172**
dropping
indexes, 175-176
integrity constraints, 60
tables, 172-173
views, 60, 179
dropping tables, 59
duplicate rows
eliminating, 74
preventing, 184
duplicate values, 461
**dynamic binding (columns),
310-314**
**dynamic cursor model
(dynasets), 234, 392-393, 414**
Dynaset objects, 376
dynasets, 391-395
ADDNEW method, 403
creating, 394-395
DELETE method, 403
dynamic behavior, 392-393
EDIT method, 402-403
methods, 391-392
opening record sets as, 302
REFRESH method, 402
UPDATE method, 402-403
Visual Basic, 351-355
LRU algorithms, 354-355
methods, 353

E

E/R diagrams, 17
**EDIT method (dynasets),
402-403**
editing
field exchanges, 308
table structure, 59
tables, 176-178
end of table function, 289
enforcing data integrity
entry time, 463
post-processing, 463-464
SQL
foreign key validity, 467
null fields, 466
primary key validity, 466
restricting field values,
466
update time, 462
entities
defining, 29-33
dependent entities, 30
parent entity, 30
subtypes, 30-33
supertypes, 30-33
entity integrity, 23, 460-462
default values, 461-462
duplicate values, 461
null fields, 461
primary key validity, 460
restricting field values, 461
**entity-relationship diagrams,
17**
environments, 524
allocating, 508
creating, 122
deallocating, 509
freeing, 123, 437
equijoins, 80
**error information (functions),
435-437**
errors
debugging, 495-496
exception handling, 298-300
catch blocks, 299
exception types, 300
try blocks, 299
handling, 370-372
ODBC 2.0 API, 416
trapping, 124-128
Visual Basic, 435-437
**evaluating SQL queries,
360-361**

Excel, 15
exception handling
catch blocks, 299
exception types, 300
try blocks, 299
executing
commands, 524
SQL statements, 453
statements, 156-158, 509
asynchronously, 159-160
directly, 156-157
prepared, 157-158
setting execution mode,
160-161
synchronously, 159
EXISTS condition, 485
expressions (columns), 77
extended fetching, 242-245
**extended functionality
(ODBC), 423-424**
**extended grammar (drivers),
116**
Extension Level 1
API conformance, 114
Extension Level 1 functions,
510-512
Extension Level 2
API conformance, 114
Extension Level 2 functions,
513-516
extensions, 524
extracting column values, 162

F

fetch directions (cursors), 252
fetching (result sets), 525
see also retrieving
field exchanges, 308
fields, 523
Fields collection, 376, 384-386
file server-based networks, 475
files
help files
API reference, 496-497
drivers, 498
release notes, 497
tech notes, 497
SETUPWIZ.INI, 348
filters, 10, 295-298
parameterizing record sets,
323-324
record sets, 298
first normal form, *see* 1NF

foreign keys, 23-24, 514, 525
one-to-one relationships, 37
SQL data integrity
enforcement, 467
SQLForeignKeys() function,
144
Forms Collection objects, 377
forward scrolling, 288-289
FoxPro, 15
freeing
connections, 437
environments, 123, 437
query statements, 214-215
statement handles, 155-156
**front-end changes
(applications), 473-474**
functions, 77-78
aggregate functions, 86-88,
307-309
API conformance level, 113
API reference, 496-497
APIs, 10
applicability, 78
asynchronously executable,
161
AVG, 307
BOOL CanAppend(), 301
BOOL CanUpdate(), 301
BOOL IsBOF(), 289
BOOL IsDeleted(), 305
BOOL IsEOF(), 289
calling with Visual Basic,
335-339
catalog and statistics, 106
catalog functions, 137-138
categories, 77
CDatabase::Open, 325
core, 12
core-level functions, 508-510
COUNT, 86, 307
count(), 162
cursor usage, 256
decoding function calls, 442
diagnostic functions, 281
driver support, 113, 511, 516
drivers, 12
error trapping, 124-129
Extension Level 1, 510-512
Extension Level 2, 513-516
GetDefaultSQL, 280
MAX, 307
message handler functions,
297
MFC (Microsoft Foundation
Classes), 14
MIN, 307

ODBC 2.0 API, 408, 416-421
declaring, 421-426
handles, 421
sequence, 417
summary, 418-421
ODBC API functions, 123
OpenDatabase, 383
QLFreeEnv(), 124
scrolling tables, 288
SQLAllocConnect(), 128, 508
SQLAllocEnv(), 122-124, 508
SQLAllocStmt(), 155, 200,
508
SQLBindCol(), 202, 208, 434,
508
SQLBindParameter(),
219-222, 510
SQLBrowseConnect(),
133-134, 513
SQLCancels, 508
SQLColAttributes(), 202,
205-207, 508
SQLColumnPrivileges(),
149-150, 513
SQLColumns(), 140-141, 510
SQLConnect(), 130, 508
SQLDataSources, 513
SQLDescribeCol(), 202-206,
508
SQLDescribeParam(), 226,
514
SQLDisconnect, 437, 509
SQLDriverConnect(),
131-132, 429, 511
SQLDrivers, 514
SQLError(), 125-128, 197,
436, 509
SQLExec(), 197
SQLExecDirect(), 156, 453,
509
SQLExecute(), 197, 453, 509
SQLExtendedFetch(), 208,
214, 242-245, 514
SQLFetch(), 162, 213-214,
509
SQLForeignKeys(), 144, 514
SQLFreeConnect, 437, 509
SQLFreeEnv(), 123, 437, 509
SQLFreeStmt(), 156, 163-164,
215, 230, 261, 509
SQLGetConnectOption, 511
SQLGetCursorName(), 238,
509

SQLGetData(), 162, 212-213,
434, 511
SQLGetFunctions(), 511, 516
SQLGetInfo(), 77, 166-167,
177, 191, 249, 449. 511
SQLGetStmtOption(), 158,
245, 511
SQLGetTypeInfo, 511
SQLMoreResults, 515
SQLNativeSQL, 515
SQLNumParams(), 226-227,
515
SQLNumResultCols(),
201-203, 509
SQLParamData(), 223, 512
SQLParamOptions(), 225,
515
SQLPrepare(), 157, 202, 217,
509
SQLPrimaryKeys(), 143-144,
515
SQLProcedure(), 145
SQLProcedureColumns(),
146-147, 227-230, 515
SQLPutData(), 223-224, 512
SQLRowCount(), 162, 187,
207, 510
SQLSetConnectOption(),
134-135, 167, 193, 197,
438, 440, 512
SQLSetCursorName(), 236,
510
SQLSetPos(), 212, 240-241,
248-249, 516
SQLSetScrollOptions, 258,
440
SQLSetStmtOption(), 159,
161, 202, 438, 455, 512
SQLSpecialColumns(),
142-143, 512
SQLStatistics, 512
SQLTablePrivileges(),
148-149, 516
SQLTables(), 139-140, 512
SQLTransact(), 168, 194, 510
status information, 435-437,
509
SUM, 307
testing, 493-495
tracing code, 456-457
virtual member functions,
280
WritePrivateProfileString(),
348

G

GetDefaultSQL function, 280
GetDefaultSQL method, 318
grammar (SQL), 17-18
GRANT command, 66
granting privileges, 66-67
grouping statements
  (transactions), 166

H

handles
    connections, 427-429
    ODBC 2.0 API functions, 421
handling errors
    catch blocks, 299
    exception types, 300
    try blocks, 299
    Visual Basic, 370-372
hardware platforms
  (downsizing), 475-479
header files, 121
help
    API conformance levels, 113
    files, 496-498
        API reference, 496-497
        drivers, 498
        release notes, 497
        tech notes, 497
    South Wind Design, 519
hints (refreshing views), 297
history tables
    many-to-many relationships,
    47
    relational databases, 46-48
    rows, 48
host names, 132

I

ID_RECORD_ADDRECORD
  message handlers, 303-304
ID_RECORD_DELETERECORD
  message handlers, 306
ID_TRAINS_BROWSEINFO
  message handlers, 314
ID_TRAINS_EMPTYWEIGHT,
  308-309
ID_TRAINS_SELECT message
  handlers, 294
IDC_UPDATE message
  handlers, 313

IDD_RAIL_FORM, 316
IDD_RAIL_FORM dialog, 276
implementing subtypes, 31-33
IN predicate, 75-76
indexes
    ascending key order, 61
    clustered indexes, 60, 174
    creating, 173-175
    descending order, 61
    dropping, 175-176
    joins, 60
    performance issues, 484
    table info, 512
    unique indexes, 23
Indexes collection (Table
  objects), 386-387
Indexes Collection objects,
  376
Informix, 132
Ingres, 19
initializing
    connections, 128-129
    member variables, 322
    ODBC, 427
    statements, 155
inner joins (Visual Basic), 358
input parameters
  (procedures), 146
input screens, 182
INSERT command, 70-71, 183,
  525
inserting rows, 181-184
installing ODBC
  Administrator, 109-111
INSTCAT.SQL, 347
integrity
    dropping constraints, 60
    relational databases, 21-24
    see also entity integrity;
        referential integrity
intercepting function calls,
  442
interfaces, 93-99
    client/server model, 96-99
    local, 94-96
intersection operator, 27
ISAM drivers, 348
isolation levels
    precautions, 192-193

J

JET Database Engine, 14,
  350-351
join operator, 26
joins, 315-320

creating functions, 319-320
DoFieldExchange method,
  318
equijoins, 80
GetDefaultSQL method, 318
indexes, 60
list boxes, 317
member variables, 317-318
message handlers, 317
multi-way joins, 83-85
precautions, 81
recursive joins, 83-85
tables, 79-83
three-way join, 84
updating IDD_RAIL_FORM,
  316
see also inner joins; outer
  joins

K-L

keyset size (cursors), 259
keyset-driven cursors, 235,
  414-415
keysets, 525

layers, 100
Level 1/2 functionality
  (ODBC), 423-424
libraries, 121
linking controls (AppWizard),
  277
list boxes, 317
list variables, 292
listing
    available data sources, 513
    driver info, 514
    parameters, 227-229
listings
    5.1 ODBC Log File, 112
    7.1 TableList class header,
      150-151
    7.2 TableList class example,
      151-152
    14.1 CRailSet, 279-280
    14.2 COwnerSet
      (ownerset.h), 283-286
    14.3 COwnerSet
      (ownerset.cpp), 284-286
    21.1 SQL integrity
      enforcement, 465
loading lists to dialogs,
  292-293
local database interfaces,
  94-96
local model, 525

lock types (cursors), 252-253
logging (ODBC
   Administrator), 111-112
logical data independence,
   20, 61
login timeout (connections),
   135
lpszConnect parameter, 326
lpszDSN parameter, 325
LRU algorithm, 354

M

Macintosh systems, 10
managing transactions,
   403-405
manual commit mode, 193
many-to-many relationships
   defining, 38-39
   history tables, 47
   recursive, 45
MAX function, 307
member variables
   appending to dialogs, 292,
      303
   initializing, 322
   joins, 317-318
   parameterizing record sets,
      322-323
   removing from classes, 308
   storing selections, 296-297
memory
   allocation, 300, 349
   concurrency, 523
   environment, 524
menu commands
   appending records, 303
   browsing, 314
   deleting records, 306
   table navigation, 291
message handlers
   appending to dialogs, 293,
      303-304
   BN_CLICKED, 293
   creating, 297
   ID_RECORD_ADDRECORD,
      303-304
   ID_RECORD_DELETERECORD,
      306
   ID_TRAINS_BROWSEINFO,
      314
   ID_TRAINS_EMPTYWEIGHT,
      308-309
   ID_TRAINS_SELECT, 294

IDC_UPDATE, 313
   joins, 317
   WM_INITDIALOG, 292-293
message maps, 313
methods
   Direct method, 412, 431
   dynasets, 391-392
   Prepared, 431-432
   Prepared method, 412, 430
MFC (Microsoft Foundation
   Classes), 14
Microsoft Developer's
   Network (Level II), 14
Microsoft Query, 125, 340,
   359-360
mid-ranged processors, 476
MIN function, 307
minimum SQL grammar, 115
mixed cursors, 235, 415-416
modeling systems
   (downsizing)
   performance elements, 480
   software compatibility,
      480-481
   testing, 481
monitoring transactions, 442
multi-way joins, 83-85
multiple data sources, 324-330
multiple driver support,
   118-119
multiple-tier drivers, 102-104,
   117, 525

N

naming
   columns, 70, 83
   columns in views, 65
   cursors, 236-239, 253
   SQL objects, 56-57
   tables, 172
natural joins, 26
navigating tables, 287-294
networking
   file server-based networks,
      475
   host names, 132
   local database interfaces, 95
   see also downsizing
NEW keyword, 396
nonrepeatable reads, 192
normal forms, 39
   1NF, 40
   2NF, 41
   3NF, 41

normalization, 39, 448, 483
null values, 461
   columns, 91
   preventing, 466
null-terminated strings, 158
numeric expressions
   (columns), 77

O

object variable arrays, 380-382
objects
   CDatabase, 325
   constructs, 20
   Controls Collection, 377
   Dynaset objects, 376
   dynasets
      creating, 394-395
      dynamic behavior,
         392-393
      methods, 391-392
   Fields Collection, 376
   Forms Collection, 377
   granting privileges, 67
   Indexes Collection, 376
   naming (SQL), 56-57
   operators, 20
   qualified object names, 56
   Query objects, 376
   QueryDefs, 375
   Recordset, 376
   Snapshot objects, 376,
      387-391
      creating, 388-389
      row pointers, 389-391
   SQL, 57
   statement handles, 154
   Table objects, 376
      Fields collection, 384-386
      Indexes collection,
         386-387
   TableDefs objects, 375-384
      class definitions, 378
      defining, 378
      object variable arrays,
         380-382
      pointers, 380
      TableDefs collection,
         382-384
   see also dynasets
OCX controls, 341, 368-369
ODBC (Open Database
   Connectivity)
   advantages, 13-14
   definition, 9

development, 12
functionality, 12
implementations, 14-16
Level 1/2 functionality,
  423-424
scope, 9
ODBC 2.0 API, 407
  applicability, 407-416
  conformance levels
    APIs, 425-426
    core level, 423
    extended, 423-424
    SQL, 424-426
  debugging tools, 440-442
  declaring functions, 421-426
  function calls, 416-421
    handles, 421
    sequence, 417
    summary, 418-421
  function categories, 408
  performance issues, 410-416
    cursors, 413-416
    error information, 416
    SQL statements, 410-413
  result sets, 438-440
    cursors, 440
    structure, 439-440
ODBC 2.0 SDK, 15
ODBC Administrator
  data sources, 117
  installation, 109-111
  logging, 111-112
ODBC API functions, 123
ODBC Log File (listing 5.1),
  112
ODBC Options dialog box,
  111
ODBC Spy program (SDK),
  495-496
ODBC Spy utility, 442
ODBC Test program, 493-495
ODBC Trace log, 441
ODBC White Paper, 521
ODBC.DLL, 122, 347
ODBC.LIB, 122
ODBC32.DLL, 110, 122
ODBC32.LI, 122
ODBCCP32.LIB, 122
ODBCINST.DLL, 347
ODBCINST.H, 122
ODBCINST.HLP, 347
ODBCINST.LIB, 122
OLE 2.x Automation, 369-370
one-to-many relationships,
  37-38
one-to-one relationships,
  36-37

OnUpdate message, 328-329
open cursors, 250-251
OpenDatabase function, 383
opening
  ClassWizard, 277
  tables, 287
operational errors, 300
operators, 20
  Cartesian product, 27
  difference, 27
  intersection, 27
  join, 26
  projection, 24
  selection, 24
  set operators, 27
  unary operators, 77
  union, 27
  UNION operator, 83
optimized drivers, 449
optimizers (queries), 60
option settings (statements),
  511
optional data sources, 131-134
options (statements), 158-159
Oracle, 19
order of operations (queries),
  201-202
ordering rows (queries), 74-75
outer joins, 26, 358
ownerset.cpp (listing 14.3),
  284-286
ownerset.h (listing 14.2),
  283-286

P

Paradox, 15
Paradox demo, 518
parameterizing record sets
  filters, 323-324
  member variables, 321-323
  updates, 324
parameters, 218, 525
  bExclusive, 326
  binding, 510
  binding values, 219-222
  bReadOnly, 326
  bUseCursorLib, 326
  clearing, 230
  counting, 226-227
  descriptions, 226
  listing, 227-229
  lpszConnect, 326
  lpszDSN, 325
  markers, 218

multiple values, 224-225
passing, 229-230
passing data, 222-224
statements
  returning, 515
  returning info, 514
parent entities, 30
passing parameters, 229-230
passwords, 130
pattern matching strings,
  72-73
PC databases, 476-477
performance issues
  asynchronous mode, 452
  binding primary key
    columns, 454-455
  bookmarks, 455
  connections, 451-452
  database design, 448-449
  downsizing
    bottlenecks, 486-487
    database design, 482-484
    dedicated processors, 486
    SQL, 485
  drivers
    capability checks,
      449-451
    optimized, 449
  executing SQL statements,
    453
  indexes, 484
  ODBC 2.0 API, 410-416
    cursors, 413-416
    error information, 416
    function calls, 416-421
    SQL statements, 410-413
  retrieving result sets,
    453-454
  synchronous mode, 452
  tables, 483
  tracing code, 456-457
  transaction isolation,
    455-456
permissions, 115
phantoms, 192
pointers (TableDefs objects),
  380
porting, 471-472
positioned deletes, 69
positioned operations,
  253-254, 525
positioned updates/deletes,
  246-249
  SELECT FOR UPDATE clause,
    246
  SQLSetPos() function,
    248-249

WHERE CURRENT OF clause, 246-248
positioning cursors, 239-241, 248, 516
post-processing (data integrity), 463-464
PowerKeys, 99-100
prepared execution (statements), 157-158
Prepared method, 412, 430-432
preparing statements, 217-218, 525
  ODBC 2.0 functions, 419
  parameters, 218
    binding values, 219-222
    clearing, 230
    counting, 226-227
    descriptions, 226
    listing, 227-229
    markers, 218
    multiple values, 224-225
    passing, 229-230
    passing data, 222-224
  queries, 202-203, 358-359
  SQL, 430-432
preventing duplicate rows, 184
primary keys, 21-24, 29, 525
  binding columns, 454-455
  data integrity, 466
  entity integrity, 23
  one-to-one relationships, 36
  single-column, 448
  SQLPrimaryKeys() function, 143-144
  tables, 58
  updates, 184
  vaiidity, 460
printing result sets, 366-368
privileges
  client/server model, 148-150
  column-level, 149-150
  granting, 66-67
  revoking, 68
  search patterns, 148-149
  tables, 516
procedures, 91-92
  input parameters, 146
  passing parameters, 229-230
  stored procedures
    SQLProcedure() function, 145-146
    SQLProcedureColumns() function, 146-147
  triggers, 187-188, 196, 477

program generation (AppWizard), 274
programming Data Access Object variables, 375-376
programs
  administration, 503-504
  cursor demo, 502-503
  QueryDemo, 501
  Quick Test utility, 506
  Spy (SDK), 495-496
  Test (SDK), 493-495
  VBDEMO, 422
  VIZDATA, 422
projection operator, 24
properties (Visual Basic Data Control), 355

Q

QLFreeEnv() function, 124
qualified object names, 56
queries, 10, 199, 526
  column binding, 208-211
  cost-based optimizers, 60
  Data Access Object variables
    result sets, 398-400
    SQL statements, 397-398
  freeing statements, 214-215
  order of operations, 201-202
  ordering rows, 74-75
  preparing statements, 202-203
  range queries, 76
  refreshing views, 297
  result sets, 161-163
  returning table names, 318
  row-wise binding, 210-211
  rows, 207
  SELECT statements, 200-201
  subqueries, 88-89
  union queries, 90
  updating views, 297
  Visual Basic
    evaluating, 360-361
    Microsoft Query, 359-360
    preparation, 358-359
    submitting, 360
  see also result sets
Query objects, 376
Query, *see* Microsoft Query
QueryDefs objects, 375
QueryDemo program, 501
Quick Test utility, 506

R

Rail program, 279-282
range queries, 76
RDBMS (Relational Database Management System), 526
  see also relational databases
read-only mode (drivers), 197
reconnecting, 451-452
record sets
  aggregate functions, 307-309
  appending CRecordset class, 301-314
  bookmarks, 399
  closing, 289
  creating with ClassWizard, 282-286
  Data Access Object variables, 401-403
  deleting records, 305-306
  dynamic binding (columns), 310-314
  dynasets, 302
  field exchanges, 308
  filtering, 295-298
  multiple data sources, 324-330
  parameterizing
    filters, 323-324
    member variables, 321-323
    updates, 324
  sorting records, 296-298
  updating, 301-305
  writing records, 304-305
records, 10, 526
Recordset objects, 376
RECORDSOURCE (Data Control), 356
recursive joins, 83-85
recursive relationships, 44-46
REFERENCES clause, 58
REFERENCES privilege, 67
referential integrity, 24, 448, 462, 526
  constraints, 58
  dropping tables, 173
  foreign key validity, 467
  rows, 188-197
  transaction processing, 190-196
    dirty reads, 192
    nonrepeatable reads, 192
    phantoms, 192
  triggers, 188-197
  updating databases, 184

REFRESH method (dynasets),
354, 402
refreshing views (hints), 297
rejecting database edits, 189
Relational Database
Management System, *see*
RDBMS
relational databases, 17
advantages, 19
constructs, 20-21
design, 28-51
attributes, 39-44
entity definition, 29-33
history tables, 46-48
many-to-many
relationships, 38-39
one-to-many
relationships, 37-38
one-to-one relationships,
36-37
recursive relationships,
44-46
relationship definition,
35-39
history, 19-20
integrity, 21-24
operators
join, 26
projection, 24
selection, 24
union, 27
referential integrity, 24
see also data integrity
relationships
defining, 35-39
history tables, 46-48
many-to-many
defining, 38-39
history tables, 47
recursive, 45
one-to-many, 37-38
one-to-one, 36-37
recursive, 44-46
release notes, 497
releasing cursors, 261
removing member variables
from classes, 308
RESTRICT clause, 59
restricting field values, 461,
466
result sets, 161-163, 526
bookmarks, 245
browsing, 365-366
caches, 239
catalog functions, 152
column privileges, 513

columns, 510
attributes, 205-207
counting, 201-204
descriptions, 204-205
updating, 246
Concurrency control, 440
cursors, 233
auto-commit mode,
256-257
bookmarks, 251-252,
260-261
checking options, 261
concurrency, 258
concurrency locking, 254
connection options,
255-257
driver support, 249-255
dynamic, 234
extended fetching,
242-245
fetch directions, 252
forward-only
implementations, 235
function usage, 256
info types, 250-255
keyset size, 259
keyset-driven, 235
lock types, 252-253
mixed, 235
naming, 236-239, 253
positioned operations
support, 253-254
positioned updates/
deletes, 246-249
positioning, 239-241, 248
releasing, 261
retrieving data, 259
rollbacks, 251
rowset retrieval, 259-260
setting options, 257-261
simulating, 260
static, 234
static sensitivity, 255
types, 258-259
Data Access Object variables,
398-400
data sources, 511
fetching, 525
ODBC 2.0 API
cursors, 440
structure, 439-440
printing, 366-368
retrieving, 433-435, 453-454
column info, 508-509
current row, 212-213
multiple fields, 434-443
multiple rows, 214

row data, 509
rows, 514
sequentially, 213-214
single values, 434
rowsets, 242, 526
SELECT FOR UPDATE
statements, 246
SQLColumnPrivileges()
function, 149-150
SQLColumns(), 141
SQLForeignKeys() function,
144
SQLProcedure() function,
145-146
SQLProcedureColumns()
function, 146-147
SQLSpecialColumns()
function, 142-143
SQLTablePrivileges()
function, 148-149
SQLTables(), 140
tables, 512
Visual Basic
bound controls, 361-363
programming strategies,
363-364
retrieving
result sets, 453-454
current row, 212-213
multiple rows, 214
sequentially, 213-214
statement options, 158-159
returning subsets from
columns/rows, 24
reusing statement handles,
163-164
REVOKE command, 68
revoking privileges, 68
rewriting applications, 473
ROLLBACK command, 165,
168
Rollback statement, 404
rollbacks, 526
cursors, 251
transactions, 510
row pointers, 389-391
row-wise binding, 210-211
rows, 10, 21, 526
adding to tables, 70-71
bookmarks, 245
cascading deletes, 187
concatenating, 27
counting, 162, 187-188, 207
cursors, 233, 248
DELETE operations, 510
deleting, 69, 186-187
duplicate rows, 184

IN predicate, 75-76
INSERT operations, 510
inserting, 181-184
keysets, 525
ordering (queries), 74-75
positioned operations, 525
referential integrity, 188-197
result sets, 526
retrieving data, 509
retrieving from result sets, 514
returning subsets, 24
selecting, 75-76
set processing, 19
UPDATE operations, 510
updating, 90-91, 184-185
rowsets, 242, 259-260, 526

S

scrollable cursors, 233
scrolling
    cursors, 440
    tables, 288
SDK (Software Development Kit), 15, 341, 493, 526
    administration sample, 503-504
    DLL viewer, 504-505
    help files
        API reference, 496-497
        drivers, 498
        release notes, 497
        tech notes, 497
    ODBC Spy, 495-496
    ODBC Spy utility, 442
    ODBC Test program, 493-495
    ODBC Trace log, 441
    Quick Test utility, 506
    sample drivers, 505
    Visual Basic sample program, 421-422
search patterns, 137, 148-149
searched statements, 247
second normal form, *see* **2NF**
security, 63-64
SELECT command, 71-72, 526
SELECT FOR UPDATE statements, 246
SELECT privileges, 68
Select statement, 24
SELECT statements, 200-201
selecting data sources, 326
selection operator, 24

set operators, 27
set processing, 19
setting
    connection options, 134, 512
    cursor options, 257-261
    execution mode (statements), 160-161
    statement options, 159, 202
    statements options, 512
Setup Wizard dialog box, 347
SETUP1.MAK project file, 348
SETUPWIZ.INI, 348
shareware, 520
simulating cursors, 260
single driver support, 119
single-column primary keys, 448
single-tier drivers, 100-101, 116, 196, 526
Snapshot objects, 376
    creating, 388-389
    row pointers, 389-391
snapshots (Visual Basic), 349
software compatibility (downsizing), 480-481
sorting records, 296-298
special columns, 141-143
Spy program (SDK), 495-496
SQL (Structured Query Language), 11, 526
    aggregate functions, 86-88, 307-309
    conformance, 54, 114-116, 524
    Data Access Object variables, 397-398, 401
    data integrity, 465
        foreign key validity, 467
        null fields, 466
        primary key validity, 466
        restricting field values, 466
    data types, 54-56
    DDLs, 57-66
    development, 54
    Direct method, 431
    executing statements, 453
    grammar, 17-18
    integrity enforcement (listing 21.1), 465
    object creation, 57
    ODBC conformance levels, 424-426
    performance issues, 485

Prepared method, 431-432
preparing statements, 419, 430-432
procedures, 91-92
Query, 340
SELECT statements, 200-201
statement processing, 410-413
submitting statements, 432-433
subqueries, 88-89
tables, 57-60
union queries, 90
Visual Basic
    evaluating queries, 360-361
    Microsoft Query, 359-360
    preparation, 358-359
    submitting queries, 360
SQL Analyzer, 350
SQL.H, 122
SQLAllocConnect() function, 128, 508
SQLAllocEnv() function, 122-124, 508
SQLAllocStmt() function, 155, 200, 508
SQLBindCol() function, 202, 208, 434, 508
SQLBindParameter() function, 219-222, 510
SQLBrowseConnect() function, 133-134, 513
SQLCancel functions, 508
SQLColAttributes() function, 202, 205-207, 508
SQLColumnPrivileges() function, 149-150, 513
SQLColumns(), 140-141, 510
SQLConnect() function, 130, 508
SQLDataSources function, 513
SQLDescribeCol() function, 202-206, 508
SQLDescribeParam() function, 226, 514
SQLDisconnect function, 437, 509
SQLDriverConnect() function, 131-132, 429, 511
SQLDrivers function, 514
SQLError() function, 125-128, 197, 436, 509
SQLExec() function, 197

SQLExecDirect() function,
156, 453, 509
SQLExecute() function, 197,
453, 509
SQLEXT.H, 122
SQLExtendedFetch() function,
208, 214, 242-245, 514
SQLFetch() function, 162,
213-214, 509
SQLForeignKeys() function,
144, 514
SQLFreeConnect function,
437, 509
SQLFreeEnv() function, 123,
437, 509
SQLFreeStmt() function, 156,
163-164, 215, 230, 261, 509
SQLGetConnectOption
function, 511
SQLGetCursorName()
function, 238, 509
SQLGetData() function, 162,
212-213, 434, 511
SQLGetFunctions() function,
511, 516
SQLGetInfo() function, 77,
166-167, 177, 191, 249, 449.
511
SQLGetStmtOption() function,
158, 245, 511
SQLGetTypeInfo function, 511
SQLMoreResults function, 515
SQLNumParams() function,
226-227,515
SQLNumResultCols()
function, 201-203, 509
SQLParamData() function,
223, 512
SQLParamOptions() function,
225, 515
SQLPrepare() function, 157,
202, 217, 509
SQLPrimaryKeys() function,
143-144, 515
SQLProcedure() function,
145-146
SQLProcedureColumns()
function, 146-147, 227-230,
515
SQLPutData() function,
223-224, 512
SQLRowCount() function,
162, 187, 207, 510

SQLSetConnectOption()
function, 134-135, 167, 193,
197, 438, 440, 512
SQLSetCursorName()
function, 236, 510
SQLSetPos() function, 212,
240-241, 248-249, 516
SQLSetScrollOption()
function, 258, 440
SQLSetStmtOption() function,
159, 161, 202, 438, 455, 512
SQLSpecialColumns()
function, 142-143, 512
SQLSRVR.DLL, 347
SQLStatistics function, 512
SQLTablePrivileges() function,
148-149, 516
SQLTables(), 139-140, 512
SQLTransact() function, 168,
194, 510
stand-alone systems
(downsizing), 475
starting AppWizard, 271
statement handles, 154
statement-specific options,
438
statements, 153, 526
    allocating, 508
    asynchronous execution,
    159-160
    BeginTrans, 404
    binding to columns, 508
    canceling, 508
    CommitTrans, 404
    configuration options
        retrieval, 158-159
        setting, 159
    creating, 155
    deallocating, 509
    executing, 509
        directly, 156-157
        prepared, 157-158
    freeing handles, 155-156
    freeing query statements,
    214-215
    granting privileges (objects),
    67
    initializing, 155
    naming cursors, 510
    option settings, 511
    parameter info, 514
    parameters, 525
        binding values, 219-222
        clearing, 230
        counting, 226-227
        descriptions, 226
        listing, 227-229

    multiple values, 224-225
    passing, 229-230
    passing data, 222-224
    returning, 515
    preparing, 202-203, 217-218,
    525
    returning cursor names, 509
    reusing statement handles,
    163-164
    Rollback, 404
    searched statements, 247
    SELECT, 24, 200-201
    SELECT FOR UPDATE, 246
    setting
        execution mode, 160-161
        options, 202, 512
    synchronous execution, 159
    testing, 493-495
    transactions, 164-168
        grouping statements, 166
        modes, 166-168
        processing, 527
static cursors, 234, 414
static sensitivity (cursors), 255
status information
(functions), 435-437, 509
stored procedures
    SQLProcedure() function,
    145-146
    SQLProcedureColumns()
    function, 146-147
storing selections with
member variables, 296-297
string pattern matching, 72-73
submitting
    SQL queries, 360
    SQL statements, 432-433
subqueries, 88-89
subtypes, 30-33
SUM function, 307
superstations, 486
supertypes, 30-33
supported databases, 15
synchronous execution
(statements), 159
synchronous mode, 452
System R, 54

T

Table objects, 376
    Fields collection, 384-386
    Indexes collection, 386-387

TableDefs objects, 375-384
    class definitions, 378
    defining, 378
    object variable arrays,
        380-382
    pointers, 380
    TableDefs collection,
        382-384
**TableList class example
(listing 7.2), 151-152**
**TableList class header (listing
7.1), 150-151**
tables, 527
    adding table names to
        columns, 318
    appending rows, 70-71
    beginning of table function,
        289
    cascading deletes, 187
    columns, 523
    combining, 26
    creating, 57-60, 169-172
    dropping, 59, 172-173
    editing, 176-178
    editing structure, 59
    end of table function, 289
    equijoins, 80
    foreign keys, 23-24, 144
    history tables
        deleting rows, 48
        relational databases,
            46-48
    index information, 512
    indexes, 60-61
        creating, 173-175
        dropping, 175-176
    inner joins, 358
    joins, 79-83, 315-320
        creating functions,
            319-320
        DoFieldExchange
            method, 318
        GetDefaultSQL method,
            318
        list boxes, 317
        member variables,
            317-318
        message handlers, 317
        updating
            IDD_RAIL_FORM, 316
    lists, 139
    logical data independence,
        61
    multi-way joins, 83-85
    naming, 172
    navigating CRecordset class,
        287-294

normalization, 483
opening CRecordset member
    function, 287
outer joins, 358
performance issues, 483
primary keys, 21-24, 58
    entity integrity, 23
    SQLPrimaryKeys()
        function, 143-144
    updates, 184
privileges
    column-level, 149-150
    returning, 516
    search patterns, 148-149
recursive joins, 83-85
referential integrity
    constraints, 58
result sets, 512
returning names, 318
scrolling, 288
selecting with AppWizard,
    273
temporary, 172
temporary tables
    creating, 172
    dropping, 173
    restrictions, 173
three-way join, 84
updatable snapshots, 288
views, 61-66
    creating, 178-179
    dropping, 179
    see also columns; record sets;
        rows
tech notes, 497
temporary tables
    creating, 172
    dropping, 173
    restrictions, 173
terminating
    SQL statement processing,
        420
    statements (Visual Basic),
        437
Test program (SDK), 493-495
testing downsize changes, 481
third normal form, *see* 3NF
three-way joins, 84
thunking, 104
Time literals, 79
Timestamp literals, 79
tracing
    code, 456-457
    data sources, 441
transaction isolation, 455-456

**transaction processing,
190-196, 527**
    connection mode, 193
    dirty reads, 192
    nonrepeatable reads, 192
    phantoms, 192
    single-tier drivers, 196
    triggers, 196
**transactions, 164-168, 478,
527**
    AUTOCOMMIT mode, 167
    behavioral characteristics,
        438
    committing, 510
    Data Access Object variables
        management, 403-405
        record sets, 401-403
        SQL statements, 401
    grouping statements, 166,
        194
    isolation levels, 192-193
    modes, 166-168
    monitoring, 442
    open cursors, 250-251
    rollbacks, 510
    updating databases, 184
Translation Spy, 505
trapping errors, 370-372
triggers, 187-188, 196, 477
    cascades, 189
    rejecting database edits, 189
    types, 196
True Grid Pro Version 2.1, 365
try blocks, 299
tuple, 21, 527
turning off bookmarks, 455

U

unary operators, 77
UNION operator, 27, 65, 83
union queries, 90
unique indexes, 23
**updatable snapshots (tables),
288**
**UPDATE command, 90, 184,
527**
**UPDATE method (dynasets),
402-403**
update triggers, 189
updating
    columns in result sets, 246
    IDD_RAIL_FORM, 316
    parameterized values, 324
    query views, 297

record sets, 301-305
rows, 90-91, 184-185
user defined data types, 56
user IDs, 130
user permission concept, 115

V

VBDEMO, 422
VBX library, 368
VBX-style custom controls, 342
vendor listings, 517
views, 61-66
AppWizard, 275-278
columns, 65
creating, 178-179
deleting, 65
dropping, 60, 179
logical data independence, 61
security, 63, 64
UNION operator, 65
virtual member functions, 280
Vista, 125
Visual Basic, 14, 333-339
API function calls, 335-339
application design guidelines, 343-345
BeginTrans statement, 404
bookmarks, 399
closing connections, 437
CommitTrans statement, 404
Crystal Reports Pro v3.0, 367
custom controls
browsing result sets, 365-366
data-aware, 368
OCX, 368-369
printing result sets, 366-368
Data Access Object variables, 335-339, 374-395
cloning databases, 397
creating databases, 395-397
dynasets, 391-395
programming, 375-376
queries, 397-400
Snapshot objects, 387-391
Table objects, 384-387
TableDefs objects, 377-384

transactions, 400-405
Data Control, 334-339
data sources, 357
dynaset, 351-355
properties, 355
data sources, 427-430
Data Widgets Version 1.0, 366
database architecture, 348-355
distributing applications, 346-347
DLL functions, 422
error handling, 370-372
error information, 435-437
inner joins, 358
ISAM drivers, 348
memory allocation, 349
NEW keyword, 396
ODBC 2.0 API
applicability, 407-416
declaring functions, 421-426
error information, 416
function calls, 416-421
function control, 408-410
performance issues, 410-416
result sets, 438-440
OLE 2.x Automation, 369-370
outer joins, 358
result sets, 361-364
bound controls, 361-363
browsing, 365-366
printing, 366-368
programming strategies, 363-364
retrieving result sets
multiple fields, 434-443
single values, 434
Rollback statement, 404
sample applications, 498-499
SDK sample program, 421-422
Setup Wizard dialog box, 347
SETUP1.MAK project file, 348
SETUPWIZ.INI, 348
snapshots, 349
SQL queries, 357-361
evaluating, 360-361
Microsoft Query, 359-360
preparation, 358-359
submitting, 360

SQL statements
preparing, 430-432
submitting, 432-433
status information, 435-437
terminating connections/statements, 437
True Grid Pro Version 2.1, 365
VBX library, 368
workbench design, 340-343
Visual Basic JET engine, 410
Visual C++ 2.0, 14
aggregate functions, 307-309
exception handling, 298-300
joins, 315-320
records
adding, 301
deleting, 305
filtering, 295
updating, 301
SQL statements, 330
Wizards, 265-266
AppWizard, 270
ClassWizard, 282
VIZDATA, 422

W-Z

Watcom SQL, 13
WHERE clauses, 72, 87, 88, 201
WHERE CURRENT OF clause (cursors), 246-248
Windows NT, 486
WINDOWS.H, 122
Wizards, 265-266
application development, 266-270
AppWizard
building applications, 274-275
class generation, 274
data source selection, 273
database support, 272
linking controls, 277
opening ClassWizard, 277
operation, 279-282
program generation, 274
starting, 271
table selection, 273
views, 275-278

WM_INITDIALOG message handlers, 292-293
workbench design (Visual Basic), 340-343
WOSA (Windows Open Systems Architecture), 12
WritePrivateProfileString() function, 348
writing
   drivers, 112
   records, 304-305

Licensing Agreement

By opening this package, you are agreeing to be bound by the following agreement:

This software product is copyrighted, and all rights are reserved by the publisher and author. You are licensed to use this software on a single computer. You may copy and/or modify the software as needed to facilitate your use of it on a single computer. Making copies of the software for any other purpose is a violation of the United States copyright laws.

This software is sold *as is* without warranty of any kind, either expressed or implied, including but not limited to the implied warranties of merchantibility and fitness for a particular purpose. Neither the publisher nor its dealers or distributors assume any liability for any alleged or actual damages arising from the use of this program. (Some states do not allow for the exclusion of implied warranties, so the exclusion may not apply to you.)